Best Wis

Curse
of the
JUNGLE BOY

Ray Crawford

with

Michael Wood

First published in November 2007 by PB Publishing

ISBN 978-0-9549446-3-6

PB Publishing
www. pbpublishing.co.uk

PB Publishing can be contacted by e-mail at
info@pbpublishing.co.uk
or by writing to: PB Publishing, PO Box 689, Portsmouth,
Hants, P06 2WX. UK

Contents

"I would like to dedicate this book to Eileen and to my mother and father. Eileen gave me four lovely daughters and stood by me wherever I went or whatever I did and, although Mum and Dad never had much, they always made sure that we had food and clothes and, above all, that we were loved.

I would also like to mention my lovely wife Carol for all her help and support"

Acknowledgements

I would like to thank the following people who have worked so hard to put this book together.

Firstly, Michael Wood, the son of the former Ipswich Town doctor who contacted me nearly 2 years ago with the idea of writing this book. He has since put in hundreds of hours compiling the book as well as researching details, collecting facts and verifying stories. Thanks for all your efforts Michael.

Thank you to Jake Payne who agreed to publish the book through his company PB Publishing. He has been heavily involved in the design of the book, sourcing the photographs and putting the scrapbook together. He has also done a fine job with publicity and marketing.

I must also mention Pat Godbold, the Ipswich Town archivist and Ian Hunneybell, the assistant club archivist who gave their time when I needed to find dates, statistics, etc. They have proven to be a fountain of knowledge. Many thanks also to John Motson who wrote a marvellous foreword.

Also:

Elvin King and Mel Henderson - The Ipswich 'Evening Star'
Tony Garnett - former sports editor 'East Anglian Daily Times'
Francis Ponder - the Colchester 'Evening Gazette'
'The News', Portsmouth
The Suffolk Records Office
Steve Gordos - former sports editor Wolverhampton 'Express and Star'
Peter Creed - Honorary Secretary of the Wolves former player association
Peter Knowles - former Wolves player
Jimmy Leadbetter, John Elsworthy, Ted Phillips, Andy Nelson, Billy Baxter, Dennis Thrower, Colin Harper, Ken Hancock, Joe Boadfoot - former Ipswich Town players.
Dr Patrick Wood MD - Former Ipswich Town club doctor.
Ralph Morris - www.prideofanglia.com

Foreword

Although I was born in the north of England, my father's work as a Methodist minister took our family to many different places before we moved to the East End of London when I was a young teenager. As I had hopped from school to school and to get some continuity into my education, my father sent me to Culford Methodist School, just outside Bury St Edmunds in Suffolk. It was a boarding school but you were allowed home at weekends to be with your family. This led to my first association with Ipswich Town as my father was as keen on football as any other man you are ever likely to find in the ranks of the clergy. In my last two years at Culford, when Ipswich were playing at home, he would drive down from London on the Saturday morning, pick me up and take me to Portman Road. For my father, a day could not be better spent than by taking me out and watching a football match as well! When people ask me which team I support it is difficult to say but my earliest and fondest memories of football will always be of going to watch Ipswich Town.

The first game I ever saw at Portman Road was at home to Plymouth Argyle, as exciting a match as you could wish to see, a six-goal thriller ending in a 3-3 draw. It was the first time I saw Ray Crawford and Ted Phillips in harness, 'the terrible twins' as they came to be called. Their physical presence was a frightening prospect for any defence as the top teams in the country were to find out in 1962 when, under the guidance of manager Alf Ramsey, Town took the 1st Division Championship by storm. It was my last term at Culford School and I got down to Portman Road twice, to watch them crush Manchester United 4-1, including two 25 yard thunderbolts from Ted Phillips, the power of which you had to see to believe and the 5-2 demolition of Chelsea in which Ray scored a hat-trick. Ray was lethal in the air and on the ground if he got any sort of reasonable service in the six-yard box.

I continued to watch Ipswich Town when they came to London that famous year, joining a crowd of over 51,000 to watch them beat Spurs 3-1 at White Hart Lane, completing an unlikely but brilliant double over their illustrious opponents. Perhaps the two most crucial games for Town that season were over the Easter Bank Holiday weekend of 1962 when I saw the 2-2 draw with Chelsea at Stamford Bridge, followed two days later on Easter Monday by a majestic performance at Highbury, sweeping aside Arsenal in an emphatic 3-0 win. As Burnley faltered with the finishing line in sight, Ipswich Town took full advantage by clinching the 1st Division Championship five days later with the 2-0 win over Aston Villa at Portman Road with Ray scoring the two goals.

It was over twenty years later in the mid eighties when I actually got to meet and interview Ray with Jimmy Leadbetter who possibly made more goals for Ray than any other player in his career. It was for a programme called 'Champions' about clubs who had won the League Championship in the 1960's. As Jimmy had travelled all the way down from his native Scotland to do the interview, I thought it would be a good idea to get Sir Alf Ramsey to take part as well if I possibly could. I remember going to his house in Valley Road, Ipswich but, as much as Lady Ramsey tried to persuade Alf to come out, he was staying put. What I didn't know at the time was that the great man rarely gave interviews or got involved with the media unless he absolutely had to!

The last time I met up with Ray was when I hosted the launch of the new FA Cup sponsors "e-on" last year at the Savoy Hotel in London. Ray was there of course, on account of his two goals for Colchester United in their epic 3-2 win over Leeds United in the FA Cup in 1971 that many think was the greatest giant-killing of all time. Ray was nearly thirty-five years old at the time and thirty-five years later at the age of seventy, he thought I might not recognise him when he playfully popped up in front of me at the opening ceremony and asked me if I knew who he was. As Ray has obviously taken good care of himself and still almost looks sprightly enough to be banging in goals, I recognised him immediately.

In this book, Ray refers to one of my fellow professionals of the past, the late and great football commentator, Brian Moore who once described Ray as "one of the most devastating strikers of all time" which is hard to disagree with, especially when you read his statistics in a career that spanned three decades in the game.

I hope Ray continues to get the acclaim he deserves for being one of the great players of his era and an ambassador for the game he served so well; and even more so for a man who seeks to make no profit from his memoirs as Ray has commendably declared that he will be putting all proceeds he may receive from sales of this book towards charity. Well done Ray, and thanks for all the years of entertainment you not only gave me, but also thousands of soccer fans as well.

John Motson

Introduction

"A Conversation with Sir Alf"

It's a late summer evening and the sun has set but it's still light enough to see the head of a wise man silhouetted against the darkening blue sky. It's great to see him again, so lifelike, just as I remember him. He changed my life in many ways and I just felt it would be nice to see him once again before I catch my train home tonight. Ipswich Railway Station isn't far away, only a few minutes walk and I could probably get there blindfolded, as I know where I stand so well. This town was like a second home to me during my life here as a professional footballer and, though they may have forgotten me here now, some of the greatest moments of my life took place here; the birth of three of my daughters, the winning of the League Championship in 1961-1962 and today has been another one I shall remember for the rest of my life.

It was not only a great privilege to be invited to a ceremony that took place on this very spot earlier today but also to be chosen by Lady Ramsey to unveil the statue of her late husband, Sir Alf Ramsey (1922-1999) was perhaps the greatest honour of my life. It was a great day but also a sad one. I lost my Eileen earlier this year; my wife of forty-two years and it would have been nice to have her by my side today. She was a fiery lady and would stand up and shout, cheer and swear at matches because she always wanted the Town to do well, unlike some who would quietly accept defeat.

"Alf, I can't imagine what you're really thinking up there; no one ever really knew did they? That is, until you spoke your few words of wisdom," I say quietly, looking up at him.
"Well I can tell you exactly what I'm thinking, Ray. Yes, you are right, there is little justice in life but I'm also thinking 'Come on Ray, don't be too sad.' I can tell you, Eileen has been by your side all day and I'm in a better position to tell you that than most."
"No, I know I shouldn't be sad but.....what?...Alf?... Is that you?"
"Well I can assure you it's not your fairy godmother and I was hoping you'd come and see me again before you left today."
"Christ Almighty! You mean you've been watching and listening all day from up there Sir

Alf?"

"Yes of course, from the very moment they dropped me here early this morning, those wretched carriers!"

"What was the problem Sir Alf?"

"Well, not only was it an extremely bumpy and uncomfortable ride but they insisted on binding me from head to foot with ropes as if I were some desperate criminal, liable to try and escape at any moment!"

"Oh, that was just to stop you from falling over Sir Alf."

"Ray, do I honestly look as though I am about to fall over?"

"No, of course not Sir Alf."

"I suppose I should count myself lucky they didn't gag me as well and Ray, please stop calling me Sir Alf every minute; every two minutes will be fine enough, thank you."

"Sorry Sir Alf, I mean Alf."

"Anyway, since then I have been standing here all day like a statue, posing for the crowds and Press to take their photographs and I can tell you, it's not that easy to stand still for so long, not easy at all."

"Well you've been brilliant from the moment I unveiled you this morning, Alf, as I know you always hated people making a fuss of you, even at the best of times."

"And it was a good job that you did unveil me. As you know, patriot that I am, it was becoming stiflingly hot under that heavy Union Jack flag before you pulled it off me. If it had been Madame Tussaud's wax model of me, 'Ramsey Mark 1' as I call it, I may very well have started to melt and that would not have gone down at all well with the photographers I'm sure, a soft focus Sir Alf Ramsey!"

"No, of course it wouldn't, but you've come through it all it brilliantly, Alf."

"But the worst of it, Ray, is that I missed the game with Manchester United this evening. I thought when they left me here this morning, it was merely temporary, just so you could unveil me, before they came back and hoisted me to my permanent position, possibly on top of the Cobbold Stand perhaps, in time to see the match against Manchester United this evening."

"No, I'm afraid this is to be your final position, Alf."

"Ray, I can well remember as a boy, standing on a box when my father took me to see games but this is either taking the mickey a bit too far or an outrageous miscalculation by who ever designed this concrete box for me to stand on! It is quite obvious to me that I need to be at least another two hundred feet up to see the games properly, then the crowd can wave at me every time Ipswich score a goal."

"Two hundred feet, Alf? You'd almost be in the heavens that far up!"

"And that's exactly where I am used to being, Ray, so please could you have a word for me with the organizers of this event as I'm sure there's just been some simple misunderstanding somewhere along the line."

"But Alf, there hasn't been any misunderstanding. This is where you'll always be, so people will be able to see how you really looked, and it's an incredible likeness of you."

"Well it's kind of you to say so, Ray, but I just felt like a glorified match programme seller after the game had started tonight, standing out here by myself. Also, I have been left in a road that is the most notorious 'Red Light' district in Ipswich and I don't think that my wife Lady Ramsey will approve of it at all! To add to that, a man and his dog walked past during the first half; the dog stopped, gave me a brief look as if to say 'never seen you here before mate' and then cocked his leg and left his opinion of me on this concrete box that I have been stood on and, from now on, I will be a sitting duck for every single incontinent pigeon in town. I'm not actually sure which model I prefer at the moment but at least there are no pigeons in 'Madame Tussauds'. If people will insist on making models of people, at least give them the chance to see what made them famous. Just look at poor Horatio Nelson for example, stuck there in Trafalgar Square forever, watching tourists feed fat pigeons all day. How on earth will he ever be able to see the English Channel from there?"

"I know what you're saying but I'm sure you'll get used to it, Alf. It'll just take a while to settle into your new surroundings, just like my very first day's training here after I'd signed for Town, when I was left with the worst of the training kit, remember?"

"Yes of course I do, as you've never been slow to remind me of it in the past. You looked as if you'd been savaged by some sort of wild animal!"

"Yes, I thought that might cheer you up a bit, Alf, reminding you of that!"

"No, I am sorry and I do apologise for that even though it is about forty years too late. It's just that we had just spent £6,000 on buying you, Ray, so you must understand, funds were a little short at the time. Anyway, tell me what happened in the game tonight as I heard a loud cheer not too long after the kick-off and I assumed Ipswich had scored?"

"Yes that's right, Alf. Town's right fullback Fabian Wilnis scored to give Town the lead, then..."

"Sorry to interrupt, Ray, but do you mean to tell me an Ipswich fullback actually scored a goal?"

"Yes Alf, he did, what's so surprising about that?"

"It's just I cannot recall our fullbacks Larry Carberry or John Compton ever scoring a goal in the entire time they played for Ipswich Town."

"I'm sure one of them scored once, but I just can't remember when at the moment."

"I suppose it was my fault as a coach; I should have drawn them a map of where the opponent's goal was. No, only joking, as I always preferred my fullbacks to defend. Anyway, about twenty minutes later I heard another cheer, not so loud so I thought that was probably an equaliser?"

"Yes, David Beckham scored with a free-kick to equalise for Manchester United."

"Ah, fine player that Beckham and some compare him to Bobby Charlton but Bobby was a different sort of player, a central midfield player whereas Beckham's strength is

11

somewhere on the right flank in my opinion. Bobby was a wonderful player, so much skill, a wonderful passer and striker of a football, so graceful in everything he did. He even looked good if he was having a poor game which was pretty rare of course."

"Ah, I remember now who scored that goal at fullback in your time here. It was Larry Carberry in a friendly game at the end of my first season at Town, in a Testimonial at Gorleston in 1959 and I think it was from the penalty spot."

"Hum, can't remember it myself but then you always did have an amazing memory for names and places Ray."

"Talking about memory Sir Alf, I'm thinking of writing my story."

"That sounds like a good idea, Ray. They say everybody has at least one book in them."

"I hope so, so I'm going to give it a try anyway."

"So when do you propose yours to start, Ray?"

"Well, I thought I might start it from today, Alf."

"That's interesting but why today?"

"Because even though I finished playing football a long time ago, I've been writing notes about my life and career in football for some time now, so I think today is a good a time to start as any, the crowning moment of my career, I mean the honour of unveiling you today."

"It's very kind of you to say that, Ray."

"That's alright Sir Alf, oh Alf I mean, sorry it's just the way I always refer to you now."

"It's alright, Ray. I was actually getting a bit worried as you had not called me Sir Alf for at least a couple of minutes."

"Sorry, Alf. Anyway, this is how I intend to start it."

"Yes, please go on, Ray."

"Well, it starts that I was well prepared for this day, having collected my suit from the cleaners the previous afternoon and made sure I had a clean white shirt and well polished shoes ready for today's trip up to Suffolk. I was so worried I might oversleep that I not only set my alarm clock for 5:00am but also arranged a wake-up call. When I woke up this morning, I didn't even bother with breakfast, just had a cup of tea before setting off in my car to Portsmouth railway station. I was in good time so I bought the morning papers and caught the 6:20 train to London that was right on time. I started to read the papers but couldn't take in what I was reading as I found myself looking out of the carriage windows, thinking more about all that had happened in my past, leading up to this day. I sat back thinking of my first meeting with you at the Ipswich Town game at Leyton Orient in London in 1958 when you told me you wanted to sign me."

"Yes I remember that day well and I sensed you were not keen to sign then but I got my man in the end. Sorry to interrupt again, please continue, Ray."

"I was standing up waiting by the doors, ready to get off the train as we pulled into Waterloo Station, as keen as a dog to get out of the front door for the morning walk. Then

it was through the gates and down to catch a tube that was packed like a can of sardines. I stood there squeezed shoulder to shoulder with commuters but thankfully it's only a short trip from Waterloo to Liverpool Street where I arrived about fifteen minutes later. I sat by the window in the next train for Ipswich where I settled down for the last part of the journey. When the train was nearing Colchester, it brought back memories of the great FA Cup game against Leeds United in 1971 that I took part in and Colchester won 3-2. I was nearly thirty five years old at the time and scored two of the goals that knocked out the Division 1 Champions."

"And you always had a knack of scoring when you played against big Jack Charlton I remember so it's just as well you weren't playing for Germany in 1966! Sorry for interrupting again, please carry on, Ray."

"As the train neared Ipswich, I noticed my hands were shaking slightly as I adjusted my tie in the reflection of the window of the carriage. It worried me a bit, making me think back to when I was a nervous, very shy child. Then I thought to myself, just think of it like a big match day used to be, sitting there in the dressing room, counting down the minutes before you ran out onto the pitch. Then you would come along and look at me with that reassuring smile, with a sort of power that could calm the worst nerves saying 'Don't worry, just relax and be yourself, you know exactly what you have to do and you will do it well I am sure, so just try and go out and enjoy yourself' which made me smile and then I noticed that my hands were no longer trembling."

"I arrived in Ipswich just after 10:00 that morning. The sun was beating down as I made my way from the station to the ground, past the Station Hotel where I stayed many times, then across the old bridge over the river that leads to the docks. It was so hot, I took off my suit top before I reached the ground. When I arrived at the reception in the club, a kind young lady made me a cup of coffee. Shortly afterwards, familiar old faces began to appear; Larry Carberry from Liverpool, John Compton from Bournemouth, Jimmy Leadbetter all the way from Scotland and Billy Reed from Wales and those who still live locally; Kenny Malcolm, Dennis Thrower, Len Fletcher, John Elsworthy, Ted Phillips and Len Garrett. We sat together in the Ipswich Town's Centre-Spot restaurant, talking and sharing our memories once again. Just before midday, we made our way outside the ground where the speeches were to be made just the other side of the road, about thirty yards from the corner of the North Stand where your statue had been placed earlier that day. I thanked Lady Ramsey for choosing me to unveil your statue. She replied that she thought it would be appropriate that a former Town player should be given the honour as it was more important that Ipswich had won the 1st Division Championship in 1961-1962 than England winning the World Cup in 1966."

"After speeches and tributes from Ipswich Town Chairman, David Sheepshanks, Sir

Bobby Charlton and John Elsworthy, it was time for me to unveil your statue. I said a few brief words but was becoming so overcome with emotion, I just wanted to get on with the unveiling."

"Yes I wanted you to get on with it as well, Ray. As you well know I was never much for ceremonies and, as I told you a little earlier, it was becoming uncomfortably hot under there."

"There were tears in my eyes as I stepped up onto the temporary wooden stand beside the statue, then I pulled the strings on the Union Jack which was draped over your statue and there you were, in front of us again, looking down with that familiar expression, greeted by a huge applause from the big crowd that were there to witness the event. The likeness to you, Alf, was brilliant and the sculptor Sean Hedges-Quinn who'd been commissioned to do the job couldn't have done it better. It was one of the greatest moments of my life. Everything had gone very smoothly up until that point. That was, until I started to step down from the wooden stand. Suddenly it started to wobble, causing me to lose my footing and I started to topple backwards off the stand. Luckily, standing close behind me were Sir Bobby Charlton and George Burley who would have caught me and broken my fall."

"Yes, I couldn't help but see you nearly fall over after you took the flag off me but, although I thought it was quite amusing, I managed not to laugh; as usual not changing my expression at all!"

"Well you may have laughed at the time, Alf, but as I slipped, I cut my leg on a sharp corner of the stand and hadn't noticed it because of the occasion and all the adrenaline running in me, just like when I was cut in my playing days."

"Oh dear, what bad luck ahahah! Please forgive me, Ray, for seeing the funny side of it. I just couldn't help imagining Jimmy Forsyth in his old blue tracksuit bursting through the crowd, running out to your rescue with his yellow bucket and magic sponge! Sorry, Ray, you know what my sense of humour was like, please excuse me. Do carry on, Ray."

"It was nearly an hour later, after we'd done all the interviews and photographs and were about to go to the reception in Ipswich Town's Centre-Spot restaurant that I had a chance to look at the injury which had started to throb a bit and wasn't a pretty sight as the blood had now dried, sticking my suit trousers to my left leg. I was taken to the club's treatment room where the trouser leg was peeled away to reveal a nasty looking gash. On hearing of my accident, some of the lads came to see me with the inevitable leg-pulling and comments like 'Oh no, Crawford's on the treatment table again!' After I'd been patched up, I went to the reception for all the guests then did another interview for the club's next home match programme before joining Ted Phillips and Larry Carberry with their wives at John and Anne Elsworthy's house for tea. It was good to see them again and we never run out of things to talk about, from the distant past to the present every time we meet."

"Then it was off to the match which Town drew 1-1 with Manchester United, outplayed

them for much of the game and probably deserved to win. I thought the players out there were a credit to the club tonight. After the game, I had a couple of beers with players past and present, trying to speak to as many old friends as possible before saying goodbye. When I left to catch my train, I'd allowed some time to have a last look at your statue, Alf, just so I could relive unveiling you again after all the crowds had gone home and that's just about where I came in this evening, Sir Alf, sorry, I mean Alf."

"Ray, that was very entertaining and I was very touched by many of the things you said but I hope you don't mind me asking, isn't it a little short for an autobiography?"

"No, Alf, that was just the start of it."

"Oh I see, so I take it you are now going back to the beginning?"

"Yes, that's right, Alf."

"Well, I would very much like to hear it, Ray, if you have the time so please start from the very beginning. I can assure you I will be listening intently to every word as I have all the time in the world now and I promise I will not interrupt you this time."

"Thanks, Alf, I was born..."

"Oh, Ray, just one last thing, please try not to mention that I liked the occasional cigarette now and again?"

"Okay, I'll try not to, Sir Alf, I mean Alf!"

Curse of the Jungle Boy

Chapter 1

"My Childhood and Youth"

I was born the eldest of four children in a small flat in Fratton Road, Portsmouth on the 13th of July 1936. In those days, natural childbirth at home was still more customary than going into hospital to give birth but my mother Muriel, as well as being an attractive woman, was also made of stern stuff. My two brothers, Alan and Colin, and my sister Barbara were also to be born at home. Although the flats where we lived were very basic and ordinary, it was far from being a slum and not a bad place to live in those days. We had little or nothing in the way of luxury as was the case of most families who lived in the area but you rarely heard people complain and you just went on with life the best way you could. Our flat was just a mile away from Fratton Park, home of Portsmouth Football Club which perhaps foretold my future as it was to be the focus of my early youth and career. Although it was a tough area, even as a child you could sense the strong feeling of community which helped us get through the terrors of the Portsmouth Blitz of World War II and people rarely stole from each other. It's old fashioned and too risky now but, in those days, you could leave your front door keys hanging on a piece of string through the letter box.

At the time, my dad, George Crawford, had just retired from professional boxing. He was a tall powerful man, about six foot two inches tall, very lean in build and without an ounce of fat on him but he was the gentlest of fathers. He never laid even as much as a finger on us, even though sometimes, if he shouted for any reason, he could nearly frighten the life out of you! He wasn't very strict nor was my mother but mostly there wasn't any need for them to be because, as children, we did what we were told. If we did misbehave, Mum would say "I'll tell your father!" That was usually warning enough. Once she caught me setting fire to matches on the top of the oven in the kitchen and chased me with a broom giving me a clout with it! She followed it up with a fierce, finger-pointing lecture on the danger of matches but that's about the worst roasting I ever received as a child.

My Dad, in later years, came to remind me of the actor John Wayne, often with a hand rolled cigarette, strangely almost never lit, hanging from one side of his mouth. I suppose, if you'd given him a tuxedo and a cowboy hat, he could have looked like a high plains drifter. He boxed at light heavyweight, mainly in London under the name 'Boy Crawford' with his main claim to glory being a win over an ex-American 'Golden Gloves' Champion. That was just about his last fight as, when he returned home bruised and battered, after paying his trainer, his rail fares and meals, he'd only about fifteen shillings (now 75 pence) left. Not long after that fight, he finally turned his back on boxing to the relief of my long suffering mother. I think my Mum had a lot to do with his retirement from boxing. Even though Dad took all the blows, hundreds of them during his career, I think she felt the pain of them too because she hated to see him hurt. One of my earliest memories of my Dad was of him sitting in a chair by the kitchen table with me sitting on his lap, with one hand in a bowl of water with blood spotted rags floating in it. Mum was sitting by his side, gently bathing his cuts and bruises, frowning and 'tut tuting' at the state of his face as it must have been a particularly brutal fight the night before. Boxing was a much tougher sport in those days as fighters were allowed to take a lot more punishment than they are now and I can remember her saying words to the effect of 'George, do you have to do this, take all this for so little money. There must be something else you can do?' I reached out with childish curiosity and nearly touched his cuts with my tiny fingers but, even though I was only a nipper, I realised how sore and tender they were so I never dared touch them.

When I was old enough to understand, Dad told me he'd once gone down to Portsmouth Docks to fight a bare knuckle, 'winner take all' fight. These fights took place now and again and, if they could get two good fighters, bets would be laid and the last man standing would win. At the time, he needed some extra money to support the family even though 'street fighting' was against the law. Not long into the fight, the police, who must have been given a tip-off, arrived and it was everyone for themselves. Dad escaped by diving into the waters of the docks so all he received that night was a soaking for his troubles.

In 1939 at the outbreak of World War II, he joined the army but, just before his ship was about to leave for North Africa, he was taken ill and rushed to hospital with appendicitis. By that time, we'd moved into a house in Crown Street. My brother Alan was born during a bombing raid in 1940. Mum and baby Alan were carried to the nearest air raid shelter and, in all the rush, Alan took a heavy bang on his head but he survived and was fine a day or so afterwards. Later that summer, our house was blown to pieces in one of the many German bombing raids of August 1940. Although we lost all of our possessions and belongings apart from the clothes we were wearing, we were lucky to be alive as a lot of people were killed in the bombing that night. We were re-housed in a two bedroom council flat in Craswell Street in the centre of Portsmouth where many of the bombed out families lived and these buildings are still there today. It was a small flat with only very basic things; a table, some chairs and a moth eaten looking sofa. Mum had to go shopping most days, especially in summer, as we hadn't a fridge to store any fresh meat or milk that she was able to buy. There was rarely any meat but you could usually get some liver or kidneys which she would cook with potatoes and boiled cabbage. I remember one day during the war when it became known that there was fresh whale meat available at a butchers in Portsmouth. We had to wait for ages in the usual log queue to get a few steaks of it but it was so tough after cooking that you had to spit most of it out, leaving it piled up in those nasty looking, chewed up messes you leave on the side of your plate when the meat has been too tough. You tasted some flavour chewing it but it was almost inedible.

Also living in Craswell Street at the time were Mum's four married sisters, granny Elverson, her mother and Aunty Phyllis and Uncle Bert who had a close shave once when a bomb ripped through their veranda but, luckily for them, it didn't go off. We were now poorer than ever and the Salvation Army supplied us all with new clothes. When we returned home from the bomb shelter after air raids, those brilliant ladies from the RWVS (Royal Women's Voluntary Service) would come round, always happy and smiling whatever the situation was, to give us hot tea and buns.

Though the Germans bombed military and industrial targets in the area, civilian and shopping areas were also hit. During daylight raids, some of the German planes strafed the streets with their machine-guns and people out in the open had to quickly take cover. By 1942 the bombing raids had become so regular we would get the bus out to Wymering Heights and stay there until the raids stopped. It was a huge air raid shelter consisting of a series of large tunnels, carved out of the chalk hills behind Portsmouth. It had everything there from a canteen to proper toilets and three-tier bunks to sleep in and although they weren't very comfortable, at least you were safe from the bombing which you could still hear in an eerie silence apart from the occasional cry of a baby. There was always a lot of condensation and dampness in the air that sometimes brought on my asthma from which I was to suffer for many years to come.

Almost every summer during the war in late August, we took the twenty mile train ride from Portsmouth to Buriton along with many other poor families, to help with the annual hop picking. Each family had a hut to sleep in with straw on the floor for beds and we lived just like the gypsies who were always there with their beautifully painted wagons. We worked together by day and I played outside on the long summer evenings with the other children of my age. The pay wasn't much but Mum managed to save most of the money we earned; more than many others who used to spend their earnings at the local pubs. One year, I was taken ill with very bad asthma so we all had to come home with no pay and no chance to earn any money.

One exception to our annual hop picking was in 1942 when I was six years old. We went to Lincolnshire for a few months where my father was stationed with his regiment at the time. We lived on a farm and it was good to be away from the bombing although the bombing wasn't as bad as the previous two years and the danger of invasion was over. To pay for our keep there, Mum helped out with cleaning chores, washing and cooking in the main farmhouse. I remember one day, a small pig escaped and the farmer, quite an old boy, was doing his nut chasing it around the farm. Mum told me to catch it for him so I started to chase it but, when I dived to catch it, I only ended up falling flat on my face in a pool of farmyard muck! "Careful not to put your hands near its mouth if you catch 'im as them little buggers have sharp teeth you know!" the farmer said. I eventually caught it and the farmer was so pleased that he gave me sixpence for my efforts. I also had my first proper English breakfasts that summer with fried bacon, sausages and a free range fried egg on top with fresh creamy milk from the cows on the farm to wash it down; a meal I'd never tasted the like of before.

When the war was over, Dad went back to his job in the Parks department of the local council. Even so, we were still poor and didn't have much but Christmas was always a happy time and Mum and Dad always did their best for us. To pay for the extra expenses at that time of year, Dad would do gardening jobs in his spare time for the posh as we called them and, in wintertime, I would go with him to help clear snow from their pavements and driveways. Some of them were very kind, bringing out tea, biscuits and cake as well as giving us a few bob for our work. I remember one occasion we took home a lot of clothes a family no longer needed. Christmas presents were given to us in a pillowcase filled with a few small toys, colouring books and other small gifts such as sweets and apples. In those days that's about the closest you would come to getting 'Playstation'! As well as football I also loved cricket from a very early age and, when I was nine years old, Dad made a home-made cricket bat for me as my main present. With some old tennis balls, this provided hours of entertainment and fun playing in the streets.

Although the war had ended, there were still bombsites that hadn't been cleared and one day I was playing football on one of them and gashed my leg quite badly. Mum washed and bathed it but we had no antiseptic cream and within a few days I developed a high fever and had to be rushed to hospital with blood poisoning. I was very ill for a few days and lucky not to lose my leg.

On the whole I was a happy youngster but my health wasn't good as I was still suffering from asthma attacks in my early teens. A doctor told me if my asthma hadn't gone away by the time I was fourteen, I'd probably suffer from it all my life. It affected me most in the cold months of winter during the football term when I played for my school in the second team. Luckily I was okay the day Bert Barlow, the famous Pompey player came to coach us one afternoon. Bert was a Pompey star at that time who'd also played for Wolves. I was totally star struck being so close to him and he showed me skills with a football I hadn't seen until that day.

I wasn't put off by what the doctor said and joined Sultan Boys, a local football club run from a big old house in Kingston Crescent, Portsmouth. They had about sixteen teams with ages from 12 to 18 so you were virtually guaranteed a game every week. On match days we would all meet at the club then travel by a car which dragged an eight by four feet trailer behind it in which most of the team were crammed. One day, on the way to a game, it fell off and some of us fell out onto the road. Apart from a few grazes and bruises, no one was badly hurt. These days it would have made the headlines in the local newspapers but we just thought it was a bit of a laugh.

In 1949, when I was thirteen years old, my father took me to see my first ever game at Fratton Park and we saw Portsmouth beat Derby County 2-1 in the 6th Round of the FA Cup. Ike Clarke scored both goals. We were all packed into one huge stadium of excitement with the roar of a crowd of over 51,000 cheering Pompey on and the constant 'clickety click' of the now banned football rattles and the sickly-sweet reek of cigarette, pipe and cigar tobacco and the aroma of baking pasties and hot pies at half time. Pompey were in line to become the first team to do the double for twenty years but, surprisingly, lost 3-1 to 2nd Division Leicester City at Highbury which I remember listening to on a crackly old radio at home. It was really disappointing but nothing could dampen my enthusiasm for football and Pompey after my first visit to Fratton Park.

I don't think football is anywhere near as exciting now as it was then for a young teenager. The one scary part of it was the sway of the crowd in moments of great anticipation or when we scored a goal but I was hooked on football from that day on. I wanted to be out there on the pitch with them, with the likes of Tom Finney of Preston North End and Stanley Matthews of Blackpool. I wanted to be like them and nothing was going to stop me. From that point onwards, if I wasn't playing for the Sultan Boys, I'd go and watch Pompey. They soon made up for their exit from the FA Cup by winning the 1st Division Championship that year for the first time in the club's history and repeated the feat again in 1950-1951, the greatest triumphs in the club's history making me even more determined to play for Pompey one day.

At that time, the problem with my ambition to be a footballer was that, as well as my asthma, I was very frail and small for my age which seemed strange considering my Dad's height and physique and Mum's average size. I was also quite a nervous, slightly insecure youth. Maybe it had something to do with the war that I had been through as a child and coming from such a poor background. When I met someone I didn't know, especially if they were very tall and much older, I used to get tongue-tied and go red in the face. Well into my thirteenth year, I was still well behind others of my age in physical development but, almost from the day I turned fourteen, I suddenly started to fill out in height and weight. My asthma attacks almost finally stopped altogether allowing me to take part in other sports that I'd missed out on before. I changed quickly from a skinny, shy, asthmatic youth into a strong young athlete, representing Hilsea Modern School and Portsmouth Schools in cross country running and in the 440 yards. I felt almost as if I could run forever, getting stronger by the month and giving me a growing self-confidence I'd never had until then. Perhaps my father's genes had finally kicked in as physically from that time onwards I never looked back and I never felt quite so unsure about myself again.

In my last two years at school I played for the First XI cricket team and represented Hampshire Schools at cricket. I felt a bit left out when I used to turn up with no cricket whites or my own bat whilst most of the others had all the gear; new bats, pads, the lot. I was above average at cricket for my age and Hampshire County Cricket Club invited me to one of their practises the year I left school. However, I'd decided by then to concentrate on football as I felt cricket was just for the posh.

Just before my fifteenth birthday, I bought my first ever pair of new football boots with the money I'd managed to save from my paper round. With great excitement and my hard earned wages, I went to the Co-op with 34 shillings (about £1.70

now) to buy a pair of the 'Stanley Matthews Boots' that I'd seen advertised in the newspapers. They were red leather and fitted me like a glove. Even though my left foot wasn't anywhere near as strong as my right at the time, I still played as a left-winger at school and scored a lot of goals cutting in from the left and striking the ball with my right foot. I will always remember my Uncle Albie's advice one day as he watched me kick a tennis ball backwards and forwards against a wall using mainly my right foot. "You won't be any good if you can't kick with your left foot," he said and, after that, I made a conscious effort to practise with both feet.

That year, at just fifteen years of age I left school which I'd never taken to much. Apart from Maths, I was poor at most subjects - you didn't get any homework in those days and that might have helped. Apart from the sport, one of the best things about my schooldays was the free bottle of milk everyday! A few days before the end of my last term, the headmaster Mr Street asked me what plans I had for the future.

"Well sir, I would like to be a professional footballer," I told him confidently. "Crawford, you've have no chance," he replied, advising me to forget it and get a sensible job.

I left school not long after my fifteenth birthday on July 23rd 1951 with no qualifications. It didn't matter as I received my first offer of a job a lot sooner than I'd expected. A few weeks before leaving school, I'd applied for a job at 'Pickfords Removals'. They hadn't even replied to my letter but, on the Friday evening of the very day I finished school, the son of our next door neighbours, Geoff Bampton, came round to tell me there was a job with the Portsmouth City Council if I was interested. Geoff was doing an apprenticeship with them and had just moved up a grade to assist a groundsman in the area, leaving his job vacant. I jumped at the opportunity as it seemed tailor-made for me being mainly an outdoor job and involved sport in one way or another. I arrived at the Council Offices at 7:30 the next morning where I was hired for the job and was told my job title was that of a 'Runner Boy'. This meant going out on a bicycle delivering letters to various places around the city including sports fixtures to the foremen who organised the preparation of council sports pitches.

I took to it like a duck to water. Sometimes I had to go to Southsea, a good four mile ride from Portsmouth, to deliver letters to the Town Council there so, as well as having a job, it kept me very fit as well. By coincidence, Dad was the head groundsman there by then, having totally mastered his craft. He was able to do anything from pruning a hedge, preparing a cricket pitch or a tennis court to laying a bowls green. On the days I went there, I was always very proud to be recognised as his son. Apart from running errands, I had to clean the Local Sports Council dressing rooms on Mondays after weekend games. As well as cleaning the shower and bath areas and mopping the floor, I also had to clean the toilets which had to be spotlessly clean on inspection. I continued to work for the Council for the next two years. Although my wages were poor, just £3:10s.0d a week, I gave half to my parents for my keep. It didn't leave me much spending money but, as my sister Barbara had been born the year before, there was now an extra mouth to feed in the family.

I continued to play football for Sultan Boys and just after the turn of the year 1952 at sixteen years of age, a chance that I had been waiting for came about. One of my best friends George Watts who played for the Portsmouth Youth team told their manager Mark Brooks, the headmaster of Milton School, that I was a goal scoring left-winger. The youth team trained on Tuesday and Thursday evenings at the Gas Company ground at Tipner. After a couple of training sessions, I'd impressed enough to be asked to come back on a weekly basis. Although I wasn't asked to put pen to paper at the time, at least I had my foot in the door of Portsmouth FC.

When I attended my first full training session at Fratton Park, all the first team players were there as well. As I was a winger at the time, I was asked to chip a ball in from the touchline into the penalty area. I felt very embarrassed for a moment because I didn't know what they meant by 'chip'. Luckily help was close at hand. Cliff Parker, a winger himself and one of the Pompey heroes of my youth, walked over to me and put an arm round my shoulder. "I bet you thought a chip was something you had with your fish eh?" he said with a smile and a laugh so as not to make a fool of me. It was the first time a first team player ever spoke to me. I was in total awe of him after that because, as well as being a brilliant footballer, he was also a nice person. Cliff had been known as quite a fiery competitor in his career but, like so many players, he was as gentle as a lamb off the field. It was nearly two years later and just a few weeks before I started my National Service that I was signed for Portsmouth Football Club who were to pay me a retainer of one pound a week during my two years in the army. Everybody in my family was very happy for me as football then was big time just like it is now although the wages in those days of even the top players bore no comparison to what they're paid now.

In the meantime, I'd started to work for the Portsmouth Trading Company making concrete and breeze blocks. My main job there was to lift concrete blocks, about 500 of them every day, onto a series of trestles at varying heights from floor to chest high where they were left to dry. As well as having to lift them correctly to avoid injuring my back, I had to be careful not to drop any of them on my feet, my most precious assets at the time! It was like doing keep-fit exercises, bending and stretching up and down with weights for eight hours a day and, though it was very hard work, it helped strengthen my whole body - I was still only seventeen and still growing. The money was better too. I was now being paid £5 a week. The job helped build up my stamina and I stayed in this job until I was called up to do my National Service in 1954.

Chapter 2

"National Service"

On 21st of October 1954, I went into the army to do my two years of compulsory National Service. A few weeks before I'd received a letter telling me to report to Winchester Barracks, home of the Royal Hampshire Regiment at 3:00pm that afternoon. At lunchtime that day, I went to say goodbye to all my work mates. They offered to take me out for a drink but I turned down their offer as I was worried it could turn into one of those farewell occasions that end up like an out of hand 'stag night'! I didn't think it would be a very good idea to arrive at my new barracks all the worse for drink although there were a few who did. I'd already said goodbye to my family earlier that day and Mum was very tearful. It was the first time in my life I'd been separated from the family for more than a few days.

After saying goodbye to my work mates, I made the five minute walk to Cosham Railway Station and caught the train for the thirty mile journey to Winchester Barracks. I was a bit nervous on arriving there. It felt like the first day at a new school with strange faces all around you in unfamiliar surroundings and the uncertainty all the time of what was going to happen next. I'm sure most of the other recruits felt the same way even though some of the cockier ones were better at hiding it than others. Our initial introduction from the CO (Commanding Officer) confirmed what we'd received in writing a few weeks before, that we were to be paid twenty eight shillings a week minus two shillings tax and that our parents were to be paid one pound for every week we served abroad. We were also expected to open a Post Office Savings account which I'd already done with the idea of saving about ten shillings (50 pence now) a week. It didn't leave you with a lot of pocket money as the rest of your wages had to go towards buying razor blades, shaving soap, 'Brasso', 'Green Blanco', boot polish, haircuts (only the first one was free), dusters and cigarettes (I didn't smoke because of my asthma).

I'd only just had my haircut a few days before but, even so, we were still all given an army regulation haircut which left you shaved at least an inch above your ears. Then, like newly sheared sheep, we were taken to the army stores warehouse to be issued with our kit. This included a best uniform, a second best uniform, best boots, second best boots, headwear, PT (physical training) kit, a gas mask, bed linen and an ex-army service rifle with its firing pin removed. Our NCOs (non commissioned officers) then showed us to our billets.

"Alright you lot, I know it's probably not as comfortable as home but you'll soon get used to it," one of them said. It didn't seem very likely at the time. Beside our beds each conscript had his own six foot tall metal wardrobe in which you stored most of your kit and a small foot locker beside it for smaller items and the few personal effects you were allowed to keep. I say 'allowed to keep' as we were instructed straight away to change into our uniforms; all our clothes, the civvies we'd arrived in, were to be sent back to our families. We didn't know it at the time but it was all part of the process to separate you from the world and family life you'd known up until then into the very different demands of being a soldier and life in the British Army.

Supper was a stinking dish of boiled fish that hardly anyone ate, including me. There wasn't much to do in our billets that evening. A few little groups formed, some playing cards and others talking about their girlfriends and families. Every evening after that, we had to make sure our kit was neat, clean, shining and tidy for the next day. Our thick woollen army trousers had to have a straight crease down them, done the army way with an iron and damp brown paper. Items referred to as 'webbing' included anklets and belts which had to be treated almost daily with the regulation 'Green Blanco' as it scuffed up easily, leaving marks you were likely to be pulled up for. Good old 'Brasso' was for polishing cap badges, belt buckles and buttons. Melting black shoe polish in a spoon then pouring it slowly over the toe area of your boots was a good though expensive trick many of us used. When the polish dried it left the toe end of your boots looking like two little black mirrors you could almost see your reflection in. Those of us who mastered the technique were often complimented by our sergeant major and NCOs who monitored your kit maintenance almost daily. The results were well worth the extra expense. It certainly helped you to get in their good books. Failure to come up to scratch on self-presentation was punishable by having a Company Order brought against you with a CB (confined to barracks) which could be anything up to seven days. More serious offences (such as being late for the curfew on returning from weekends) could result in having your pay stopped and internment for a month. Other punishments included washing the latrines, cleaning the barracks or 'spud bashing' which meant peeling hundreds of potatoes in the canteen kitchen, sheer hell. Anything you could do to keep the NCOs off your back was worth doing. Mostly they were a bad tempered lot and given the slightest chance would swear and shout, tearing a strip off conscripts if they failed to come up to standard. If they'd been banned from swearing, it would have left some of them almost speechless.

At 6:00am the next morning, the lights went on, like blinding little suns. "Wakey wakey, wakey wakey!...early morning rise and shine!...hands off cocks and on with socks if you please gentlemen!" an NCO shouted, striding through our billet, tugging at the bed clothes and swearing at the deepest sleepers not awoken by the lights or his first blast. We didn't know what to expect for breakfast after what they'd served up the previous evening but it was a big improvement with porridge, eggs, bacon and toast with plenty of hot tea. In the next few weeks, I soon worked out if I didn't like what they were serving up in the canteen I could use the one pound a week retainer that Pompey paid me to buy something decent to eat in the NAAFI (the Navy, Army and Air Force Institute). Otherwise there was never enough left of your wages to treat yourself to a good slap-up meal.

By the time breakfast was over it was only 7:00am so a long day lay ahead. The worst fitting uniforms were, in time, tailored to the size of the individual but, before our first parade at 9:00am that morning, some of the recruits were in a terrible panic, mostly with the trousers they'd been issued that were far too short or miles too long. By the time we were assembled for our first day's training on the parade ground, most of us looked reasonably well turned out. There were still a few weird and wonderful looking would-be soldiers amongst us. After taking a roll call, the drill sergeant confronted the more unfortunately dressed recruits, standing in front of them looking them up and down before lifting his eyes to heaven in dismay. It was probably all part of his usual routine. After forming ranks, we marched off round the parade ground for a few minutes before the drill sergeant brought us to a screaming "HALT", followed equally loudly by "BLOODY SHAMBLES". I think that, whether you were good or bad, this again was all part of his first day routine. By the end of the day, we were slowly getting better, learning to react to the different commands of marching drill. The drill sergeant said he didn't expect miracles at first and would be patient to begin with but that we had to learn fast and any of us who didn't were in for a rough time because we had only six weeks before our passing-out parade. Anyone who failed to listen or pay attention to his commands or advice were eventually singled out for an ear shattering lecture on the parade ground and, in some cases, for punishment drill.

During the first week, the drill sergeant had told me a few times not to drag my feet along so much which I thought I'd improved on until one training session when he brought our ranks to a sudden halt. He then started to move towards me and I knew straight away his frowning eyes were focusing in on me this time. "Here we go," I said to myself as he came to a boot-crunching attention right in front of me with his hands held tight together behind his back, eye-balling me with worrying menace.

"Private Crawford," he started.

"Yes sergeant," I replied, trying not to look him directly in the eye.

"For the last time of asking, would you please try and pick up your legs when you march and not look like some bloody German peasant dragging along a couple of bloody tree trunks! Do you think you could possibly manage that for me Private Crawford?" he shouted.

"Yes sergeant," I said, quaking in my shiny black boots.

"I mean, I'm not expecting you to do a stupid bleedin' German goose-step am I for Christ-sakes?"

"Yes sergeant."

"Because at present Private Crawford, I dread to think of you in the passing-out parade. At the moment you stand out a bloody mile for all the wrong bloody reasons and I'm not going to let you be just the one bloody idiot to turn it into a bleedin' shambles! Is that quite clear Private Crawford?" he continued to shout.

"Yes sergeant," I said, keeping my replies short, as I'd seen others dig an even bigger hole for themselves by trying to make excuses or giving too much backchat.

"So just pick them up a bit okay, just try and at least make them look as though they're attached to your body in some way?... Do you think you could possibly do that for me Private Crawford?" he said more quietly and I sensed the worst was over.

"You're a footballer I believe Private Crawford?"

"Yes sergeant."

"And what football team do you play for?" he asked, beginning to smile and looking down at my boots.

"Portsmouth sergeant."

"Portsmouth!...Well, God help them if you keep on carrying your legs round like you are at the moment Private Crawford!"

"Yes sergeant," I kept replying. To my relief he then started to grin but only briefly before casting his pinpoint eyes at some who were giggling at my expense.

"And all those I can hear sniggering, and you know who you are, can bloody shut it because he's a bloody sight better than most of you! Do you understand you horrible lot?" he barked.

"Right. Quick...march," he roared and that was the end of my one and only grilling on the parade ground.

Most of the recruits had a roasting one way another during our training, some worse than others. It certainly made you listen and correct any faults he found with you. As with most drill sergeants, his bark was a lot worse than his bite. When he was off duty he was great to talk to with a brilliant sense of humour and, if any of us had a problem, you knew you could confide in him. He would advise and help you as much as he could. He also told us of his experiences as a soldier in World War II, having us spellbound by some of the stories he had to tell.

After nearly six weeks of almost non-stop square-bashing (marching drill in the army) and 'Field Training' in which we learned how to march with and present a rifle on parade, we were all good enough to be 'passed-out' on the parade ground in mid November, witnessed by my proud parents, my brother Colin and sister Barbara who came to watch me that day. It also meant I had some leave too. It was great to travel back to Portsmouth on the train together and spend a welcome three days at home where I knew Mum would cook up some good dinners for me.

In the month before Christmas, I was sent to Exeter to do my small arms training in the use of the new FN rifle, the Sten Mark 5 machine-gun and the Bren Gun. You were taught how to take them apart bit by bit, then clean and re-assemble them, sometimes against the clock. The Bren Gun, famous for its use in World War II, was the most complicated weapon and pretty heavy if you had to carry or run with it for any sort of distance. The Sten gun had a love-hate reputation amongst the regular army for its habit of sometimes jamming. In the army, it was known not very affectionately as 'The Plumber's Nightmare' owing to its barrel looking like a sawn-off piece of tubing that you were just as likely to find under your kitchen sink, stuck on top of a very basic wooden frame. The jamming problem was caused by a combination of badly made magazines and poor maintenance but, in my training, I never had one jam on me. It was devastating at close range with thirty two 9mm rounds in the magazine and capable of firing 600 bullets a minute that ripped through your cardboard target of the enemy, completely decimating it in a few seconds. You were also strongly advised not to drop the Sten gun on any sort of hard ground, especially concrete. This had been the cause of numerous accidents in World War II with many soldiers being wounded or killed as the Sten had a nasty habit of re-cocking itself and spraying the whole unwanted contents of its magazine all over the place, forcing those nearest to it to show a sudden talent for break-dancing! We were constantly told "If you look after your weapon, it will look after you" which was probably true though I never quite came to fire one in anger or war.

Just before Christmas that year, I passed the practical and written exam and was promoted to Lance Corporal. We had five days off and it was a great luxury to have four consecutive nights in a soft warm bed at home. I slept like a log every night just basking in the luxury of it. When it was time to return to Winchester Barracks, Mum locked herself in the bedroom and I could hear her crying. She knew our regiment was about to be posted out to Malaya within the next few weeks which was, at the time, Britain's equivalent of America's Vietnam in years to come.

The forecast was not good the day we left Southampton docks on the troopship 'Empire Orwell'. By the time we had left the English Channel and reached the Bay of Biscay, the weather had roughened up and everything that could possibly move was battened down. It wasn't long before the stormy sea took its toll on us and most of us were sea sick. We were just young soldiers who'd never been to sea before, not like the sailors aboard who were more used to a constantly rolling ship. It was my first time at sea and I fared no better than most of my fellow recruits, being seasick for well over twenty four hours. It was no use staying in bed either. It just seemed to make it worse as the hammocks we slept in seemed to roll around even more than the ship. Getting used to the hammocks was also a skill in itself. At first, most of us ended up on the floor when trying to get in or out of them.

Our first stop was Port Said where we stopped for eighteen hours to take on supplies. We were allowed ashore there, the first time I'd ever set foot on foreign soil. The day before, the Captain of the Royal Hampshire Regiment had warned us about mugging and the possible dangers involved when individual servicemen were offered women. He advised us to stay in groups of three or four and to be wary of being lured off the beaten track. He'd also shown us a film, warning us of some of the pitfalls and perils of travelling with the army abroad, especially in hot climates. It was mainly about food poisoning through contaminated food or water, followed by sunburn and how best to avoid or treat it. It finally finished with the full horrors of venereal disease with nothing left to the imagination. He then went to the desk at the front of the lecture room and picked up a length of rolled white towel to show us what we were in for if any of us caught the clap.

"Oh, just one thing I've must to show you lads," he said, unrolling the towel in front of us. "I popped in to see the ship's doctor on my way here and he lent me this to show you all. If you're not careful, you'll be getting one of these stuck in your bum," he said with a bit of glee, holding up for all to see a large, wide syringe with a hypodermic needle of no less than six inches long on the end of it, bringing 'ooh's' and 'ouch's' and some brave laughter from a few of us assembled. I think we all literally got 'the point'!

When we went ashore in our khaki uniforms, we stood out like sore thumbs and were constantly approached by street traders, some of them offering their goods and women too. Our few hours of shore leave went without any major alarms and we set sail for the Suez Canal and Aden at midnight. When we arrived, some of the troops on board disembarked but there wasn't enough time to go ashore as our ship was on a tight schedule for our arrival in Singapore. We were looking forward to getting there. After three weeks at sea, we were keen to get our 'land legs' back as soon as possible. As there wasn't a great deal to do to kill time during the trip, our senior officers organised keep-fit sessions for the mornings and weapon drills to occupy us in the afternoons. I took my section for both these activities, using some exercises I'd learned training with Pompey. It mainly involved running around the decks and up and down the stairs between them. In the afternoon under scorching hot sunshine, all the different types of guns we had were dismantled, time and time again, until many of us could almost have done it blindfolded.

When we reached Singapore, a lot of the lads had been hoping to try their luck with the local talent. They were disappointed as there was no time for shore leave. We were marched off in ranks, rifles and kit over our shoulders, straight to the railway station. We travelled overnight to Kuala Lumpur with an escort of highly trained armed guards, bristling with weapons who told us that rebel bandits sometimes fired at the trains on this route. "Don't stick your head out of the windows - you might get it blown off," we were warned. It wasn't very comforting or sleep-inducing. I don't think many of us slept much anyway as it was so hot and sticky; conditions most of us had never experienced before. It didn't help that we were still wearing our cold climate army gear and it wasn't until we reached our new barracks just outside Kuala Lumpur shortly after sunrise the next day, that we were issued with our new kit. It was to be our base for the next sixteen months and certainly one of the most exciting times of my life. I was to use my football boots that I had packed for the tour a lot sooner than I'd expected.

After we'd been issued with our hot climate kit and shown our billets, I was told to report to the Support Division Office. There I was informed that I would be in charge of the Supplies Store which had everything you would need out there, from uniforms to tents and 'billycans'. I think they'd known quite a lot about me in advance of my arrival and that I was a young professional footballer because that same afternoon, after I'd finished unpacking, I was summoned to the Sports Sergeant's office. He was very welcoming, asking me if I'd like to play for the barracks football team that evening at 6:00pm (in army time, at 1800 hours) and, though I was tired, it was an offer I was only too pleased to accept.

I scored a hat-trick in a 6-1 victory, a great start to my posting, with our team that evening including two other professional footballers; John Thomas, the Bournemouth youth keeper and Alan Wicks of Reading. Others I remember in that team were Len Pickard, Brian Holland, Dave Mitchell, Jack Softley, Ian Hunt, Nobby Rule, Peter Salt and Clive Newton. Sport in the army then was just as important as it is now with the desire to win, just like in battle, being of major importance. If you were good at any of the major sports, representing the army gained you more privileges. You were given as much time off as necessary for training, giving you regular breaks from some of the more tedious daily routines and duties that the other recruits had to endure.

Not long after my army debut, a Chinese gentleman called Mr Lee came to the camp and was given permission to talk to me with an offer of playing for Selangor Rangers of Kuala Lumpur, the biggest club in Malaya. I think he'd made some sort of attempt to pronounce my name before our first meeting but it came a long way short of it in practice.

"Ah! Mistar Ramone Crawfords! Vely pleeze to meekyu," he said, introducing himself with a huge smile and a bow which continued through as vigorous a handshake as I'd ever had, leaving my arm shaking like a crossbar after being hit by a Ted Phillips thunderbolt.
"No....me... Raymond... Crawford," I replied slowly, pointing a finger at my chest, trying to correct him. Unfortunately, his next two attempts at pronouncing my name turned out to be even more alarming than the first so I thought it best to settle for his first effort which had been 'Ramone Crawfords' as it sounded a lot better than a cross between 'Mistar Rayving Crawlforwards' and 'Mista Raymo Clawforwards' which had roughly been his next two attempts although it did make me sound like some sort of drag artist on the camp entertainment committee from the old comedy programme 'It ain't Half Hot Mum'.

Although I couldn't make much sense of what Mr Lee had said to me, the words 'football, team, play and pay' had a lot of appeal to the young impressionable eighteen year old that I was; to be paid for what I loved doing best. The Sports Sergeant had told me it wasn't the first time Mr Lee had approached the army looking for professional footballers so I gladly accepted his offer. After confirming my first game would be in two weeks time and another sweat-wringing shake of my hand, he left.

The day of my debut for Selangor Rovers, Mr Lee came to collect me in his chauffeur driven Mercedes. It was a day that I will never forget. It was exciting to see parts of Kuala Lumpur that I might never have seen otherwise. We drove through the outskirts of the town on our way to the ground of Selangor Rangers. On our way through one of the poorer suburbs of the town, our driver brought our car to a sudden halt. We had come face to face with a large, horned ox and cart, one of hundreds on the streets there which were a constant source of accidents and traffic hold-ups. We were stuck there for a while, not being able to move backwards or forwards, with our driver hooting madly which made no impression on the ox whatsoever. It just stood there, looking poker faced at us through the windscreen with saliva dribbling heavily from both sides of its mouth. As its owner tried to move the ox, shouting and shaking a stick at it, a very young frail looking young girl ran up to the car holding a tiny baby in her arms. She held out her hand, obviously pleading for money, through the open window that I sat by in the back of the car. I started to fumble through my pockets to try and find some money but quickly realised I hadn't brought any with me. All my expenses were to be paid along with my match fee. She kept on begging with the palm of her tiny hand almost under my chin but I was both powerless and penniless to be able to help her. Then Mr Lee leaned across and gestured her away angrily with language I can only think was not very charitable. The ox and cart shifted and we began to move on again, leaving her standing there, a slight tiny figure holding a baby in her arms by the road side. When I looked back over my shoulder, she was still standing there, looking at us as our car drove away into the distance and I felt really bad about not being able to give her some money.

"Don'woree Mistar Ramone, it ap'en all times here," Mr Lee said. Maybe she was having me on, I don't know, but there were all too many beggars and poor looking people around, far too many of them for them all to be taking you for a ride. I knew well enough from my own childhood what it was like to be poor but we'd never starved. As I was young and all this was so new to me, I forgot the encounter quickly but it's the sort of thing you remember more when you get older, when you've more time to think about the past. That's when it catches up with you and some moments like that start to come back and haunt you a bit. I wish we'd been coming home after the game that day as I could have given her some of my match money.

I played as often as I could for Selangor Rangers and the few pounds Mr Lee gave me for every game I played came in handy. We won the league they were in that year and also two cup competitions. I suppose I could look back at it as the first loan period of my career; from Portsmouth FC to Selangor Rangers. I quickly became renowned locally for my goal scoring feats and it wasn't long before I was approached by the Malayan Federation who invited me to go on a tour to Cambodia and Vietnam. The army couldn't have looked after my professional interests outside my national service any better and gave me permission to join the Malaysian team for the two weeks of the tour. I had a brilliant time though I had one setback. After we'd played Cambodia winning 3-1, in which I scored one of the goals, I suddenly came down with a respiratory infection and a heavy fever. It was unbelievable how quickly it hit me. No sooner than I had showered and dressed after the game, I felt like death warmed up. In a few hours, I was in such a delirious state, I can't even recall the flight from Cambodia to Saigon, apart from saying "Christ! What the bloody hell are you going to do with that? I haven't caught the bloody clap" at the sight of a doctor holding up in front of me, a huge syringe with a six inch needle, just like the one the captain of our regiment had shown us on our ship out here. The sight of it was enough to make anybody come out of a heavy fever and sit up in their sick bed with eyes agape at the size of it. It did the trick though and, being very fit and strong at the time, I was up and playing again a few days later against Vietnam in the national stadium in Saigon. Before the game, the Malaysian team were introduced to the recently appointed Ngo Dinh Diem, president of what was then The Republic of Vietnam. I shook hands with him as he moved down the row of our team but his years were numbered. He was executed in the political coup d'etat in 1963 which was the start of the Vietnam War.

Whilst I took part in many more football matches in Malaya than military exercises, I did go out into the jungle on a few occasions with the battalion when our senior officers had received information of any terrorist movement in areas near to our camp. Apart from that, the most scary part of it as a soldier had been guard duty at night on your own. Two hours on then two hours off under searchlights with shadows flickering everywhere as they moved around. It certainly made you stay awake as night time was bandit time when they were most likely to kill soldiers.

On the night of our first operation in the jungle at 10:00pm, our sergeant major did a quick recap on what we'd already been told in lectures on the 'do's and don'ts' of jungle warfare; especially on night operations. It was just like a manager's pre-match talk before a football match except, in this case, people would be shooting not at goal but at you instead. We boarded light trucks and made our way to the edge of the jungle with our nerves starting to jangle at what might lay ahead of us. Those who'd done the full weapons training course at home, including myself, were carrying the standard army Sten machine-gun of the time and those who hadn't with rifles with long stainless steel bayonets to be used if it came to hand to hand combat with the enemy. These were fearsome looking weapons and enough to confirm what Corporal Jones was to say years later in the TV comedy series 'Dad's Army' that the enemy would certainly not like to have one of these 'up 'em' as he used to put it!

Apart from mosquitoes and snakes, the heat and humidity were the worst things you had to combat out there. Even if you'd been out in that climate for some time, the rebels were much more used to it, giving them a big advantage over us in that type of guerrilla warfare. After our support group had been dropped off, we were left with our officer by a small, forty yard long wooden bridge that army engineers had constructed which we'd already been told how to negotiate. To go over in one large group would have made a nice big target for the enemy if he were lying in wait for us so we went over one by one. When the man in front of you reached the other side of the bridge, you would follow when he signalled the all clear and, when you reached him, he would tell you which direction to take then you would do likewise with the soldier who followed you.

Unfortunately, when I arrived on the other side of the bridge, the man in front of me had disappeared. 'Trust my luck to have a fucking idiot right in front of me!' I swore loudly to myself. When the next man joined me, it was down to potluck as to which route I should take. There were two tracks to choose from. I told my fellow soldier to wait and I ran as fast as I could down one of the tracks, holding my Sten gun out in front of me with the safety catch off, ready to fire if necessary. After about a hundred yards there was no sign of our company. Feeling the panic rising in me, I turned around and sprinted back to the bridge, fearing a bullet might come fizzing past my ear or banging into me at any second. I was relieved to get back the bridge in one piece where a few men had congregated including our officer who'd backtracked to sort out the confusion started by the one irresponsible idiot. After we'd re-grouped, we were instructed, as in training, to split up into twos with thirty yards between each pair, taking up positions of cover, crouching or lying down behind trees or vegetation, in wait for the rebels. One of you looked at the jungle in front of you, the other keeping his eyes out for any movement on your flanks and behind you. The never ending screech of the crickets was so loud you could hardly hear yourself think. The sweat poured off us and endless squadrons of blood-sucking mosquitoes gave us no respite but we had been told not to swat them or flap at them as the slightest noise or movement could give not only your own position away but the whole company's as well. It was to be one of the most important lessons I ever learned about teamwork and certainly the most dangerous team game I had ever played in.

I had paired off with my trusty mate John Thomas and we just lay there bathed in sweat; the Bournemouth Youth team goalkeeper and Portsmouth's Youth team centre forward, waiting for the enemy to arrive. We were both very nervous, clutching our machine-guns tightly and, after a few minutes, our nerves started to jangle even more when there was a loud rustling noise some thirty yards to our side; roughly where the next pair of soldiers would be. We couldn't be sure it was them making the noise or if they'd been taken by surprise by rebels who were masters at getting within killing and knifing distance without being detected. John moved quietly into a firing position, lying face down with his Sten gun pointing in the direction that the noise was still coming from.

"Do you think I should let 'em have it Ray?" John whispered in a hoarse voice. "No, give it a while John. We can't be sure it's one of them yet," I whispered. I think we both thought the moment of truth had finally arrived for us, kill or be killed. Then we heard a another sound, this time more familiar. It sounded like someone having a piss and that's exactly what it turned out to be. We both allowed ourselves a quiet sigh of relief when it turned out to be one of our blokes relieving himself in the bushes. The rest of the night passed without further incident.

By the time we arrived back to camp early the next morning just before sunrise, we were tired, covered with mosquito bites but in high spirits. All of us were laughing and joking, relieved that our first operation in the jungle was over. We'd also found out that the idiot who relieved himself in the jungle was also the bastard who'd left his position at the bridge when he should have been waiting for me. The bollocking he received later that day must have been pretty bad as he was reported as being in tears when he came out of the CO's office. In a way, you had to feel sorry for him; he just wasn't cut out for the army. He didn't want to be there and had never wanted to be a soldier. There were others like him who were equally hopeless. To have advised any of them to make a career of the army would have been as cruel as suggesting to a man with only one leg to consider a career in professional football. A sobering fact was brought to our attention later that day when we were informed that earlier that morning after our night in the jungle, ten local Malay workers had been found beheaded in the rubber plantation next to the jungle. The rebels, mainly Chinese communists, had most probably outflanked us. It was just like the Vietnam War which started a few years later, trying to fight an enemy you rarely saw.

I went into the jungle on two more occasions but nothing out of the ordinary happened on either operation. It was shortly after one of these night operations that, having all returned safely to our billets, the one tragedy of the whole tour happened. It was the death of Brian 'Smudger' Smith who came from the same Hilsea area of Portsmouth as me. Even though he wasn't in the same Company as me and I didn't know him that well, we had both come from very poor backgrounds. We'd met a few times and talked about our past, our childhood and being brought up during the war. Brian was a good footballer too. The fatal accident happened in his billet after Brian's 'A' Company had been out on an operation when, as was customary drill on returning, they were cleaning their rifles before handing them in. Some idiot on the bed next to him had forgotten to remove a loaded round from the firing breach of his rifle, pulled the trigger and a few seconds later Brian lay mortally wounded on the floor beside his bed. He never regained consciousness and died a few days later in hospital.

It was the first funeral I'd ever been to, so I didn't know what to expect or how I would react. On the day, I cried my eyes out. I just couldn't believe Brian's life was over as they carried his coffin out of the small chapel on the camp. That afternoon I put on my training shoes and started to run round the camp. By then, I was now doing that every day to keep fit but, after a while, I ignored the warning we'd been given not to stray too far from the camp and made for the jungle. At the time, I wasn't thinking about some rebel who was going to chop my head off or about to take me hostage as it just seemed the events of the day and the funeral outweighed the normal thoughts I may have had regarding my own safety. This was the best way to get it out of my system. It was silly to put myself at risk. There had already been one death through negligence but, in times of high emotion, we sometimes react to impulses we usually suppress. I just ran and ran, as fast as I could for as long as I could. If there were any rebels out there watching me running, stripped to the waist sprinting through the jungle as if my life depended on it, they might have thought I was trying to escape from the British Army. They'd have to have shot me that day to stop me. After that first rash venture, I became more confident and did the same run almost every day after that though not going quite so deep into the jungle. I used to take quite a bit of stick from my mates about my obsession with fitness. It didn't worry me as I think some of it was jealousy on their part for the extra privileges I received playing football for the Army and Selangor Rovers. All I was concerned then was to be as fit as possible when I arrived back in England and Portsmouth FC.

Apart from the tragedy of Brian Smiths death, I'd had a great time out there, not just because of all the football I was able to play but also the good friends I made. I still keep in touch with a few today. What it gave me most of all was an all round, self confidence that put me in good stead for years to come. Problems I would have had doubts about tackling myself before my National Service now became quite simple to overcome. My one disappointment on leaving was the failure of Selangor Rovers and also Mr Lee to give me the Gold Medal they'd promised me after we'd won the Malaysian Gold Cup, their equivalent of our FA Cup. I kept on asking almost to the day we left for home but I never received one. Maybe that's where they drew the line. Even though I had helped their team to win the cup, I was possibly regarded as a foreign football mercenary and therefore not considered as far as receiving medals was concerned. However, it would have been nice to take one home to show to my family and the lads at Portsmouth FC but it just wasn't to be.

It took three weeks longer to get home than the outward trip. By then, the Suez Canal was closed because of the troubles at the time, forcing our ship the 'Captain Cook' to take the long route around South Africa. We eventually arrived home, docking at the quayside of Liverpool harbour on a cold, wet October day and the first thing I did after setting foot on British soil again was to fall flat on my arse! It wasn't the best advert for eighteen months of National Service. That was the end of my life as a soldier, one of the best times of my life. It was then only a day's train ride back to Portsmouth and my family.

Chapter 3

"Eileen and my dream comes true"

It was just one month after I had returned from Malaya on Saturday November the 26th 1956 that I first sighted the lady who was to be my wife for the best part of the next forty three years. I was walking off the pitch at Fratton Park after we'd beaten Reading Reserves when I had my usual quick glance at the crowd. It gave me a good feeling to see happy contented faces when you'd played well and won. That afternoon as I neared the tunnel, I couldn't help noticing an attractive young lady smiling at me. I smiled back and our eyes locked together for a few seconds before I disappeared down the tunnel back to the dressing room. I didn't think a lot more on it at the time until later that evening.

Saturday nights were drinking and dancing nights and I joined some of my mates as usual for a few drinks in a local pub before we took the bus to Southsea where there were two dance halls; the Savoy and the South Parade Pier. We usually ended up at the Savoy but, that evening, one of us said we'd try the Pier for a change. When we walked in, I saw the same young lady I'd exchanged smiles with after the game that afternoon. She was chatting with some other girls. On noticing me, she smiled at me again. Although I was still a bit on the shy side, I smiled back, mouthing a 'hello' at her as I walked past her which was quite brave for me as I was quite shy with the ladies at the time. I couldn't stop looking at her as the evening went on and, though she was looking back, it took me a few pints and more than a few words of encouragement from my mates before I plucked up enough courage to ask her for a dance. When I eventually did, she made me feel comfortable straight away. I wasn't much good at dancing so I just shuffled around the floor. However bad I looked, I just wanted to get to know her. I asked what her name was and she said 'Eileen'. Straight away, she told me I was a little shy and that she'd seen all the games I had played for Pompey Reserves and that Elvis Presley was her favourite singer whose records she played so loud at home the whole street could hear. I think I knew straight away that she was a kind person with a strong personality which, in the future, I found out could be very fiery at times but, without Eileen, I doubt that I would ever have achieved anywhere near what I did as a footballer. After the last dance, I took her home. On the way back, she went through the entire Portsmouth squad, telling me that her favourite Pompey player was Jack Froggatt who'd also played for England. At the doorstep of her house, I asked her if I could see her again and perhaps take her to the pictures. She agreed and from that moment we started to see each other two or three times a week.

As I started to get to know Eileen, I found out her upbringing had been very different from my own. She'd never really wanted for anything as her father had a well paid job in Portsmouth dockyard. He was coming up to retirement age, a veteran of the 1914-1918 war about which he had many stories to tell, most of them horrific with just a few that were very amusing. He accepted me straight away as did Eileen's mother who was quite a lot younger than her father. She had a part-time job in a pub called 'The Mermaid' as well as being a confirmed 'Bingo' addict with a lucky habit of winning money more often than not. Not long before I met Eileen, their family had been hit by tragedy. Her eighteen year old brother Tim had been killed in a motorbike accident. The consequences of this, regarding Eileen's relationship with her mother, came to light many years later.

After our first meeting, Eileen never missed a game for the rest of the season when I was playing for the reserves at Fratton Park. Strangely, she never commented on how well or badly she thought I'd played and always seemed to be a nervous wreck after games. In fact, even more shattered than I was. It was something that never changed in all the years and hundreds of games she watched me play. She had a good job working for a firm called 'Canda', a supplier to the multinational clothes retailers C&A. The factory was directly above their branch in Commercial Road, Portsmouth. She was a supervisor on a line making dresses at which she was brilliant. She could make a dress out of anything from an old curtain to a used tablecloth if she had to. I remember in years to come, when she made about twenty dresses for herself and our three daughters for a holiday in Italy and all our curtains and tablecloths were still intact the day we left for that holiday! It was nearly a year later, as we danced again at the place of our first meeting at the South Parade Pier, that I asked Eileen to marry me and it was only a few seconds before she agreed. We decided to wait until after the following Christmas to get married.

I continued to have a good season in the reserves, scoring 'almost for fun' as they say these days, especially over Easter when I notched up nine goals in three games, four of them in a 7-1 demolition of Ipswich Town Reserves at Portman

Road. In 39 combination league games, I had scored 33 goals. It was enough to convince the Portsmouth manager, Eddie Lever, that the moment pre-season training started in the summer of 1957, he included me in the 1st team squad. I was very nervous at first. In those days, as a young player, you really respected the senior players. Some of my childhood shyness' came back. I was now training with the likes of Jimmy Dickinson, Peter Harris, Jackie Henderson, Alex Wilson and Norman Uprichard; all international players. At first, I wasn't too sure whether to address Jimmy Dickinson as 'Mr Dickinson' or not. I wondered, shall I call him 'Jimmy' if he had the ball? No, better not, it might upset him, me being so forward. I decided it was best not to speak until spoken to. It didn't last long though as Jimmy was a kind person who made me feel welcome in the squad. After he'd called me 'Ray' a few times, I had the courage to say 'Jimmy' in return. He was a very cultured left half, comfortable on the ball, rarely giving away possession and, if he had time, he would always pass the ball. I learned a lot from watching the great man play.

A week before the season started, we had a practice match at Fratton Park with the 'possibles' against the 'probables'. I must have done enough to impress Eddie Lever to give me the chance I'd been waiting for. My childhood dream had come true. I made my debut at Fratton Park against Burnley in the first game of the new season on the 24th of August 1957. My nickname of 'Jungle Boy' had come about the day before the game. I'd done an article for the Daily Mirror with the football reporter Mike Langley about my time in Malaya. Jack Mansell, who was the comedian of the team, immediately started to call me 'Jungle Boy' and it stuck for the rest of my career.

My debut in the 0-0 draw against Burnley wasn't a great curtain opener for the season. I didn't do myself justice. It was mainly due to nerves and I think Eddie Lever realised this. Though I'd tried my best, harrying and chasing down everything and pressurising defenders as I always did, I was doubtful if I'd be in the team to play Tottenham Hotspur the following Wednesday evening but Eddie gave me another chance. At home to the mighty Spurs, with a crowd of over 33,000, I set about repaying Eddie's faith in me by scoring two goals in two minutes that night. I was also brought down in the box allowing Peter Harris to complete his hat-trick from the penalty spot in a 5-1 thrashing of our famous visitors. I was so happy as I thought I'd finally made it and this was the start of a long career with Pompey. It was all I'd ever wished for and I felt life couldn't get any better at the time.

We went into the next game confident that we'd do well against Preston North End side at Deepdale. They had veteran players Tom Finney and Tommy Docherty playing for them. It was known to be a home fortress, a hard place to come away with anything and they overwhelmed us 4-0 on the day. Confidence was still high though when, a few days later on a rainy North London evening, we did an early season double over Spurs in a thrilling match at White Hart Lane. Before the game, our team coach was held up in traffic after a serious accident in North London and the police had to give us an escort to the ground. To save time, Eddie Lever told us to change into our strips on the coach. When we reached the ground, we virtually ran straight from the coach onto the pitch. Although I didn't score that night, I laid on the fourth goal for Syd McClellan and Jackie Henderson added another to seal the points for us in a 5-3 win. It was Pompey's first post war win over Tottenham Hotspur at White Hart Lane and I was just glad to be part of it all. It was three days later in early September, just five games into the season, when my luck literally broke. I scored in our 3-1 win at home to Sheffield Wednesday but, in the game, picked up the most serious injury of my career, breaking two bones in my left ankle. They decided not put it in plaster, just binding it up with heavy criss-cross bandaging that the surgeon at the hospital thought would be enough. It took over two months for the injury to heal, much longer than anyone had expected.

I made my return to the first team in late November in the SFCC, a cup competition for league clubs in the south, part of what eventually became a national tournament called the League Cup, the lesser version of the FA Cup. I made a good comeback on a chilly late November evening in London, scoring twice in a 3-2 win over Millwall under floodlights at the 'Den' - I think Joe Broadfoot, later of Ipswich Town, told me lately that he'd played in that game.

A couple of days later I was happy to see my name back on the 1st Team sheet to play Blackpool away on the Saturday. We lost the game 2-1. A week later we were back on song, destroying Luton 5-0 at Fratton Park. I scored two of the goals so I thought I'd taken up where I'd left off. The next game was at Roker Park against a struggling Sunderland; we weren't that far above them in the table. With their fanatical fans, it was never going to be easy to come away with anything. I also had the bones of my newly healed ankle fully tested that day. I started the game on the left wing. After about twenty five minutes, myself and Peter Harris changed over to try and unsettle their fullbacks. I was just taking on their left-back when a crunching tackle came in from nowhere leaving me in a heap on the ground wondering what had hit me. I looked up to see their left winger ex-England international Bill Elliot, standing over me with his hands on his hips, glaring down at me.

"Now Ray, you can fuck off back to your own bloody wing and don't come back if you know what's good for you!" he growled. I didn't reply, settling for a free-kick as I limped back to the left wing. We managed to draw 1-1 that day, a good result those days as we were usually hammered there, ankles and all.

The game at Turf Moor against Burnley a week later, just four days before Christmas, was probably the turning point of my career at Pompey. They were a very good up and coming side. Despite playing bad, we came in 0-0 at half-time. When we entered the dressing room, the club chairman Mr Jack Sparshatt, a huge bullish man of near 18 stone, was waiting there with a face like thunder. After a few words telling us how poor we'd been, he started to tear into me as if most of it was my fault. Just as little boys and sticks don't go well together, club chairman and half-time team talks are an equally bad mix. A chairman's place is in the boardroom and he shouldn't interfere with the manager's job. When you come in at half-time, the adrenaline is still pumping in you and Sparshatt went on for just a few seconds too long. "Fuck off, will you," I snapped and complete silence followed. Sparshatt left without saying another word and, from that moment, never spoke to me again to the day I left Pompey eight months later. Though we played better in the second half, we lost the game 3-1. There were four senior internationals in the team that day; Jimmy Dickinson, Peter Harris, Alex Wilson, Norman Uprichard and Phil Gunter who was an England 'B' cap, yet I took the brunt of the chairman's attack in front of them. I was only 21 at the time, still learning the game and apart from Derek Dougan, the youngest player in the side that day. It left a bitter taste in my mouth like a nightmare you can't get out of your head.

A day later, though I'd not forgiven him for what he'd said, I regretted swearing at Mr Sparshatt and wondered what the consequences would be. Having been in the 1st team squad since the beginning of the season, I'd a fair idea by listening to the rest of the team talking. It was the chairman who was having the final say on team selection, not Eddie Lever. I wasn't summoned to the chairman's or manager's office for a dressing down or fined or suspended but it was no surprise to me when I saw I wasn't on the team sheet to play Chelsea at Stamford Bridge on Christmas Day. It turned out to be the best game to miss all season as we lost 7-4! We did put matters right on Boxing Day turning Chelsea over at home 3-0 but I was still left out of the team. It was nearly a month and two more defeats later (Preston completing the double over us 2-0 at Fratton Park and 4-2 at Sheffield

Wednesday) before I was back in the team to play Manchester City at home.

I was picked to play centre-forward with Derek Dougan as my strike partner which was the first time we'd played up front together. Derek was a year younger than me, two inches taller, strong in the air with some good ball skills and tricks on the ground. The 'Doog', as he was to be known at Wolves in years to come, had been signed from the Northern Ireland club Distillery the previous summer for a fee of about £5,000. He had made his debut shortly after my injury earlier that season. Derek was a great character and a handsome, six foot two, quietly spoken Irishman with a kind smile and a touch of the showman about him. He was one of the few players at the club who owned a car at the time, an open top Ford Consul which was a luxury car in those days. He could be seen on most afternoons parked opposite fashionable coffee houses or driving round Portsmouth with some of his team mates on board. I was very envious of him. I would have loved to have a car then but I was saving for the extra expense of married life so Eileen and me had to be content with our bikes.

We beat Manchester City 2-1 and I scored both goals, made more pleasing than usual as they were against City's legendary German keeper Bert Trautmann, an ex-POW who'd been voted 'Footballer of the Year' the season before in 1957. My first after nine minutes was about the best I scored for Pompey. When Peter Harris ran to the bye-line and crossed for me to volley into the roof of the net from about ten yards and even the great Bert was nowhere near that one. I could have had a hat-trick and several others would have increased our lead had it not been for Trautmann's brilliance. Unfortunately we pushed forward too much with too many players looking for a second goal, leaving ourselves too thin at the back and they equalised just three minutes before half-time. All the crowd rose to Trautmann as he walked off at half-time for his brilliant exhibition of goalkeeping. Ted Phillips, my strike partner in years to come at Ipswich, always rated him as the best and bravest keeper he ever played against. True praise from a man whose ferocious shot was the hardest in British football at the time and the like of which I've never seen again to this day. I scored again in the second half, pouncing on a slight error from Trautmann, to give us a 2-1 win, though Bert certainly didn't deserve to be on the losing side that day. The next goal I scored wasn't of much consequence as far as the result went, in the 5-1 thrashing at Wolves in the Third Round of the FA Cup. It was however, the only game I ever played against their legendary centre-half Billy Wright, capped by England 105 times who was marking me that day. It was slightly more than just a consolation goal for me.

At the time, Eileen and I were finalising the arrangements for our wedding. I went to see Eddie Lever to check if the date we'd chosen, Saturday the 12th of April would be okay. Eddie agreed at the time, saying there was no problem. On the Friday morning the day before we were to be married, just out of curiosity, I took a casual look at the team sheet pinned up on the dressing room notice board for Pompey's game against Blackpool at home that weekend. Within a few seconds, it quickly turned into more than just a glance as my eyes nearly popped out when I saw my name 'R. CRAWFORD' chalked in to play for the first team against Blackpool at home the next day, my wedding day! I rushed straight away to see Eddie, entering his office, almost at a gallop to ask him what was going on.

"Ray, you look worried, what's the matter?"
"Eddie, have you forgotten I'm getting married tomorrow. You said it was okay a couple of months ago that I could take tomorrow off?" I replied.
"Oh, sorry about that Ray, it must have slipped my mind but I really do need you to play tomorrow. As you know, Alex Govan has picked up an injury and we've already have four other first team players on the injured list at the moment. I need you to play on the left wing for us," he said.
"But I can't just cancel it, everything's been arranged from the church where were getting married to the reception and what about all the people we've invited, we can't just call it off like that?"
"Where are you getting married Ray?" he asked after a few seconds thought.
"At St Mary's Church on Fratton Road."
"And what time is the wedding Ray?" he asked.
"Half past one give or take a few minutes either way."
"That's alright Ray, kick-off isn't till three o'clock and you don't have to be here before two fifteen," he said calmly.
"Eileen will be hopping mad when I tell her!" I said.
"Ray, I'm sorry. I know it's not very convenient and I am sorry but I really need to field my strongest available team" and that was the end of it; another factor being that since Eddie had agreed to let me have the day off, Pompey had slipped into a desperate relegation struggle. I was very worried what Eileen would say about the change of plan When I told her, she said it was great that I should play for Pompey the same day as getting married though my version of the musical 'My Fair Lady' was now 'just get me to Fratton Park on time!'

All went as planned and we were married shortly after 1:30 pm on Saturday the 12th of April 1958 at St Mary's Church which overlooks the small house in Fratton Road where I was born. As notice had been given of our marriage in the local paper 'The Evening News' a few days before the wedding, quite a large crowd of well-wishers, mainly teenagers, had assembled outside the church. I waited patiently for Eileen to arrive constantly looking at my watch and signing dozens of autographs for the youngsters. Eileen arrived with time to spare at the entrance to the church with her hand resting on the arm of her proud father, wearing as beautiful a wedding dress as you are ever likely to see and that she'd designed herself. It was a perfect ceremony witnessed by over fifty family and friends and not, as I'd feared, rushed in any way. Perhaps the most touching part of the whole day was when those beautiful youngsters, most of whom I knew were poor and couldn't afford a ticket to go to the match that day, were waiting patiently to cheer us when we came out of the church.

It wasn't long after the wedding photographs before I was speeding towards Fratton Park in a chauffeur driven car we'd hired for the day. The chauffeur looked more like your local milkman and was without doubt the fastest one in Portsmouth that day! There were a few laughs and raised eyebrows when I arrived in the Portsmouth dressing room a few minutes after 2:15pm that afternoon with bits of confetti in my hair, still dressed in my wedding clothes, white carnation and all. Eddie Lever and the lads all congratulated me before I proudly pulled on the Pompey shirt that day. When we saw the Blackpool team sheet shortly before the kick-off, neither Jimmy Armfield who was injured nor Stanley Matthews were playing. Stanley rarely played at Portsmouth because of the severe physical battering he usually received. It was a tough game in those days.

We lost 2-1 and I left the pitch thinking I'd had a poor game until I read a report on the game in the 'Football Mail' the next day. It was written by 'Nimrod', the most respected local sport writer on Pompey matches, who said that I'd played well on the day and was unlucky to find their keeper George Farm in such great form. The one saving factor of the day was Sunderland's 3-1 defeat to Manchester City, slightly easing our relegation worries. As it turned out, with three games of the season to go, if they had won or even scored a point that day we would have been relegated that year.

When I came out of the dressing room, probably in the quickest time I had ever showered and changed after a game, Eileen was waiting for me with the chauffeur in the players' car park. Despite losing to Blackpool, there was a large crowd of well-wishers waiting at the gates to cheer us on our way as we left the ground with the milkman-like chauffeur still at the wheel, speeding us off to our wedding reception. There was more loud applause with another shower of confetti and cheers when we arrived at a place called 'The Hut', a small community centre in Binsteed Road that we'd rented for the reception. I put behind me the disappointment of the game and, after thanking all the guests for being so patient waiting for me to get back from the football, everybody tucked in to the superb buffet Eileen's parents had organised, the centrepiece being a huge dressed salmon. Thanks to my new mother-in-law, who'd done a very good deal with the Mermaid pub, it pleased all no end, especially some of my mates who were to arrive later that evening to find out that all the drinks were free!

Later that evening, more guests began to arrive, mainly friends who'd had to work that day and some of my mates who played for local teams on Saturdays (making you wonder if football is more sacred than marriage!) It was one great evening, with everyone dancing and singing to a local band hired for the occasion. They played everything from the top of the charts music of the time to jazz. I didn't dance much that night, just with Eileen for the traditional dance of bride and groom. I was just happy to sit back and watch everybody enjoy themselves, talking to Eileen's father for much of the evening. By eleven o'clock, all the excitement of the day was beginning to catch up with me; the build up to the wedding, the football, and the beer and the wine. So, with Eileen by my side, we were driven off to the loud cheers of all our family and friends with the usual tin cans tied with string to the bumper rattling along behind us, all the way to our flat in Copnor to begin our married life together.

Less than forty eight hours later, I was carrying a fully loaded dustbin outside our flat for collection when I felt my back go. As you can imagine, when I reported to the ground with an injured back later that morning, the stick I received from the rest of the team was merciless! The club physio was more sympathetic. After examining me, he said that, although it wasn't a serious injury, it was bad enough to keep me out for the next match. I was bitterly disappointed because I was hoping to play in the last three games, especially against Manchester United. It was to be a momentous but sad occasion as it was the new United, rebuilt after their tragic loss of so many great players in the Munich Air disaster. I watched the game from the stand and the point we gained in a 3-3 draw at Fratton Park turned out to be the difference between survival and relegation. It put us two points clear of Sunderland who we still had to play with two games to go. We lost 2-1 away to Luton Town but Sunderland lost as well and, although they beat us 2-0 at Fratton Park in the last game of the season in which I played, Pompey survived by the skin of their teeth on goal difference and the 'Black Cats' were relegated. I finished the season with 9 goals in 17 league and cup games and was looking forward to a long future at Pompey or would the curse of Jungle Boy rear it's ugly head?

Chapter 4

"Farewell Pompey"

Shortly after the end of the season in the summer of 1958, Eddie Lever, after thirty years of loyal service to the club was sacked and replaced by Freddie Cox from 3rd Division Bournemouth. I was very disappointed with the decision. The club had struggled for a few years but it wasn't all Eddie's fault. To me it was no coincidence that Eddie's sacking was the start of the worst decline in the club's history and also a change that was to turn my whole career upside down. The chairman Mr Sparshatt and the Board thought Pompey were under-achieving. The glaring fact was that although they'd been a great team winning the 1st Division Championship (now the Premier League) two years running in 1949 and 1950, that was nearly ten years before and the players weren't getting any younger. Four of the team were the wrong side of thirty by a few years and, without myself and Derek Dougan, the average age of the 1st team was over 28 years old. Pompey had lived in the past and rested on their laurels for too long.

Sparshatt said he was going to invest in a youth scheme but he was about five years too late. I saw exactly the same thing happen at my next two clubs, Ipswich Town and Wolverhampton Wanderers. I remember when I shook hands with Eddie the day he left Fratton Park. I thanked him for giving me the chance to prove myself and said I was very sorry to see him go. He told me not to worry as he was going back to school teaching for which he'd qualified before his playing and managerial career. He also said he'd made a special point of saying to Freddie Cox the new manager "Whatever you do, don't sell Ray Crawford!" His final words to me were that he thought I had great potential and would play for England one day, a prophesy that came true. It was still one of the saddest moments of my career when I watched Eddie walk away that day.

His replacement Freddie Cox had once played for Arsenal as a winger before retiring to manage 3rd Division Bournemouth. He was given the job at Pompey on the strength of reaching the Sixth Round of the FA Cup the previous season with the giant killings of both Wolves and Spurs. This had led Freddie to believe that third division players were well capable of adapting to the much higher demands of 1st Division football and he bought a centre-half, Basil Hayward from Port Vale and paid out £10,000 for Harry Harris, an inside-forward from Newport County. Although Harris scored 13 goals as a striker that season, his final record of 48 goals in 377 appearances for Pompey shows that although he served the club well, he was not a natural goal scorer. Only Ron Saunders, a centre-forward signed from Gillingham, managed to bridge the gap between the divisions with any success. To sum it all up, Freddie Cox brought 3rd Division players to the club and that's exactly where Pompey ended up a few years later, in the 3rd Division.

We lost the first game of the season 2-1 at home. I wasn't in the team that day but was recalled for the next game two days later on the Monday away to Aston Villa. Although we lost 3-2, I scored my first goal of the season and Villa Park came to be a happy hunting ground for me throughout my career. This turned out to be my last ever goal for Pompey. If anybody had said that to me at the time, I'd have thought they were either joking or crazy.

My last game for Pompey was the third game of the season away to Nottingham Forest where we were hammered 5-0. Two days later on the Monday, Ron Saunders, the Gillingham centre-forward was signed. I never even stopped to think it might signal the end of my days at Pompey. I was now happily married, Eileen was expecting our first child and I was playing for my hometown club where I intended to stay for my whole career. I was also hoping to play up front alongside Derek Dougan. We'd begun to build up an understanding that had been noted by the local press. I was in for the shock of my life. On the Tuesday morning, just a day after Saunders had been signed, Freddie Cox called me into his office shortly before training. I knew Alf Ramsey, the Ipswich Town manager, had already watched me a few times and approached Pompey after Eddie had been sacked. He had been refused to talk terms until a new manager had been appointed. I didn't think anything would come of it until Freddie spoke to me that day.

"Ray, you won't be in the team to play Aston Villa tomorrow night. I have to inform you that yesterday Ipswich Town contacted us with a view to buying you and it's been decided we will accept any reasonable offer concerning your transfer to that club," he said bluntly. It took me a few seconds for what he'd said to sink in and reply.

"What? But I haven't asked for a transfer, I'm not even on the transfer list!" I said.

"Well, I'm sorry Ray, you are now," he replied.

"Well, I'm sorry as well to say I don't want to be on the transfer list! I want to play for Portsmouth. I love the club and I don't want to go to Ipswich Town or anywhere else for that matter!" I could hardly believe what I was hearing.

"Ray, we have to do what is in the best interests of the club and your future," he continued.

"But what about my interests. My wife is expecting our first child. We've just moved into a nice club flat. All our family live here. Why should I want to leave Portsmouth?" I almost shouted but it was obvious he had no intention of listening to anything I had to say. After a brief pause he delivered his final verdict which felt like I'd been found guilty after a very short, unfair trial.

"Ipswich are playing Leyton Orient in London on Thursday evening and I want you to go and watch them. I've already told their manager Alf Ramsey you'll be there as he's very keen to meet you for a chat, okay?" he said, and I made no more comments, storming out of his office without saying another word.

After I'd cooled down a bit and my thinking became clearer, I thought the matter was possibly out of the manager's hands and he was just another 'mouthpiece' for the chairman Sparshatt. There were nearly forty players on Pompey's payroll then and I wondered whether Freddie could have been acting on orders from a higher level; to thin out the squad at the slightest opportunity and consider any half decent offers for any player to get some money coming in, thereby reducing the payload at the same time. I also had to consider the exchange of words I'd had with Sparshatt in the game at Burnley the previous season. I know it's never a good idea ever to swear at the club chairman but I knew I would get goals that season. What you do on the field and not what you say in a flash of temper in the heat of the moment, especially in a dressing room, a place that should be 'no man's land' for a chairman at half-time during a game, is what should really count.

But from that point on I really had no choice, so I took the train up to London to watch Ipswich Town play Leyton Orient at Brisbane Road the following Thursday evening. I was cursing to myself a lot on the way, wondering what the hell I was doing there, sitting on a train I didn't want to be on, wasting my time going to a game I had no wish to see. When I first met Alf Ramsey and shook his hand, I felt as if I was about to ask for an overdraft facility or to borrow some money. He looked more like a bank manager, immaculately dressed in suit and tie, without so much as a hair out of place. I watched the game with Alf from the Director's box. Ipswich lost 2-0 and, but for their keeper Roy Bailey, it could have been a lot worse. To be honest, they were terrible. I was tactful enough not to offer this opinion to Alf after the game. I just referred to it as one of those off-days you sometimes have, where nothing goes your way and all the luck seems to be against you. Alf though, forever honest, put the record straight just saying "Ray, we played badly tonight. We can play a lot better than that, I can assure you", before inviting me to join him on the team coach back to Liverpool Street to have a chat. I accepted his invitation and we stopped for a meal on the way where Alf introduced me to John Cobbold, the Club Chairman and some of the directors of the club. It was also good to see Reg Pickett again, the ex-Pompey player who Alf had bought the previous season, even though he was also a little embarrassed by Town's performance that evening.

I had a long talk with Alf in which he spoke very slowly but clearly, leaving me in no doubt as to the meaning of what he said. He told me of his plans for Ipswich Town and thought the team had great potential but he was still a few players short of having a team that could challenge for promotion to the 1st Division. He said I was one of the players he felt could help Ipswich achieve this. He also arranged the payment of all my expenses for the trip and, if only one thing impressed me that evening, it was the quiet honesty of a man who knew exactly what he wanted and, little did I know it then, a man who was going to change my whole career, putting it quite definitely on the right track. As we parted company that evening, I told Alf I would need a little time to consider a move to Ipswich and would have to discuss it with Eileen which he accepted with a firm handshake and a knowing sort of smile that suggested it was not going to be our last meeting.

But it didn't take long to think about it. Before the train had barely left Waterloo Station, I'd made up my mind that I didn't want a transfer to Ipswich Town. There were many logical reasons at that time in my career. Why should I move from Portsmouth who were in Division 1 to a team in Division 2 who didn't appear to be very good, even though Pompey had narrowly escaped relegation the previous season. Joining Ipswich at the time seemed to be a long way short of improving my career and also a good hundred and fifty miles away from both my family and Eileen's. There seemed to be no real incentive to move there. I wouldn't be getting a pay rise which I'd just had at Portsmouth. Any fair-minded young player in my position would surely have come to the same conclusion that it would be taking a step backwards to have joined Ipswich Town at the time.

I'd played at Ipswich once at the end of the 1956-57 season for Portsmouth Reserves on an Easter Bank Holiday Monday. There was only a small crowd being a reserve game. We were strong for a reserve side that included two full internationals, Alex Wilson, a Scottish fullback and goalkeeper Norman Uprichard. We were far too strong for the Town Reserves winning 7-1. I scored four of them so perhaps my performance that day filtered back to Alf Ramsey on his return, sparking off his interest in me. At the time, Ipswich were in the Third Division South and that same day won 2-1 at Carrow Road against their arch rivals Norwich City and did an Easter double over them winning 3-1 two days later at Portman Road. That year Ipswich won promotion to the 2nd Division and Norwich were relegated.

The evening I arrived home from London after seeing Town play and meeting Alf for the first time, I asked Eileen what she thought of a possible move to Ipswich. As I'd expected, she said that she'd prefer to stay in Portsmouth but it was my decision and she would support me whatever I decided. I'd already made up my mind. I was Pompey born and bred and proud to be playing for my home town. There was no way I wanted to move to Ipswich at that time or anywhere else. The next morning, I expressed the same feelings to Freddie Cox as I sat opposite him in his office. He wasn't at all happy with my decision which I'd half expected anyway.

"Ray, I'm sorry to have to tell you this but you do not figure strongly in the future of this club. I advise you to reconsider what has been offered to you," was all he had to say.
"But I scored nine goals in seventeen games last season. I know I was out injured for a while but...." I started to plead my case.
"Ray, look! Please just take my advice. Be grateful that another club has come in for you. You'll get regular first team football and roughly the same pay as you get here. Just take my advice and sign for Ipswich Town. It's the best offer you have at this very moment. I also have to tell you that you've played your last game for Portsmouth. As far as I'm concerned, that's the end of the matter," he said, before walking out of the office leaving me sitting there, shaking slightly like a child after a telling off for something I hadn't done.

Whether this was really coming from him I still couldn't be sure of at the time. I knew there was also talk amongst some of the players that some of them were getting the same treatment as me. I thought in my case it was a bit more personal, on account of my run-in with the club chairman after our dressing room exchange at Burnley the previous season. Wherever you go, wherever you play, whatever job you do, there is always liable to be just the one person you don't get on with. However much you try, they won't change their opinion of you and, if it's the club or company chairman, you've no chance really.

After thinking over my almost non-existent options, I went out to join the rest of the squad for the morning's training. I spoke with a few of them about the position I was in. They said I should take the offer. Johnny Gordon, a man I thought I could confide in more than most said he thought that Portsmouth was only going one way and that was down. He strongly advised me to go to Ipswich Town. Johnny was to leave the club just a couple of months later as well, a huge blunder as he was a terrace hero and the powerhouse of our midfield who always scored his fair share of goals. That morning I had to concede that this was the end of the line for me and the club I'd been so proud to play for and worshipped since I was no more than a child. It was hard to believe, at the age of twenty two, I'd played my last game for them. I had a reasonable option, not one I would have chosen myself, but at least it was a chance for a fresh start somewhere else. Although Ipswich hadn't played well when I saw them, their manager Alf Ramsey had left a strong impression on me. I kept on thinking of that moment we had said goodbye after our first meeting, that 'knowing look' he gave me, as if he knew that our paths were destined to meet sooner or later. The more I thought about it, the more I believed that he'd really left me with the genuine feeling that he wanted me at Ipswich Town, as had their chairman John Cobbold. So I said to myself: 'Sod you, Cox and Sparshatt, I'll go where I'm wanted and two fingers to both of you!' At least Ipswich had one thing in common with Portsmouth - they were both ports near the sea where I'd always prefer to live. I'd possibly been as good as an Ipswich Town player for the last few weeks or 'Ports-wich Town' player ever since that first meeting with Freddie Cox, the deal probably agreed, done and dusted to the last detail, all but me putting pen to paper and signing. Maybe the days of the old navy 'press-gangs' weren't quite over yet?

It was after training that morning, on Friday September the 5th, having made only two first team appearances that season, I decided enough was enough and went to see Freddie Cox. I'd rehearsed a few lines but didn't bother with them or sit down and was as blunt and brief as he'd been with me earlier that day. I told him I'd sign for Ipswich Town and, without a second's delay, he picked up the phone and rang Alf Ramsey, quickly arranging for me to meet up with him at Craven Cottage in London where they were to play Fulham the next day. I had no idea at the time that this would eventually turn out as one of the best decisions I ever made in my life.

It was a much happier journey when I travelled up with Eileen to London the next morning. Just two days before, I had been cursing my luck and been an unwilling guest at the Orient game. I felt as if a huge weight was about to come off my shoulders. I was going to make the very best of the opportunity for which I was about to sign. It was a good flowing game with Ipswich impressive in attack but shaky in defence. Fulham fielded a strong side that had gained promotion that season. The team included Johnny Haynes, Jimmy Hill, Jim Langley and Tosh Chamberlain, a forward line that would have tested the best of defences at that time. Fulham won 3-2 with a late goal but I'd definitely seen some of the potential Alf Ramsey had told me about two days before. I signed for Ipswich Town Football Club shortly after the game in the presence of Alf Ramsey and John Cobbold in the office of the Fulham manager, Bedford Jezzard, on Saturday September the 6th 1958.

Chapter 5

"Ipswich Town"

It was six o'clock the following Wednesday morning when I left our flat in Portsmouth, carrying a suitcase containing a few changes of clothes, my football boots and a few sandwiches Eileen had made me for the trip up to Ipswich. I boarded the first train to London that morning, starting a journey I was to make many times over the next two months. After making my way through the maze of the London Underground from Waterloo to Liverpool Street, packed with early morning commuters, I just had time to grab a newspaper and a cup of coffee before catching the next train to Ipswich. As the train rumbled through the Essex and Suffolk countryside, I wondered what the future might hold for me. I was so sad to leave Pompey but I had to be positive, put the past behind me and take my move as a challenge, a new adventure in my life.

The train arrived shortly after nine o'clock at Ipswich Station and I walked the short distance to Portman Road, not much more two hundred yards away. When I crossed over the bridge between the station and the ground, it was good to see the river running underneath and, to my right, the docks in the distance that led to the estuary and the sea. At the entrance to the ground, I met Freddie Blake, Town's groundsman at the time who'd produced about the finest of all football pitches in England. It was almost like a huge bowling green, mowed in neat criss-cross squares, perfect for a team with a passing game. Freddie directed me to the old converted cricket pavilion which I quickly remembered from my one game there eighteen months before when playing for Portsmouth Reserves. It wasn't easy to forget as it was about one of the most basic of dressing rooms you were ever likely to see, probably one of the worst in the entire football league at the time. It was nicknamed by the players as the 'Chicken Hutch'.

Jimmy Forsyth and Charlie Cowie, Town's first and reserve team 'Z Trainers' as they were called, were there waiting for me. In those days if you'd referred to them as 'coaches' as they're called today, they would have thought you were talking about a bus! Jimmy was a funny looking chap, totally bald with a long, square chin, not as famous as Jimmy Hill's but no less interesting. Jimmy Forsyth was both first team trainer and club physio. I felt a little weary on my arrival, not just because of my journey but also totally drained mentally. I think all the uncertainty and events that had overtaken my life so rapidly had all suddenly caught up with me as I stood there two hundred miles from home, about to start my first day's training at a new club. I'm sure Jimmy sensed this. He was not only a very good physio but also a good psychologist, always knowing what made players tick in all situations. I quickly grew to respect this kind efficient man more than any other trainer I ever knew. I wish I could have taken his gentle wisdom on all the travels of my career. He was always there to talk to if you needed to confide in someone and always there when you were lying poleaxed in a game on some ground in a distant part of the land, perhaps on a darkening floodlit afternoon on a freezing cold winter's day. Out Jimmy would rush in his light blue tracksuit, sprinting towards you with the slight limp he always carried from an old injury, his shiny bald head standing out against the dark background of the stands, both arms weighed down straight to his sides as he ran with his yellow bucket of cold water with floating 'magic sponge' in one hand, towels and a blue bag of assorted remedies in the other. Jimmy was always the same reliable person you knew from the first time you met him. Whilst Alf Ramsey was waiting to see me in his office, Jimmy made me a large mug of sweet strong tea to revive me. "Take your time, no hurry, just take things easy son" the first of many times he was to say this to me in the coming years.

Alf was equally welcoming and, from the moment I set foot in his office, he made me feel at ease. First he sorted out the money side of things, confirming my wages were to be £20 a week playing for first team, £17 a week when not playing and the same in the summer months as a retainer fee. I was also to get £300 that was the maximum signing-on fee to cover moving costs and expenses. I soon found out that Alf was known for building up information not only on the strengths and weaknesses of every player on the club's books but also every player we would come up against in the whole 2nd Division. He told me my main strengths were scoring goals, running, heading the ball and my willingness to scrap and tackle but my left foot needed working on as well as my positional play, first touch, first time passing and hold up play. It was a fair assessment and I was willing to learn and improve. As he'd said to me in London the previous week, he wanted to get Ipswich into the 1st Division within the next two years. The more he spoke I sensed whatever disappointment I still felt on leaving Pompey was soon going to be forgotten.

It was then time to be introduced to the players. Alf took me back to the ramshackle old dressing rooms where they'd arrived for morning training. I quickly recognised two ex-Pompey players, Reg Pickett, Town's captain by then and Derek Rees who'd both moved there the year before. The rest of the squad was a real mix of local players with the usual sprinkling of Scottish and Welsh, one Irishman and a Yorkshireman. There were a few London lads as well, including 33 year old Tom Garneys, a six feet two inch tall East London cockney and a living legend at Ipswich having scored 126 goals in 248 games. The crowd had a special chant for him when Town were in need of a goal of "Give it to Garneys, give it to Garneys, give it to Garneys!" Tom was a great bloke and we got on very well but it was a chant that was to haunt me even after he'd retired. Playing alongside him was local boy Ted Phillips from Leiston, also well over six feet tall, who had scored 46 goals in 44 games in winning promotion to the 2nd Division in 1957, equalling Derek Dooley's post war record in 1952 playing for Sheffield Wednesday. It was a hard act to follow. At the time I joined, Tom was struggling with constant knee injuries and Ted was fighting to get back to full fitness after a cartilage operation, forcing Alf into the transfer market bringing 26 year old Dermot Curtis from Bristol City to the club the week before he signed me. From this point on, as Alf Ramsey, Ted Phillips and John Cobbold crop up so many times, I will refer to them as Alf when I was at Ipswich, otherwise Alf Ramsey, Ted, and Mr John.

After the introductions, Charlie Cowie came in with the training kit in an untidy bundle held with outstretched arms in front of him, so large you could hardly see him behind it, before dumping it in the middle of the old wooden floor of the 'Chicken Hutch'. What followed was like a loose ruck in a rugby game as they all dived into the mound of kit with some of them swearing and cursing, 'Ah, they're mine today, thank you very much!', 'Oi, that's the one I usually have you bugger!', 'Bloody hell! I've a matching pair for once!' and 'Ey, get your thievin' 'ands off 'em you bastard!' as I just stood there looking slightly bemused. When the mad scramble was over, it left what you could only describe as a small pile of assorted old rags for me to choose from. This wasn't anything like what I'd been used to at Pompey. There, they looked after us well in this respect with clean shirts, socks, tracksuits and woollen jumpers for when it became cold during winter. It was all ready for you when you came in for training at the beginning of the week, all freshly laundered, hung up on peg with your name on it.

When I'd put on the best of the remaining rags, I stood there wearing a shirt with most of its sleeve missing, a pair of badly ripped shorts and one of my big toes sticking out of the end of a sock. I realised then why there'd been such a mad rush for the kit as I looked like I'd been attacked by a ferocious animal! It was cause for great amusement amongst my new mates.

"Ah, you have to be quick in the morning here Ray, survival of the earliest and the quickest it is!" came a Welsh sounding voice from somewhere in the dressing room.

It wasn't long before Reg Pickett carried forward my nickname at Pompey of 'Jungle Boy' and, as Reg had an obsession about hair, announced to all that I would be bald by the age of thirty. Well, I'm sorry to say Reg, if this is ever printed and you get to read it, even though mine is now almost white, I still have most of it, unlike you thank you! After training, we went to 'Jimmy's Place' in Princes Street where we had coffee and tea and something to eat before the cards came out and some of the lads played poker for money. I just watched as I was never a gambler. I remember many occasions in the future when the pots grew very big and I saw players lose as much as a week's wages there. Somehow, professional football and gambling have always gone together. Nothing seems to have changed as you still hear players' stories of how their careers have been ruined by gambling.

I'd expected to stay in a hotel until Eileen moved up Ipswich but Charlie Cowie had kindly agreed to let me stay in his house in Granville Street, just off the Norwich Road until Eileen was ready to come up and choose from one of the club houses Ipswich owned. Although Town weren't a fashionable club at the time, they owned about a dozen town houses you could rent for £1:10s a week (£1.50 today) and Jimmy Leadbetter later told me this was almost the main reason why he moved to Ipswich.

Although Town had lost at Fulham the previous week, Alf told me it would be best if I had a few games in the reserves whilst I settled in so the first time I pulled on an Ipswich Town shirt was for the reserves away to Charlton Athletic that weekend. Both Tom Garneys and Ted were playing but neither of them was anywhere near fit at the time. We missed a lot of chances and the game ended in a 0-0 draw. Playing for Charlton at inside forward (midfield) that day was 25 year old Mickey Stewart who also played cricket for Surrey and went on to play for England. His son Alec Stewart followed in his father's footsteps playing for Surrey and England as a wicketkeeper/batsman. Mickey was on Charlton's books for a couple of years and retired from football that season to concentrate on cricket which seems a little strange as, in the nine games he played in the Charlton 1st team, he scored three goals; not bad for a midfield player.

Playing in London that weekend worked out well for me. I was almost halfway home already. With Eileen being six months pregnant at the time, Alf had agreed to let me stay in Portsmouth for the first two days of the week, coming up to Ipswich on Wednesdays for the rest of the week. At first Pompey had agreed to let me train with their squad on Mondays and Tuesdays but this arrangement was to change as the weeks went on for reasons that I can only call 'sour grapes'. When Ipswich started to flourish and Pompey to struggle, I was told that I could only train at Fratton Park in the afternoons by myself. It didn't matter as it wasn't long before we moved to Ipswich.

It was just a month later after a few games in the reserves that I was given the chance that I'd been waiting for to break into Town's first team. Dermot Curtis was called away on international duty to play for Eire. It was my second visit to Swansea in a week. I'd played there the week before for the reserves. On that trip, I'd forgotten my football boots, having to borrow Charlie Cowie's and, although they were slightly too big, I scored one of our goals in a 5-2 win. What more could I ask of Charlie? He was putting me up in his house and now I wanted to borrow his boots as well!

My first game against Swansea Town was on a mud bath of a pitch at the Vetch Field. We lost 4-2 but, with both Reg Pickett and Derek Rees encouraging me, I scored my first two goals for Ipswich Town. We returned to Wales a week later where we beat Cardiff City 2-1 at Ninian Park. It was the first time that I had played alongside Jimmy Leadbetter who had a hand in both goals from Derek Rees and myself. Jimmy's nickname was 'Sticks' because of his very thin legs. He was a lot a stronger than he looked, elastic and wiry, with a sweet left foot that could cross a ball with great accuracy; exactly what a centre-forward who is strong in the air wants. He was so accurate that Ted and myself used to pull his leg by asking him to make sure the ball was the right way round when it reached us so that we didn't head the laces that footballs were tied with in those days. They could give you a nasty bump or even a cut if you caught them flush on the forehead. A year or two later, they started to seal footballs with a plastic coating and laces were no longer used. This was good news for players like myself who loved to head the ball and, being a bit lighter as well, made Ted's shooting even faster and more of a handful for keepers to deal with.

Jimmy didn't have the easiest task as Alf had already asked him to play as a deep-lying winger, an original position that most, including Town's fans, didn't understand at the time. It left opposing fullbacks with a dilemma as it seemed they had no-one to mark, and if they committed themselves forward to go and seek out Jimmy, they risked the danger of leaving huge gaps in the defence behind them. As a result, Jimmy was getting quite a lot of stick from the crowd. They thought he should be getting forward more as wingers normally do. Just like our opponents, they didn't understand Alf's system and he was not about to broadcast it in the national papers. It was to be the key to Town's eventual triumph in 1962 and England's victory in the 1966 World Cup. I remember that season. I was once queuing up for some bread in a bakers shop on the Whitton Estate when I overheard a man rubbishing Jimmy, saying "Anat' Leadbetter, donno what the 'ell eeh's doin', do 'eeh?" Nobody knew me there and he didn't either. I hadn't been at Ipswich very long so I asked him if he'd ever watched Town play lately. He said he hadn't. I told him it might be a good idea to go and watch Town. Jimmy was playing a role few understood which was the test of a system that helped Ipswich win the championship and England, with their 'wingless wonders' as they were once described, the World Cup.

My first game for Town at Portman Road was a 0-0 draw with Huddersfield Town. Apart from a couple of shots, I ran around huffing and puffing like an angry young bull from the south coast, chasing down everything, trying to impress the crowd and win them over. I was shattered by the end of the game, leading to some of the local press saying I wasn't fit. Alf came to my defence saying that I was one of the fittest but needed to learn how to even out my energy over the course of a game. Meanwhile, Ted was scoring a hat-trick for fun in the reserves win at Brighton. More seriously, John Elsworthy came back with a fractured cheekbone that required surgery. Not long after that, John also had to have a cartilage operation which put him out for almost the rest of the season. It wasn't until the following year when he returned for an extended run in the team that I began to realise what a great player John was, a pure footballer much like Jimmy Dickinson of Portsmouth. Most, who ever saw him play, will tell you that John was almost without doubt the greatest ever un-capped Welshman. There was a saying at Ipswich that 'When Elsworthy is playing well, so are Town' which I came to believe with ever greater certainty over the next few years.

Two weeks later I played alongside Ted for the first time in a league game. He laid on one of the goals for me to score in a 3-1 win against Charlton Athletic at Portman Road. It was reported that we showed a good understanding. Over the next few years, we came to be known as the 'terrible twins'. Our initial partnership only lasted two games because Ted was injured again the following week in a 2-0 defeat at Sheffield United. Whenever Alf had to be critical of a player, he rarely did it after a game when he only spoke of the overall performance of the team unless you'd done something really stupid. He would wait well into the next week, usually on a Thursday, then quietly take you to one side and tell you how he thought you could improve your game and exactly what he expected from you. Almost a week after the defeat at Sheffield, he quietly gave me strict instructions to stop straying out to the wings, asking me "If you're not in the middle, who is going to score the goals, Ray?" What he also meant was that with me on the wing we were not attacking with enough players in the box. Sometimes you hear commentators talk of games being like a game of chess and, just like football, you are less likely to win a game if you don't attack with enough pieces. As an old fashioned type centre-forward, Alf wanted me to be in the six-yard box, drawing as many defenders in as close to goal as possible, allowing our midfield players and wingers to get in the box as well. Taking his advice on board, I stopped charging around like a mad thing and it immediately paid off in the next game with my first football league hat-trick in a 5-3 win against Brighton at Portman Road. The sports editor of the local Football Star wrote of my performance *'He moved like a footballer, used his brains and, in short, looked very nearly capable of filling the gap left by the illustrious Garneys'* and after I'd scored two more in a 3-2 away win at Grimsby Town, he commented 'One is becoming increasingly puzzled as to how Ipswich managed to persuade Portsmouth to part with this young player. I know Mr Ramsey was most persistent but it really does seem that Portsmouth have made a mistake they will come more and more to regret. Crawford's record of 9 goals in 8 games, must make Freddie Cox at Fratton Park think more than somewhat'.

Everything seemed to be settling down. That month Eileen and I finally moved into an Ipswich club house on Guy Fawkes' day, November 5th 1958. A few weeks earlier, Eileen had come up from Portsmouth to look at Ipswich Town's club houses and we stayed together at Charlie Cowie's house in Granville Street where I was still lodging. Charlie and his wife Chris, as well as being a very kind Scottish couple, were fresh air fanatics as well. They arose very early every morning and opened all the windows and doors and God, it was fresh living in Ipswich that November! Alf kindly spent a couple of afternoons with us, personally driving Eileen and myself around Ipswich until we'd seen all the available club houses. Eileen chose one in Cedarcroft Road on the Castle Hill Estate. It was best to keep quiet when Eileen was choosing houses. She knew exactly what she was looking for. I just stood there quietly, keeping whatever thoughts or reservations I had to myself. The house was very modern for the time, unfurnished with three bedrooms, a 22 feet diner and a big garden. The rent was incredibly reasonable, only 30 'bob' a month, in today's money £1.50. There was no garage but we didn't have a car at the time so it didn't matter. Only a few of the players had cars;

probably the most skilful player on Town's books at the time, Yorkshireman Brian Siddall, Basil Acres owned a van he used for his pet business in the Norwich Road. Other car owners were John Elsworthy and George McMillan, Town's Scottish reserve team keeper who lived in a small cottage a little way out of town. George was notoriously mean with how much petrol he put in his car, only about a quid's worth at a time. On more than one occasion that season, George and the other players he gave lifts to were late for training as he'd run out of petrol again. George also came up with one of the most original excuses I'd ever heard for being late for training. One day when he was late again, Alf asked him "Run out of petrol again, George?" to which George replied that he couldn't get to his car because there was a huge bull in his front garden! It had everybody in stitches and Alf, who had a great sense of humour, just smiled and raised his eyes to the heavens.

The one downside to my first two months at the club, was that although I'd received quite a few letters from Town supporters wishing me a happy stay at Ipswich Town, I also received others of a type I'd never seen before, poisoned pen letters. Some were very nasty with a lot of four-letter words made up in old newspaper print stuck to paper, telling me I'd never be able to replace or be as good as Tom Garneys. I just had to ignore them and keep on doing my best and score as many goals as possible. I never told Eileen about them. I realised that being away from her native Portsmouth was going to be difficult enough as it was without showing her the poisoned notes.

By the turn of the year, I'd established myself as first choice centre-forward. Alf Ramsey's tuition was slowly improving my all-round game. I scored my 17th goal in 16 games in the 3rd Round of the FA Cup at home to Huddersfield Town. It was a tough, bruising game, played on a pitch more suitable for skating. We were awarded a penalty five minutes before half-time. As Ted was out injured, I volunteered to take it. I powered it past their keeper Ray Wood who hardly moved an inch as the ball flew into the net. What could be easier I thought at the time. It was enough to win us the game 1-0 but it was to be my last goal for some time. My parents were at the game. They'd come up to stay for the weekend, the first and last time in all my years at Ipswich. It was also almost the last penalty I ever took for Town.

It was just over a week later, the day after we lost 2-1 to Fulham at home, on Sunday the 18th of January 1959 that Eileen made me a father for the first time. We quickly settled into our new life with a young baby although most nights, as is normal, I had to attend to the cries of young Jane so that Eileen could rest. Alf always put great emphasis on helping new players and their families to settle in the area. Frequently he asked if everything was alright, hoping that we were happy. Needless to say, Eileen thought the world of Alf. After the birth of Jane, my form took a dip in terms of goal scoring as I failed to find the back of the net in the next five games which included four defeats in a row, the worst being a 5-2 mauling by Luton Town in the 5th Round of the FA Cup. Strikers go through lean spells without scoring, just like batsmen or bowlers in cricket when sometimes the runs or the wickets dry up. Maybe the additional responsibilities of becoming a father and a few sleepless nights didn't help but I took to fatherhood like a duck to water, changing nappies, bathing and most afternoons pushing baby Jane in her pram to the local park and back. I loved her to bits so I never found it a chore. I wanted to give her everything that I may have missed out on as a child.

Jane's pram was the old fashioned type, nearly four feet tall with huge wheels and a large folding hood, built like a tank compared to the modern ones. On home match days, Eileen would walk the two miles to the ground, pushing the pram in front of her with baby Jane on-board. In those days, all the entrances were still left open for the whole game and, at half-time, she would walk the pram slowly past groups of supporters near the refreshment stands and listen to what they were saying. She told me that during those weeks when the goals dried up for me, she hardly heard a decent word said about me but all I could do was to keep trying and working hard though I knew I was still living in the shadow of Tom Garneys. Tom wasn't playing any more having announced his retirement and taken over as the landlord of the 'Mulberry Tree' pub in Ipswich. Some of the crowd were still shouting the old chant of 'Give it to Garneys!'. Like the poisoned pen letters, I just had to try and ignore it. I played with a smile on my face, trying to build up a rapport with the crowd even when things weren't going right for me. You might think supporters are impatient these days with so much more at stake but, in those days, if you didn't score for a few games, the crowd was on your back a lot quicker. What they expected from me was goals every game and that's what they got when I put an end to my goal drought by blasting a hat-trick in the 3-2 home win against Swansea Town on February the 21st.

Ted returned two games later and scored in the 3-1 win against Barnsley but the inconsistency that had dogged Town for most of the season came back when we lost 5-1 at The Valley to Charlton Athletic a week before Easter. The away game at Bristol City on Good Friday of the Easter bank holiday programme was a bad day for me, both on and off the pitch. We were given a penalty and, although

Ted was deadly from the penalty spot having never missed one for Ipswich, as I'd taken the last one, I confidently picked up the ball and put it on the spot. I ran up and hit it going for power but my boot struck well underneath the ball and I stubbed my toe in the ground, sending the ball more like a back pass and, after a few bounces, into the grateful hands of their keeper. It was one of the most embarrassing moments in my whole playing career. It didn't affect the result too much as we lost 3-0. After the game, Alf took me to one side and was brief and to the point saying quietly 'Ray, that is the last penalty you will ever take for Ipswich Town' and it was. It was also my worst game since I'd joined Town. Although I scored in the 3-3 draw against Cardiff City the next day, Alf decided to rest me, saying he thought I'd lost a bit of confidence and sharpness. I wasn't happy with his decision. I'd scored 22 goals in 28 games by then. Dermot Curtis replaced me in the 1-1 draw against his old club Bristol City on Bank Holiday Monday at Portman Road and Ted continued to improve banging in our one goal that day.

I was also left out of the next game against Brighton & Hove Albion. Alf wasn't pleased to say the least after a 4-1 defeat at the Goldstone Ground. That day I was playing in the reserves against Bristol City at Portman Road and, at most football grounds in the country that day, a minute's silence was observed before the kick-off in respect of Jeff Hall, the 29 year old Birmingham City player who'd died of polio earlier that day. On the Monday morning, we were told that all members of the squad who were under 26 years old were to be vaccinated by the end of the week. Because of the shortage of vaccines in Great Britain, they were being imported in their thousands from America as fast as they could produce them and, as the younger were more likely to get polio, the regulations were that all people under the age of 26 received priority. A few days after Jeff Hall died and along with a few others, I was given the polio vaccine by the club doctor. Jeff didn't die in vain. He must have saved many lives as his death highlighted the danger of this frightening disease, hurrying up the process of getting everybody immunised. Rest in peace Jeff.

After the defeat at Brighton, Alf made no less than seven changes for the next game at home to Grimsby Town. We were still not clear of the threat of relegation and needed at least a couple of wins to be safe. I was recalled and scored both goals in a 2-1 win, both in the space of three minutes in the first half. I peppered the Grimsby goal with headers, helped by it being a dry sunny day and the ball not carrying the extra weight it did in wet conditions. I always loved heading the ball and I think that gave me an advantage in the air over many defenders who were not so keen to. The old fashioned ball was heavier than the ones today even in the best of conditions. The previous weekend, 64 year old Mr Fred Davies, chairman of Handforth FC in Cheshire, had died after being hit by a football on the head whilst watching a pre-match kick about. I can remember many occasions of players not heading the ball on wet days, just letting it drop to the ground before playing it and you couldn't blame them for it. I think that, just as boxers who take too many punches to the head during a career can end up a bit punch-drunk, some footballers of that era were affected in a similar way. The Coroner of the inquiry into the death of the former West Bromwich Albion and England centre-forward Jeff Astle, concluded that he'd died of a 'degenerative brain disease', most likely caused by the constant heading of heavy footballs during his career.

Four days later, on the evening of Wednesday the 15th of April, was one of mixed feelings for me and a day that Pompey fans of that era will never forget. Peter Harris was defiant right to the end scoring twice for Portsmouth but they lost 3-2 at Fratton Park to Everton and were relegated to the 2nd Division for the first time since 1927. I still loved the club but not the powers that existed there for the way they'd treated not only me but also other players as well and the disastrous way it had been run since they'd sacked Eddie Lever. Since I'd left, Johnny Gordon had been sold to Birmingham City, Jackie Henderson to Wolves and Derek Dougan to Blackburn Rovers. Ron Saunders had scored 21 league goals as Pompey went down but, with my return of 24 goals in 29 games for Ipswich Town, I'm sure I'd have scored goals for Pompey that season if they hadn't sold me. Just imagine what a forward line it could have been with the 'Doog', Ron Saunders, Peter Harris and me. We'd have scored buckets of goals. About six weeks after Pompey had sunk to the 2nd Division, two monkeys called 'Able' and 'Baker' were sent rocketing up into space at 10,000 mph from Cape Canaveral in Florida, America on a 1,500 mile space flight. I wondered whether, if we'd had our own space program, 'Cox' and 'Sparshatt' would have been prime candidates for the mission?

With three games to go, Town still had an outside chance of being relegated so it was vital to win the game against Rotherham United at Millmoor. It was the first time I'd ever played there and the dressing rooms were almost worse than our own. On the way up to Yorkshire on a warm April evening, one of the lads had said "We'll be in the boiler room tonight!" I found out exactly what he meant when we were put on the side of their dressing rooms where their boiler was and it was like walking into a pressure cooker. They were clever like that. If you played there on a freezing cold winter's day, they would put you on the other side of the dressing rooms where you'd virtually be breathing fog whilst they were sitting in the warmth of the boiler room!

Another thing I found out that evening was that although Ted was the team's main practical joker, he was not the only one capable of conjuring up practical jokes for his unsuspecting victims. The one I witnessed that night was about the most anti-social one I ever saw and was kept a secret for years. Jimmy Forsyth had prepared his usual yellow bucket of cold water with the magic sponge floating in it and also an old football bladder used to squirt water over the faces of players recovering from knocks on the head. Jimmy had left it in our dressing room, just there long enough for Roy Bailey, giggling hysterically, to empty his bladder into it! The first one down in the game was going to get it in what you could have called a game of 'Roy's Roulette'. Unfortunately for Vic Snell, he was left lying flat on his back just about out cold after a nasty clash of heads only a few minutes into the game. Out of the dugout came Jimmy, sprinting to Vic's rescue. He gave him the full works with the magic sponge followed by a few squirts from the old football bladder all over his head and face! A few of the team didn't know what Roy had done and looked at the others wondering why they were virtually pissing themselves laughing after poor Vic had taken such a bad knock. Vic had received an unfortunate baptism nobody ever dared tell him about. Vic was a tough guy, probably the strongest man at the club, so this was a long kept secret at Portman Road. I suppose if Don Revie had been in charge (he was reputed to be an incredibly superstitious manager years later at Leeds United), you could have imagined this becoming part of the pre-match ritual. I can never imagine Alf asking Roy before every game "Have you peed in Jimmy's bucket, Roy?" We won the game 2-1 with Doug Millward and myself scoring the goals.

We were now clear of any threat of relegation when we lined up two days later against Middlesbrough at Portman Road. By that time Brian Clough had scored 43 goals for them, just three short of the record held by Derek Dooley and our own Ted with 46 goals. Vic Snell, sporting two black eyes as a result of his injury at Rotherham, had a blinder (excuse the joke) against Brian Clough who never had a chance in the game. Ted scored our two goals, both shots of awesome power; one of them a penalty. Whenever Ted was on the ball, it was exciting. Something was going to happen; sometimes totally brilliant, sometimes terrible but the crowd always roared with expectancy. One thing was for sure, I'd never seen such powerful shooting before in my life and never since. Ted played in all the 11 remaining games scoring seven goals and I began to see why other clubs were regularly being linked with his name.

At the end of my first season at Ipswich, I'd scored 25 goals in 30 league games. The next highest goal scorers were Derek Rees with 12 and Ted with 8 but he'd been unlucky with injuries and had only played 22 games. Town finished in 16th place, twelve points above the relegated clubs. When I think back, without my goals that season, they may have come a lot closer to being relegated. At least by then I think most of the doubting Town supporters who'd tried to hang on to the memory of Tom Garneys were beginning to accept me. There were still some who refused to and, for some reason, never would.

Chapter 6

"Lethargic, Sluggish, Slovenly Individuals"

During the summer of 1959, Mr John gave many of Town's players thirst quenching jobs at his Tolly-Cobbold brewery in Suffolk. Eileen was keen to spend the close season at home so I worked with Reg Pickett for a timber merchant called 'Bailey and White's' in Portsmouth. The work mainly involved going down to the docks in a broken down old lorry to pick up stacks of timber unloaded from ships there. Most of it was heavy work with us stripped to the waist, lifting plank after plank of wood under the baking hot sun. As well as keeping us fit and as brown as berries, it reminded us that we were lucky to be professional footballers even in those days. We were paid £9.00 a week and, with our retainer from Ipswich Town of £14.00 per week, we were no worse off than in the playing season.

By the time we were back for pre-season training, Alf had strengthened the squad for the new season by buying Andy Nelson, a six feet tall centre-half from West Ham. Andy was a hard player but by no means a 'Basher', a term used for rugged defenders without much skill. We had a poor start to the season losing five of our first seven games; two of them heavily, 4-1 in Andy's debut at home to Huddersfield Town and by the same score away to Leyton Orient. It didn't help that John Elsworthy picked up a knee injury in the very first game, putting him out of action for three months.

We started to put things together in early September, reeling off four consecutive wins, including a 6-1 rout of Sunderland at Portman Road with Ted and Dermot Curtis who'd returned for a run in the side, both scoring hat-tricks, a feat never equalled at Town since. Dermot went on to score all four goals in the next home game against Stoke City but faded from the picture soon after that. Up to Christmas, we slumped to eleven defeats in fifteen games. During the poor run, Alf once made us train without footballs for almost the whole week. It was incredibly frustrating. It was his idea of punishment for poor team performances, his theory being that it would make us doubly keen to get hold of the ball and keep possession of it in the next game. It wasn't the first time Alf had done this in my time there and wasn't to be the last. When he'd first started this, it had almost driven Ted bonkers, like a man having to go without cigarettes. During training once, Ted tried to kick the lock off the shed door where the training balls were kept, cursing loudly, before Alf came out and told him to stop. Alf was worried he might injure himself. Ted eventually came up with a solution which was to hide as many footballs as he could in various places, in case Alf ordered us to train without them. His favourite hiding place was behind the coal bunker which was never discovered. The first time Ted put this plan into action was pure comedy as he sprinted across the practice pitch (now the all weather pitch at Portman Road) with a football under each arm and with trainers Jimmy Forsyth and Charlie Cowie in hot but hopeless pursuit as Ted was much too fast for them. Alf, who'd seen the funny side of it, could be seen smiling at the window of his office. It became a kind of ritual in the end and Alf gave up with Ted on this. He finally did on all his unpredictable and wayward habits as Ted was also the number one practical joker at the club with a wicked sense of humour and mischief.

We rarely trained on the main pitch at Portman Road, only when Alf was with us. One Monday morning, we were jogging round the 'Holy Turf' when the tannoy system started to crackle and make some strange noises. This was followed by a familiar voice saying "Good morning everyone, it's a lovely morning here at Portman Road and training seems to be going well, though there are a few I reckon who could be trying a bloody sight harder!" The commentary continued by telling most of us that we weren't running fast enough and to get our fingers out! It was of course Ted who'd been having treatment from Jimmy Forsyth for an injury. Afterwards, he had managed to get into the little room that overlooked the pitch where the tannoy was. Ted went on until Alf finally brought things to a halt, standing hands on hips, shouting out to Jimmy Forsyth "Get that bloody man off the mic!" Then all Alf could do was smile, saying "God, what can I do with him!"

Many of Ted's practical jokes were carried out with the help of another local lad David Deacon. Luckily for the rest of us, David rarely played in the first team. Together they would have created merry hell on away trips. One of Ted's most annoying habits was hiding clothing, having a particular liking for shoes and socks with the most likely victims being players who were in a hurry to get away after a game. Dennis Thrower once told how he'd been on the receiving end of possibly Ted's greatest ever shoe prank whilst staying at a hotel one night before an away match. All the players had left their shoes outside the doors of their rooms overnight for polishing, only to find they'd all disappeared by the morning. Ted had hidden them all around the foyer of the hotel. Most of the players managed to get their shoes back but Dennis and Roy Bailey turned up for breakfast that morning in their socks! Another of Ted's unpleasant habits you had to watch out for was in the elephant bath after training or games. If he didn't like or agree with what you were saying or singing, you were likely to get a bar of soap raked across your teeth. This seemed to give Ted great pleasure. Bobby Johnstone, a Scotsman whose liking for singing opera in the bath always annoyed him, once had a bar of soap almost pushed down his throat, leaving poor Bobby literally frothing at the mouth. He retired at the end of that season to take up a career in Opera singing in Canada, a long way out of Ted's reach!

After our poor run up to Christmas, we finally managed to turn things around, completing a quick double over Brighton, 3-0 at home on Boxing day then 4-1 away two days later, followed by a crushing 6-3 defeat of Leyton Orient at Portman Road just two days into the new year. Despite being dumped out of the FA Cup by 3rd Division Peterborough United in the 3rd Round (3-2 at Portman Road), we made it six league wins in a row by doing the double over Sunderland at Roker Park in the first week of February. That day I was up against Charlie Hurley, the Republic of Ireland international, rated by many experts to be the best centre-back in Britain at the time. Charlie was not only a tough opponent but a very skilful ball-playing centre-half and I never played against a better defender except possibly against Maurice Norman of Spurs. As a pure footballer, Charlie took some beating; the equivalent of Roy Keane in today's game who, at this time of writing, now manages Sunderland. We fought a rearguard action for most of the game until I sneaked a winner three minutes from time. The Sunderland players and supporters could only look on in disbelief when the final whistle blew.

It was the start of one of my most memorable few days at Ipswich. After the game we boarded our coach and made straight for Scotland where I'd never been before, to Mr John's house in the Highlands of Perthshire near the banks of Loch Rannoch. It was like a small castle set amongst stunning scenery in an estate of dark evergreen forests with snow capped mountains all around us. I will always remember the sweet smell of burning pinewood. It was as old castles have a reputation for, extremely cold at that time of year, so we took in turns to bring in pine logs to keep the large fires in the main lounge and dining rooms constantly burning. There was one place that had no heating; the large long dormitory where the players slept. We were given an endless supply of blankets as it was absolutely freezing. Reg Pickett, who always complained about the cold, wasn't happy until he had over a dozen blankets on his bed!

Mr John had told us before we arrived there that it wouldn't be complete luxury like being in a hotel but more like a self-catering holiday as there were only a couple of daily staff on duty. There was little food in the house apart from porridge oats so, on our first day there, a few of the lads went out with the gamekeeper on a deer hunt. I didn't go as I was a bit squeamish about that sort of thing. Kenny Malcolm, who had once worked in the fish market in Aberdeen before he went into pro-football, was made chief cook with Ted as his assistant. Mr John took charge of the bar, of course. It was certainly well stocked as he had everything there from beer, lager, scotch, malt whiskies and the best wine I'd ever tasted. When the hunting party came back with a large deer, the gamekeeper prepared it before giving it to Kenny with his filleting skills to do the rest. With Ted's help, who we knew was quite an authority on game already, especially pheasants, a side of deer was put into the large kitchen oven to roast. There was so much of it Kenny said "How thick do you want your steaks, three, four or five inches?" I don't think any of us had ever eaten venison before. With some of Mr John's best claret, we all enjoyed it and it was our main meal for our stay there. Almost all of us had come from working class backgrounds and it was an education to us into some of the finer things in life that Mr John wanted to share with us.

On the Monday morning we went for a nine mile hike across Rannoch Moor as we'd put the boat out a bit the night before. When we became thirsty, we drank from the little brooks that ran down into the loch. I'd never tasted water so refreshing and delicious before. There were also little trout racing around in the streams. They were a bit too small to arouse Ted's poaching instincts! Quite often, Ted used to turn up to training in the morning carrying a few braces of pheasants. We were never quite sure where they ended up or from where Ted had found them. Most probably they ended up hanging from a rail in a local butcher's shop. Whenever we asked Ted how he'd found them, we always received the same answer, "From me local woods, where d'yer think? I get 'em at night. I just shine a torch up into the trees and they just fall off the branches into my hands, easy as wink it is."

The long trek built up our appetites for another feast of roast venison that evening. When Alf and most of the lads had gone to bed, a few of us stayed up with Mr John, drinking into the early hours of the morning in front of a roaring log fire in the big lounge, listening to all the stories he had to tell about his life. He loved being with the players. Although he came from an aristocratic background, it was always easy to be in his company. He had a great way with all people, whatever walk of life they came from. He had a brilliant sense of humour too, with a mischievous sort of giggle when he laughed. The conversation never dried up, neither did our glasses.

Whether you were on a train, in a restaurant or in a pub with Mr John, things were always likely to turn into a small party and Alf was the only one who had any control over him in these situations. I can remember on more than one occasion when Alf became angry with him, even swearing at him once, when he thought he was overindulging his players. But although Mr John believed life was to be lived to the full, his total dedication to Ipswich Town and his great will to see them succeed at the highest level, eventually made him one of the greatest club chairmen of all time. Above all though, you knew how much he cared for the players. When you came out onto the pitch, you wanted to win for him as much as anybody else. I think all the players loved and respected Mr John.

On our final night there, a few of the lads who worked on Mr John's estate organised what is called a 'Ceilidh' (pronounced 'Kay-Lay') and some local ladies came around to help out. It always makes me laugh when I remember Jimmy Leadbetter, one of the lightest of us, being hurled around the shoulders of our young hosts which was all part of the dance. It wasn't a complete holiday away from football. On the way back, we stopped in Glasgow on a Wednesday night to play a friendly with Third Lanark which had been arranged in advance. The game was drawn 2-2 and we were impressed with the skill and creativity of the Scottish players. Looking back it was not surprising that many Ipswich managers and scouts in future years went in search of young talent north of the border. We were treated royally after the game with food and drink fit for a king and they couldn't have been more hospitable. It was possibly one feast too many.

The three day break was as memorable as the 1-1 draw against Portsmouth at Portman Road the following Saturday was forgettable. We played badly. We were described as **'lethargic, sluggish, slovenly individuals'** in the local press, questioning the need for our holiday in Scotland, having missed out on the chance of setting a new club record of seven consecutive league wins. Maybe we'd eaten too much venison and drunk too much vintage claret. We made up for it a few days later, although it was a pity there were no points at stake, when a crowd of over 15,000 came to Portman Road to witness the official opening of the newly installed floodlights. The ceremony was carried out by Lady Blanche Cobbold, Mr John's mother who switched on the lights for the first ever floodlit game staged by Ipswich Town and no less than the mighty 1st Division Arsenal were there to play a friendly match to celebrate the opening. It was a great night for the supporters and club alike. Arsenal were like cannon fodder for us as we blew the 'Gunners' away 4-0 with goals from Ted, Doug Millward and two from me. Alf had been opposed to having the floodlights because he wanted the £15,000 the supporters association had made available to be spent on new dressing rooms and offices. He was unhappy with the poor facilities that existed for his players and staff, especially the old 'Chicken Hutch'. Alf was outvoted and the floodlights were given priority. This was one of the rare times he didn't get his own way at Ipswich. The previous summer, Liverpool had put in a big offer for Ted which Alf had turned down point blank. It was rumoured that the Board were willing to sell him to pay for the much needed ground improvements but Alf stuck to his guns and Ted stayed. The right decision as without him there's no way we'd have won the championship two years later. Possibly only Ted and Jimmy Leadbetter would have been mildly disappointed for the old 'Chicken Hutch' to be replaced at the time. As there were no toilets there, you had to go outside some ten yards behind it to where four of them were set up against a wall. There was a nine inch gap at the top of the doors, and one of Ted's favourite and most unpleasant tricks was to chuck a bucket of water through the gap to drench unwary players who stood or sat there just a moment too long! As for Jimmy, he was quite a heavy smoker and hid his favourite 'Player's Untipped' there where he would go for his half-time fags.

We were due to play under floodlights again a few nights later at the Victoria ground against Stoke City but it was postponed because of a frozen pitch, giving us a break of nearly two weeks without a game. The day after the birth of the Queen's third child, Prince Andrew, we beat Scunthorpe 1-0 at home then thumped Rotherham 4-1 at Millmoor where I scored my 16th goal in 30 games. Although just over an average of a goal every other game is normally thought to be a good return for a striker, I finished that season playing for the reserves. The 1-1 draw against Derby County at home just a week before Easter was the turning point. The ex-Norwich City player Ken Oxford was the Derby keeper that day and was a pretty frightening looking bloke, like a slightly more human version of Frankenstein without the nuts and bolts sticking out of his ears. Suffolk locals like Ted would have described him as a pretty 'Rum looking bloke' although I never knew how the 'Rum' came into it? I thought I'd scored near the end to win the game but Ken made the most incredible save. From that point on, the curse of Ken Oxford must have been on me as I was left out of the last four games and hated every minute of it. If you are used to playing for the 1st team every week, it comes as a hell of a shock. There is nothing like a few games in the reserves to make sure you never give the manager a reason for ever dropping you again.

When the retained list comes out at the end of the season, it's sometimes hard to find the right words when you say goodbye to a player who's been released without a club to go to. David Deacon was one of two players not retained that year. The day he finally left Portman Road was his final double-act with his arch ally in wind-ups and practical jokes, Ted. David said he wanted to take away a few of the training footballs with him and asked Ted if he could help him. Ted took a large net of about a dozen training balls to the shooting practice wall at the far end of the ground which seemed a bit over keen seeing the season was over. David drove out of the ground and took up a position the other side of the wall and waited by his car. Ted then proceeded to belt the majority of the balls over the wall where David collected them and put them in his car. When Ted came back with only a couple of footballs left, Jimmy Forsyth wanted to know where all the rest had gone. Ted's story was that his shooting was way off target that day and that most of them had gone over the wall but by the time he'd gone outside to fetch them back, somebody must have nicked them!

Chapter 7

"Promotion"

In the summer of 1960, I worked with Reg Pickett in the timber yard in Portsmouth again. I also passed my driving test and bought my first car, a yellow and white Triumph Herald for £460. The advert for the car had really caught my eye as it said 'THESE CARS ARE DESIGNED TO GIVE YOU A NEW EXPERIENCE IN MOTORING' and this one certainly did in our drive from Portsmouth to Ipswich for the start of the pre-season training in early August. We left at 8:00am on a sunny morning but the problems soon started as we were driving up the old A3 road where the engine kept on cutting out whenever we came to a set of traffic lights or stopped. By the time we reached London, the weather had roughened up and Eileen and baby Jane had to retreat to the back of the car to avoid being soaked with rain which was seeping through a crack in the windscreen. We eventually arrived exhausted in Ipswich at 4:00pm after a drive that had taken eight hours! I took the car straight to a garage the next day where they put in a new carburettor and fixed the leak in the windscreen. We also had a phone by then and Eileen rang up Alf to ask if we could have a garage put in. Alf said it would be no trouble and, being a man of his word, just a few days later it was done.

During the summer Alf, with the small budget the club allowed him, had bought Wilf Hall for £2,000 from Stoke City, John Compton from Chelsea for £1,000 and Roy Stephenson an inside-forward from Leicester City for £3,000. Roy or 'Rocky' as he was nicknamed, was very quick off the mark just having that ten yards of pace to get him round opponents who may have beaten him over 100 yards, but not ten. He was a good passer and crosser of the ball and had an eye for goal as well. Alf almost immediately asked him to play on the right wing (like Alan Ball in the 1966 World Cup) to fit into the system he wanted to play with two deep-lying wingers with Jimmy Leadbetter on the left. Perhaps the most important signing was Billy Baxter, a twenty year old Scotsman who was doing his National Service at Aldershot, for the giveaway fee of £400 from the Scottish junior club Broxburn Athletic.

Curse of the Jungle Boy

Before the new season started, I bought an expensive pair of new boots from a sports shop in Ipswich. We were given an allowance of £14.00 for new boots every year but these cost me twenty two quid. When I asked Alf if the club would give me the extra eight quid I'd paid, he told me I had expensive taste and gave me a typical, blunt Ramsey "No". Alf said that if I had the extra cash, everyone would want it as well. This little extra investment was to bring rich dividends to Town and me by the end of that season. The day I bought the boots, I was almost as excited as when I'd bought my first 'Stanley Matthews Boots' when I was fourteen years old. I started to break them in straight away as you did in those days by wearing them in a bowl of warm water. After a few soakings, this softened the very hard leather of which they were made and moulded them to the shape of your feet. Once broken in, they were very comfortable and the thick leather gave you plenty of protection. I don't go for the modern trend of multi-coloured boots that many players seem to prefer today. It looks as if they're playing in their bedroom slippers. Not only that but more players seem to be getting fractured bones in their feet. When I first heard the word 'Metatarsal' I thought it was some sort of prehistoric monster but both David Beckham and Wayne Rooney had theirs broken. Players with feet like dinosaurs? - ridiculous I thought!

As I wasn't happy at being dropped at the end of the previous season or with my return of 18 goals, unknown to most of my team mates, I started to go back for afternoon training. Most of those afternoons, Reg Pickett and Derek Rees would be there too and we used it mainly for shooting practice. Alf had set up an exercise with numbers from 1 to 11, painted on a part of the old red brick that surrounded the ground. A ball would be passed or lobbed to you, then the trainer, usually Jimmy Forsyth, would shout out one of the numbers. After one touch with foot, thigh, chest or stomach, you had to try and hit that number. I concentrated mainly on my left foot, allowing myself one touch with my right foot then bang with the left. "10!", one touch, bang with my left foot, "4!", one touch, bang with my left again, "7!", one touch, bang with my left foot again. This could go on for some minutes before you had to have a rest as it was surprisingly tiring. I soon found out that trying to strike the ball harder with my left foot wasn't the way to improve it. I was scuffing too many shots well off target with some of them just trickling lamely into the bottom of the wall. Then Jimmy Forsyth told me "Look son, don't try and hit the ball so hard, just relax your whole body from head to toe and stroke the ball at the target." His advice was brilliant. Slowly, my left foot became a more powerful weapon. Since those days, I've noticed many rugby players who are about to take a conversion let their shoulders go flop to relax themselves before they run in to strike the ball. I think it's just the same with the round ball game, especially if you are about to take a penalty. I spent literally hours every week, peppering the numbers on that old brick wall with footballs.

We won our first game at Leyton Orient 3-1 but we couldn't have looked less like promotion challengers in our next game, going down 4-0 away to Scunthorpe United. The only disadvantage of having floodlights was that we were now able to play at any time at home during the week, not giving as much rest as we were used to. We beat Scunthorpe 2-0 less than a week later in the first ever floodlit league game at Portman Road. I scored my first hat-trick of the season a week later in a 4-2 win against Brighton at the Goldstone Ground. We carried on our good form beating Bill Shankly's Liverpool 1-0 at home on a baking hot afternoon with a fantastic goal from Ted which must have annoyed Shanks after trying to buy him the year before. A few days later, we completed an early season double over Brighton with Rocky Stephenson making a brilliant debut and Ted and myself getting two goals each in a 4-0 win. This took us to first place in the table. While we were tearing Brighton to pieces that evening, a barman was knifed to death after a dispute with four men in the Rainbow Inn in St Matthews Street, no more than a few hundred yards from Portman Road. The case eventually went to The Old Bailey in London where one man was convicted of manslaughter and sent to prison for five years. Alfred Hitchcock's murder thriller 'Psycho' had just been released. As I loved the movies, going almost every week, I watched it with Eileen at the Gaumont Cinema in Ipswich just the week after the killing at The Rainbow. I've always been a great Hitchcock fan. Perhaps he summed up the world at the time. Although it was an exciting time to live, it was an even more dangerous place to live than it is now.

The Rainbow Inn was a pub I'd been to many times. It was a rough pub, the sort of place you only stayed for one or two at most unless you were a regular. Usually there were a few drunks and trouble makers there and if you were recognised as a Town player, you were liable to get targeted for trouble a lot quicker than others. One night I went there with Reg Pickett, 'Bunny' Rees and Brian Siddall to watch a Hula-Hoop contest between a dozen or so young ladies. While the competition was going on, Bunny soon attracted the attentions of a very amorous woman, much to the annoyance of her boyfriend. The moment the competition was over, we dragged Bunny out as quickly as possible as he was already a bit the worse for wear. We went to another pub where, by the end of the evening, Bunny was virtually legless and Brian, who was never a drinker, drove us back to Bunny's house where we almost had to carry him to the front door. We managed to find his front door key and I opened the door and went in first with Bunny staggering in behind me. I'd barely passed through the doorway when I was hit with a barrage of pillows from the top of the stairs. His wife Shirley was cursing and shouting at her husband for waking her up at one o'clock in the morning. When we switched the porch light on, she put her hand to her mouth and apologized to me for being the target of what was meant for Bunny. Shirley's maiden name was Shirley Broads. I'd known her since I was a teenager as she'd also lived on the Hilsea Estate in Portsmouth. She also knew my best mate Brian Cross who only lived a few doors away from her.

In our next home game, Ted scored two goals in a 3-3 draw against Southampton. It was therefore a surprise when he put in a written transfer request at the end of the next week. Ted's reasons were that he was fed up with having to travel the 18 miles by train from Colchester to Ipswich and back everyday and gave another reason which surprised me, saying that "I think I should score more goals if I had better support. I run into spaces and nothing happens." I think Ted had been unsettled by Liverpool's interest in him the previous summer and there always seemed to be rumours of other clubs wanting to sign him. The club had tried to help Ted settle and offered him a club house in Ipswich but he didn't want to live there and thought a move would help his football. Ted had a reputation for putting in transfer requests both verbal and written on the spur of the moment if anything annoyed him. He was upset that this one was leaked to the press the day before our away game against Leeds United. He said he didn't want to unsettle the rest of the lads on the eve of such an important game. In what Alf described as Ipswich Town's best ever performance during his time there, Ted had a brilliant game scoring a goal and I scored my second hat-trick of the season in the 5-2 win at Elland Road; more goals than Leeds had ever conceded in a home game since the war. Jack Charlton was marking me that day and it was the start of a very good record I had against him. Ted was all smiles afterwards. After a talk with Alf the next week, he withdrew his transfer request. In the return game at Portman Road later that season, we gave them another battering. We were soon two up with goals from Ted and myself. Ted's second, just a few minutes before half-time, was the best goal I ever saw Ted score. Our defence cleared the ball high over the halfway line, I sent a looping header onto Ted who headed it back and I, in turn, headed the ball into his path for him to hit a spectacular volley that must have been travelling at over 90 miles an hour as it hit the net. The Leeds players, including Jack Charlton and Billy Bremner all just stood there mouths agape as their keeper Alan Humphries walked slowly back with an air of disbelief to retrieve the ball from the back of the net. Ted's goal killed off the game. 'Bunny' Rees scored another to complete a 4-0 rout. Ted and I never worked on any set pieces or planned anything in training; it just sort clicked naturally between us. Alf never tried to analyse what made us tick with a view to making us an even stronger combination. It makes me wonder if sometimes players get over-coached and perhaps lose that instinctive understanding.

Two weeks before Christmas, we beat Plymouth Argyle 3-1 at Portman Road, after which the local sports editor reported *"On the form he showed in this match, there are not half a dozen better centre-forwards in the country than Ray Crawford."* I scored my third hat-trick of the season when we tore apart Leyton Orient 6-2 a week later. The sports editor then wrote *"Once again Ray Crawford, worthy successor to the great Tom Garneys, played a major part in the success, showing magnificent ball control and an eagle-like eye for any opening"* and I was beginning to think that only a small minority of Town fans still had doubts about my ability.

Over Christmas we played two, back to back, local derby games against arch rivals Norwich City, the first on Boxing Day in front of a large crowd of 30,884 at Carrow Road. As our coach slowly approached the ground that day, making its way through the crowds, there was a full size wooden coffin with a blue and white sheet over it with the words 'WE'RE GOING TO BURY IPSWICH TOWN TODAY' painted on it. 'The Canaries' were certainly very chirpy and confident at the time as they'd not lost at home for over a year. We just laughed at the coffin and their jeering supporters. It turned out that if anyone was going to buried that day, it was Norwich City. After seven minutes, I quickly turned and shot to put us one up. Then Ted latched onto a poor back-pass to make it 2-0 at half-time. They never recovered and we struck again after seventy minutes when Sandy Kennon could only block a thunderbolt from Ted, leaving me with a tap-in for number three. The 'terrible twins' had struck again.

The coffin idea had backfired on them. There may also have been another bad omen working against City that day. A few days earlier Sir Edmund Hillary, the famous conqueror of Mount Everest, had flown into London airport after an expedition in Nepal, claiming to be in possession of the two hundred and fifty year old scalp of a Yeti. With him was Klumbo Chambi, guardian of the scalp and the headman of a small village called Klumjung where Hillary had discovered it. It was believed to be a good luck charm by the villagers but would bring bad luck to them if it was ever lost, stolen or to anyone who took it away; a bit like the curse of the Pharaoh's if anyone broke into their tombs. Before leaving the airport, Sir Edmund said he was going to have talks with the Royal Geographical Society before going to join his sister for Christmas in Norwich, so was the curse of the

Yeti on the whole of the City of Norwich at the time?

The same evening as all of Suffolk were celebrating our win, a young footballer's career was coming to an end as he lay trapped in the wreckage of the Sheffield Wednesday team coach in a ditch just off the Great North Road. The accident happened as they were travelling back north after playing Arsenal in London that day. After several attempts by the rescue team had failed to remove the 19 year old reserve team player Douglas McMillan from the stricken coach, there was only one option left. No other way to get him out other than to amputate his right leg just below the knee. Other casualties in the accident were England international centre-half Peter Swan and Under 23 international Tony Kay who were released from hospital a few days later. Young Douglas McMillan's playing days had tragically come to an end. I am by no means a cynical person but I've always taken the turn of every new year with a large pinch of salt. If I'd been young McMillan, I dread to think what I might have done but for my family.

The return match against the Canaries the next day was my 100th league appearance for Ipswich. It was also the debut of a player who was to become a legend at Ipswich Town. In my mind, Town's greatest ever player; a young man from Scotland, 20 year old Billy Baxter. With Billy's introduction, one of the final pieces of the jigsaw Alf had been building for the last few years snapped into place. Though Billy wasn't very tall, about five feet eight inches in height, he was very tough and had the ability to leap higher than players who were a lot taller than him, much like Billy Wright the great Wolves and England centre-half. He was also fierce but fair in the tackle and a good passer of the ball; everything you could wish of a young player. Being very broad chested with his shoulders held tightly back and his head held high, he looked every bit like a highly trained soldier, the very picture of discipline on a football field. Billy had his chance at left-back coming in for Kenny Malcolm who'd been injured in the game at Carrow Road.

Again, I ruffled up the Canaries feathers by scoring another brace in a 4-1 win at Portman Road. Ted crashed home his second in two days from the penalty spot and Doug Millard, who'd often been the brunt of the home crowd when things weren't going well, hammered the final nail in City's coffin with a thunderous shot five minutes from time. Even though I was a neutral to the area, you couldn't help getting involved in all the passion that surrounded the games. The Canaries must have been as sick as parrots having been doubled by their greatest enemy in the space of just two days. We were now back on top of the table. As we were in the festive season, you could say it had been more like a Norfolk turkey shoot for Town and the Canaries had well and truly been stuffed. I was now the leading scorer in the whole football league with 27 goals in 24 games. I felt I was now closer to becoming the complete centre-forward and all the extra training and hours of practice I'd put in were beginning to pay off.

The goal aggregate in the two derby games was 7-1 to Ipswich. As they say 'pride comes before a fall' and just a week later we were thrashed 7-1 in the Third Round of the FA Cup by Southampton at the Dell. Most of my family and many of my old mates bought tickets for the game, hoping that Town were going to put one over their south coast rivals. It couldn't have been more embarrassing. We were 6-0 down by the interval! We were expecting a minor rocket even from the usually unflappable Alf as we sat waiting for him in the dressing room at half-time. When he arrived, he'd barely passed beyond the doorway before announcing calmly "If you play like that again in the second half, it'll probably be twelve," before walking out and leaving us to ponder the obvious. Probably a record on the least amount of words a manager has ever said to a team losing by six goals at half-time in the history of professional football. But those few words had their effect and we rallied in the second half. Though they scored again, Rocky Stephenson pulled one back so you could definitely say it was a game of two halves. We had at least drawn the second half 1-1! Unfortunately, it still remains Ipswich Town's heaviest defeat ever in the FA Cup. Billy Baxter missed the game due to his National Service duties. He played for the rest of the season and was a vital factor in our eventual promotion.

Apart from that, the team was knitting together well with Rocky Stephenson looking every inch like a goal-scoring winger. He was also proving to be of considerable interest to the players wives. The wooden ceiling of the 'Chicken Hutch' was very low and Rocky, not being very tall was the only player who could stand on the benches without banging his head on the ceiling. The advantages of this were to avoid the mud, dirt and the splinters on the wooden floor whilst putting on your socks. After games, the players wives used to wait outside the dressing rooms and towels were put up to stop anybody looking in. One day the tiniest gap was left between the towels and the top of a window. It was just wide enough for the wives to get a sneaky look in to see Rocky standing on a bench, bollock naked, drying all his 'bits and pieces' (also a good record by the Dave Clark Five!) Before the next day's training, compliments were passed to Rocky by many of the players on behalf of their wives, that they thought he had a very nice bum! Rocky was a bachelor. In fact the only one in the team, so I suppose he was the likeliest target for this sort of curiosity. That was players wives for you in the 1960's. Maybe things haven't changed that much. This is just a preview in words as you can see the real thing, Rocky, in the section of photos as he is about to enter the elephant bath the day we won the Championship. It was vetted slightly for fear of giving too much away about other parts of Rocky's anatomy. We also had some insight into Rocky's past just before his second game for Town, away to one of his previous clubs Rotherham United. When our coach pulled into the car park at Millmoor, there was the usual small crowd of people there waiting for our arrival. Just as we were about to get off, Rocky suddenly threw himself to the floor of the coach and shouted "Oh no, it's her! For God's sake don't tell her I'm here! Tell her I'm not playing if she asks you, I'm just not here okay!" We were all in hysterics including Alf. We assured Rocky that even though we didn't know which lady it was, if anyone asked we'd say he wasn't with us. It was all of ten minutes later that Rocky turned up in our dressing room looking like a haunted and hunted man, still slightly stooping as he peered out of the window to make sure the dreaded woman hadn't tracked him down!

In the home game with Rotherham just over a month into the new year, we dropped a point in a 1-1 draw which was unlucky '13' for Ted. Just six minutes from time, he missed his first ever penalty for Ipswich Town when their reserve team keeper Jack Wren dived the right way to save his shot that had been hit with slightly less power than usual. Two days later, the Spurs and Northern Ireland captain Danny Blanchflower was in the news for a different kind of miss. He became the first person to refuse to go on the show 'This is Your Life' since the show had started in 1955. The very next day Freddie Cox, after three years of disaster parted company with Pompey by 'mutual agreement' as it was called. This was the nice way of saying he'd been sacked, almost like I was and Pompey were on their way to the 3rd Division where Freddie said the players could be every bit as good as 1st Division players!

Our next game, away to promotion rivals Southampton and was my 100th appearance for Town. The draw was enough to keep us in second place on the table. It was a big improvement on the 7-1 mauling we'd received in the cup but it was our third successive draw and we needed to string together some wins which we did winning the next five games including the 4-0 rout of Leeds United at Portman Road. This took us to the top of the 2nd Division. The last of these wins was against Plymouth Argyle who'd been banned from playing at their ground Home Park for 14 days the week before as punishment for crowd disorder in a home game a few weeks before. The FA had given White Hart Lane in London as the ground where the game would be played which I would have loved as I always scored there. When our nearest promotion rivals Sheffield United, Liverpool and Southampton Town heard of the venue they all complained to the FA saying it would give us an unfair advantage as Plymouth would have to travel near on 250 miles whilst our journey would be a relatively short train trip to London. What they were trying to do was to get Town involved in a fixture pile up at the end of the season. The FA rightly ignored their complaints and Plymouth agreed to play at White Hart Lane. That was, until nearly a week later, when they asked if Town would be willing to play at Torquay, giving only two days notice before the game. Alf could have stood by the FA ruling but agreed to play there so instead of having a large following of fans to London, only a few hundred fans travelled to Torquay which was even further away than Plymouth! It seemed Town were the ones being punished for a situation that was none of their making.

As if this wasn't enough, on the journey down to Devon, Alf came into our carriage and told us Bill Shankly had phoned him shortly before we'd left Ipswich that day, saying it would be 'ungentlemanly' for us to play anywhere else than at Home Park and that Ipswich Town should wait until the ban was lifted to play them there, again trying to get Town into a fixture pile up in the run-in to the end of the season. This was the final attempt to play on Alf's insistence in always doing things the honest and proper way. Despite all of Shankly's great qualities, this was nothing but pure gamesmanship and Alf rightly just ignored it. I think there'd been a little bit of a niggle between them ever since Alf had insisted on Huddersfield Town changing their strip for a cup tie at Ipswich because of a colour clash when Shankly was manager there. Furthermore, Alf had also refused to part with Ted Phillips who'd rubbed it in by scoring a superb goal in a 1-1 draw at Anfield earlier that year. I doubt if the two great men ever exchanged Christmas cards!

Plymouth were a good side then and it was 1-1, looking like a draw until five minutes from time when their keeper and centre-half both went for a cross and collided. As they lay in a heap on the ground, the ball came to me just a yard inside the bye-line. Jimmy Leadbetter and Ted were calling for me to pass it to them for an easy tap-in for either of them but I wanted the goal and walked the ball into the empty net. Ted called me a greedy bastard. There was always a sense of competition between us as Ted wanted to score more goals than me and vice versa. There were no hard feelings and without the friendly rivalry we probably wouldn't have scored so many goals between us as we did. As it was too late to catch the last train to London after the game, we had plenty of time to kill until we caught the overnight sleeper later that night. After dinner at our hotel, we went into town and were there almost until the pubs closed. By the time we stepped on the train shortly before midnight, most of us were fairly pissed to say the least. Mr John joined us in our carriage to continue the party, handing out miniature whiskies of which he seemed to have an endless supply in the pockets of his famous sheepskin jacket. All was fine until Alf entered giving us a stern glare, leading to a stony silence for a few seconds which Mr John broke, perhaps unwisely, by offering Alf a whisky. Alf, on one of the rare occasions we'd ever heard him swear, told him quietly to ef....off and go to bed and the same went for the players. After all the uncertainty and difficulties Alf had had to deal with leading up to the game, I think this was about the last straw for him that week. All was forgiven and forgotten the next day.

On Easter Friday, Middlesbrough came to Portman Road with a big reputation and free scoring centre-forward Brian Clough. Andy Nelson never gave him an inch of space, frustrating him the whole game. It must have finally pushed Cloughie too far. After a harsh exchange of words with left-winger Eddie Holliday, Cloughie went over to him, grabbed him by the throat and told him what he thought of him. It was a nasty and embarrassing moment which Alf would have come down on like a ton of bricks if a Town player had done that to one of his colleagues. I scored twice and Jimmy Leadbetter scored the third in a 3-1 win to keep us top of the table. Straight after the game, we travelled north for our game at Huddersfield the next day. We continued our good form with a 3-1 victory but our luck ran out two days later on Easter Monday away to Middlesbrough. Things started to go wrong after twenty five minutes when Clough hit a full-blooded volley from almost point blank range into Roy Bailey's face leaving him almost unconscious and with a broken nose. Roy recovered but was obviously still dazed when a shot he normally would have saved flashed past him just a minute later to put Boro' ahead. Ted equalised just five minutes from time but we lost concentration conceding a penalty, albeit a dubious one, from which they scored two minutes later. We were rattled with so little time to go and threw almost everyone forward, only for Clough to score on a breakaway to give Boro' a flattering 3-1 win.

We stayed top despite dropping another point in a 2-2 draw with Portsmouth who, by then, had come to their senses and bought back ex-player Johnny Gordon. George Smith, who'd once been at Ipswich as coach and assistant manager to Scott Duncan, had replaced Freddie Cox as their new manager. After the game Jimmy Dickinson said "If only we'd had Johnny Gordon and Allan Brown with us a few weeks ago there would have been no question of relegation" but Pompey were on their way to the 3rd Division.

Just a few days later the Russian Yuri Gagarin became the first man in space and we beat Lincoln City 4-1 away. Promotion was all but there and Norwich City did us a big favour winning 2-1 against Liverpool at Carrow Road putting us six points ahead of them with three games to go, leaving them with only the slightest mathematical chance of catching us. All we required was just one point from our last three games to be sure of getting one of the two promotion places but the 4-0 win in the next game at home to Sunderland was all we needed. The game was a strange experience for me. About an hour before the kick-off, Reg Pickett offered me what was called a 'purple heart' in those days. He told me it would really lift me and give me endless energy so I took it. They were not actually purple or heart shaped but more of a blue colour and triangular and were very popular amongst the young swingers of the early sixties and for years after. On looking them up, I found what I'd taken was 'Drinamyl', a mixture of amphetamine which made you feel like superman, Mr Hyde if you like, and some downer in it which made you come back to Dr Jekyll when the effects wore off. Reg was on them as part of some treatment he was having at the time as a sort of tonic for minor depression. Having given up the club captaincy at the beginning of the season to Andy Nelson and then lost his place in the 1st team with the arrival of Billy Baxter, I knew Reg well enough to know he felt very left out when promotion to the 1st Division was finally about to be achieved. He knew his playing days were nearly over and it was hurting as he loved to play.

As for the game, I rushed about for the first half hour feeling like 'superman' and that I could run the hundred yards in record time, feeling my body was capable of anything until just before I scored our second goal. Usually, I liked to celebrate in some style but I felt totally flat and could hardly remember my name as the effects were wearing off. It wasn't an experience I ever wanted to repeat. Many players took them all the time as they were legal in those days. You'd receive a lengthy ban and fine for taking the equivalent of them these days. Strangely enough, that goal is one of the bits of commentary from old games in the introduction to Radio Suffolk's Saturday afternoon coverage of Town games that goes *"and that was Crawford scoring his 39th goal of the season!"* I hope they don't edit that bit out now I've admitted this. I like the introduction. But neither do I want to see a headline in the papers when this book comes out reading something like *"Drug crazed Jungle Boy tells of his addiction"* as they do tend to exaggerate to say the least. I promise I only ever took the one and never did it again.

Needless to say, I was up for the champagne which flowed in the dressing room after the game to toast Ipswich Town. It was the first time in the club's history that they had been promoted to the 1st Division. We went one better beating Derby County away 4-1 in a twice postponed game two days later to win the 2nd Division title outright, one point ahead of Sheffield United. That evening Mr John invited us for a buffet supper and drinks at his house in Kirton village near Felixstowe. The next time I saw Mr John, he asked me if I had any idea who'd sewn up his pyjamas! "I bet it was Eileen and Reg's wife who did it!" he said with his usual playful smile. I just smiled back and we had a good laugh about it.

Losing our final game at Swansea 2-1 was disappointing. We were a bit off-guard by then with the job already done. Alf had allowed us out the night before so some of us were literally not quite focused as usual for the game! Ted scored a magnificent goal which was fitting for Town's 100th league goal of the season. Ted had scored 30 and myself 40. We played no less than four testimonials the following week. They were usually happy affairs but the one for 27 year old Ipswich Town player Peter Berry was quite a sad occasion. Peter had been advised to quit the game a few weeks before after badly damaging some knee ligaments in a reserve game earlier in the season. It was a good night though and over ten thousand supporters turned up to watch a Town side play out a 3-3 draw with West Ham United. Peter had been unlucky just like his elder brother John Berry who'd played over 200 games for Manchester United before the Munich air disaster in 1957. Although he had survived, he never played again because of the injuries he suffered in the crash. Peter and John returned to their native Aldershot to open a sports shop together. There were always bad luck stories in football and tragic ones too. You just had to keep reminding yourself to make the most of it before injury or age caught up with you. I was in my prime, and about to do just that.

Chapter 8

"The Taste of Honey"

The following summer we stayed in Ipswich for the first time since I'd joined Town. Shortly before the end of the season Eileen and I been looking around the carpet department of the Co-op in central Ipswich when the manager there, a Mr Savage, recognised me. We talked for a while and I said I was going back to Portsmouth to get a job there for the summer at which he offered me the alternative of a job there. After speaking with Eileen about it, I accepted his offer. By now we had quite a few friends in Ipswich. The hours were 9am to 5pm, six days a week with a half day off on Wednesdays. The work wasn't hard physically but my mind had to work overtime, calculating the costs of carpets from the measurements given by the customers. As a footballer, I was used to being told what to do, not having to work much out for myself, so it was quite testing in that respect and a modern day pocket calculator would have come in very handy. It was an interesting experience but I was relieved when pre-season training started in mid July.

The 19th of August 1961 was Town's first ever game in Division One (the premiership now) away to Bolton Wanderers. It was also Doug Moran's debut, Alf's only signing that summer from Falkirk. Doug was an attacking midfield player whose goals were to be vital to us that season. He was also a great lad, a little shy and very unassuming. We scored a point from a 0-0 draw, more than was expected by most of the critics and so-called experts who'd said we were certain to be relegated that year.

Three days later we travelled north again to play Burnley at Turf Moor. They were football giants at the time with England internationals centre-forward Ray Pointer and winger John Connelly who was always menacing in attack and with the brilliant Irishman Jimmy McIlroy pulling the strings in midfield. They took the lead three times. Three times we equalized; two blockbusters from Ted and one from me but Burnley scored again and won 4-3. We weren't outclassed in any way. There was even better to come. Ted's power shooting that evening left the home crowd gasping at the ferocity of it. I don't think they'd seen anything like it before. But for the woodwork, Ted would have had a hat-trick. He was soon to be featured on the wrapping to 'Bazooka' chewing gum which read *'Who can stop Ted Phillips 87mph shooting?'* There was a different kind of shooting that night. On the coach back to Suffolk, we passed very near to a place appropriately called 'Deadman's Hill' where a few hours later a man called John Gregson was shot dead in what was to become known as 'A6 murder', the Hanratty case, probably the most controversial murder trial of the sixties.

The following weekend we ran out onto the Portman Road pitch to the cheers of 21,000 supporters for Town's home debut in the 1st Division against Manchester City. The famous Bert Trautmann was still their keeper and it seemed a long time ago since I'd scored twice against him in a Pompey win against City three years before. I was hoping to do the same that day but it wasn't to be. The score was 2-2 with only four minutes left when a clearance by John Elsworthy bounced off the referee straight into the path of Peter Dobing who took full advantage of his luck to put City ahead. As we threw players forward in search of an equalizer, he scored again to give City a very flattering 4-2 win. I think it would have been fairer if the referee, Mr Fussey, had given a drop ball, as a draw would have been a fair result. You could just about forgive Mr Fussey for that as those who ever saw him referee will tell you he had to be the funniest and most eccentric ref of all time. It still brings a smile to my face when I think of the way he signalled for a corner. First he would rush to the edge of the box, stand bolt up right to attention, then point to the corner flag and blow his whistle. With the crowd cheering, he would then tear off with his knees pumping up and down like old railway engine pistons to the goal line, a few yards to the side of the goal, then pivot round coming to parade ground military attention, before pointing goalwards and blowing his whistle for the corner to be taken. I don't know if John Cleese ever saw him referee but, if he did, it could have led to the Monty Python's sketch 'The Ministry of Silly Walks'. Mr Fussey was similar in build, very tall with long thin white legs. He was hugely popular with the crowds and also the players. There was always some comic compensation for having a corner awarded against you. Just to see him going through his routine - even if you were losing 5-0 - he could still make you laugh and remember it's just a game. Unfortunately there's no room for characters like Mr Fussey in the game any more. Purely as a referee, I think he would have been equal to the task in today's game although he did allow a dodgy goal I scored once. I will come to later.

We were not down for long and in the next two weeks reeled off four wins in a row including revenge over Burnley in a 6-2 demolition at Portman Road. The last of those wins at home to Birmingham City 4-1 in which I scored before getting a full blooded kick in the calf which left me hobbling around in a lot of pain. As there were no substitutes in those days, I stayed on as a virtual passenger for the rest of the game. Roy Bailey picked up a more serious injury. After he had been dead-legged, he was admitted to hospital with a severely bruised and swollen thigh. Roy was kept in for over a week and missed the next six games with Wilf Hall taking over in goal. We were due to play Manchester City two days later on the Monday evening in the 1st Round of the League Cup at Portman Road. After our unlucky defeat in the league, I was desperate to play and have another go at them, as were the rest of the lads.

When I arose on the Sunday morning, my calf was so stiff and sore that I could hardly walk or put much weight on it. I didn't hold out much hope of playing. It was still early September and, as the weather was still good, a few days before we'd arranged with our neighbours and friends, June and Derek Francis, to go to their beach hut in Felixstowe for the day. We were very lucky in this respect. Two of our other best friends, Val and Buddy Hutchinson, also had a beach hut there so we were never short of invitations to the seaside which, of course, the kids loved. Val was a brilliant hairdresser who Eileen had met at prenatal classes before Jane was born. Years later she became Bobby Robson's wife.

I'd found in the previous two years, that if I had any cuts or bruises, the sea seemed to have instant healing powers. By 8:00am that morning we were in the beach hut, tucking into a large English breakfast that June and Eileen had cooked. After a look at the Sunday morning papers, I walked the forty yards or so down to where the waves were breaking and stood there about knee high in the near freezing water, letting the waves and surf flow round my injured calf. It was a familiar sensation as each wave broke and receded of the fine sand and shingle moving backwards and forwards around my legs, feet and ankles, giving them an unusual but pleasant sort of ticklish massage. I suppose you could call the sand the ashes of the world as they're millions of years old and it was like I could feel the power of it all healing me, slowly taking away all the pain. When my feet were almost numb with the freezing cold water of the North Sea, I went back to the hut to warm them for a while. Eileen made me one of my favourites, a hot cup of all milk coffee and I read the Sunday papers for a while before going back to the sea for some more treatment. I did this many times that day until it was time to go home. When I'd arrived at the seaside that day I could hardly walk. By the time I left, it was amazing what the sea had done for me as most of the stiffness and pain had gone from the injury. All this was minor though compared to the fatal accident in the Italian Grand Prix at Monza that afternoon as I stood there in the North Sea. The German racing driver Wolfgang Von Trips had tragically lived up to his nickname of 'Count Crash', leaving the track in his Ferrari at over a hundred miles an hour, spinning and scything through a wall of unprotected spectators. Von Trips was amongst the 13 killed and several others were seriously injured, putting into perspective Roy's dead leg and my bruised calf muscle.

When I reported for training the next morning, Alf had brought Dermot Curtis into the 1st team squad fully expecting me not to be fit to play. Alf asked me "How's that leg, Ray? You were limping round like a lame duck on Saturday." I replied that it was funny he should put it like that as I'd spent most of the previous day just like a duck, paddling around in the North Sea, then said I was fit enough to play that evening. Alf jokingly said I should go into business bottling up saltwater from the North Sea! Nowadays it's all high technology in the treatment of injuries and club physio's are paid thousands of pounds for their undoubted skills. I wonder sometimes whether they ever think about more natural remedies which don't cost a penny? I know they used to make injured race horses stand in fast flowing rivers to heal their injured legs. Maybe the sea works on humans in a similar sort of way. Near the end my career. I was often referred to as the 'Old War Horse'; as a young war horse, the sea helped to heal many of my wounds and injuries. I think they call it Complementary Healing these days. We beat Manchester City 4-2 that night with the lame duck of two days scoring twice and Doug Moran bagging the other two. They sometimes call it the 'cruel sea' but it can be kind as well and so it proved for me throughout my playing career.

After a great start that no one had predicted, the landlord of the Station Hotel in Ipswich where I had stayed many times in my years with Town, was the only one who'd put a quid on Ipswich winning the championship that year though we were bound to come a cropper sooner or later. Everton, after a poor start to the season hammered us 5-2 at Goodison Park, with fast attacking play I don't think we saw the like of for the rest of the season. The real test of our metal came on a hot sunny day in late October when the mighty Tottenham Hotspur, the reigning league champions came to Portman Road. They had a reputation for playing attractive free-flowing football and were the biggest crowd-pullers of the time, with seven internationals including Danny Blanchflower, Maurice Norman and Johnny 'The Ghost' White. Jimmy Greaves was yet to be signed. The crowd record was broken with over 28,000 packed into Portman Road. The referee was the notorious Mr Tinkler from Boston, Lincolnshire. You could never say he was ever biased towards any one team or another and was generally a good referee but he was capable of huge blunders. Just the mention that Tinkler was to referee your game was enough to send a tingle of nervous anticipation down the spines of both players and crowd. As with all the other games we'd played by that time, we had no fear of Spurs or all the big names in their team as we had nothing to lose. Being the newly promoted club from nowhere, almost everyone expected to be relegated.

The game started at a hectic pace. Despite this, both sides played entertaining skilful football. Spurs went in front after 20 minutes when their Welsh international left-winger Cliff Jones scored with a diving header. Ted thundered in an equalizer. On the stroke of half-time, we took a sucker punch as Jones headed in his second for them to go in 2-1 up. I had to rush off the pitch as I'd suffered quite a bad cut after Dave Mackay had raked his studs down the back of one of my calves. Jimmy Forsyth had taken a look at it and told me to carry on but that it would need stitches at the interval. The club doctor Patrick Wood, was waiting for me in the treatment room, ready with the dreaded needle and thread. As he was putting the stitches in, he said "Ray, you've skin like leather," and a few seconds later cried out "Ouch!" as the needle pierced one of his fingers. I reminded him of this when I met up with him last year. He said the worst stitch up job he'd ever had to do was on another Town centre-forward David Johnson who had received a nasty kick in the knackers in the 4-0 home win over Lazio at Portman Road in the UEFA Cup in 1974. "Just a little prick," he warned as he gave him a local anaesthetic before stitching him up, to which David said " You must be bloody joking Doc!"

Alf was his usual calm self when he gave us our half-time team talk, telling us to get the ball out to the wings as much as possible to Jimmy and Rocky who'd just come back from their usual half-time fags in the outside toilets. It didn't take long. Only about eight minutes for his advice to work. Coming from a Jimmy Leadbetter throw-in to their box, I ran onto it, flicked it past one challenge then picked my spot in the far corner of the net and the crowd went mad. I only had to wait a few minutes for my 100th league goal, made by Rocky Stephenson with a peach of a cross. Bill Brown their keeper suddenly came hurtling off his line to catch the ball but completely missed it, leaving three defenders flat footed in the six-yard box. Perhaps the sun peeked through Bill's country gent style cap that he always wore or Rocky's cross beat him in the flight like a bowler's out-swinger in cricket at which Rocky was very good at as well. It didn't matter to me as I volleyed the ball into the net then rushed to the crowd to celebrate with them, standing with my arms outstretched and my shoulders shrugged, as if to say as one commentator reported, 'No Problem!'

We hung on to win a great game 3-2. When Mr Tinkler, who thankfully had a good one as well, blew the final whistle, amidst the celebrations there were one or two who were not quite so happy. As we were walking off, Maurice Norman, the England centre-half at the time, came up to me and said with a snarl "I'm gonna kick the fuckin' 'ell out of you when you come up to our place!" Maurice was a Norfolk man and played for Norwich City before going to Spurs which perhaps made defeat even harder to swallow that day. Andy Nelson had the same promise from their England centre-forward Bobby Smith. He just smiled calmly as was Andy's way and replied "I'm looking forward to seeing you as well Bobby!" Nobody ever got the better of Andy if that's the way they wanted to play it. That win put us into 4th place in the league that day, two places ahead of Spurs on goal difference. The Spurs manager Billy Nicholson praised Town after the game and said "If we'd had Ipswich's strikers, we would have paralysed them." The same week in Ipswich, one of the most famous films of those times was showing, 'The Taste of Honey' with Rita Tushingham. Whenever I think back on that great season and the early sixties, the classic soundtrack of that film always comes back to me. I'd always loved going to the movies and working up a thirst by eating loads of peanuts, followed by ice cream or strawberry lollies, in fact everything on the tray with which the young ladies with torches used to walk up and down the aisles. At that time it had never tasted so good.

I had a lot of good write-ups in the national press that weekend, saying I should be leading the England attack. Part of my success was due to Alf's system of playing two deep-lying wingers which was still confusing almost everyone we played. The lack of instant replays every Saturday night which you get nowadays helped keep Alf's system under locks, as Ipswich Town games were rarely televised. All the evidence of his system was lost. These days even players are given their own personal DVD's on their opponents to study. Alf's system would have been rumbled quicker though there was a downside of not having your games and goals televised every week. Although I was to play for England twice that year, they were my only two caps. I think that if Town's games had been viewed every week and with the amount of goals I was scoring and the different ways I was scoring them, it may have been difficult for the FA Committee, who picked the team, to deny me further England caps in view of what the whole nation would have witnessed almost every Saturday night. Exactly the same applied to Ted. He would have been my first choice to play up front alongside me in those two England games.

Three weeks after the Tottenham game, the England team to play Northern Ireland in a friendly was announced. I was in Ipswich town centre doing some shopping for Eileen when, by chance, I bumped into Reg Pickett. He shouted across the street to me "Congratulations, Ray!" I thought he was joking. He told me he'd heard it on the radio just before coming out that I'd been picked to play for England. I could hardly believe it till I arrived home. Eileen opened the door to me and said with a large smile "Someone is waiting to see you!" When I entered the living room, there was a beaming Mr John, waiting to shake my hand and congratulate me as this was the first time an Ipswich Town player had ever been capped by England. It was only a matter of seconds before a champagne cork was blasted into the ceiling of our living room! Later on that day, the room was full of press, cameras and flashlights, the works but those moments celebrating with Eileen and one of the great men of football in that era Mr John were the highlight of that day.

A few days later we played Manchester United at home and Walter Winterbottom, the England manager, was at the game. I can only think he'd come to watch Ted who obliged with two typical scorchers with myself and John Elsworthy completing a fine 4-1 win over the Reds in which we were almost toying with them by the end of the game. Just as in life, in football there is sometimes no justice. Ted was at his peak of his ability but he was never chosen to play for England. This was sad not only for him but all the England soccer fans who never saw one of the most exciting players in the game of that era grace the turf of Wembley. Ted's shot made Bobby Charlton's almost look like a back pass to his keeper.

On the Monday morning I drove up to London to join the England squad at Lancaster Gate Hotel where I met up with the England squad, including Ron Springett, Jimmy Armfield, Ray Wilson, Bobby Robson, Peter Swan, Ron Flowers, Bryan Douglas, Johnny Byrne, Johnny Haynes, Bobby Charlton. From there, we went to play a 50 minute practice match with a Fulham team at Craven Cottage. There was no tactical talk from Winterbottom before the game in which I played up front with Johnny Byrne who was also winning his first cap; he was playing for 3rd Division Crystal Palace at the time and was a fine player in the making but we had little idea about each others playing styles. I scored one and Bryan Douglas scored two in a 3-0 result. After the game, Winterbottom was quoted as saying of Johnny and me "I thought the two fitted in well and showed promise for Wembley." The truth was, that after about quarter of an hour Johnny seemed to play more of the game in midfield, helping out Johnny Haynes who moaned if the slightest thing went wrong and sulked if he didn't get the ball for any length of time but he seemed loath to do his share of the chasing, fetching and tackling. Don't get me wrong, Johnny was a fantastic player but perhaps the best way I can put it, is that he was used to being waited on in football terms.

Johnny Byrne was an education to me, so self confident in every way on and off the pitch. After dinner at our hotel in Hendon that evening, he said "Come on Ray, we're going out!" Johnny had a big car, a top of the range Ford of that time and drove us for miles and miles, past the lights of Piccadilly Circus well into a part of the capital I didn't know before stopping outside a big house in the East End of London. We stepped out, Johnny knocked on the door and a well stacked, good looking woman welcomed us in. Johnny went to the kitchen, pulled me a beer out of the fridge then disappeared with the lady upstairs leaving me to watch the TV. Half an hour later Johnny returned with a big smile on his face and drove us back to our hotel.

I was naturally a bit nervous before the game. A few of the players were helpful and friendly, especially Ron Springett and Jimmy Armfield. Jimmy, as well as being a great player and a bubbly personality, was also a good team man. All Winterbottom said to me before game was 'Just play like you do for your club'. That's the only advice I had. Ireland were much more up for the game with Blanchflower and Jimmy McIlroy controlling the midfield for long periods, playing around the grumpy figure of Johnny Haynes. I ended up trying to help out in midfield as I wasn't getting an ounce of service upfront. I didn't have a good game even though I tried my best and at least supplied the pass for Bobby Charlton to score our goal. I did have one chance ten minutes from time but blasted the ball just over the bar from about ten yards. I thought that might be the end of my England career after just one game and ONE bloody chance missed. When you think of how many games players get these days to prove themselves, I might at least have had a few more chances and, but for an injury to another player, it might well have been my one and only cap.

I drove back to Ipswich with Eileen who'd driven up to Wembley to see the game. It was a quiet journey back. I knew I'd not shown my true potential. I'd been starved of the sort of passes and crosses I was used to getting from Jimmy and Rocky when playing for Ipswich. Alf had also watched the game and told me the next day I'd done far too much running for the England midfield, especially Johnny Haynes. I told him that I'd waited so long for the ball to be passed to me, running into the right channels so many times but it had never arrived, so I eventually went looking for it. Alf agreed that most of the England team were playing for themselves as individuals that night. He would change this when he was given the job of national coach. Most of the London based newspapers reported the next morning that Johnny Byrne and I hadn't showed much understanding which was a complete joke as we'd only played together for sixty minutes before the game. Our local reporter had a very different impression of the game saying that England were *"barren of ideas and devoid of enthusiasm. If they had played to any kind of plan, Crawford would probably have been able to fit in well enough. He moved the ball smoothly and made at least three openings in the first half, one from which Bobby Charlton scored the England goal, but for the most part was running into open spaces, waiting for passes that never came."*

That summed it up pretty well. What saddened me most was that my Dad had travelled up from Portsmouth to watch the game and I didn't even know he was there. He always thought he was a bad omen for me when he watched me play so he didn't tell me he was going to the game that night, bless him.

I now felt even more strongly that Ted should have been playing alongside me. The night before the England game, he'd reminded whoever was on the FA committee that picked the England team then, as Winterbottom certainly didn't, that he was in prime form scoring twice in the 3-2 away win against Aston Villa in the 3rd Round of the League Cup.

To stay with the leaders in the league we knew we had to win more away games. We beat Cardiff City the following weekend 3-0 at Ninian Park. After ten minutes, Ted deflated them with one of the most incredible goals I ever saw. The ball bounced towards him about forty yards out near the touchline and, noticing that their keeper had come off his line, hit an angled drive with ferocious power and swerve on it, leaving their 17 year old keeper Dilwyn John stranded as the ball sailed over him into the net. There was a gasp of disbelief followed by almost complete silence from the crowd, amongst them leader of the opposition Labour Party, Hugh Gaitskell. When Ted came in at half-time, Alf asked him if he was trying to set a new record for long distance shooting to which Ted replied "Well, there was no one to pass to was there!"

I lost some of the frustration I was still feeling after my England debut by scoring a hat-trick in the 5-2 win against Chelsea at home. Our away form continued to let us down and after losing 3-0 away to Aston Villa, we went out of the League Cup two days later, 4-1 away to Blackburn Rovers. It was probably the best result for Town in view of the fixture pile up that was to follow because of our FA Cup exploits that year. Just over a week before Christmas, we played one of the hardest games of the season against Bolton Wanderers at home. They scored just before half-time, a lead they hung onto with desperate tackling. A dangerous foul by their left back, Syd Farrimond, brought the game almost to fever pitch with the crowd, by then almost baying for blood, angry with Bolton's continual fouling and time wasting tactics. With just seven minutes to go, I went into a shoulder to shoulder challenge with their keeper, England International Eddie Hopkinson as he went to collect a corner from Rocky, taking both him and the ball over the line. He was an agile, spectacular type of keeper but not the tallest and therefore making himself vulnerable to this sort of challenge which was allowed in those days. When the ref signalled a goal, Hopkinson went literally hopping mad. I had to abandon any thoughts of celebration near the crowd. He chased me fly-hacking and swearing at me as I beat a hasty retreat back to the halfway line. The rest of the Bolton team protested to the officials but they only managed to rattle themselves in the end. Their defence fell apart two minutes from time when I swivelled to shoot past Hopkinson after he'd only managed to block a fierce drive from Doug Moran. After the game, their chairman and great ex-player Nat Lofthouse, one of the most renowned 'keeper chargers' of all time, said that he saw nothing wrong with my challenge on their keeper as it was all just part of the game.

On the Saturday just before Christmas, Manchester City brought us back down to earth thumping us 3-0 on a frost-bound Maine Road pitch that was more suitable for skating on that day. On Boxing Day, we played Leicester City at home. As the players warmed up on the pitch, everyone in the crowd wanted to know who the fearsome looking new Town No. 10 was? It was actually Ted who had certainly taken up the festive spirit by wearing a red wig and beard which he only took off just before the kick-off. Their keeper, a young man called Gordon Banks, kept us at bay with some brilliant saves until Aled Owen, deputizing for Jimmy Leadbetter who was injured, supplied the perfect cross for me to score the only goal of the game. I drilled in an unstoppable shot that even the best keeper in the world couldn't stop. Frank McLintock was marking me that day who, in later years, became a famous double winner with Arsenal.

Even though it was a bitter pill for Town fans to swallow, we went out of the FA Cup in the 4th Round to Norwich City. We reeled off five wins in the next six games including a 4-2 rout of Everton, the club's first ever victory over Fulham 2-1 at Craven Cottage and a brilliant win away over the mighty Spurs in front of a crowd of over 51,000 under the floodlights at White Hart Lane to complete an unlikely double over the League Champions. They'd just signed Jimmy Greaves from AC Milan who I'd always admired. After 8 minutes, I gave Maurice Norman the slip, leaving him stranded to put Town ahead but Greavsie only took a minute to equalize. After that, Billy Baxter kept a tight reign on him and Ted scored twice with Town running out 3-1 victors and the first team to do the double over Spurs in three years. One report said of my performance *'Ray Crawford has confirmed his booking to Chile, of that there can be no doubt. He was superb, worrying the giant Norman into complete misery and stamping his personality on the whole game like no one else.'*

Well, it just shows you how wrong you can be. Two weeks later, the day we were travelling up to play a re-arranged midweek game against Leicester City at Filbert Street, the squad was announced for England's next international, a friendly with Austria at Wembley. I was very disappointed not to be included. Alan Peacock, the Middlesbrough centre-forward had replaced me. He'd scored quite a few goals that season but Boro' were struggling in the wrong half of the 2nd Division whereas I was scoring goals against some of the best centre-halves and defences in Europe. By that time of the season, I'd notched up 28 goals in 36 league games. I couldn't understand the logic of it. I just had to try and put it behind me and get on with the job of keeping Ipswich's challenge for the title going. We were in second place in the table at the time. Ted wasn't having the best of times either. He had one hand in plaster after breaking a thumb in the 1-1 draw at home to Blackpool the previous week.

We beat Leicester 2-0 that night with goals from Rocky and my second against Gordon Banks that season. As we travelled back to Ipswich that night, Alf made a special point of coming to the back of the coach to talk to me. Up to that point, he had not said a word to me about my omission from the England squad that day. He sat down beside me. After a slight pause, he said "Ray, well done. It must have been hard for you knowing you had been left out of the England team. I would like to thank you for all the effort you put into your game tonight." After a brief chat about the game, he gave me a gentle pat on the knee before returning to the front of the coach. Alf rarely singled out individuals for praise or criticism but this great man-manager had a lot of compassion for his players. His words at that moment couldn't have been better timed or chosen. England didn't want me so I was going to put all my efforts into winning the championship for Alf and Ipswich Town.

Three days later Burnley were playing their FA Cup semi-final against Fulham and we had the chance to go top of the 1st Division for the first time. We were at home to Wolves. It was good to have Ted back at my side although Dermot Curtis had deputized well for him in the two games he'd played. Ted was soon back amongst the goals with a brilliantly taken penalty in the 20th minute after I'd been hauled down in the box. We didn't have the lead for long. Five minutes later Ron Flowers, their England defender, equalized with a 25 yard pile-driver. It was end to end stuff before I notched up my 30th league goal of the season to give us a 2-1 lead at half-time. They really tore into us in the second half and Peter McParland equalized on the hour. Shortly after that, Ron Flowers fell into an unconscious heap on the ground after challenging Ted for a header. Ted was wearing a protective rubber glove over the plaster-cast of his broken hand that day which made it look like a huge claw, like something out of a Hammer Horror movie. In going up for the header, he had caught poor Ron flush on the jaw with it. Happily, Ron was quickly revived by a quick dowse of the magic sponge, a bit dazed but none the worse for his encounter with Ted's plaster 'claw'. Ted had been a little worried about Ron as he was one of the most liked and respected players in the game and was standing close by to shake Ron's hand when he recovered. Ron asked Ted "What the fucking hell have you got in there?" pointing at Ted's larger hand. With a wry smile, Ted showed him the plaster cast under the glove and all Ron could do was laugh about it as well!

Two minutes from the end of the game, I whacked in a shot hard across the goalmouth. It was blocked but Dougie Moran was waiting at the far post to score from the rebound, bringing the house down as Town had gone top of the 1st Division for the first time in the club's history. It was a great feeling. I think from that moment we thought we could win the championship although Alf never mentioned it. The minus side of the game for me was that I had a very sore ankle having landed badly on it after scoring my goal which had slowed me up for the rest of the game. The next day I could hardly put any weight on the ankle. I was mobile enough though to be decorating our kitchen which I'd promised Eileen I'd do that weekend. At about eleven o'clock that morning there was a ring at the door and Eileen went to see who it was.

"Ray, it's Alf!" she shouted to me in the kitchen. I thought she was joking until I limped through to the hallway with a paintbrush in one hand, to find Alf standing there.
"Hi Alf, what's up?" I asked.
"Ray, you have been picked to play for England against Austria on Wednesday afternoon, congratulations!" Alf said. He then told me that Alan Peacock had broken a cheek bone playing for Middlesbrough the previous day and that the FA had rung him that morning, asking him if I was fit to join up with the England squad at Lancaster Gate the next day on the Monday morning. I was in a bit of

a dilemma. Alf was also concerned about my injury. I wasn't going to miss the chance of playing for my country again and told Alf I'd play.

"I'll see you after the game then okay?" Alf said, then left. Eileen asked me how I could possibly play with my injured ankle and she was probably right. I thought I could play through the pain and knew this was likely to be my last opportunity to prove myself. I had to take the chance and thought that if I could score just once, it might open the door to a long England career. We quickly changed arrangements for the day and went to Felixstowe where I stood once again in the sea for as long as I could until my toes and feet were almost like two blocks of ice. As usual, it helped my injury a lot.

The next morning I went up by train (2nd Class for England players in those days) to join the squad at Lancaster Gate. The format was the same as my first outing with England. We had another warm-up game against a Fulham side in the afternoon. My ankle was still very sore but I just had to play through it. On the day of the game, we arose for breakfast at nine o'clock, about an hour after BBC Radio had announced that James Hanratty had been hanged at Bedford Prison for the 'A6 murder'. A lot of people thought he was innocent, right up until a few years ago when his grave was dug up and a DNA test confirmed his guilt. Personally, I was against the death penalty at the time. I thought that even if they convicted 9 out of 10 cases right, it didn't justify hanging the one innocent man. The next day, the London press were to virtually string me up in football terms although I was innocent as far as effort went, compared to the other ten outfield players.

Austria proved a good side and we had to work hard to beat them. I was playing alongside Roger Hunt. He was a very good player but I still would have preferred Ted to be up alongside me that day. I had one clear-cut chance in the game and this time I made no mistake. John Connelly, the Burnley right winger who'd also been my roommate the night before the game, hit an accurate cross, the sort I was used to from Rocky and Jimmy at Ipswich. Having lost my marker, I volleyed in England's first goal from about ten yards. It was the first goal of the game and we went on to win 3-1. After the game I had no feedback from Walter Winterbottom who just thanked me for playing at such short notice. I met up with Alf as arranged and travelled back with him on the train to Ipswich.

During the journey, I'd no idea that I was talking to the next England manager. Alf, with his incredible ability to re-create games as if he had a modern day video recording of it before his eyes, went through it from start to finish. When it came to my performance, just as in the Northern Ireland game, he said I was hardly given any service. He still thought I'd done far too much running for Johnny Haynes and the other midfield players. I said that running and chasing was part of my game. We couldn't agree. After a few short and sweet exchanges, Alf put up his newspaper between us and the rest of the journey home to Ipswich passed without much comment. Alf knew the right time to say something. Probably more importantly when not to. I was never given another cap after playing two internationals for England in which I'd had two chances and scored one goal. Eddie Lever's prophesy that one day I would play for England had come true. I'd had a ridiculously short time to prove my worth in just two international games. Some strikers can play ten or more games without scoring yet they still get selected. I don't really understand that as natural goal scorers should be on the score sheet more consistently at international level. As I see it nowadays, it still seems that playing for England still depends on who you know, who you play for; much like being an accepted member of a select club however mediocre the members are and I don't think I qualified on any of these counts.

The day after the Austria game, my ankle injury stiffened up and became quite swollen. After Jimmy Forsyth had taken a look at it, he told me there was no way I was going to be fit enough to play against Manchester United that weekend. On the Friday, the squad was announced for the Home International against Scotland to be played at Hampden Park the next weekend. I was left out along with John Connelly and Roger Hunt, with Jimmy Greaves and Bobby Smith recalled, having not been available for the Austria game because of Spurs European Cup semi-final against Benfica at home which they'd won but lost on aggregate. I was disappointed again. Having to miss the game against United as well increased my frustration as this was one game I really wanted to play in. As it turned out, it was probably the best game of that season to miss. We took a real hammering at Old Trafford where the Reds tore us apart in a 5-0 thrashing, our worst defeat of the season.

Chapter 9

"The Taste of Rejection and Victory"

The next week the preliminary 40 strong England squad was announced for the World Cup in Chile and I wasn't even amongst the names. Then the penny slowly began to drop, confirming that, in life, it is not how good you are but who you know if you want to get to the top. In that respect, it is my belief that Harold Sheperdson, the Middlesbrough coach at the time and assistant to Winterbottom and the England squad, had enough pull to persuade the FA Committee to pick Peacock ahead of me for the World Cup in Chile. Although Peacock had proved himself a good striker scoring 26 goals that season, it had been against mostly average defenders in a Middlesbrough side that was to finish only halfway up the 2nd Division table. On paper, it didn't compare with my 33 goals in the 1st Division against some of the best defenders and goalkeepers in the world at the time including Maurice Norman, Bobby Moore, Peter Swan, Ron Flowers, Dave Mackay, Gordon Banks, Peter Bonetti, Bert Trautmann and Ron Springett to mention just a few; the list was endless. I think Alf was even more upset than I was and expressed his opinion with rare anger. *"I just do not understand it and I will go as far as saying it is downright unfair but probably the less said about it the better."* I think Alf knew perfectly well what was going on but was too diplomatic to go public in any more detail than he did. As for me, I just had to put the whole thing behind me and concentrate on helping Town win the Championship. The next weekend, as England were losing 2-0 to Scotland, we beat Cardiff City 1-0 at Portman Road giving us two vital points. Tony Garnett wrote of my performance that day *"Crawford seemed somewhat subdued. I should imagine he is still suffering from the cavalier treatment he has received from the England selectors."*

From that point on, I scored freely to the end of the season with a passion bordering on anger as I slammed the goals in with both head and foot. I thought of my days at Pompey, at being virtually kicked out and my Dad taking all those punches to help our family just survive when I was a child, then the night he came up to Wembley to see my first international game against Northern Ireland when I didn't even know he was there. It all came back to me and spurred me on.

The Easter Bank Holiday games looked tough on paper; two games against Arsenal and Chelsea away in the space of four days. We drew 2-2 with the 'Gunners' at Portman Road on Good Friday. I scored in the 2-2 draw the next day at Stamford Bridge with Town coming from behind in both games. Then came the crunch game on Bank Holiday Monday against Arsenal at Highbury. I really wanted to give the two-fingered salute to the FA that day. I did with two of our goals and Ted getting the third. We outplayed them with some brilliant football in a 3-0 win keeping us top of the table with just one game to play. My first goal was very similar to one of the two I scored for Colchester United against Leeds in the 1971 FA Cup giant killing except it was with my right foot and from an even more acute angle. You might say it became my 'laid-back style', hooking the ball home as I lay on my backside in the six-yard box. My second was possibly the best that I scored all season, nutmeg-ging their centre-half Terry Neill before blasting a shot past their keeper Jack Kelsey. I celebrated both goals with clenched fists and gritted teeth. I couldn't have stated my case any better. There were two more goals in my locker to come and, without doubt, the most important ones in the history of Ipswich Town and my career.

Burnley were two points behind us with a game in hand when it came to our last game against Aston Villa at Portman Road. We knew that, if Burnley won both their games against Chelsea and Sheffield Wednesday, they would take the title whether we won or not. Villa were a very good side placed 8th in the League with a very strong defence led by their tall centre-half John Sleeuwenhoek who marked me that day. Chelsea, although a talented young team who were to come back with a vengeance, had already been relegated but we were hoping they might scrape a draw away at Burnley. Whatever the result was at Turf Moor, we knew we had to win to give us the best chance of winning the championship.

In his pre-match talk, Alf put the emphasis on patience and told us just to keep passing and make the ball do the work as he'd always said and not be tempted to go rushing madly at them from the word go. Alf prepared us well. There were the usual jitters when we ran out onto the pitch but we were all as relaxed as possible. I'd never seen the ground so packed and the roar that greeted us made the hairs on the back of your neck stand up. There was also was a small section of Tottenham Hotspur fans in the crowd holding a painted message on a large white sheet saying 'Good Luck From All At White Hart Lane'. It was a great gesture especially as we'd done the double over them that year.

When the referee for the game, Mr E. Crawford from Doncaster (no fixed relation!) blew the whistle for the game to start, I just knew I had to chase everything down, to get rid of the adrenaline levels that were running in me. Adrenaline is a powerful force of strength but can be destructive if you don't control it. You feel powerful, headstrong and bold which can lead to overconfidence. That's why you see even the best football teams just boot the ball up field after getting control after the kick-off. Very often you can feel weak after you've worked off the adrenaline but your strength and fitness soon returns and your mind clears. I had a half chance in the first couple of minutes after being put through by Jimmy Leadbetter but sliced my shot wide. A few minutes later I probably would have scored.

We didn't look like scoring until twenty minutes from time when I was given the chance to change the whole history of Ipswich Town. We were awarded a free-kick on the right touchline in front of the Churchman's Stand. Of all of us, Rocky Stephenson had been the one player on top form all afternoon and the cross he delivered was perfectly met by a fierce header from John Elsworthy which crashed against the underside of the bar and bounced down perfectly into my path, only a few feet in front of me. Their keeper Sims had been wrong footed and was rooted to the goal line. I'd managed to lose my marker John Sleeuwenhoek for the first time in the game. All I had to do was throw myself forward to head the ball and I was still off the ground when the ball went into the net, a typical Crawford six-yard box goal. I couldn't hear what my team mates were saying to me as they picked me up off the ground to celebrate, such was the deafening roar from the crowd.

Villa had played well up to that point. After going behind, they started to throw men up into attack even though there was still quarter of an hour to go. One of these attacks broke down with a long clearance from our box and I managed to turn John Sleeuwenhoek with a quick burst of pace taking me racing towards their goal. Sims saved my first shot but I quickly ran round to hammer the loose ball into the back of the net. All hell broke loose amongst the crowd. Word had gone around that Chelsea were drawing with Burnley at the time. We cruised the rest of the game with Doug Moran and Ted Phillips netting but both efforts were disallowed. When the final whistle went, the crowd invaded the pitch. We didn't know the result of the Burnley-Chelsea game yet. When the public address system announced that Burnley had only managed to draw and that Ipswich Town were champions, along with Jimmy Leadbetter, I was hoisted onto the shoulders of two strong lads, one of them aptly named Jim Crane, from Haughley, immaculately dressed for the occasion wearing a suit and a bow tie. They carried me round the pitch for some of the greatest and most memorable minutes of my life.

When we finally returned to the dressing rooms, the champagne corks were popping; some of it supplied by the famous commentator Kenneth Wolstenholme who had promised Ipswich Town half a dozen bottles of bubbly if we finished above Spurs that year. This we had done by two places. It was some of the last to flow in the Ipswich Town dressing room for many, long barren years. Town's achievement of winning the third, second and first divisions in the space of five years had never been done before and what Alf had achieved was like a fairytale, turning a small club into 1st Division champions. It reminds me of an old John Wayne movie in which he plays an old football coach who gets his players from here, there and everywhere, just like Alf did, then moulds them into a winning team. Every time I see that movie, I think of Alf and those days at Ipswich. Everyone had played their part in a fantastic achievement, none more so than Jimmy Forsyth who we were going to throw him in the elephant bath that day win or lose but, rather than been thrown in, Jimmy chose to jump in himself!

A few days after winning the championship, the England squad were training at Roehampton and about to leave for the World Cup in Chile. I was on a post season tour with Ipswich Town in Vejle, a small town in Denmark watching line after line of poor squealing pigs hung upside down by their trotters then being electrocuted and having their throats cut; their idea of a local sightseeing trip before we played the local team that evening. It seemed a strange thing to be doing having just won a 1st Division championship medal the weekend before. Just over a week later, after playing a few friendly games in Germany, we docked at Harwich harbour. On the train back to Ipswich, there was blue and white everywhere, draped from house to house and fence to field to welcome us home. This was just a light starter compared to the reception we received the next evening as we stood together on an open-top bus that took us from Portman Road to the Town Hall in the centre of Ipswich. It was raining blue and white paper and confetti from the buildings around us as a 40 strong band of Royal Marines from nearby HMS Ganges led the procession in front of us. It was a very emotional moment when the thousands of Town fans who lined the road around us sung with all their hearts 'Keep right on to the end of the Road' that was always a favourite song with both supporters and players.

When Andy Nelson was offered the greatest trophy in British football and held it high above his head for all to see, it was the greatest moment in the history of Ipswich Town Football Club. My turn soon came to hold the cup as well, then also with Ted, the 'terrible twins' together in glorious celebration. We'd terrorised some of the best defences and defenders in the world that year. Between us, in all competitions, we had scored a staggering 73 goals. Three days after the civic reception, the same day as the England squad left for Chile, the 1st Division Trophy again occupied the place of honour at the top of the table at a banquet put on by the Ipswich Town Supporters Association at their Manor House Headquarters. Kenneth Wolstenholme was there, now remembered mainly for his famous commentary at the end of the 1966 World Cup when some of the Wembley crowd started to run towards the pitch. "They think it's all over," Kenneth said as Geoff Hurst broke away towards the German goal, followed by "it is now!" as Geoff lashed in England's fourth goal. Strangely enough Sir Geoff had a word for almost every striker in the game in that era in his autobiography apart from me. Perhaps he didn't want to admit that I outscored him by miles in our careers.

At the time, I was still just 25 years old and at the height of my powers as a striker. If anyone had told me my England career was finished, I wouldn't have believed them but, as Wolstenholme again may have said, it was 'all over'. My total of 37 league and cup goals that season plus my 40 league goals in the previous promotion year, gave me a total of 77 goals in 94 games over the two seasons. Since those times, I've read many articles by various people about my career and many of them have described me as a 'goal-scoring machine'. That is what I was and continued to be.

Just for the record, in the table below is where I stand in games/goal average in all the league games I played in compared with the career totals of my main challengers for the England centre-forward position in that era. I played a total of 475 league games in my career in which I scored 289 goals at an average of a goal every 1.6 games. I was surprised when Ian Hunnybell, assistant archivist at Ipswich Town, informed me that 207 of these games were played in the 1st Division in which I scored 130 goals at an average of a goal every 1.5 games, higher than my average of a goal every 1.6 games in my 2nd Division games for Ipswich and the one season in the 4th Division with Colchester United. It seems that the higher the level, the more I scored. Only Jimmy Greaves, my hero and the 'Prince of the Penalty Area' as George Best once described him, outscored me on this count.

Football League Games only

		Appearances	Goals	England Caps	Games to Goal Ratio	Strike Rate (%)
1	Jimmy Greaves	514	357	57	1.4	69
2	Ray Crawford	475	289	2	1.6	61
3	Bobby Smith	376	217	15	1.7	58
4	Roger Hunt	473	269	34	1.7	57
5	Derek Kevan	436	235	14	1.8	54
6	Alan Peacock	284	153	6	1.8	54
7	Joe Baker	299	146	8	2.0	49
8	Fred Pickering	353	168	3	2.1	48
9	Ray Charnley	464	217	1	2.1	47
10	Ray Pointer	416	179	3	2.3	43
11	Jeff Astle	393	169	5	2.3	43
12	Johnny Byrne	410	171	11	2.3	42
13	Geoff Hurst	523	212	49	2.5	41

Chapter 10

"Flat Champers, Beetroot and Bribes"

When pre-season training started in mid July, I was lying in a wing of the Anglesea Road Hospital in Ipswich, the other side of Ivry Street opposite Christchurch Park, recovering from an operation on my tail end. It was an old fashioned hospital, and during my few days there, one sunny afternoon, I was wheeled out onto the sunroof to get some fresh air along with all the other patients, many of them with various limbs plastered from head to toe and one bloke who kept shouting like a lunatic. Town wanted to get all the necessary operations players needed done at the same time so Andy Nelson and Kenny Malcolm were also there for a couple of days having their broken noses reconstructed. Whatever was wrong with you, we were all out on that roof, the players, the plastered and one lunatic, all recovering together.

Possibly some own fans thought me insane as well. At the time, I'd turned down Ipswich Town's new contract for the next season. I was on a monthly contract of £15.00 a week, the standard minimum wage set down by the Football League for players who weren't able to agree new terms with their clubs. Billy Baxter had been the only other player reluctant to accept the new contract but had signed just before the deadline at the end of June. All Town players who'd helped win the championship had been presented with a silver tray but the new contract only offered a guarantee of further years of employment at the club. There was no increase in pay in the new terms. Ipswich had a policy of not paying individual players more than the rest of the team. I thought as an England International and with my prolific goal scoring the season before, I was justified in expecting a pay rise. In my two outings for England the previous season, I'd talked to some of the players who told me they were being paid more than twice as much as me. Everyone knows football is a short career so you have to make the most of it especially when you have no other trade to turn to when your playing days are over. Just like the man in the next street, if he knows he can get a better paid job in his profession, nine times out of ten he'll take it.

The same week I'd been in hospital, Joe Baker had been signed by Arsenal for a reputed £65,000 from Torino of Italy and a few days later Denis Law for £115,000 by Manchester United also from the Turin club. You could say they had been the equivalent of Ted and myself, the terrible twins of Torino but more off the field because of their constant breaking of club rules. The most serious one involved both players in a car crash in which Joe had been quite badly injured. I was to play alongside his brother Gerry at Ipswich in the coming years whose driving turned out to be no better than Joe's! As well as the abolition of the maximum wage the previous year, players were now entitled to negotiate a signing on fee. It was reported that Joe Baker was to receive the sum of £12,000 over two years from Arsenal, a lot of money in those days and enough to prick up the ears of any footballer at the time who knew they could command a large transfer fee. Though I hadn't asked for a transfer, it was rumoured in the press that Tottenham Hotspur, Everton and Chelsea were all interested in signing me. I personally never heard a word though it wasn't unusual in those days for players to be kept in the dark about another club's interest in them for fear of unsettling or losing them. I will always maintain that Ipswich Town had many clubs wanting to talk to me who were not allowed to and that I was never informed of these approaches.

During the summer, Ipswich had spent a new record fee of £15,000 to buy Bobby Blackwood, a fierce looking ginger-haired striker from Hearts. Though Bobby was a decent bloke and a good team man and I know it's easier to say with hindsight, we needed to a top class defender more than anything else. As Bill McGarry believed, and it still stands today, the basis of a good team is built around a reliable goalkeeper, a commanding centre-half, and a good centre-forward. The day after I came out of hospital, I had a meeting with Alf but still couldn't agree with the new terms so I had to tell him I was going to put in a transfer request. It was all in the papers the next day and I received a few letters from angry Town supporters. Then in stepped Gordon Betts, a local businessman. He rang me at home inviting Eileen and myself out to his luxury Tudor Mansion in Kesgrave just outside Ipswich to discuss a financial offer he hoped might change my mind about leaving Town. It involved setting up a Family Trust for my daughter Jane which you had to leave for 16 years before cashing in on the interest. We were very impressed and accepted his offer. Alf said he had no objection to it so I finally signed a new contract for the coming season. Mr Betts said he would do the same in future for any player in the same position, meaning any Ipswich Town player who was married with children and had also played for England.

Less than a week after the death of one of my favourite actresses, Marilyn Monroe in America (some say it was suicide but I doubt it myself), we were hosts to

Tottenham Hotspur in the pre-season Charity Shield Cup at Portman Road. By then, their manager the great Bill Nicholson, had done his homework on Alf's system and we were torn apart 5-1 on the day. Larry Carberry was injured early in the game and it was the start of an injury ridden season, the complete opposite the previous year. As expected, Ted and I weren't being given so much space as before. I could now almost feel my markers breathing down my neck every game. We were giving almost as good as we were taking, scoring 15 goals with 13 against, though only eight points from the first nine games with only two wins was a sign of things to come. It wasn't helped by Jimmy Leadbetter picking up a injury which ruled him out for nearly two months shortly before Town's first venture into European Cup football against Maltese champions Floriana of Malta.

The trip out there didn't start well. Just as we were about to fly from Gatwick Airport, our scheduled plane, a Vanguard airliner was grounded because of engine trouble which was a bit unnerving when we took off two hours later especially for Kenny Malcolm and Jimmy Forsyth who'd not flown before. The flight turned out to be very smooth, in contrast to the bone shaking ride in a very old bus to our hotel after landing in Luqa Airport in Malta. When we arrived, you could soon see why the Germans had never managed to invade the island. It's like a huge fortress surrounded by rocky cliffs. The locals were football crazy and couldn't have been friendlier as the Brits had helped them defend their island against almost impossible odds in World War II. We were told not to eat the local fruit and drink bottled water although the same rules didn't apply to Mr John who said that to counter the blistering heat "I shall merely have two blocks of ice in my drink instead of one!"

On the day of the game, it was great to be up in the cool of the morning before it became too hot and to watch the sun rise on the horizon in the west over a calm Mediterranean Sea whilst Billy Baxter my room mate still snoozed away. We usually roomed together in my time at Ipswich and Billy always said I could sleep on a clothes line if I had to! As the equivalent of their Wembley there, the Empire Stadium, had no showers or baths, we changed in our hotel rooms then travelled to the game by bus in full playing kit, ready to leap out and play. Floriana had won the Maltese title without dropping a point and over 15,000 locals were there to cheer them on plus another few hundred watching from the roof tops around the ground. We had more support there than we'd expected, not only from the few hundred Town fans who'd had made the trip out there but also from the many Servicemen who were still stationed in Malta. Further support came from almost the entire crew of HMS Hermes which was docked there at the time. Strangely enough, we were literally playing on home soil as the pitch was bone hard lime with a layer of sand on top that had been specially imported from a river bed somewhere in England! There was no way the pitch would take a stud so we all played in flat rubber soled boots apart from Doug Moran who always played with studs whatever the conditions.

Although we started the game in the late afternoon, the heat was still intense and things took a turn for the worse after only four minutes when Andy Nelson had his nose broken. Billy Baxter took over at centre-half as Andy left the pitch with blood pouring down his face. The locals also sensed blood, cheering on their local heroes even louder. Luckily their goal area turned out to be much less of a fortress than the island was. I took some of the sting out of the game, heading us in front just before Andy returned fifteen minutes later, slightly concussed and very shaky, slotting into Billy's position where he played bravely on for the rest of the game. Ted demoralized them heading in our second just before half-time and after the break we took complete control. I scored another before Ted completely silenced the home crowd with his second ten minutes from time, a pulverizing drive from all of 30 yards. They scored a consolation goal just before the end but, despite the sweltering heat, we were far too strong for them winning 4-1.

It was a great experience playing in Europe. Travel in those days was a lot slower and I think this took its toll on the team as a whole. Individuals vary on their recovery time from travelling and playing. If you haven't a big enough squad allowing you to rotate the players as they do these days, the pursuit of European glory can be disastrous. Early evidence of this was the weekend after returning from Malta when we conceded two late goals in a 3-2 home defeat at the hands of Wolves. Andy Nelson had put off his operation to have his nose reset and played through the pain. He was in a bad way by the end of the game. I scored my 10th goal of the season making me the top goalscorer in the 1st Division with Jimmy Greaves in second place behind me with 8. On the Monday after the game, Andy went in for his nose operation. I might well have joined him as that day, in effect, I had mine put out of joint too. I had hoped to be named in the England team to play France in the European Championship at Hillsborough the next week but was again disappointed only to find myself amongst the 11 reserves for the game. Hunt, Hitchens and Peacock had all been dropped after mediocre performances in the World Cup. I could hardly believe it when I saw that another Ray, the Blackpool centre-forward Ray Charnley, who'd never played a representative game for England, was to play alongside Greaves. Charnley was a tall, bean-pole of a striker in the mould of Liverpool's present day Peter Crouch but he wasn't even on the goal scoring charts at the time. As Johnny Haynes was out of the picture having broken an ankle in a car accident, Jimmy Armfield of Blackpool had replaced him as captain for the game. I suppose it was no coincidence that Charnley, also of Blackpool, was selected before me. I was in pretty good form to put it mildly and, just to remind the FA selectors, the next day I banged in 5 of our goals in the 10-0 rout of Floriana in the return leg of our European tie at Portman Road. In the process I broke the goal scoring record for any player in the European Cup at that time. Just for good measure, the following weekend I scored our two goals when we lost to Aston Villa 4-2. That made it ten goals in just over a week and wondered how many I had to score to convince them. To be honest, I think even if I was scoring a hat-trick every game, it still wouldn't have been enough!

Four days later, England were slow handclapped and jeered as they just managed to scrape a 1-1 draw with France at Hillsborough, saved by a late and dubious penalty from Ron Flowers. One report said that *"None of the England forwards came out of the game with any credit."* I thought that I had a good chance of being selected to play in the next international, a friendly against Northern Ireland in Belfast. Again, my hopes were dashed when the squad was announced the next week. Out went Ray Charnley, back came Roger Hunt and Alan Peacock so the Harold Shepherdson/Middlesbrough/England club/who you know membership/ had struck again. I was always a far more prolific goal scorer than Peacock but my chances of playing for England again would have been a lot better if I'd been playing for 2nd Division Middlesbrough at the time and not the leading scorer in the 1st Division playing for Ipswich Town.

I had some consolation by being picked to play for the Football League against the Irish League. A few days later, the bombshell dropped when Alf accepted the appointment to be the new manager of England on the 26th of October 1962. It was a great day for Alf but a bad and sad one for Town. Ted told me he saw Mr John coming out of the boardroom in tears, having done everything in his power to try and persuade Alf to stay. He'd even offered him a better salary than he was going to get from the FA but Alf's mind was made up and you couldn't blame him for taking the top football job in the country. Alf had turned down the job the month before. The chairman of the FA, a Mr Doggart at the time, had personally come down to see him in Ipswich. Alf had then accepted what I can only imagine were new terms in that Alf had refused the original ones that were probably the same as in the 16 year reign when Walter Winterbottom was in control or perhaps 'not in control'. At that time, it was well known that Walter didn't pick the team. I'm sure

Alf insisted he wouldn't accept the position unless he alone was allowed to select the squad and that the FA Committee wouldn't have any say in it. Alf agreed to stay at Ipswich for the rest of the season before starting as national coach. The champagne moments of the championship winning year were well and truly over. Town were on such a slide that many were already talking of us as relegation candidates. Everything had gone flat and some of the players were struggling with injury but, with the average age of the team creeping up to almost thirty, in a game that was becoming faster and more physically demanding by the year, it wasn't surprising. Added to that, many of our opponents had also begun to rumble Alf's system and tactics which had baffled them for the previous two seasons.

A few days after Alf had taken the England job, I scored all three goals with a hat-trick in the 3-1 win against the Irish Football League at Carrow Road. I was given some good service especially from Johnny Byrne and scored two of my goals with headers from his accurate crosses. A lot of people assumed at the time that I would now be the automatic choice for England centre-forward position when Alf eventually took charge. This turned out not to be the case. Although Alf was uncompromising, every England manager had (and still has) to go a little bit with the flow of the London press. At the time, Jimmy Greaves and Bobby Smith were in harness together at Spurs so it probably wouldn't have been popular with either of the two players or the press if Alf had broken up their partnership.

Possibly as a reaction to Alf's appointment, we lost our next two games to Everton 3-1 at Goodison Park, followed by a 5-3 defeat at home to Manchester United with Denis Law getting four of them. On the bright side, Jimmy Leadbetter had returned after his injury. Even though we lost, we realized not just how much we'd missed his skills but also his constant cheery smile and his never say die attitude. The weekend before we flew to Italy for our 1st Round tie in the European Cup against AC Milan, we stopped the rot with a 2-1 win against Leyton Orient at Brisbane Road. It was only our third win in 17 games that season. Even though we'd dropped to the bottom of the table, we were all looking forward to our trip to Italy, though that was to leave a bitter taste in our mouths. When we arrived at Milan Airport there were no AC Milan club officials to meet us off the plane. Alf was furious at this, thinking it a deliberate snub on their part. It was just a taste of what was to come from our hosts both on and off the pitch.

As we slept in our hotel in the centre of Milan that night, there was a huge storm which continued on and off until the next afternoon when we went to have a look at the pitch. There were pools of water everywhere. The match should really have been cancelled. We all admired what we'd seen of Italian football and were quietly confident of our chances of causing an upset. There were only just over 7,000 spectators who could hardly be seen in a ground with a capacity of 80,000. They were taking shelter from the rain high up in the stands but there were to be no hiding places for us when we found out what the Milan players had in store for us that night. In 1959, Manchester United had gone out of the European Cup after losing 4-0 at the famous San Siro stadium so history was stacked against us from the very start.

It wasn't long after Andy Nelson had exchanged club pendants and handshakes with their captain and the referee had blown for the game to start that both teams were soaked through to the skin as we slithered around on the slippery surface. The English-style conditions should have suited us better but we were quickly distracted by the more sinister side of Italian football. They started to behave like thugs, body checking, pulling hair, stamping, spitting, the whole works, with Cezaro Maldini who was marking me that night (father of the now more famous Paolo) giving me toe kicks in the Achilles and lower calf area at every opportunity. It was all no doubt designed to put us off our game, not helped by the referee who was a blatant 'homer'. Both Jimmy Leadbetter and myself were brought down in their box, both 'stonewall' penalties as they're now called.

What seemed so unnecessary about their attitude was that they had so many really gifted players, including Brazilian centre-forward Altafini who'd just helped Brazil win the World Cup in Chile, Trapattoni and nineteen year old Rivera, the 'Golden Boy' of Italian football who really was world class. It was one of the filthiest nights I have ever played football on and some of the Italian players were a mirror of the weather. There was also hardly any need for floodlights when we were defending crosses or corners because Roy Bailey and Larry Carberry reckoned that, of the gang of over half a dozen photographers behind our goal, only a few of them were taking pictures. The others were using their flashlights to try and put us off whenever the ball was crossed into our box. We lost 3-0. We were seething with anger at the reception after the game. They sat at one table and us at another and there was no conversation or contact between the teams. At the end of the dinner, the Milan players were whisked away without even so much as a goodbye or a handshake.

By the time AC Milan came to Portman Road for the 2nd leg of our tie, we'd lost our next two games and slumped to second to bottom of the table. On the evening of the game my car broke down, even refusing to start in my driveway.

There was nothing else for it but just run as fast as I could down to the Norwich Road where I managed to flag down a car although he didn't have much choice really as I was almost standing in the road waving frantically for him to stop! We had some consolation winning 2-1 and, but for three or four shots hitting the woodwork, we might have won the game. It just wasn't to be. They were good defenders and scored a breakaway goal just after half-time to put the tie almost out of reach. I scored after 80 minutes and Bobby Blackwood won the game 2-1 with a late goal. It was the end of a very physical tie. Even more violent had been the hanging of James Smith earlier that day in Manchester for the murder of 57 year old Sarah Cross. He'd battered her to death in her sweet shop in Manchester the day before the Burnley versus Tottenham Cup Final six months before while we were on tour in Germany and less than a week after we had won the 1st Division Championship. She was a Burnley fan and had tickets for the final for herself and her husband but she never made it to Wembley. Those were the times we lived in where football, life and death were closer than ever. I didn't know it at the time but I had also made my last appearance at Wembley. AC Milan went on to play there that year, beating Benfica 2-1 in the European Cup Final.

The two most controversial goals I ever scored in my career came in Ipswich Town's 2-0 win over Sheffield Wednesday, three weeks before Christmas that year. We'd done the double over them the season before so we expected to win but none of us realized at the time that three of their players, David 'Bronco' Layne, Peter Swan and Tony Kay had taken bribes to chuck the game. All I can say, is that the kicks I suffered from Swan hurt just the same as usual and they were no worse than the rest of the Wednesday players that day. Tony Kay was even named as their man of the match. It wasn't until over a year later when it all blew up and shook the whole of English soccer. On the evening after the game Eileen, who liked to surprise me with her cooking which could be anything from an Indian to a Lancashire hot-pot, cooked a Russian dish that I've since found out is called 'Borscht' and is made almost entirely from beetroot. Having had a good game and scored both our goals that day, I was hungrier than usual and after a few second helpings had eaten the lot. A few hours later, I was sitting in front of the Ipswich Town club doctor, Patrick Wood, having driven myself round to his surgery in Fonnereau Road in Ipswich shortly after midnight. I told him that just before I had gone to bed, I'd gone for a pee and, to my horror, it had come out red and I thought I was pissing blood. He asked me questions about the whole day, starting from what I'd had to eat and if I'd been kicked in the game, especially in the kidney area. After examining me, he said there was no damage to any of my major organs. I drove back home with his words ringing in my ears after he'd diagnosed me. "Ray, you have being passing beetroot juice, not blood!" It was a strange end to a day that was to turn out one of the most controversial in the history of English football. We won two of our next three games, only to finish what had been a great year for me and the club on a low note, going down 5-0 at White Hart Lane to Spurs on Boxing Day on a bone hard icy pitch with Jimmy Greaves scoring a hat-trick in the last five minutes. It was the start of what was to be called 'The Big Freeze' in years to come.

Our 3rd Round tie away to Mansfield Town in the Third Round of the FA Cup just after the turn of the year, was memorable to me for more than one reason. Most of the game was played in a snowstorm and Jimmy Leadbetter scored the only hat-trick of his long professional career in our 3-2 win. Jimmy was absolutely thrilled after scoring his third. I know some teams have a sort of rehearsed act after scoring a goal these days, maybe it's gone a little bit out of fashion now but it was a total one-off when Ted and I picked up Jimmy and carried the nicest person I ever knew in football across the snow covered pitch back to the halfway line. I was equally thrilled when I returned to the dressing room to get the news of the birth of our new baby, Liza Anne.

At about that time, Jimmy Leadbetter had just passed his driving test and bought his first ever car. As Jimmy always wanted to do everything exactly in the right way and in the right order with no detail spared, he listened to any of us who had any advice on cars especially as we were going through a cold spell that was one of the worst on record. One tip that Jimmy took on-board, was to put a blanket on top of the engine overnight to stop the frost getting to it, making it easier to start on freezing cold mornings. A few days later, he arrived in a terrible fluster for morning training and not his usual cheery self. He said he'd had to walk to Portman Road from the centre of the town where his new car had conked out on him. Jimmy was a little embarrassed when we asked him what he thought the trouble was with his new car. He explained he was mystified too until he'd had a look under the bonnet. To Jimmy's horror, he saw that a large part of the tartan blanket he'd forgotten to remove that morning when starting out, had wound itself round the fan belt in a hell of a tangle, more or less strangling and bringing the car to a complete standstill. Jimmy was obviously well known in town and said the most embarrassing thing about it had been the comments of passers-by, like "you'll have to get the bus, Jimmy!" and "we know you're Scottish Jimmy, but putting a tartan blanket over it is going a bit far, isn't it?" After training, a couple of the lads who knew a bit about cars took Jimmy back to his stranded car in the middle of town to sort it out for him. There was no damage to the car but the tartan blanket was a write-off. Another Scot, Billy Baxter, also bought his first car that year but had a different problem. On most Wednesday nights, we used to play for Roy Bailey's darts team which Alf didn't mind about as it was in aid of a charity for the blind. On one of those nights, we were right out in the sticks of Suffolk at a country pub. After Billy had finished his game, he said he wasn't feeling too well and was leaving to get an early night. About fifteen minutes later, the pub door opened and there was Billy, looking a bit sheepish and covered in mud. He shouted out "Anybody got a tractor here?" Straight away one of the locals called out in a deep broad Suffolk voice "I ain't, but I know someone ooh'as!" and off he went with Billy to rescue his car from a countryside ditch. Perhaps Town's modern nickname 'The Tractor Boys' has some reason behind it!

In our only game for six weeks during January and February of that year, we slithered and slipped to a 3-0 defeat in the 4th Round of the FA Cup at Leicester City in the ice and mud of Filbert Street. The former Newcastle and England centre-forward Jackie Milburn watched the game with Alf. The day before he'd been appointed as the new manager of Ipswich Town. Jackie had previously been player-manager of Yiewsley in the Southern League so it was a huge step up to manage a team that had just won the 1st Division Championship. I think most of us were quietly confident he'd be up to the job. He was a nice guy too, probably too nice as it worked out. My first meeting with him could have led me personally to doubt this.

The day Alf introduced Jackie to the team, we were waiting in the usual line to shake his hand. When my turn came, he just smiled and said "Nice to meet you Ray, you won't be here long!" before moving onto the next player. What an amazing thing to say! What did he mean by it? Did he think I wasn't good enough? No, he can't have meant that as I'd scored 37 goals the season before. I also wondered if he'd had heard of my transfer request earlier that season and thought I was a troublemaker? I was dumbstruck at the time. I forgot it soon enough because if you took to heart every comment made about you in football or life for that matter, you would soon go completely bonkers. As it turned out, I probably should have taken it as a compliment.

On Jackie's first day's training with us, Alf was away at Hendon with the England squad to meet France in a qualifier for the European Championship. Jackie was waiting for us on the frozen practice pitch at Portman Road wearing a tracksuit with one foot on a football, a cup of coffee in one hand and a cigarette in the other. This was to become Jackie's customary pose at training sessions and I don't think Alf approved of it one bit. Alf had big, dark expressive eyebrows and that, with a narrowing of his eyes, could give you a real brow bashing without him even saying a word if he was unhappy with you for some reason. You had the feeling that the way Alf glared at Jackie that he wanted to say something like "What the ef...g hell do you think you are doing? I thought you had been asked to come here to manage a football team, not to look like some poser in a hairdressing salon who fancies himself as a football manager!" But of course Alf never did, it wasn't his style. From the very start, I don't think Alf had much time for Jackie. In fact, I don't think they connected well at all, although Alf, for all his great qualities as a manager, wasn't an easy man to get to know or get close to. I also feel that Alf found Jackie's ideas about coaching and tactics much too naive at the level he was about to take on. From a player's point of view, I think Jackie wanted to get to know the players too well, treating us too much like buddies. In the process, he failed to keep that respectful distance there should always be between manager and player. Unfortunately, the saying 'familiarity breeds contempt' comes to mind. In comparison, you could have likened Alf to an old fashioned headmaster in his style of management which demanded mutual respect from both pupils and master. You could just imagine him, walking into a pre-match talk wearing a long black cloak, holding some dusty old books on the history of football tactics. Alf would look after you if you toed the line, but if you crossed him in terms of discipline or how he wanted you to play, he would come down on you like a ton of bricks whilst, on the other hand, Jackie was far too easy going.

The one good thing about the weather, was that it gave all the players who'd been carrying injuries the chance to recover and for the whole squad to rest and re-charge their batteries. In a small club, injuries are felt far more as, usually, they don't have the resources to cover their best players. It certainly cost Ipswich in the Championship of 1981 when Town also had a brilliant team but were distracted by too many cup games at home and abroad. A very big mistake although winning the UEFA Cup was some consolation. Both Alf's and Bobby Robson's teams were smoothly running machines only when all the top 11 players were fit. If you removed any part of it, almost any one player, the wheels could easily come flying off as there wasn't anywhere near enough quality to replace them if any one of them were injured.

During the big freeze, it wasn't easy to find anywhere to train or have any practice games. Unlike the rest of the country, the whole of Suffolk was ice bound apart from some areas on the coast. During a milder spell, we managed to play a full game at Harwich and once travelled to Felixstowe taking the ferry, which wasn't much bigger than a ship's lifeboat, across the estuary to Bawdsey, a beautiful secluded place by the sea. We had permission to play a game on the local rugby ground which was soft enough to take a stud. It was mighty cold but very invigorating. It made the fish and chips in Felixstowe on our way back taste better than ever!

When the eventual big thaw set in at the end of February, I think there was still an icy distance between Alf and Jackie that was never to thaw. Strangely, Alf's last game in charge was against Burnley at home. We thought Alf was going to stay to the end of the season. We won 2-1. After a lean season, Ted had found his shooting boots again. In scoring one of the goals, he managed to bust the net with a typical blockbuster and the ball flew on into the crowd behind the goal! It was a good send-off for Alf, though typically he didn't want any fuss to be made of him and slipped quietly away from Portman Road after the game. The problem was that with four games still to play, we were still not safe from relegation. It seemed a little premature for him to leave at such a crucial time. We knew that relations between Alf and Jackie had never been exactly warm but we weren't aware of any bust-up between them behind the scenes. This only came to the surface shortly after Jackie had resigned well over a year later. As it was, with Jackie now in sole charge, it took three of our last four games to make sure of survival, which we finally did by beating Bolton wanderers 4-1 at Portman Road and I scored my 25th league goal of the season.

Town finished 17th in the 1st Division and Everton won the championship. In all competitions I'd scored 33 goals in 49 games. Billy Baxter and myself had been the last to sign new contracts the year before so, maybe now, we'd made our point as to our worth; we were the only two players who played in every game that season.

Chapter 11

"Sent off and sold"

With Jackie now in charge as full-time manager, we went on a post season tour to East Germany and Slovakia (now Czechoslovakia). Our first game was against an East Berlin XI on the east side of the Berlin Wall which had just become communist East Germany. We played before our biggest ever crowd; 70,000 people. We were winning with a goal from Ted but conceded twice in the last ten minutes losing the game 2-1. Four days later, I scored both goals in a 2-0 win over SC Empor Rostock before we crossed the border to Slovakia where I scored a hat-trick in a 5-1 win over 1st Division side Jednota Trencin. I was enjoying playing against European teams. For all their skills, they didn't like playing against an old fashioned style English centre-forward who wasn't afraid to mix it in the six-yard box. I scored again in a 3-1 win over another Czech 1st Division team, Provazska. I can safely say that most of the matches were full-blooded encounters with both sides doing their best to win and certainly, in our final game of the tour, our hosts Kosice FC of Slovakia were taking no prisoners.

Things seemed destined to go wrong the day of the game not long after we'd checked into our hotel. Jackie went into the hotel kitchen to sort out our pre-match meal and we sat down in the dining room waiting for our main course of boiled chicken with creamy rice pudding to follow but Jackie had his own ideas about the menu. A few minutes later, both the boiled chicken and creamy rice were served up on the same plate. We all had a good laugh about it; some of us asking Jackie if we were behind schedule, others if they needed any help with the washing-up in the kitchen or if there was a national plate shortage! As in East Germany, what we missed more than anything else was real butter. Their equivalent of it was about half way between lard and margarine. Good English butter would have been wasted on them, certainly on the team we played a couple of hours later. It probably wouldn't have melted in their mouths. We were to find out that, after Jackie's all in one dinner, Kosice FC had no intention of playing the game in the spirit and comradeship that we'd shared as allies in World War II. I suppose football will always be a totally different kind of war when it becomes football between clubs and nations. In this game, I was sent off for the first and only time in my career.

Before the game started, we were all presented with bouquets of flowers that we gave to some of the ladies in the crowd. They may just as well have been bouquets of thorns. Kosice was also known for its large zoo and the game was about as friendly as playing eleven football versions of King Kong. By half-time, they were 4-2 up. Most of us had been clattered from pillar to post. I'd been hounded by their centre-half who was kicking the living daylights out of me. He was a huge man, at least six feet four inches tall, the equivalent of 'Jaws' in the James Bond movies but without the silver fangs and the largest and most violent defender I'd ever played against. Perhaps 'offender' would have be a better word as what he'd done to me was criminal!

It was in the second half, after being flattened by him yet again that I retaliated but only in a comic sort of way. After peeling myself up from the local mud, I gave the giant man a playful side foot on the backside. He should have been sent off long before then. The referee took exception to my small act of defiance and pointed me towards the dressing rooms for an early bath. To be honest, that was the safest place to be at the time. So much for our wartime allies I thought. Mr John also decided he'd had enough as well. As I slowly walked off to the jeers and boos of the partisan home crowd, he stood up from the touchline bench where he'd been sitting next to Jackie and led a one man pitch invasion shouting back at Jackie "For god's sake, Jackie that's enough, let's get them off!", making rounded 'come off' signs with his arms to the whole team. Jackie remained unmoved on the bench and with his usual smile shouted back "Come and sit down John, it's only a friendly!" Thinking back, I wonder if Jackie took too many games we played in a similar spirit? A furious Mr John, frowning with red faced anger and puffing heavily on a 'Players Untipped' duty free, reluctantly took his place back on the bench next to Jackie. It was rare for Mr John to lose his temper. When he did, it was usually with good reason. The incident emphasized not only how much he cared for all his players but also that Jackie was far too easy going in his attitude which was to be part of his downfall at Ipswich. The very same day, England, who were also touring Europe, thrashed Switzerland 8-1 in a friendly in Basle. Alf had obviously started to get things right. I couldn't help feeling a bit envious of the forwards when I read a report on the game which stated 'The Kay-Melia link operated very well and kept a constant supply of opportunities going up to Charlton and Byrne'. Little did I know that I was going to link up with Jimmy Melia in the next season or that it would be Tony Kay's last as a professional footballer.

Jackie Milburn signed six players that summer of 1963, five of them Scotsmen. First came Jim Thorburn, a 25 year old part-time professional goalkeeper from Raith Rovers who'd just been relegated from the Scottish 1st Division conceding no fewer than 114 goals in the process. More than a few eyebrows were raised at this but Jackie claimed it was because of a poor defence in front of him. It was even more of a surprise when he bought one of those defenders, centre-half Jack Bolton for a similar fee two months later! Although you couldn't wish to meet two nicer lads, they were just not up to English 1st Division standard. Why he bought them was a mystery at the time. When a manager brings in new players, they should at least be as good as the ones you already have.

He also brought in two full backs on free transfers, Joe Davin, a 24 year old fullback from Hibernian and Jimmy Nelson, a nineteen year old from Sunderland who was yet to make his league debut. When Jimmy left Town nearly a year later, he still hadn't. The forward line was strengthened by the signing of Danny Hegan and John Colrain. Danny was a brilliant 20 year old Scottish midfield player from Sunderland, probably Jackie's best buy for Town. John, 'Horse' as he came to be nicknamed, was a massively built six feet one inch striker from Clyde. All these buys were around the £5,000 mark. Only Danny turned out to be 1st Division material and was a real bargain. Jackie certainly had more of an eye for attacking players than defenders but had frittered away about fifteen grand on players you have to say were no improvement on the squad at the time. If he'd bought one good solid defender of 1st Division standard and experience as Town were still crying out for, I think the money would have been more wisely spent. Jackie, likewise in management, had no previous experience in the transfer market at this level.

On Jim Thorburn's first day at training, before Jackie left he instructed Jimmy Forsyth to give him a workout which would also give us some shooting practice. It had been a long session and Ted wasn't very happy with the idea as it meant he was probably going to miss his usual train back to Colchester that morning. Ted didn't like having his daily routine altered one bit! I think Jim was possibly unaware that Ted, even though his knees were nearly shot to pieces, still had the hardest and most destructive shot in British football at the time. Jim, anxious to prove himself in front of his new team mates, tried as any goalkeeper should to get his body behind the flying leather punches of Ted's near eighty seven mile an hour shots, taking them all over the body and I mean all over. It was not long before he took one full in the face and crumpled to a heap on the ground. On this, Jimmy Forsyth declared the session over and we trooped off back to the 'Chicken Hutch'. Jackie, who had just come out of the showers and was rubbing himself down, asked why the shooting practice had ended so quickly.

"Well, it's Jim," said Ted.
"Why, where is he?" asked Jackie.
"They're just bringing him in on a stretcher," replied Ted.

Apart from Town's keepers not many went in goal for shooting practice when Ted was around. Tony Garnett, for many years the sports editor and football reporter for the East Anglian Daily Times, was one of the few who were brave enough to do this. Tony, who was a good all round sportsman himself and sometimes took part in our five-a-side training games, asked Ted if he could go in goal for a while to see what it was like facing his 87 mph shots. Ted agreed after asking Tony if he was sure as Ted hated all goalkeepers, even in training. Tony replied that he was up for the challenge and, after taking off his suit top and tie, he went between the posts. After Ted had blasted a few thunderbolts past him, one of them nearly taking his head off, and with Tony already covered in dirt and dust, Alf's voice suddenly bellowed out of his office window, "Get him out of there! He'll kill him!"

Our first pre-season friendly was a 5-0 win against Jackie's previous club, non-league Yiewsley. Two days later, one of the most daring crimes of the century took place, the 'Great Train Robbery' An overnight mail train from Glasgow to Euston London was robbed of over two and a half million pounds in used bank notes. I bet Jackie wished he'd had that amount to spend on new players. He had had to settle for a tiny fraction of that. Although Jackie's early signings for Town hadn't been very shrewd, in the coming months his good ones made up for the poor ones. However, he had to get some money in before he made them, so inevitably I became involved in the equation of finances concerning the long term future of Ipswich Town. Not being arrogant, I was the only asset they had to sell.

A week later we travelled to Switzerland to play in a tournament for the Uhren Cup. We did well beating Sparta Rotterdam of Holland 4-2 and the host club FC Grenchen 5-2 in the final. Jackie gave me the honour of being Town captain on the day. As well as bringing some silverware home, Town were also awarded a large clock which went in the club's boardroom when we arrived back home. Possibly there was some sort of message or warning as it sat there, that even though we had won the tournament, Town's time as a 1st Division club was starting to run

Family photo taken when I was four sitting on my Dad's knee. My Mum Muriel is holding brother Alan.

'The Crawfords'
Alan and Me,
Barbara, Mum, Dad and Colin

My Dad, George 'Boy' Crawford,
Professional Heavyweight boxer in the 1930's

Hilsea Modern School 1949/50.
My first team at the age of 13. I am front row, second on the left.

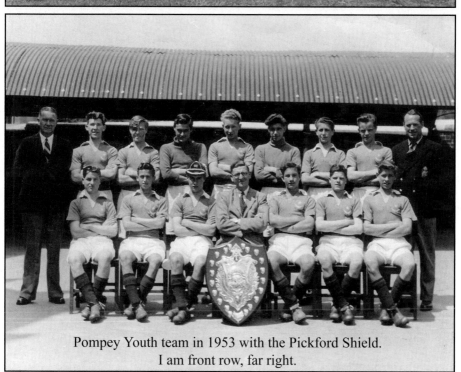

Pompey Youth team in 1953 with the Pickford Shield.
I am front row, far right.

Me scoring for Pompey Youth against Southampton at Fratton Park in 1952. Always a good feeling.

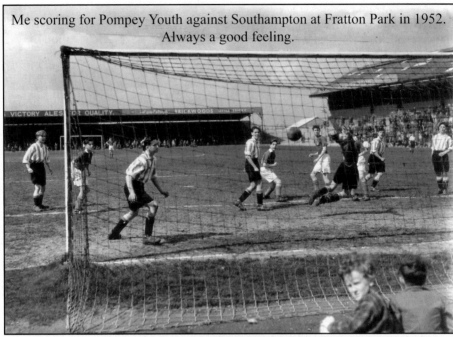

1st Battalion, The Royal Hampshire Regiment

(1ST XI)   MALAYA 1956

Runners-Up CALDBECK CUP (FARELF)

Cpl TERRY E,   Pte THOMAS J,   Bdsm HELLARD B,
Pte RULE P,   Pte SAIT P,   Pte PICKARD L,   Lcpl CRAWFORD R,   Pte HUNT I,   Pte NEWTON C,
Capt G.W. ALDERMAN,   Lcpl MITCHELL D (Capt),   LT COL A.H.T. HOGGE,   Pte SOFTLEY J,   ORQMS G. STREET.

'The Jungle Boy' on National Service in Malaya.
I didn't think joining the Army would be such fun.

Me looking the part in Malaya.
I never fired this rifle in anger.

Playing for the Hampshire Regiment against the Scottish Fusiliers in the Malayan Cup Final.

Sid, Roy, Tommy, Brian, John, Me, Les at my Wedding Reception in April 1958.

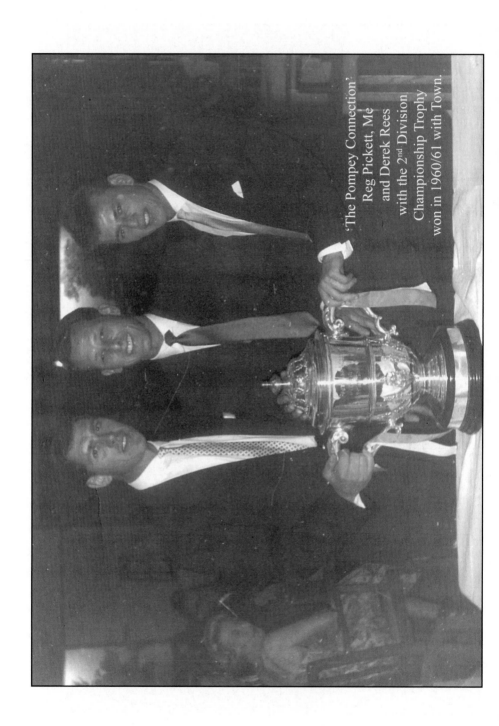

'The Pompey Connection' Reg Pickett, Me and Derek Rees with the 2nd Division Championship Trophy won in 1960/61 with Town.

Me scoring for Ipswich against Chelsea on our way to winning the championship. I managed to bang three past Peter 'The Cat' Bonetti (2nd December, 1961)

Town v Aston Villa during the championship season 1961/62.
I scored a brace past big Villa goalie, Nigel Sims.

Parading the 1st Division Champions through Ipswich Town centre. A Great Day.

The Championship winning team 1961/62.
'Up the Town'.

Celebration time with Mr Smith (Director). The Supporters Club Chairman, Captain Andy Nelson, Ted Phillips and me.

'The Terrible Twins', me and Ted Phillips. In the championship year, we scored 61 goals between us.

My second game for England v Austria at Wembley in 1962.
I missed this time but scored in the second half.

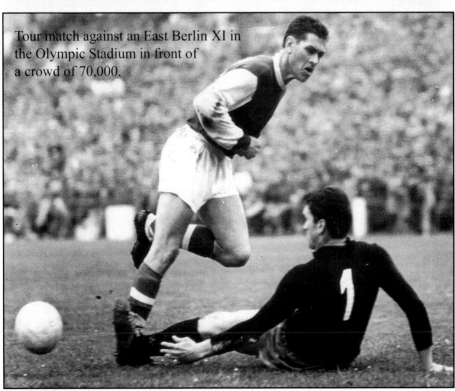

Tour match against an East Berlin XI in
the Olympic Stadium in front of
a crowd of 70,000.

Me signing for Wolves on Sept 16th 1963
with Manager Stan Cullis (left) and
the Club Secretary looking on.

out faster than anybody could have imagined. Also that my time at Ipswich Town was also coming to an end.

We started well enough that season and I scored twice in the first game of the season 3-1 at home against Burnley. It was four days later on the Wednesday morning, as we travelled back from the north by train after losing 2-0 away to Manchester United the night before, when I witnessed a brief but telling conversation between the Mr John and Jackie Milburn. I was sitting opposite them when Jackie suddenly brought up the subject of starting up a youth team. Mr John was either not listening or not interested at what Jackie was saying. He was paying more attention to a pig field we were passing at the time.

"Good God! Look at the size of that pig's bollocks!" shouted Mr John pointing out of the window. Jackie just looked at me with a resigned look, shrugged his shoulders and then just laughed. Perhaps 'pig's bollocks' just about summed up the non-existent forward planning of the Board. Alf had never been keen on the idea of having a youth set-up. He didn't like the thought of having to tell young lads they were not good enough. It would also have needed more funds to run it and Town were always struggling to make ends meet in those days.

The train took us straight to London where we were due to play West Ham on the Friday evening at Upton Park. With time on our hands, we decided to go to the Theatre that was never closed (not during the 2nd World War either) 'The Windmill' just off Piccadilly Circus. The star of the show was a crude comedian called Arthur English, like an earlier version of Bernard Manning but with a support act of almost totally nude dancing ladies adding a lot to the attraction. When we were queuing up to go in, Lionel Blair happened to walk past and Ted, never one to miss out on a chance of instant entertainment, asked the great man if he would give us a quick dance. Lionel just smiled and politely declined Ted's request. When Ted was about to let go with one of his thunderbolts, defenders and keepers were given a brief warning; he used to do a quick shuffle with his feet before striking the ball. It was Ted who did a little dance as he always did after scoring the next evening against West Ham in a good 2-2 draw at Upton Park but the writing was soon to be on the wall. The following Tuesday evening, Manchester United completed an early season double over us in a 7-2 massacre at Portman Road, Town's worst home defeat in their entire history at the time. This was followed by a 3-1 defeat away to Sheffield Wednesday and things were getting out of hand with only five matches of the season gone. The same day, the reserves lost 7-1 to Arsenal at Portman Road, emphasising Town's overall weakness in defence. In less than a week, the 1ˢᵗand 2ⁿᵈ teams had conceded 17 goals between them in just three games. Jackie had tried to encourage us to express ourselves but we had no real system. We were playing with too much freedom and not enough creativity to justify it. It was not helped by Jimmy Leadbetter being sidelined through injury. No one else in the team quite had Jimmy's guile for opening up defences. Larry Carberry had also not figured having picked up an injury on our pre-season tour and we were missing his no-nonsense defending at the back, having conceded 15 goals in five games, far too many and a recipe for relegation.

It quickly became obvious that Jackie was beginning to find it hard adjusting from managing a non-league club to the much heavier demands of running a 1ˢᵗ Division football club. There was no throwing of teacups in the dressing room, no ranting or raving but neither was there any real authority in his leadership. Things were slipping away fast and he didn't seem to have any answers to what was happening. Jimmy Forsyth still took training sessions and Jackie watched but he had very little serious input of his own. We were a team used to being given precise instructions and were missing the tactical awareness and discipline that Alf had engrained in us. Even though the average age of the squad was about thirty, we still had some ability. Alf, who'd been the catalyst to activate it had gone. It was at that point, having just turned 27 years old, I thought it was time, just as Alf had done, to move on to another challenge as well. Although I'd almost given up all hope of ever playing for England again, I knew I had little chance of realizing this with Town as things were going at the time.

Jackie never asked me if I was happy at Ipswich or whether I wanted to leave or not. I think he was resigned to losing me eventually. He knew and Mr John no doubt as well, that the only way he could build a new team was by selling me. Another matter that influenced me at the time, was the rumours going around about Eileen having an affair with Gordon Betts. These rumours were totally untrue. After his intervention in persuading me to stay at the start of the previous season when Alf was still at the club, he'd turned up at various official functions and in the process became very friendly with most of the players and their wives as well. It was obvious he wanted to get onto Town's Board of directors. For some reason, Alf hadn't taken to him although Gordon was a very generous man. It seems strange he was not welcomed with open arms. He could have been the much needed 'sugar daddy' that Town desperately needed to invest in the club (and are still in need of today by all accounts). Another thing that helped me make up my mind up that I needed a move at that time in my career, was some gossip going around that I was seeing some lady who was pregnant with my child. That, just like the rumours about Eileen, was also rubbish.

On the Monday morning after the game at Sheffield Wednesday, I went to see Mr John and asked to be put on the transfer list. I told him my reasons. He said he would have to arrange an emergency Board meeting to discuss my request. He wouldn't stand in my way, even though he could have held me to the new contract I'd signed the summer before. When I spoke to the press later that day, I said I had no quarrel or dispute with Ipswich Town. My request was for 'personal reasons'.

'RAY CRAWFORD TRANSFER REQUEST SHOCK' were the headlines in the local papers the next day. I was a little embarrassed. It was the first time I'd ever been on the transfer list at my own request. I thought I might get barracked at the next home game against Everton the coming Saturday. I needn't have worried. The crowd were still loyal to me and had been ever since I had won them over all those years ago when I arrived at Portman Road as a rough diamond. I had been ready to learn which I had done from the master of football, Alf Ramsey, and then helped them win their first ever 1st Division Championship Trophy. I think they knew, like me, that times were changing rapidly at Ipswich. Perhaps they understood that my transfer request was not unreasonable or totally unexpected at the time.

I knew there were more than a few managers and scouts watching me against Everton, including Stan Cullis from Wolves and Joe Mercer from Aston Villa. I was so keen to impress that I probably was trying too hard and didn't score in the game which ended in a 0-0 draw. I had turned the then England centre-half Brian Labone once, leaving him like a statue and laid on a chance that Rocky Stephenson should have scored from. In the dressing room after the game, Jackie Milburn took me aside to tell me that Stan Cullis, with my permission, would like to come round to see me at my home in Ipswich that evening to talk to me about signing for Wolves. I agreed to this and was very excited at the prospect. I told Eileen the news as we drove the few miles home. I knew if Cullis wanted to buy me, it was an offer and opportunity I couldn't afford to refuse in the interests of my career at the time. It was also the end of 'the terrible twins' as Ted and myself had been called. The next time I spoke to Ted, he told me that after I'd left that afternoon, Jackie had approached him to ask him if he would lead the line in the next game against Bolton Wanderers. Ted had replied "Why, what's wrong with Ray?" to which Jackie replied he'd just sold me to Wolves. Ted told him in effect that he was a bloody fool in that case. For his reaction, he was dropped for the next game against Bolton!

As always, Eileen was quite exhausted after watching me play. When we arrived home, I told her to have a rest and made a large pot of tea. I brought down baby Liza's small bathing tub to the living room and switched on the TV. I was kneeling on the floor having just started to bathe nine month old Liza, wearing my customary waterproof plastic apron when a knock came at the front door. Eileen went to answer it and a few seconds later, a man I recognized straight away walked into the living room.

"Hello Ray, I can see you're a good family man!" he said as I bathed Liza.
"I'm Stan Cullis, manager of Wolverhampton Wanderers." As if I didn't know!
"Forgive me for coming round at such short notice but Jackie said it would be alright to come and see you," he said, towering over me. He was a tall, smartly dressed man; everything I'd expected with an unmistakable Midlands accent.
"No not at all, pleased to meet you too," I replied, wiping my hand on a towel then shaking his outstretched hand. He came straight to the point.
"Ray, I've followed your career with interest over the years and I think you are just the sort of player I would like to have at my club. I have some good young players coming through and we need someone with your experience and ability to help them. I know we're not doing too well at the moment but I hope to be buying a few other players as well to add to the experienced players we already have like Ron Flowers, Peter Broadbent and Gerry Harris. Also, as far as I'm concerned you're still the best centre-forward in England. That's why I am here tonight. I'd very much like you to come up to Wolverhampton tomorrow, just to have a look round to see if you could be happy playing for us."

It was high praise and very flattering coming from a man so highly respected in the game for what he'd achieved as both a player and a manager. I was not unlike any other player and always thrived on the confidence a good manager can give you and Wolverhampton Wanderers as they still are today were one of the biggest clubs in the country.

"Well, yes..." I started to reply.
"I have also picked out some houses you could look at in a nice area with a good school for your daughter Jane to go to. What do you think?" he asked.
"Yes, that's fine, I'd love to thanks!" I replied knowing it was an opportunity I couldn't afford to refuse. I took to Stan from the moment I met him and I was

also impressed that he'd done his homework knowing the names of Eileen and my two daughters. I don't want to sound disloyal to Ipswich Town but I knew I had to go and it was a very straight forward decision accepting his offer.

"That's great Ray!" he said and we shook hands again.

"Assuming all goes well, I'd like you to play for us against Liverpool on Monday evening so I'll book you in at the Heathfield Hotel which is very near the ground for tomorrow night" to which I agreed. Stan had obviously planned my move down to the last detail.

"Should I ring Jackie and let him know about this?" I asked.

"No that's okay, I told him I would be going back to Portman Road to see him later. Well, I'll let you carry on bathing young Liza now!" he said and, after another handshake and complimenting Eileen on the colour scheme in our lounge, the great man left.

We set out for Wolverhampton early on the Sunday morning with Jane who was four years old by then. Although they were already used to babysitting for us, we left nine month old Liza in the safe hands our friends and neighbours June and Derrick Francis who kindly agreed to look after her at short notice for a couple of days.

I signed for Wolves shortly before lunchtime on Monday the 16th of September 1963. My wages were to be £45.00 a week with an extra £10.00 for a draw and £20.00 a win. In those days, players were beginning to negotiate signing on fees, even if they had asked for a transfer but I asked for nothing and just received the standard £300 moving costs you automatically received. There was no doubt that Cullis had been determined to get me as he said to the press that day "I went to Ipswich with my mind already made up because Crawford's record speaks for itself. I did not go to Portman Road to watch Crawford but to buy him."

My transfer fee was first said to have been around was £55,000 which was a lot of money in 1963. Jackie Milburn said a few days later that it was well short of that which incensed many Town supporters who thought the club had been ripped off; Ipswich's version of the 'Great Train Robbery' at the time. Having said that, it was still the highest fee Wolves had ever paid for a player. I left Ipswich having played just six games that season and everything had happened so fast there'd been no time for goodbyes or anything. I felt a little guilty leaving Town as they were a club on the slide but there comes a time in most players careers when you come to the crossroads as they say and, having just turned 27 years old that year, this was right for me at the time. I had many regrets about leaving a club that had been very good to me and we were leaving a lot of good friends in the area. Little did I know then but I had not pulled on an Ipswich Town shirt for the last time, not by any stretch of the imagination.

Chapter 12

"Black and Gold Country"

Wolverhampton Wanderers were the first team I remember watching live on TV against top European sides like Moscow Dynamo and Honved of Hungary and beating them as well. Players like Billy Wright, Bert Williams the goalkeeper, half-backs Ron Flowers and Bill Slater, strikers Roy Swinbourne and Dennis Wilshaw supplied by wing wizards Johnny Hancocks and Jimmy Mullen, all came to mind. Stan Cullis had been with them for over thirty years and was a classy centre-half in his prime, winning twelve England caps. I had no reservations about joining a club that was famous all over the world having won the League Championship three times and the FA Cup four times. When I joined them, the club was going through a rough patch. They were only a few places ahead of Ipswich Town in the league and their defence was no better than Town's having conceded 21 goals in seven games including a 5-1 thrashing at home to Blackburn Rovers the day Stan Cullis was at Portman Road to watch me.

On the Monday I signed for Wolves, I was put straight into the team to play Liverpool that evening. I had a medical in the afternoon that was a very basic test in those days just to make sure you were alive and all your limbs were intact, not like these days when players have blood samples galore taken before and after heavy physical exercise. After examining me, the club doctor drove us up to Liverpool in his Mercedes saloon. I only linked up with my new team mates about half an hour before the kick-off at 7:30pm. We were hammered 6-0 that night, not helped by losing our keeper Malcolm Finlayson who was playing his first game of the season and not knowing it was to be his last not only for Wolves but also as a professional footballer. He was covering for Fred Davies who had been injured against Blackburn two days before. Malcolm was forced to come off with the fingers of one hand badly split and bleeding taking no further part in the game. As it turned out, he was probably the richer and not the poorer for it. He went on to become a successful businessman. It was a bad evening all round, finishing with some petty thief stealing the emblem off the bonnet of the club doctor's Mercedes. Two nights later, Ipswich also lost by the same score, 6-0 away to bottom of the table Bolton Wanderers. I've always believed in statistics. Like old photos, they don't often lie and are nearer to the truth than failing memories. Just one month into the season, Wolves and Ipswich had played a total of 15 games and conceded an unbelievable 48 goals between them; Wolves 27 in 8 games and Ipswich 21 in 7 games, an average of over 3 goals a game. It wasn't difficult to sense the lack of confidence in the players at Anfield and I think it hit me as well. I had a nervy game missing a couple of chances that I'd normally have put away. I made up for it in the next game scoring both our goals in a 2-1 win against Blackpool at Bloomfield Road. Their outstanding player, a young man named Alan Ball scored their goal and could have been playing for us in that game - Wolves once had the chance to buy him but Cullis thought he was too small!

Meanwhile Ron Flowers and his wife Yvonne had kindly offered to put me up in their house until we found somewhere to live. Eileen came up to stay for a few days to look for a house. We found one in Wolverhampton that we wanted to buy. We decided to buy rather than rent as I thought I'd be spending the rest of my career at Wolves. The club helped by sorting out a mortgage for us. We couldn't move in straight away as it needed a lot of work doing to it. The original plan was for Eileen to stay in Ipswich with the two girls until the house was ready. This didn't work out as Ipswich urgently needed our club house for a new signing to move into. Eileen and the girls had to leave and joined me to live with Ron and Yvonne. Things didn't turn out very well even though Ron and Yvonne couldn't have been more hospitable. Although Eileen never totally settled at Ipswich, we'd made some good friends there and we were now even further away from our native Portsmouth. Eileen became very frustrated with the situation and we began to row a lot. I understood how she felt but I started to stay at the club as long as possible after training as it had reached the stage when I dreaded going back to the house and the thought of another possible row. Eventually things became so embarrassing that I asked the club if they could help me out and they booked us into two rooms at a hotel not far from our new house. Although a high level of discipline was expected of you at Wolves, they really looked after their players.

My first two months at Wolves was quite emotionally draining. It hadn't affected my ability to score goals, one of them gaining two valuable points in a 1-0 win over Leicester City at Filbert Street. It was the same night that I played alongside a seventeen year old young lad making his debut named Peter Knowles who was to become a legend at Wolves. Peter was a born entertainer and the fans quickly came to adore him. You couldn't say the same for defenders who had to mark him. More often than not he was a total nightmare to them. As slippery as a young black and gold fish, right up there with the likes of George Best, a true football genius. Alf once said that Martin Peters was ten years ahead of his time. I reckon Peter must have been 'light years' ahead in comparison. He could play the game fast or slow and had a very unique style. If you think the step-over was invented in the last few years by Ronaldo of Manchester United and many others who have copied him, I'm sorry but they're about forty years too late to patent it as their own invention. I saw Peter do it time and time again. He could frighten and tease the life out of defenders running at them, sometimes stopping and putting his foot on the ball, followed by a couple of step-overs inviting opponents to go for it dog-like for a toy, ready to whip the ball away in a flash if they lunged in. He reminded me of Jimmy Leadbetter in many ways but Peter was a lot quicker. I was getting the best service a striker could have wished for from wingers Terry Wharton and Alan Hinton and now Peter as well, although after a few games Cullis said to Peter he should be scoring more goals.

"Thanks Stan but I'm quite happy just making them for Ray," he replied in his usual laid-back manner, one of the best compliments I ever received from a fellow player, especially coming from Peter. Playing alongside him in my first year at Wolves, I scored 26 goals in 34 games, a reflection of how good he was. I was back with Ipswich Town in 1969 when I heard of his retirement from football to become a 'Jehovah's Witness'. By that time Bill McGarry was the Wolves manager and said it would only take Peter a few weeks to come to his senses. There was nothing anyone could say or do to make him change his mind. One of the most gifted players of that era was lost to the game at the age of just 24. Perhaps it would have different if he'd been given the chance to play for England. I wish I'd had him alongside me when I played my two internationals instead of the selfish players I played with but he was possibly too much of an individual to fit in to an Alf Ramsey team. However talented a player was, Alf rarely selected players unless he thought they would combine and gel perfectly with his team. He tended to neglect what you might call 'luxury' or 'flair' players. Both Rodney Marsh and Stan Bowles were outstanding individual talents but gained a mere handful of caps between them.

Just over a month after the win at Leicester City, I scored my best goal of the season, the only pity of it being that it had to be against Ipswich Town at Molineux. As the ball came to me just outside the six-yard box, I let it go almost through my legs before bringing my left foot round and flicking it in the opposite direction, wrong footing the defenders and into the net it went. The local Ipswich papers made out it was a fluke but I can assure you it wasn't. Cullis was so impressed he called me into his office the next week to tell me what a great goal he thought it was. We won the game 2-1. My only regret was that it pushed Town even deeper into relegation trouble. Ted scored Town's goal and they deserved a draw but Town's luck was out. When I spoke to some of my old mates after the game, there was a lot of unrest amongst them with most of their criticism directed at Jackie Milburn. They told me he'd been trying to get too friendly with them, doing things like taking them Ten-Pin bowling every week where he'd wait on them, bringing them tea and biscuits on a tray. Alf would never have done that. They also said that, after Jackie had left the room after pre-match talks, Andy Nelson would say "forget all that shit, this is what we'll do!" And at half-time in games, if things were going wrong which was usually the case at that time, Jackie wasn't able to come up with anything original or tactical to change things.

It didn't take me long to find out how passionate Cullis was about football and Wolverhampton Wanderers. After the calmness of Ramsey and the far too easy going Milburn, some of his outbursts surprised me. I thought they were a bit over the top but most managers are hardly perfect in this respect. Stan also had one rare characteristic for a football manager in that he never swore at anyone or anything whatever the score or however bad the situation was. Me and the lads used to chuckle away sometimes as we were sure he was fighting back the temptation to swear. He always resisted it, one of his favourites being "just stop... stop...flip-flopping about!" Although Stan never swore, he did have a habit of singling out someone if they were having a poor game and it was almost funny sometimes when we talked amongst ourselves waiting for Stan at half-time, trying to work who could be in for a rollicking. We could usually hear him approaching the dressing room especially along the corridor that led to the home dressing room at Molineux. He always wore metal toe and heel tips on his shoes. You could hear him saying loudly even before he burst into the dressing room "Where is he? Where is he then?" I remember one game when our winger Chris Crowe, one of our most talented players, was having a nightmare of a game and was in no doubt he would be Stan's half-time victim, so he hid behind a two feet wide vertical steel girder in the dressing room. As Stan walked around the room asking where he was, Chris moved around the girder and a few of us couldn't help giggling before Stan caught up with him and gave him his usual 'two pennies worth'. No one was safe from Stan's half time rockets, it could be any one of us and my turn was soon to come.

Just for the record, as most people seem to remember where they were at the time, the week after the game against Town, I was having a quiet beer in the bar of our hotel when the news came through of President John F. Kennedy's assassination in America. It was a numb kind of feeling. The man had such charisma that even though you didn't know him personally you felt the whole world had lost a good friend, much like the feeling you had when the tragic news was broadcast that Princess Diana had lost her life in a car crash. Reading through the history of the times when Kennedy was killed, you feel the horrors of the Vietnam war might never have happened had he lived. There was a minute's silence before all league games and at Hillsborough before we played Sheffield Wednesday that weekend. We lost 5-0.

Shortly before Christmas that year, we finally moved into our new house. Things were never perfect but Eileen was a lot happier; the rows stopped and we started to live a relatively normal life again. Liza Anne was just nine months old at the time and Jane, who was nearly five, had started at a local primary school. We became friendly with an older couple, Jack and Iris Jones who lived across the road from us and who were devoted Wolves fans and season ticket holders. More than anyone, they helped us to settle there; babysitting for us when we wanted to go out for the evening. We became good friends and it was especially good for Eileen as Iris was very worldly and loved a good chat.

It wasn't long into the new year when I had my first, and thankfully last experience, of a Stan Cullis half–time rocket. Since the thrashing at Wednesday, we'd picked up just two draws and been hammered 4-1 by Fulham at Craven Cottage. Stan wasn't very happy at the time. We were away to Stoke City and I was sitting in our dressing room at half-time at the Victoria Ground with the score at 0-0 when Stan tore in with his usual bustling style and "Where is he? Where is he then?" Then "Ah! There he is!" pointing directly at me. I'd had a difficult first half up against their rugged centre-half George Kinnell who'd roughed me up quite a bit with some heavy tackles and was winning our duel hands down. I knew I'd had a poor first half but so had most of us though Stan obviously hadn't seen it quite the same way as me.

"Ray," he said, "I bought you because I thought you were still the best centre-forward in England but tonight I think I could get one of the ball boys to play better than you!" After taking the flak, I asked Stan what he wanted me to do, to which he threw his arms into the air in despair and walked out without saying another word. I'd never had a half time rollicking since Sparshatt had given me an earful at Portsmouth. That was hateful whereas Stan was critical but brief. Stan's words seemed to have the desired effect. I scored with a header from a Johnny

Kirkham centre on the hour, then wrapped up the game thirteen minutes later with a vicious cross shot, probably hit with a bit more anger than usual. Stan gave me a big pat on the back at the end of the game and all was forgotten. Stan had a soft streak in him and never bore grudges against anyone.

It was a miserable day in mid March, pouring with rain when we made the coach trip to Suffolk to play Ipswich Town. I knew that, if I scored against Town that day, it could possibly make relegation even more of a certainty for them. By the time we arrived at Portman Road shortly after 2:00pm, it was still raining heavily. Waiting for our arrival, standing under the shelter of the old 'Chicken Hutch' dressing room roof, was Mr John. The moment we started to get off the coach, he came rushing towards us, wading through some ankle deep puddles of rain as if he were wading a salmon river in his estate in Scotland, waving his arms and shouting "It's off! I'm afraid it's off chaps! I'm sorry the referee has just called it off, the pitch is waterlogged." He just kept on running until he reached me, then threw his arms around me, hugging me quite fiercely, pinning both my arms and kit bag to my sides. All Stan Cullis and the Wolves lads could do was look on, a little bemused by it all. Although Mr John was no doubt pleased to see me again, I think his joy was mixed with some relief that the match had been called off. It was a good time to play Ipswich if you were a striker and hungry for goals as they'd lost 6-0 to Liverpool the previous week and, just a week after our postponed game, they received one of the worst batterings in their history, going down 9-1 away at Stoke City.

Towards the end of the season Stan continued to rebuild the team buying Jimmy Melia, a fine passer of the ball from Liverpool and Bobby Woodruff an attacking wing-half from Swindon Town to strengthen our midfield. Jimmy was a true 'scouser' and also probably the baldest player in the Football League at the time. The day he was introduced to the team, Chris Crowe wasn't slow to remind him of it. Jimmy was all smiles until Chris said "What the fuckin'ell do you think you're doin' 'ere baldy?" In this respect, Jimmy would certainly have preferred to play in the game today where bald haircuts are very popular with many footballers. To get the best out of Jimmy, we had two good coaches in Bill Shorthouse and Joe Gardiner, both ex-Wolves players who managed to get us to play an intricate passing game in training, built around Jimmy's skills but, when it came to match days, Stan would still ask us to get the ball forward as quickly as possible, straight down the middle to me the target man. It was a system that had served Wolves well for many years. It left poor Jimmy out of the game more than often, watching the ball, tennis spectator style, as it went backwards and forwards over his head.

I think Jimmy eventually said to himself 'sod this' and often joined the chase up front, ending up with four goals in nine games by the end of the season. When Wolves were relegated the next season, it was no surprise to me when Jimmy moved to Southampton Town, just a few months after I'd been sold to West Bromwich Albion.

Near the end of the season, I had my first experience of playing as an emergency goalkeeper in a game at Bramall Lane against Sheffield United. It was 2-2 at the time and I'd scored one of our goals when our keeper Fred Davies was injured seriously enough to go off for treatment. I put on the keeper's jersey and went between the posts. It seemed like the longest twenty minutes in my career football career. The lads rallied round protecting me and, with the help of the crossbar and a few desperate saves, I managed to keep my first 'clean sheet' as a keeper even though it was for only just over a quarter of the game. When Fred came back on, Derek Pace scored to put them ahead again. It wasn't long before I scored my second goal to level the score at 3-3. I was thrilled to bits but it was only short lived as a virtually unknown 19 year old young striker named Mick Jones (later of Leeds United and England) who was making his debut for 'The Blades', bustled through the middle to slam in the winner with just a few minutes to go. You can imagine how we all felt, especially Bobby Woodruff who'd only half tackled Jones before he scored. After the game, Stan held only a short inquest, Ramsey-like brief and to the point, singling out poor Bobby as expected saying "As for you Bobby, you couldn't tackle a dog's dinner!"

The day Ipswich Town were finally relegated that season, despite a 4-3 win over Aston Villa at Portman Road, I scored twice for Wolves in a 3-3 draw against Everton at Goodison Park. By then they'd bought Tony Kay from Sheffield Wednesday and he was playing that day. It was to be the last game he ever played in the English Football League. We were 3-2 up when Everton pulled the game out of the fire with a last minute equalizer from Derek Temple. After the ref had blown for time, Tony Kay seemed to make a special point of coming up to me and, after shaking my hand, said "All the best Ray" but he seemed so sad. The next day the bombshell dropped and I think Tony must have known this was going to happen before the game. I always read most of the Sunday papers, to pick up the different angles of reporters on games, and as I'd scored twice against Everton the day before I naturally wanted to read them all. Some of them had also started to rate players performances on a scale of 1-10, making them even more interesting reading for a player. When I picked up the Sunday paper 'The People' that morning, the front page headlines was 'TOP SOCCER STARS BRIBED'. I thought that's interesting until I read on a bit and saw one of the games involved was Ipswich Town against Sheffield Wednesday on December the 1st 1962. I almost shouted at Eileen across the breakfast table "Strewth! Bloody Hell!!" when the article confirmed I'd scored both goals to win the game 2-0. I hadn't a clue about what had happened but almost felt a strange sort of guilt having taken part in a game that was to become the biggest soccer scandal of the 1960's. The article said that a betting coup had been planned which called for Brentford to beat Lincoln City, Oldham to beat York City and for Ipswich to beat Sheffield Wednesday and that all the results had finished as arranged that day. It went on to say that Tony Kay, David 'Bronco' Layne and Peter Swan had all agreed to chuck the game against Ipswich Town.

I could hardly believe what I'd read but the following day Kay confirmed it was all true when he said "This is the only match I have ever agreed to throw away, I swear that. As it turned out I didn't have to do anything to lose the game as Ipswich scored an early goal and that was that." All three players were suspended by their clubs until the allegations of bribery against them were investigated. This was by no means the first game ever fixed in English soccer and those who really knew about the game in those days will tell you it wasn't commonplace but it happened. I knew of one fixed game and Bill McGarry said the same club had tried it on when he was playing for Huddersfield Town the same season. It was only £20.00 a player, about a week's wages and, I have to say, I wasn't so high and mighty that I wouldn't have taken it if I'd played in the game.

Two weeks later we played the re-arranged game with Ipswich but, as they had already been relegated, there wasn't much for either side to play for except pride. Ipswich won the game 1-0 with new signing Gerry Baker from Hibernian scoring the goal. I was to team up with Gerry on my return to Ipswich nearly two years later. It was my old mate John Compton's last game for Town. He signed for Bournemouth later that summer. Our last game of that season was away to Bolton Wanderers who needed a win to avoid relegation. When our coach pulled into the car park at the ground, Bill Ridding the Bolton manager was there to meet us and when the coach door opened, he climbed on board and after shaking hands with Stan Cullis said something that took all by surprise.

"Would you like to buy a red headed Welshman Stan?"
"Who's that?" Stan replied.
"Wyn Davies, he's big, quite good in the air but not much else."
"No thanks, I've already had enough trouble with him!" Stan replied pointing at

me.

I think Stan was very embarrassed and, although I laughed at the time, I didn't actually find what he'd said about Wyn very funny. He was a fine player who went on to play for Manchester United. As far as being too much trouble for Stan went, I scored a hat-trick that evening in a 4-0 win with Peter Knowles scoring the fourth and Bolton were relegated. My overall goal tally that season, including my Ipswich games before my transfer was 28 goals in 40 games, 26 of them scored in 34 games for Wolves. I was bought to score goals and that's exactly what I'd done. The next highest scorer that year was Terry Wharton with nine goals and it was a great honour for me to be voted Wolverhampton Wanderers Player of the Year. Although we'd only finished 16th in Division , it wasn't all that bad considering the poor start to the season and that Stan was trying to build a new team. Building a new team doesn't happen overnight; it takes time, sometimes many years. I don't think this view was shared by the chairman or the Board in view of the money they'd given Stan to spend.

In the close season, the club treated us to the most luxurious tour you could ever imagine in the West Indies. It wasn't all leisure as the trip involved playing several exhibition matches against Chelsea who travelled out there with us and also a few games against some of the best island teams. All the matches were nothing short of full-blooded and we played to win, making it not only good entertainment for the people of the Caribbean but also a good advertisement for British football. First stop was Barbados, one of the best places I've ever visited. I scored twice in a 3-1 win over Chelsea at Bridgetown. Next stop was Port of Spain in Trinidad where I went one better scoring a hat-trick in a 4-0 win over the national side. We lost our second game against Chelsea 3-2 a few days later at the same venue with Terry Venables clinching victory with a late penalty. We then flew north to Kingston, Jamaica where we played three games. We first beat Chelsea 4-2 and I scored two more, then thrashed Jamaica 8-4 before Chelsea won our fourth match of the tour 3-0. With an aggregate of 5-4 over the two games there, the Londoner's took home a special trophy presented to them by acting Jamaican Prime Minister McDonald Sangster. We finished the tour in Haiti, playing two games in Port au Prince where we were held 1-1 by the national side before losing our last game of the trip 2-0 to Chelsea. I missed the game through injury. Believe it or not, I could have become a Chelsea player during that tour. That is, if I'd agreed to an offer from Tommy Docherty, the Chelsea manager and if Wolves had been willing to let me go. 'Tapping', that is a club directly approaching a player without the permission of his club has always gone on in the game and it happened to me out there in Jamaica of all places. One evening, I was drinking a long rum and coke in our hotel bar where both teams were staying when Tommy Docherty suddenly came over to have a chat with me. He told me that he was very impressed with the many goals I'd scored in the previous few years for both Ipswich Town and Wolves and didn't beat around the bush for long before asking me if I'd like to join Chelsea, adding that he would throw in winger Barry Bridges as well as part of a cash plus player deal. Chelsea were a club on the way up with players like Terry Venables, Bobby Tambling, Barry Bridges, Peter Bonetti, John Hollins, Ron 'Chopper' Harris and an eighteen year old youngster named Peter Osgood.

"Go on Ray, go and ask Stan if you can join us!" he said, gesturing to Stan Cullis who was also in the bar with the rest of the players.
"What! Now?" I replied. I hardly knew what to say and was totally taken aback by Tommy's approach. He was a very vibrant, irresistible sort of person, full of energy and enthusiasm with a charisma that made him one of the top and most sought after young managers of the time. It took me a little while to recover my senses.
"I'm flattered by your offer but Stan has put his faith in me and Wolves could not have looked after me better," I said to Tommy.

I would love to have played for Tommy at Chelsea but his invitation was a few months too early in view of what was to happen at the beginning of the next season which few could have predicted. As things turned out, I was to be kicking myself six months later for not accepting his offer.

Chapter 13

"Cullis out, Crawford out"

Ironically, the first game of the season was against Chelsea at home. We lost 3-0 to our fellow tourists of the summer. Five defeats in the next six games, left us bottom of the 1ˢᵗ Division with only one point from seven games. I missed the last of those games, a 4-1 defeat to Blackburn Rovers but was fit enough to play two days later on the Monday night against West Ham at home. It was a great game to play in, the sort of stirring performance the patient fans had been waiting for. I was happy as I scored two of our goals in a 4-3 win so it was a huge shock when it was announced the next day that Stan Cullis had been sacked a few hours after the game. I was very sad as, by this time, I thought the world of Stan. I think most of the players did. The majority of Wolves supporters were also angry about it. There had been friction between Stan and the chairman John Ireland for some time. We'd had a poor start to the season. Had the Board been thinking of sacking Stan, they should have done it during the summer, not just over a month into a new season. If I had to be critical of Stan, although Jimmy Melia and Bobby Woodruff were good signings, the defence hadn't been strengthened and conceded 20 goals in those first seven games of the season with only six goals scored of which I'd scored four. At least one top class defender should have been top priority to play alongside Ron Flowers. Ipswich Town, having made exactly the same mistake were bottom of the 2ⁿᵈ Division. Stan wasn't the first managerial casualty of that season. Just over a week before he was sacked, Jackie Milburn had resigned as manager of Ipswich. A third casualty was Eddie Boot, manager of Huddersfield Town who'd also got 'the boot' and, little did I know it, I was virtually going to get the 'boot' as well.

Whatever Jackie Milburn's failings as a manager at Ipswich, the one thing for which they will forever be in his debt was that, before he left, he finally managed to persuade Town to start off a youth policy. Like any investment, it takes a few years to bring dividends but it was all 'too little, too late'. Jackie had been like a lamb to the slaughter. Jackie knew football management wasn't for him . He had no trouble in finding work, going straight into a new job as the northwest football correspondent of the new 'The Sun', the first of the tabloid newspapers. Jackie quickly took the opportunity of confirming a bust-up with Alf shortly before he'd left to manage England full-time. It was just one day after Stan Cullis had been sacked that 'The Sun' Sports headlines read:

'I ACCUSE RAMSEY!'

In short, Jackie accused Alf of giving him very little advice, criticising Alf's attitude towards him, not inviting him to team talks and, when he'd asked Alf to look out for some players for Ipswich Town on his scouting trips, the answer had been a blunt 'No'. Jackie finished by saying: "I thought at the time, that's a fine attitude for someone who is supposed to have a soft spot for his old club and the man who is asking all League managers for help and assistance. I knew then that I was on my own and that I was in a ruthless jungle."

Alf avoided a slanging match with Jackie in the press but it all seemed to explain why Alf left Town whilst we were still in danger of relegation. In a similar way, things didn't work out for me after Stan left. I will always be grateful for the chance he gave me at Wolves and no one in the long history of the club had achieved the level of success as he had in his thirty brilliant years there. Stan returned to the ground about ten days after he he'd been sacked to say goodbye to the players. He stood in front of us and told us that he would always look upon Wolverhampton Wanderers as the greatest club in the country despite what they'd done to him. There were more than a few watery eyes in the room by the time he left us for the final time. One thing I think I can safely say is that if Mr John had been chairman at Wolves, he would never have allowed it to happen as I know he would have stood by Stan regardless of whatever anyone else said. The thought of sacking him would never have entered his head and he would have waited until Stan had recovered but then Mr John was a one off. Like Cullis, there will never be another quite like him. There are statues of Sir Alf and Sir Bobby outside the ground at Portman Road. Perhaps one day, there will be one of Mr John too. It would be nice to see the great man there as well.

In early October, Andy Beattie was named as caretaker manager till the end of the season. Andy was a small, quiet Scot and completely the opposite of Cullis who always wore his heart on his sleeve. I don't think the players knew how to take Andy. His team selections soon became a puzzle to us. In his playing career, he'd made just 125 appearances for Preston North End and managed Nottingham Forest for two years, getting them to a respectable 8th in the 1st Division the season before. The Board obviously thought he was the quick-fix answer at the time.

When a new manager takes over, you always remember the first things he says to the team and one of the first points he made certainly raised a few eyebrows. It was his insistence that he didn't want any of the players to smoke on match days and that anyone caught doing so would be fined. Fair enough, as smoking does use up oxygen in the lungs and is very bad for you. It wasn't a problem for me as a non smoker but one or two of the lads liked a cigarette and I think to make a big issue of it was counterproductive. I think the smokers in the team felt they were being treated like school children. He could have compromised and said just the one after your pre-match meal and that's it. From then on, they were always looking for the opportunity for having a quick fag without Andy catching them instead of concentrating their thoughts on the match ahead. I once read that Ipswich Town's former centre-half Allan Hunter, admitting that he was so nervous on the eve of the FA Cup final in 1978 against Arsenal, had smoked about 40 cigarettes that night! Understandably, he was worried about not having any puff left for the match. It turned out that he marked the dangerous Malcolm McDonald out of the game which Ipswich went on to win 1-0 although it did help that Allan was a world class defender.

With the arrival of Andy Beattie, I was given the job of being spokesman for the players, representing them for any grievances or problems they might have. As we were nearly bottom of the league at the time, morale was low and most of us thought it would be a good idea if we could have lunch together before home games to increase bonding and team spirit; this was the first suggestion I put to Beattie. His reply was that he'd already done this at Nottingham Forest but before the maximum wage was abolished! He really did have some weird ways of looking at things. I said if it was money he was worried about, we'd bring our own sandwiches as long as we could have a pre-match meal together. Whether this responsibility gave Andy the opinion of me that I was the leader of a bunch of malcontents, I don't know but I wasn't that keen on my role as players' spokesman as I thought it should have been the job of the club captain.

By the end of October and Beattie's first month at the club, Wolves had lost thirteen games, won only one, drawn one and were firmly rooted to the bottom of the 1st Division. After a brief recovery of three wins and a draw in November, we slumped again to five successive defeats in December. In that time, Beattie had been given some money to spend and bought two Scots, Hugh McIlmoyle, a striker from Carlisle and George Miller, a 25 year old wing-half from Dunfermline. That was all very well but what we were still crying out for was a couple of experienced defenders although the signing of David Wagstaffe, a very skilful winger from

Manchester City on Boxing Day, was a good long term investment as 'Waggy' went on to give great service to the club for the next ten years.

Just before the end of January, Tony Kay and 'Bronco' Layne were sent to prison for three months for their part in the fixed game at Ipswich and Peter Swan followed them a couple of weeks later. I thought this would be the end of it; enough punishment for what they'd done. I was soon to be punished in a different way as well. At the time, morale was very low at Wolves and we were still at the bottom of the 1st Division alongside fellow strugglers Birmingham City. I was doing my best having scored 13 league goals in 23 games. Everything came to a head for me after we'd drawn 2-2 in the 4th Round of the FA Cup against Second Division Rotherham United at Molineux, played on an icy, thawing pitch of half frozen mud and water. This suited our opponents more than us. I scored one of our goals but this was to be my last appearance for Wolves. The funeral of Winston Churchill took place the next day and my career at Wolves was soon to be well and truly buried as well.

On the Tuesday evening of the replay, Andy Beattie left everybody guessing what the team would be until half an hour before the kick-off. We were out having a look at the pitch. The surface was part frozen but it was thawing and took a stud. I didn't like playing on totally frozen pitches (I can't think of anyone who ever did) but I was expecting to play in the game. When Andy came up to me and told me he was leaving me out of the team that evening because of the conditions, I expressed my feelings and told him straight away how unhappy I was about his decision. I said "If they've changed at all, they've changed for the better as far as I'm concerned!" I avoided further confrontation at the time. It was difficult as I was at the stage where the adrenaline begins to kick in just before a game. I was really pumped up and ready to play.

As it was, I watched the game from the stands. Wolves won 3-0. I was furious and getting worse by the time we boarded the coach for our return to Wolverhampton. Not long into the journey home, Andy Beattie walked down the aisle of the coach and, when he passed me, asked me if I was alright. This was all too much for me and unfortunately I lost my temper. We really had a go at one another in front of the other players, ending up with me telling him I'd never play for him again. It was all on the spur of the moment and I realized soon afterwards I'd overstepped the limit. A couple of days later, I took a knock in training, not a serious injury, but enough to sideline me for the Saturday game at home to Sheffield Wednesday, whether selected or not.

On the day of the game, there was a report in the papers about me wanting a move although I don't know where they heard that as I'd not been to the press myself. I just tried to carry on as normal and went to see the 3-1 win over Sheffield Wednesday. By Monday morning, I'd recovered sufficiently from my injury to return to training although I was feeling very unsettled and no longer sure of my future at the club. I hadn't been asked by the manager for any sort of meeting to clear the air since my bust-up with him the week before. I didn't have to wait long to find out where I stood. It was the very next morning at the breakfast table when I opened a letter from the club. It informed me that I'd been suspended for fourteen days for the following reason.

1. For not reporting for Saturday's match.
2. For not reporting to the club physiotherapist that I was fit.
3. For talking to the press.
4. For swearing at the manager.

I rang up the club asking to speak to Beattie but I received an abrupt message back saying "I won't see Crawford until he apologizes." I said I was willing to apologize and a reply came back saying if that was the case he was willing to speak to me. When I went to see him in his office, I apologized as he'd requested. I had hopes Beattie would lift the suspension but although he reduced it, he insisted I was to be banned from the club for seven days without pay. I thought the matter would have best been forgotten right there and then with a shake of hands. He was obviously determined to see me punished. I didn't have a lot to lose so, before I left, I asked him about rumours that Sunderland were interested in buying me.

"Who do you think you are?" he said.
"I'm just a player and you're the manager and I'm in the game to make a living just as you are!" I replied and walked out. I'd been very happy at Wolves, scoring lots of goals and had a good relationship with my team mates but this only served to alienate me and, from that day on, I began to think that my days there were numbered at Molineux. They were. During my week away from the club, I contacted the Players Union who agreed I had a grievance and took up my case. I couldn't help thinking at the time that I may have been wrong not to have accepted Tommy Docherty's offer to join Chelsea.

It was near the end of my week's suspension when I received a call from Beattie saying that West Bromwich Albion wanted to talk to me about a possible move there. I felt that I'd nothing to lose at the time as I was sitting at home not doing much, other than torturing myself over the events of the last few weeks which had led to my suspension. I decided to accept Beattie's offer and made the half hour drive to The Hawthorns to see their manager, Jimmy Hagan. He greeted me in a very friendly manner. My interview with him shortly before I signed, was to be my first and last civil conversation with him during my entire stay there. As managers went for me at the time, it was almost like 'out of the frying pan and into the fire!'

We talked about our careers and I recalled my times with Ipswich Town and winning the championship there and about playing for Wolves and working with Stan Cullis. He told me about his days at Sheffield United where he played his whole career as an inside-forward (the old term for a midfield player) scoring 106 goals in 333 games, showing he'd certainly been a very good player in his day, representing England at school boy level and also at international. Jimmy had started his management career at Peterborough United, guiding them successfully from the Midland League to the Football League. He told me that, while he was there, he was once questioned about his tactics by three members of the Board at a meeting. "Look, you're a taxi driver, you're a butcher and you, sir, own a shop so what do you know about football that I don't!" he said and we laughed at the time. I agreed with him. I soon found out that maybe they had a point. The taxi driver, the butcher and the shop owner as some of Jimmy's methods and ideas about training were certainly a little unusual. I wasn't to know that then. I signed for West Bromwich Albion for £35,000 in February 1965. As for my appeal against the suspension, Wolves lost the case and had to pay the wages they owed me and the suspension was removed from my player's record. I never wanted to leave Wolves but, with Beattie as manager there, I really had no choice. During my time at Wolves, I scored 39 goals in 57 league games. It seemed strange that they wanted to get rid of a such a goal scoring machine.

Chapter 14

"The Baggies"

When I joined West Bromwich Albion, just like Wolves they were one of the top clubs in the history of the game. At the beginning of the 20th century, around 1905, the supporters club used to go around pubs and shops to find new members. It was 6 pence a year in those days which was collected in small bags, hence the nickname we now know West Bromwich Albion best for, 'The Baggies'. I was glad to play for them although things could have worked out better. They had a strong first team squad at the time with Ray Potter in goal, fullbacks Bobby Cram (Uncle of Steve Cram the athlete) and Graham Williams the club captain, centre-backs Stan Jones and Doug Frazer, Bobby Hope, Tony Brown and Gerry Howshall in midfield, Ken Foggo and Clive Clark the two wingers and John Kaye and Jeff Astle the two strikers. Jeff had signed from Notts County a few months before they signed me. Since his arrival both Kaye and Brown had been sidelined by injuries, forcing Jimmy Hagan into the transfer market to look for another striker, hence my transfer from Wolves.

There were also two talented youngsters coming through at the time, Graham Lovett and Ian Collard, both midfield players. Ian, even as a teenager was probably the most gifted and skilful player on the club's books at the time. You would have thought that he was destined to play for England. He was strong, a superb passer of the ball, usually with his sweet left foot and had the ability to put his foot on the ball and dictate the pace of the game; the sort of player every manager loves to have in his team. Bobby Robson saw his potential when he took Ian to Ipswich Town in 1969 in an exchange plus cash deal which took another great player, Town's Danny Hegan to West Bromich Albion. Unfortunately, as was the case with his whole career, Ian's early career was dogged by injuries. Without them, I've no doubt he would have gone to the very top of the game.

My first day's training at The Hawthorns didn't work out quite as I would have wished. It was a freezing cold day in mid February and we had been sent on a road run. By the time we reached the local countryside, it had started to snow quite heavily. One of my new team mates suggested that if a lorry came along we should try and wave it down to give us a ride back. Being the new boy, I was anxious to create a good impression but, when the next lorry came along and stopped to pick us up, I didn't have the sense to say I didn't want any part in it and jumped in the back with the rest of them. After a couple of miles, one of us unwisely decided to pop his head out of the back of the lorry only to see none other than the club trainer directly behind us! When we arrived back at the ground, Jimmy Hagan tore us off a strip and we were punished with extra training. Jimmy told me that, as a new player, I should have known better. After my troubles at Wolves, he was right and it seemed at this time of my career, trouble was starting to follow me around. I had never had any troubles at Ipswich or Portsmouth as far as toeing the line went. 'It never rains when it pours' as they say or, in my case, 'it never snows when it hails'.

The players were a decent friendly lot and I had no trouble settling there in that respect. Straight away, I sensed there was a lot of unrest with most of the players' grouses directed at Jimmy Hagan. The previous year before my arrival, there had been a players strike led by the club captain of the time, Don Howe. They told me how Jimmy and Don had always argued and things had come to a head when Hagan hadn't allowed them to wear track suits when training in freezing conditions. Since then Don had left for Arsenal. No doubt this incident had something to do with it. I soon began to understand what the players were on about. Hagan's team talks, instead of giving us the confidence you expect from a manager, tended to be only full of criticism.

I had a run-in with Hagan a few weeks later when he did exactly the same thing which had caused the player's strike the year before. All we were allowed to wear on a day when the temperatures were well below freezing was sweatshirts, shorts and trainers. I said to Hagan that it was not necessary or a good idea to be so cold in training. Players were more likely to pull a muscle or injure themselves if they were forced to wear such little protection from the cold. Hagan, in a few words, told me to mind my own business. He then told our trainer, Albert McPherson, just to run us a bit harder. Crawford the 'malcontent' again?

I don't think Hagan was very happy with me at that point and even more so when I was injured after only two games. His new striker crocked for nearly two months. After making my debut in a 3-1 win against Aston Villa, I damaged some knee ligaments in the next game when my studs became stuck in some heavy turf in the 6-0 home win against Leicester City. Luckily the ligaments were just strained and not torn, however, I was out for over six weeks none the less. Being injured is not the skive a lot of people outside the game may think it is. I had to turn up for treatment and keep-fit exercises in the gym twice a day, every day of the week, with no days off. Like most of the big clubs at the time, we had our own physio, Fred Ederly. He didn't have the sort of medical technology at his disposal as they do today. The treatment table was literally 'a bone of contention'. All you received was the old fashioned heat lamp which they seemed to use on almost every type of injury. Injuries would take months to heal rather than weeks as they do now. When players suffered painful knocks, they were usually told to get on with it. If the leg wasn't broken, you were expected just to 'run it off'. I think this was the reason why there were so many bad injuries during my time at West Bromich Albion. Lots of players played with bad knocks, pulled and even torn muscles when they should have been given time off for their injuries to heal. This was counter productive. Some of them ended up making their injuries even worse. What should have been a few weeks getting back to fitness often turned into months. During my time there, the worst example of this happened to Ken Foggo. He'd been carried off after a very heavy tackle in an away game against Northampton Town. Ken was in a lot of pain when he turned up for training the next week. There was no obvious break and he could just about walk. It was put down to heavy bruising and he was told, as was usual, just to 'run it off'. Even though Ken continued to complain about the pain he was in and didn't play in the next few games, he was not rested from training. They thought he was faking his injury. After a few weeks with the pain getting steadily worse, better late than never, poor Ken was sent for an X-Ray which revealed a hairline fracture of the leg. He was out of action for nearly three months. Even when he came back, it was obvious that he was struggling to gain full fitness and only managed six more appearances that season; little wonder, having being made to train on a broken leg for three weeks.

My injury cleared up enough for me to play in the last three games of the season scoring two goals in three games, one in the 2-2 draw away Chelsea and the other in the final game of the season in the 1-0 home win over Sheffield Wednesday. It was slightly ironic that, on the Wednesday before playing Wednesday, Denis Follows, the secretary of the FA announced that Tony Kay and 'Bronco' Layne, who'd just been released after serving 11 weeks of their 4 month sentences for their part in game-fixing, had been permanently suspended from football and football management; in other words a lifetime ban. The same went for Peter Swan who was still in prison as his case had been heard at a later date. This meant they were also banned from playing in any of the 132 countries under the ruling of F.I.F.A. including South Africa. South Africa had been axed by F.I.F.A. at the time because of apartheid but they still recognised suspensions and bans. I thought this was really too harsh and that, following the prison sentence, perhaps a year's ban and loss of earnings from football would have been sufficient punishment. Kay had possibly come off worst as Alf Ramsey rated him very highly. He may well have played in the '66 World Cup ahead of Nobby Stiles. For English football, it was a sad and bitter note on which to end the season. It was also the worst and most frustrating time in my career. My injury hadn't helped. Although my 2 goals in five games wasn't a huge return for what they'd paid for me, I thought I'd done enough for Jimmy Hagan to see my potential for the next season. As for Wolves, they were relegated along with Birmingham City and the 14 goals I'd scored before being sold to West Bromich Albion still left me as their top scorer that year. Perhaps the 'Curse of Jungle Boy' (and that of Stan Cullis as well) had struck again?

We went on tour for a month to America to play in a tournament in New York against Kilmarnock, Ferencvaros and Polonia Bytom. We stayed in groups of three in apartments and my two flatmates were Bobby Cram and Ken Foggo. They did the shopping, Bobby was the chief cook and I was volunteered to do the washing-up! When we arrived, New York was in the middle of a heat wave so we trained in Central Park in the cooler hours of the morning at 7:00am, then played our matches in the evenings to avoid the heat which was up in the high eighties most days. The first night we were there, it was absolutely sweltering. Jimmy Hagan insisted that we wore a shirt and tie for dinner as we were representing not only West Bromwich Albion but our country as well. It was the reverse I suppose of Jimmy's quirky ideas about training in sub zero temperatures with kit more suitable for the summer months. None of the lads were happy about it as it seemed unnecessary in that sort of heat. I put on my most colourful shirt together with my club tie as a sort of tasteless protest. They clashed so badly that, when we assembled to go down for dinner, Hagan took one look at me then said "Right everyone, you can take off your ties." I don't think I endeared myself to Hagan any more than I already had. He seemed determined either to freeze us to death in training in winter or half suffocate us from the heat in summer.

When the 1965-66 season started I was still out of the team. It was only when Jeff Astle injured a knee that I played a game in late October against Liverpool at home which we won 3-0. I didn't score in that game. I scored my first of the season against Spurs at White Hart Lane the following weekend in front of a crowd of 43,512. We lost 2-1. I thought I had played well enough but was left out yet again the next week. I couldn't believe it, wondering what I had to do to get an extended run in the first team. Jeff Astle came back for a couple of games. He was still obviously struggling with his knee injury and I was recalled to play against Leicester City away. I scored my second goal in three games early on in the game to put us one up at half-time. After only a few minutes of the second half, it all started to go wrong when my old mate from Portsmouth, Derek Dougan, scored two goals in quick succession to give City a 2-1 lead. In scoring his second goal, the bony old 'Doog' collided heavily with our keeper Richard Sheppard who had to be stretchered off and taken to hospital. As there were no substitutes in those days and none of the players seemed very keen to go in goal, given my brief experience in goal when I was at Wolves, I volunteered to put on the goalkeepers top and kept goal for most of the second half. At the other end was none other than my famous opposite Gordon Banks. We defended well for the rest of the game and I did quite well, making a couple of saves which I honestly didn't know much about. I managed to keep a clean sheet. I did give my team mates one anxious moment when I rushed out and tried to dribble past the 'Doog' momentarily forgetting that I was allowed to pick the ball up! He nicked the ball off me but I had just enough time to recover and dive on the ball. Although we lost the game 2-1, it was great to walk off the pitch in the company of Gordon Banks, possibly the greatest goalkeeper the world has ever seen. He complimented me on keeping a 'clean sheet' albeit for only one half of the game. I was pleased with my two emergency goalkeeping experiences. I hadn't let in a goal for Wolves or West Bromich Albion on either occasion. Not so pleased though was Jimmy Hagan. After the game, the players who were not in the team that day and had been sitting on the bench with him, told me that he'd been very critical of my performance. He thought I had been messing around when picking up the ball or clearing my lines. They must have been right about what he said as Hagan had nothing to say to me after the game, nothing complimentary. He seemed to have a thing about goalkeeping heroics, both on and off the pitch. I was told that, not long after Hagan had joined the club and not being very familiar with his new surroundings, he'd reversed out of the training ground straight into the 40 feet deep canal which was only yards from the entrance to the training ground. Tony Millington, who was the first team goalkeeper at the time, saved his life that day, yet next week he was dropped from the first team! One can only think that Hagan perhaps objected to being 'saved' by the club's goalkeeper. Given Hagan's peculiar sense of loyalty or logic, after scoring our goal at Leicester *and* keeping a clean sheet for the time I was in goal, I was dropped for the next game against Sheffield United. Jeff Astle was recalled even though he was still clearly not fit. I was annoyed about being dropped yet again. I felt the time had come for me to look for another club so I put in for a transfer request. I said that I didn't think I figured in Hagan's plans for the future and my request was granted by the Board.

It was then decided that Jeff needed to have a cartilage operation. I went with the lads to see him in hospital the day after the operation and it was sad to see Jeff almost crying with the pain he was in and Jeff was as tough as they come. With Jeff sidelined, I played six more games before being sold to Ipswich Town later that season. One of my last games was against Manchester United at Old Trafford. We were losing 1-0 until late in the game when Bobby Charlton, without looking up, played the ball back to the Red's keeper Harry Gregg. Bobby under hit his pass, giving me time to nip in and bang the ball in the net to give us a 1-1 draw. I only played a few more league games after that. My last game for the Baggies was against Peterborough United in the semi-final of the League Cup, scoring one and assisting in the other two which helped get the club into the final. The Ipswich Town manager, Bill McGarry, was at the game to watch me. He must have seen enough to put in an offer for me as Hagan called me into his office the next day to ask me if I was interested in signing for Town. I jumped at the chance. It didn't worry me that I was dropping down a division or that Ipswich were struggling at the time. I'd have gone there even if they were in the 4th Division. I knew what a great club they were and was only too pleased to sign for them for the second time in my career. It was regarded as a great bargain by Mr John. He'd sold me for £55,000 and bought me back for £15,000. I reckon he thought it was a good bit of business as far as Ipswich were concerned. Eileen was very happy with the move. We still had a lot of friends in Ipswich and she'd never quite settled in the Midlands, not because of the area so much but because it was even further away from home than living in Suffolk.

West Bromich Albion went on to win the League Cup final beating West Ham 5-3 on aggregate and finished in mid-table in the 1st Division. In my time at the Hawthorns, I played 15 games and scored 7 goals (one in the League Cup). I did my best but never had a decent run of games in the first team. It never quite worked out though I enjoyed most of my time there and the fans could not have been better. My record there has been described as a 'bad time' and I quote, 'never did well in the Midlands'. I just laugh when I read these typical press comments. I never saw it that way as my stats there reveal a very different story. I scored 39 goals in 57 league games for Wolves, then 6 in 14 games for West Bromich Albion plus two goals in the League and FA Cup, a total 47 goals in 73 games - yes I had a terrible time there! I was still in my prime at 29 years of age and still averaging at least 25 goals a season in the four years I'd played playing in the 1st Division.

When I signed for Town, they were in a precarious position and only a few points off the relegation zone. It was likely to be a hectic end to the season. Eileen agreed that we should look for a new house in Ipswich when the season was over. I stayed at the Station Hotel, just a stone's throw from Ipswich Railway Station, set right by the bridge that I'd first walked over before my first days training over seven years before. As they say, a lot of water had flowed under the bridge since then. I had plenty of time to contemplate my past and future at Ipswich, especially when Mr John joined me for a meal and a drink there every Wednesday evening. He was so happy to have me back at the club. Apart from Billy Baxter and Kenny Malcolm who was now training the youth team, I was the only other link remaining of the great days of Alf Ramsey and winning the Championship.

My fellow striker up front was Gerry Baker, a talented, cultured player that Milburn had bought to replace me when I was sold to Wolves. Gerry was a very intelligent footballer and certainly helped me settle quickly into my second spell with Town. He was also a great character and fun to be with whether you were training, on the golf course or playing cards. Gerry always had a bright outlook on life even when the chips were down. As well as being a supreme optimist, he had a brilliant sense of humour, especially when in the company of his best pal Danny Hegan - that is, if you could understand the strong Glaswegian accent they tended to use in their conversations. When it came to football they were both very professional. Though the pay was peanuts compared to the thousands of pounds players take home every week now, they played their hearts out, week in week out, for Ipswich Town, a small club tucked away on the east coast that was almost foreign to them. Gerry, Danny and also Frank Brogan should never be forgotten as great Town players of the past. Jackie Milburn brought them to the club and although he didn't make it as a manager, he was a very good scout and really had an eye for strong attacking players. While he was at Ipswich, it was estimated that he drove over 3,000 miles, virtually from John O'Groats to Land's End and back three times to find these players who were to be the basis of the forward line that would eventually take Town back into the 1st Division.

After my return, I managed to score in my first game away at Bolton Wanderers. It just seemed like the old times. They won 2-1 taking the edge off my delight at being amongst the goals for Town again. I scored with more purpose in my second home debut against Norwich City in the local derby at Portman Road. Gerry Baker set it up perfectly, leaving me with a virtual tap-in and Billy Baxter who was now Town's full-time centre-half, scored the other one in a 2-0 victory over the old enemy. I hadn't caught up with Ted since my return to Town. He was watching that day and tried to come and see me in the dressing room after the game but was intercepted by McGarry who asked him who he was and what he thought he was doing. Ted explained who he was but Bill told him to wait in reception until I came out, 'just like everyone else'. Bill was very close to being decked on that occasion and Ted told me he thought he was a 'madman' after their unfortunate first meeting.

McGarry was a good tough manager, exactly what Ipswich needed after the indiscipline of the Milburn reign. He was very much a man's man with very few social graces. He swore in front of ladies, he was blunt and to the point in almost everything he said or did; that's the way he was, the complete opposite to Alf, the gentleman admired by all the players wives. Eileen used to tell me how Bill always used to pass the ladies room in a big hurry 'with his nose to the ground' as she put it. Bill was just not suited to any event or social situation that required any amount of tact. The polite manners and the atmosphere of the cocktail party were not for Bill. He was always much more at home trying to win something whether it be on the golf course, the football field, the cricket pitch or the squash court. But it was Bill's intense desire to win, not worrying about what people thought of him, his manner or his methods, that eventually succeeded in getting Ipswich Town back into the top flight.

Billy Baxter and I were now the only surviving players from the championship winning year. On the Tuesday evening after the Norwich game, it was good to team up with two of my old mates from those years again, John Elsworthy and Jimmy Leadbetter in their joint Testimonial match against Arsenal. Only a small crowd of 7,619 saw the old masters play for the last time at Portman Road in a game we won 3-2. Jimmy scored one and I scored the other two goals on that night. They received very little financially from the evening which was disappointing considering the service they had given Town over many long years. After the game, I was lucky enough to get to talk with the legendary Billy Wright who was the Arsenal manager at the time. He had captained both Wolves and England, winning 105 caps in a brilliant career. He said to me "Ray, just keep playing as long as you can, don't give up until you really have to." Billy was 42 at the time and I really felt that he missed the playing side of the game. As I was nearly 30 years old, I took it as a compliment from the great man who thought I still had a lot of mileage left in the game.

On the Saturday after, we really needed a win against Birmingham City at home before the long trip to Carlisle away where we knew we'd be lucky to get away with a point. We lost 1-0 to a workmanlike City team managed by my former Wolves boss Stan Cullis. It was very disappointing to lose at home but it was good to see Stan well again and back in the game he'd served so well. As I mentioned in my time at Wolves, Stan never swore but, after that game, I heard the full McGarry's swearing repertoire and, for the first time in my career, I saw tea mugs fly at a rate of knots before smashing into the far wall of the dressing room. Bill was furious with us that day and certainly let us have it, both barrels, also threatening us with extra training on Sundays if we didn't improve. McGarry was not devious, he was right up front and though he was ruthless in some of his methods, you knew exactly where you stood with him. You soon learned that compliments to the team or individual players were rare and bollockings were given more often than praise. That was his way but, when you were getting results, it just about seemed to make sense.

The club afforded us the luxury of a flight for our next game with Carlisle United rather than a back and bum breaking, 400 mile coach trip up there. If you played in the South, it was a good incentive to get promoted to avoid this fixture every season. I should imagine, a mild consolation if you were relegated. We took off from RAF Wattisham at lunchtime on Friday. The game was scheduled to be played that evening so as not to clash with the home international between Scotland and England at Hampden Park in Glasgow the following Saturday afternoon. The Scottish lads on the trip had tickets for families and friends for the game but the weather was going to ruin their plans for the weekend.

The first supersonic jet, Concorde, capable of 1,400 mph, faster than the speed of sound, was being built in France as we flew in a De Havilland 14-seater Heron with a top speed of just over 180 mph. In comparison, more like the aeroplanes in the film 'Those magnificent men in their Flying Machines' starring Terry Thomas, one of my favourite actors. I was known to be pretty confident and dangerous in the air. I didn't feel quite so clever when travelling at 2,000 feet in the old Heron. De Havallind had also made the great Mosquito warplane of World War II, made even more famous by the film 633 Squadron which I'd seen two years before in a Wolverhampton cinema with Eileen. I thought we were pretty safe. Rivalry between the supporters of many clubs was getting more violent by the year. Carlisle was not the most hospitable place to play but they hadn't yet gone as far shooting down in-coming flights of opposing teams!

The North was in the grips of a bitterly cold freeze at the time. We were approaching Lancashire when the wings of our plane started to ice up, leaving the pilot no choice but to make an emergency landing in Blackpool. We were just climbing onto the coach to make the last 90 miles to Carlisle by road when we were told the game had been postponed because of heavy snow blizzards. The game had been re-scheduled to be played at 3:00pm the next day. We checked into a hotel in Blackpool for the night and, an hour later, I sat down to dinner with my new team mates. We'd just started to eat when a loud voice bellowed out "Remember, you're up here to play football, not to stuff yourselves with food!" as McGarry walked in to the dining room. I was the only one to raise my head as the others just kept on eating. I was sitting next to Ken Hancock, Town's keeper. "Don't worry Ray," he whispered, "he's always like this when he sees us eating. He'll be okay when he sits down." Ken then told me that McGarry had once stopped him from having the dessert as he'd already had the soup for starters!

The next morning we were expecting to hear the news that the game had been called off again. The Scottish lads were praying it was but their final hopes of getting to Glasgow for the international were ruined by a heavy thaw early that morning. We finally made the rest of the journey by coach to Carlisle. Having travelled all that way, the pitch was an unwelcome mud bath of melting ice and water - no wonder almost everyone lost there. They'd probably have been near the top of the Scottish League had the border been drawn about fifty miles further south but then Kevin Beattie would have been lost to probably Rangers or Celtic and certainly Scotland.

Surprisingly we were one up at half-time with an Eddie Spearritt goal. We slumped to a 3-1 defeat in the second half. Colin Harper, Town's highly promising young left-back, dislocated his shoulder in the game and was substituted by one of the disillusioned Scots, Ray Treacy who came on to make his last ever appearance for Town. The same went for fellow Scot, John 'Horse' Colrain that day. As it turned out, England beat Scotland 4-3 that day. It was probably even more to McGarry's killjoy liking that the Scottish lads weren't going to get the chance of a good piss-up in the pubs and restaurants of Glasgow after the game.

After that defeat, we knew that just drawing our remaining games might not be enough. We forged ahead with three straight wins over the Easter Bank Holiday weekend, doing the double over Leyton Orient and a home victory over Cardiff City which raised us out of the bottom three. Drawing our next two games, 1-1 against Manchester City at Portman Road and 0-0 away at Rotherham United a week later saw us finally clear of any threat of relegation with three games to go. The same day, Suffolk, who play in the Minor Counties cricket league, had been drawn to play the mighty Kent at the Ipswich School ground in Ivry Street in the one-day knockout competition of the time, The Gillette Cup, cricket's version of the FA Cup. Ted was furious that day as Suffolk had asked him to play for them in the game but Neil Franklin, the Colchester manager, had refused to release him. Kent, being a major county won the game easily as they were expected to, with Colin Cowdrey scoring a century and voted man of the match. Ted swears he'd never have scored a hundred if he'd had a chance to bowl at the great man. Ted was an extremely hostile and feared fast bowler in the area. It was sad that he wasn't given the chance to play against a major county. The great John Arlott was commentating on the game so what a listen it might have been. Perhaps big Ted making Cowdrey duck a bouncer and then glaring at him just like he did to keepers. Just imagine Arlott saying "Phillips, as merciless to batsman as he was to the finest goalkeepers in the land in his prime, comes roaring in again, with a raw frowning fury, bowls to Cowdrey and...." who knows what might have happened. We'll never know but Mr Franklin, it's too late now. You owe us all for not letting Ted play in that game. Ted was released by Colchester at the end of the season in which he scored 13 goals in 32 games before finishing his career with non-league Chelmsford City. Both Jimmy Greaves and Geoff Hurst followed to finish their careers there so they were in good company with Ted.

Our last home game of the season was against Wolves when Mick Mills made his debut in a defence that was terrorized by Peter Knowles the whole way through. Peter was made 'Man of the Match'. I managed two goals in a 5-2 win and we finished six points clear of the relegated clubs. I'd done my bit, scoring eight goals in thirteen appearances. After the season had ended, it was a nice surprise to get a letter from Bill McGarry, thanking me for helping Ipswich avoid relegation. Next to Alf, he was to be the second most important influence of my career. I wonder if those at Ipswich ever really knew how good a manager he was. His temperament and methods were almost the very opposite to Alf's but, by the end of that season, he'd done a great rescue job for Town.

Just before the 1966 World Cup started that summer, we moved into a house in Kempton Road in Ipswich. We'd been away for just under three years but it hardly seemed like that. We just carried on from where we had left off. Not too much had changed at the club either apart from all the new faces, though the old 'Chicken Hutch' had finally gone, not demolished but transferred to the Speedway Stadium at Foxhall and new dressing rooms and offices built in its place. I know it might sound a little strange having condemned it myself so many times but, in a way, it's a pity it couldn't have been saved and moved to a part of the ground and remained like a sort of wooden museum. It was very much a part of the history of Ipswich Town despite its shortcomings.

I can just imagine it if it had been kept intact with lots of photos on the walls of all the players and historic moments in that era of the club, like when Jimmy Forsyth was thrown fully clothed into the elephant bath after the we'd won the 1st Division Championship in 1962. There could also be recordings playing of interviews with Sir Alf, Mr John and the players of those great years. It would also be nice just to sit there by myself on one of those old benches for a while in complete silence. Then I'd be able to imagine Alf giving one of his half-time pep talks or a player screaming out "Ted! Where's my bloody shoe!" or Alf shouting "Put that fag out Jimmy!" and I could have a good laugh as there would be so many memories to relive.

They buried all the war planes after the World War II; now some are trying to dig them up again. Sometimes, when I hear the unmistakable sound of a Rolls Royce engine and look up to see a Spitfire flying overhead, I think what a great sound and sight it is. When I look around, nobody else seems to be looking up; perhaps most people don't care any more.

Chapter 15

"So near, so far"

By the start of the season, Bill McGarry had either sold or given free transfers to no less than eight players who'd played the season before, being especially harsh on the Scots at the club as John 'Horse' Colrain, Jack Bolton, Joe Davin and Ray Treacy were not on the retained list. He was ruthless. He reduced the wage bill and made the shrewd signing of Billy Houghton, a strong and reliable defender from Watford on a free transfer. We thought we had a good chance of promotion. If we failed, it wasn't going to have anything to do with our fitness as McGarry shouted at us in pre-season training "I'm going to push every fucking ounce out of you and you can moan, swear and curse as much as you like but I'm going to work you till you're ready to fucking drop!" He wasn't kidding either. I doubt whether there was a fitter team in that division as results were soon to confirm. It wasn't a good idea to have much of a breakfast before training. McGarry said once after he'd put us through it one morning that he was not happy the way training was going; not enough of us were throwing up for his liking!

McGarry didn't favour road work, preferring long runs on the local parks and heaths. One of his favourite places was Rushmere Heath where most of the team were members of the golf club. It became a place of both pain and pleasure to the golfers amongst us, the sort of sadistic irony McGarry loved. These long runs were often followed by circuit training in the gym. Circuit training is a mixture of exercises, jumping over wooden horses, hauling yourself up and down ropes, standing astride a bench and jumping up and down on it (the one I hated most) and climbing over high parallel bars. It's like an indoor assault course which sorts out the fit from the unfit and the old from the young. Some aspects of it are not recommended for players with long term injuries, especially those with dodgy knees.

When McGarry first came to Ipswich, he'd made circuit training a regular part of the fitness schedule and understandably a few of the older players didn't like it, nor were they used to his abrupt manner and his constant swearing. John Elsworthy never played a game under McGarry. Just over a month after McGarry's arrival,

Larry Carberry and Rocky Stephenson had played their last games for Town. By the end of his first year at Ipswich, Jimmy Leadbetter, Roy Bailey, Andy Nelson, local lad Dennis Thrower and Jim Thorburn had all left the club. Although it was ruthless, I think McGarry had to do this. If there is one criticism you could have of Alf Ramsey, he was that he was almost too loyal to some of the players who'd won the championship for Ipswich in 1962 and the World Cup in 1966. Although I thought it was a disgrace when he was sacked as England manager, perhaps his outstanding loyalty to some of his players was part of the reason for his downfall. If Alf had to have a weakness, it's not a bad one to be remembered for.

McGarry was very much a man's man with very few social graces, the complete opposite to Sir Alf, the sergeant major type, with seemingly endless combinations of swear words that reminded me of the NCOs of my National service days. He wasn't easy to like but, as he said, he wasn't there to make himself popular but to take on the huge task of getting Ipswich Town out of the shambles that the club was in when he arrived. Someone once told me that Rocky Stephenson, before one of his last games at Ipswich playing for the reserves, came out onto the pitch smoking a cigarette which he continued to smoke during the warm up. He waited until the ref was about to blow for the start the game before taking up his position by the touchline in front of the directors box, then stubbed out his fag on the velvet like turf of Portman Road he'd once loved to play on. I thought this very un-Rocky like when I heard it but maybe it summed up the morale of the club when McGarry took over from Milburn.

The bookies had us at 33-1 to get promotion that year. We started well with a 2-0 over Cardiff City at Ninian Park where I opened my scoring for the season with a glancing header, one of the best I ever scored. Frank Brogan whacked in our second with a spectacular 25 yarder. We followed this up with two home wins against Huddersfield Town and Wolves who were both strong sides in the 2nd Division. Huddersfield, who McGarry had made over 350 appearances for in his playing career, had a reputation for being a skilful side but were also known for their physical approach to the game. Their rugged centre-half Coddington was a formidable centre-half who was rarely far from my shoulder. It wasn't long before he came too close and, as I turned him, he caught me inside the box and the ref pointed to the penalty spot. Their players surrounded the ref saying I'd dived. After a couple of minutes order was restored and Frank Brogan calmly struck home the penalty. Meanwhile their manager Ian Greaves was still doing his nut and shouting abuse from the dugout. At this point, a small man in a cloth cap, looking much more like a man from the north-east, a sort of life-size 'Andy Cap', climbed over the concrete wall of the West Stand, picked up Greaves' bucket of water and threw it over him in the dugout. This was all too much for Greaves who went absolutely mad and started to chase the little man along the touchline, wildly throwing punches at him. It became comical when two policemen joined in the chase, eventually catching up with the irate Mr Greaves, managing to calm him down as the little man with the cloth cap climbed back into the safety of the stand to the cheers of the crowd. Huddersfield had only succeeded in rattling themselves and we went on to win the game 3-0 with further goals from Gerry Baker and Eddie Spearritt.

We made it three wins in a row with a 3-1 victory over the division favourites Wolves at home. I didn't score in the game. Even though Hugh McIlmoyle scored their only goal, the report of the game in the local press said of him *'astonishingly preferred to Crawford at Wolves.'* Like Andy Beattie, McIlmoyle was also Scottish so maybe there was a touch of the old clanship between them. Whatever it was, it didn't stop them from getting relegated the season they sold me.

Huddersfield had revenge for their defeat at Portman Road by beating us 1-0 in Yorkshire. We pulled things round in our next game in the local derby with a 2-1 victory against Norwich at Carrow Road. Gerry Baker and I scored the goals, mine coming from a rare gift from their keeper Kevin Keelan when he dropped a cross virtually at my feet. Mick Mills was booked in the game for bringing down their wily old winger Bill Punton once too many times. Some thought Billy Baxter, who'd tried to plead Mick's case to the ref, had gone in the book. Billy confirmed it wasn't him after the game, saying "What? Me? Of course not, I've never been booked in my life!" For such a hard tackling player, this was a remarkable record at the time. Billy was a tough defender. He always stuck to the rules and knew exactly what was in the bounds of hard but fair challenges.

The evening before that game, I'd gone with Billy to see Alf Ramsey display the World Cup at a civic reception at the Town Hall. Ted and many of the old championship winning team were there as well and it was great to witness Alf proudly holding the greatest trophy in the world. No one deserved it more than him. It makes a mockery of the reputed £5,000 bonus Alf received for winning the World Cup in 1966 and the £4,000,000 Erickson received for failing to win it in Germany 2006.

I should think that players who have had long careers in the game can usually recall at least one occasion of 'afters' as they call it these days, not during the game but off the pitch at half time or after the game. This happened to me in the very next home game against Derby County at Portman Road when I was assaulted at half time by a fellow professional for the only time in my career. After only four minutes, we were 2-0 down to goals from their strikers Ed Thomas and Alan Durban. By the interval, Billy Baxter and Gerry Baker had both scored to put us level. As we walked off, not far from the dressing–rooms, I was totally shocked by a huge thump in the back of my thigh which would have knocked me over had not Ken Hancock who I was talking to at the time been at my side to break my fall. Then alongside me was the veteran Derby keeper and ex-England international, Reg Matthews, who'd taken a fly-kick at me, Thai Boxing style but with studs as well. I had no thoughts of retaliation at the time. My father had once said to me that the first man to lose his temper was most likely to not only lose the fight but also the argument which had always been my philosophy in my playing days. I just turned to Hanks and said "Did you see that Hanks?" Hanks replied "Yes, I bloody well did!" after which Matthews said with spitting aggression "If you come so much as near me next half, I'll break your fucking legs mate!" It was a pity he'd taken this attitude as Matthews had played a blinder in the first half, making some brilliant saves. I'd challenged him strongly a couple of times as you were allowed to do in those days but I'd not elbowed him or kicked him.

No more was said until we came out for the second half and Hanks asked me what I was going to do about his assault. Hanks had a very long kick so I told him to hoist some rugby style 'up-and-unders' into their penalty area as soon as he had the chance. They took the lead only a minute into the next half and it was then that Hanks obliged with a high long kick which bounced perfectly just outside their area. Matthews came out of his goal and, with the ball falling between us, I clattered into him with more than just the usual shoulder force. We repeated the combination a few minutes later. I scored twice in the last fifteen minutes to win 4-3. At this, their keeper lost his temper. They just happened to lose the game as well.

In a similar vein, the very same day, Alf Ramsey had an apology accepted by FIFA for referring to the Argentine team as 'animals' after England had played them the previous July in the World Cup. Their captain Antonio Rattin had been sent off. I suspect that Alf was just being diplomatic. He felt so strongly about the way the Argentinians played that he actually went as far as trying to prevent the English players exchanging shirts at the end of that game. Possibly Alf hadn't forgotten the way AC Milan had fouled and cheated their way to victory in Ipswich Town's European Cup tie at the San Siro Stadium in 1962.

By the time we visited a struggling Pompey side at Fratton Park in mid October, we were lying second in the table just behind Hull City. It was a game we expected to win. Their manager George Smith had done his homework on us and we were out-thought and outplayed in a 4-2 defeat. Bobby Kellard, who Ipswich had sold to Pompey in the same week Ipswich had signed me the previous season, showed us what a good player he was, tormenting our defence and scoring two of their goals. I then found out about Bobby's unhappy short stay at Ipswich. He was by all accounts a man who spoke his mind and the players hadn't taken to him as a person and didn't think he could play either. His approach to the game was very professional. I don't think McGarry shared their opinion or wanted to sell him but they needed the money to buy me from West Bromich Albion so Bobby was sold. After the game, McGarry made his favourite entrance after we had lost games badly, kicking our dressing room door open with the usual almighty whack, before shouting "So you fucking lot don't think Bobby Kellard can fucking play do you?" before walking out in total disgust.

We made amends a week later by beating Hull City in a nine goal thriller at Portman Road. They were leading the division just one point above us so it was a good time to score my one hat-trick of the season. I scored my third just after half-time to make it 5-2. Hull refused to give up and, helped by two defensive errors, their long serving and outstanding goal-poacher Kenny Wagstaff, scored twice to bring the score to 5-4. Luckily we hung on for both points as the club would probably have had to fork out not for just one but a whole new set of tea mugs such would have been McGarry's rage if we hadn't won. If that was an avalanche of goals, there'd been a real one the day before in which 144 people had tragically died, 116 of them children in the man-made disaster of Aberfan in Wales. A huge coal tip had slid down a mountain crushing a local school. When I came home after the game that day, my children were waiting for me as they always did at the front door to give me a big hug. It made me think how I would have felt if suddenly they'd not been there any more. It didn't bear thinking about. The world in the so-called 'Swinging Sixties' was a dangerous place in those times.

Two weeks later we gave the Town fans another goal feast, hammering Northampton Town 6-1 with Frank Brogan getting a hat-trick; two of them from the penalty spot. I never saw many more deadly penalty takers than Frank in all my years in the game, possibly with the exception of Ted. Frank was a great player for Town as he not only provided that width a good left-winger gives you but he also scored a lot of goals making him in effect a third striker. Ipswich Town, just like most clubs, have always achieved more when they've had a good player on the left flank with the names of Jimmy Leadbetter, Clive Woods, Arnold Muhren and also Jamie Clapham coming to mind.

Our next game was my 250th appearance for Ipswich Town. Probably the most dreaded fixture in the whole football league at the time, away to Millwall at the notorious 'Den'. You might as well have called it the 'Coliseum' of South London, S.E.14 in those days. To continue the comparison, their manager, 'Emperor' Benny Fenton, must have given the thumbs down sign for most of us before we even came out onto the pitch. At the time, the 'Skinhead' fashion was at its height and the whole place was full of fierce aggression. The Den was a small, compact little stadium with the crowd very close to the pitch. It was best not to be an opposing winger or fullback playing near the touchline as you would only be a few feet away from the snarling abuse of yobs and hooligans. This wasn't helped by some of the Millwall players whose aggressive behaviour frequently took the already hostile part of the crowd to even higher levels of hatred. The intimidating atmosphere there made a local derby game with Norwich City seem like a Saturday afternoon picnic. At the time, Millwall had gone 54 games undefeated at home. It was hardly surprising as it really was like throwing Christians to the lions. Because of the fear of vandalism, those of Town's bravest supporters who travelled up to the game by car, had been warned not to leave any rosettes or stickers on their windows if they parked anywhere near the ground.

In the very first minute of the game Frank Brogan broke through, getting into their box before Bobby Hunt took him out leaving Frank limping for the rest of the half. Danny Hegan gained possession of the loose ball only to be fouled by Hunt as well. The ref bottled out of booking Hunt and also of giving us the clear penalty that it was; instead giving us a free-kick right on the edge of their box. It was obvious from the very start of the game that Millwall didn't want to play football and hoofed the ball in the air at every opportunity. We went behind in the 39th minute to a farce of a goal. It seemed to everybody, apart from the linesmen and referee, that Bobby Hunt was at least 10 yards offside when he received a through ball and was allowed to go on and score the only goal of the game. Hanks was so convinced that it was offside, he didn't even bother to try and save Hunt's shot. None of us could believe it when the ref blew and pointed to the centre-circle to signal a goal, perhaps fearing what the crowd might do if he disallowed it. In the light of what was to happen the next season to referee Keith Burkenshaw at The Den, he was probably wise to let the goal stand.

Soon after the second half started, Frank Brogan, who'd not recovered from

Hunt's earlier challenge, went off with a badly bruised leg, 'crippled' as McGarry referred to it as after the game. He was to be replaced by another winger, local Ipswich lad Eddie Spearritt. Up until that point, there'd been a number of scuffles between the players but the referee had just about kept the lid on things. These days, when referees seem to throw around red cards like confetti sometimes, there would hardly have been a player left on the pitch by then apart from the two keepers.

As the game wore on, our captain Dave Harper, being an ex-Millwall player came in for the worst abuse from the Millwall players and the crowd. He was getting hacked to pieces. The ref by then seemed too scared to do anything about it. Just through total frustration, Dave eventually was booked for retaliation after he'd been cynically scythed down again by the ex-Arsenal centre-forward Len Julians who should have been booked as well. The ref bottled out of it yet again.

Joe Broadfoot had just returned to his native Millwall after a period with Ipswich Town. I don't know if there was any history between him and Eddie Spearritt in his time there but Eddie hadn't been on the pitch long before they were eye-balling each other in a heated exchange of words, pushing and jostling each other after Eddie was alleged to have fouled Joe. All eyes were on Millwall organizing the free-kick when Eddie suddenly collapsed to the ground in our penalty area. As was the custom there, counted out with a chant of one to ten before Jimmy Forsyth came to his rescue with the magic sponge. Joe had punched him in the stomach. Eddie was not entirely innocent as he'd shown aggression as well. Joe said later that Eddie had called him a 'Cee U Next Tuesday' and for Joe that was just going too far.

Just a few months after the whole nation had pulled together to cheer England to victory in the World Cup, there were mini civil wars going on, in and around many of our football grounds, with young opposing supporters of different towns and cities clashing every weekend. Many Ipswich fans had their scarves and rosettes torn away from them and burnt on the Millwall terraces that day. Some even had burning cigarettes pushed into their necks. It was just the usual mindless minority causing the trouble. Some of the Town fans, who'd been hurt or beaten up, were helped and escorted from the ground by the true Millwall supporters. There was a great deal of fuss at the time about a lot of black Africans being allowed into the country. I've always wondered, how can you accept foreigners when you don't even like your own and perhaps that's been going on ever since.

By the end of the game, which we inevitably lost 1-0, you couldn't call us 'saints' either. It was difficult not to be drawn into it all after the non-stop provocation that the ref had done little to stop. Players were still pushing and jostling each other all the way to the dressing rooms. We were licking our wounds there when a Millwall official came in with a smile and a bottle of champagne with the compliments of their manager Benny Fenton for us to share the celebration of their 55th game at home without defeat. McGarry was still furious at what had happened and said "Just fuck off will you and you can tell him to stick it up his fucking arse!" A few minutes later Benny Fenton came in and asked Bill to have a word with him outside. You could have heard a pin drop as we listened to their raised voices outside with Fenton calling McGarry a bad loser to which he replied "Yes I know I am, but I don't like fucking cheats!" and that was it. After the game, Fenton called the result 'wonderful', Bill McGarry said it was 'diabolical' and Gerry Baker described it as 'murder'. I suppose you could say the ref had a good game as there hadn't been a riot; one of the soccer hooligans favourite chants at the time was "We want a riot! We want a riot! We want a riot!"

Although Millwall had a bad reputation, they were by no means the only offenders as all clubs were beginning to suffer from unwanted hooligans. Ipswich was no exception although there were relatively few who made trouble compared to other clubs. In general, the whole country was becoming a less safe place to live with many calling for a return of the Death Penalty because a number of policemen had been shot dead that year in London. Murder was on the increase including the conviction of Brady and Hindley for the killing of two children in the 'Murders on the Moor' case. Drugs were also becoming a serious problem with teenagers. I was happy to be living in Ipswich with my family. It had a very low crime rate and was one of the safest towns in the country to live.

On the Sunday after the Millwall game, Buzz Aldrin the American astronaut broke the record for a man walking in outer space. He was tethered to Gemini 12 for two hours and twenty nine minutes as it orbited the world at over 17,000 miles an hour. Given all the troubles of the world and the war in Vietnam being at its fiercest, Aldrin was possibly one of the safest men on earth, being so far away from it. He was quoted as saying on that walk "Greetings to all the people of the world who have been and will continue to strive for peace in the world." How far away could he have been from the truth? Well, just over 28,000 miles by my reckoning.

We were top of the league when we went to Coventry two weeks before Christmas where we suffered our worst defeat of the season on a rainy winter's evening at Highfield Road with Bobby Gould scoring a first-half hat-trick in a 5-0 defeat. It was the start of a run of 12 games without a win, ending any hopes of promotion we had that year.

Despite our drop in League form, we had a good run in the FA Cup run starting with a 4-1 win over Shrewsbury Town. The next week saw Joe Broadfoot, Eddie Spearritt's sparring partner in the Millwall game, sign for his second spell with Town. Joe was the fastest winger I ever saw and had once been like a secret weapon. By that time, many defences had wised up to him and played a temporary sweeper whenever Joe looked like getting possession. Joe just had one gear, a fast forward 100 metre style sprint and it was just like lighting up a rocket. You lit the fuse by passing the ball to him. Joe would pass the ball into an open space a full thirty or so yards past the fullback, then fly past him chasing after the ball like he'd had a rocket up his arse. You could say that Rocky Stephenson was the prototype of Joe Broadfoot, the difference being that Roy was nowhere near as fast as Joe. He was a very accurate crosser of a ball whereas Joe was more erratic in that skill. If you'd put their skills together, the results would have been devastating. Just like on November the 5th when you send off a rocket, you're never quite sure where it is going to end up; it was the same when Joe had the ball. That's why the crowd loved him as he was a great entertainer. After one of his famous sprints, Joe would take time to recover and you could see his head rolling from side to side as if he'd just finished an Olympic marathon. It was best to wait a few minutes whilst he recovered before you lit his fuse again. Joe said that part of the reason for joining Ipswich again was that he'd fallen out with Benny Fenton for refusing to 'dive' in a game.

As Joe wasn't cup-tied, he was in the starting line-up for our 4th Round FA Cup tie against Carlisle United at home. I opened the scoring after 69 minutes, then Frank Brogan passed a perfect ball through to Joe in the last minute of the game. One of the linesmen flagged for offside, but the ref Ken Stokes waved play on as Joe wasn't offside when the pass was made. Joe calmly crossed the ball inside leaving Frank Brogan with just a tap-in to kill the game off. It was all too much for Willy Carlin their captain, a five feet four inch terrier of a player with a snappy temper to match. He was booked for arguing, then sent off a couple of minutes later for continuing his protest. Then all hell broke loose. Ken Hancock had annoyed the Carlisle supporters who thought he'd been time wasting by bouncing the ball too many times for their liking. He started to get pelted in the goalmouth at the Churchman Stand end with anything they could lay their hands on. Even

Hanks, the bravest of keepers, had to retreat to the halfway line from a hail of bottles, coins, sweets and fruit, the lot, apart from their return tickets home. It took about ten minutes for things to calm down enough for Ken Stokes to restart the game and play out the remaining seconds on the clock. After the game, Town officials picked up about 10 shillings worth of one penny pieces, roughly 140 as there were 240 pence in the old pound then.

We were drawn against 1st Division Manchester City at Maine Road in the Fifth Round of the FA Cup. Two weeks before Easter, we travelled north to stay at our usual hotel in Southport to prepare for the game. I always liked training by the sea. It was a welcome break from our usual training routine. On one of the days that we were there, McGarry also organized a visit to the local swimming baths, followed the next day by two rounds of golf at the Highgate Club, right next to the Royal Birkdale Course. As Bill liked a sense of competition in almost everything he did and there was no such thing as a 'friendly' to him, we were split up into relay teams for the swimming and played two mini golf tournaments, one in the morning followed by another in the afternoon. Some were obviously a lot better than others at swimming and golf but all the players had to compete even if they were poor swimmers in danger of drowning or hardly knew one end of a golf club from another! Swimming is a very good way of toning up the muscles and McGarry thought golf went well with football as it improved 'eye to ball' co-ordination so there was good reason behind the schedule. I can't remember who won the swimming relays. In the golf, Frank Brogan won in the morning and Cyril Lea in the afternoon. Danny Hegan, playing with McGarry, made the shot of the day after managing not only to drive into 'no-man's land' but even worse, directly into the back of a deserted trailer. Danny with his never say die spirit, declined to take a drop losing a stroke before mounting the trailer and hitting an almighty shot which landed within a few feet of the flag! We never heard the end of it for the rest of the trip. Danny was just the same on the football pitch. Not only was he a great player, he never gave up; that's why McGarry thought so highly of him. Danny was eventually sold to West Bromich Albion before being re-united with Bill who took him to Wolves after becoming manager there.

By the time we arrived in Manchester on the Saturday, we couldn't have been better prepared for the game. We were more than a match for City for much of the game and one report said we actually 'mesmerised' them with some of our play. I put us in front with a header in the 25th minute, a lead we held onto with the help of some spectacular saves by Hanks until ten minutes from time when their left winger Neil Young equalized. We could have won with just a few minutes to go when Joe Broadfoot scored but it was disallowed because, although I was nowhere near the play, the ref said I was in an offside position. McGarry was absolutely furious about the decision and said after the game with the swear words removed "Nine times out of ten, the goal would have been allowed." It might have been on our home patch but not at Maine Road in front of a crowd of over 47,000. I really wish they would make this ruling easier for officials and players. The dilemma still goes on today. If a player is in an offside position, he should be given offside whether he is interfering with play or not. Simple as that. This would take a lot of pressure off referees and linesman. They already have enough to think about and this nonsensical ruling does nothing to help them. All it does is produce unnecessary ill will between players and supporters alike.

As was the case too many times that season, our inconsistency let us down in front of a 30,000 crowd that witnessed us tamely surrender 3-0 to City in the replay at Portman Road the following Tuesday evening. A mixture of defensive blunders and missed chances brought about our exit from the Cup. One of the best wingers the game has ever seen, Mike Summerbee, even with one thigh heavily strapped, ran rings round our defence and scored two of their goals. I missed a chance that one local reporter described as *'an astonishing piece of village green football from a top class player'* All I can say about that, is that at least I hit the target 229 times in all my other 352 games for Ipswich Town - I wonder if he saw all of those?

Promotion was a lost cause by then but we kept giving our best as there were still eleven games to go. McGarry always expected 100% whatever the game or position you were in. On Easter Bank holiday weekend Colin Viljoen, a brilliant 19 year old midfield player from South Africa and one of the greatest players ever to grace the turf of Portman Road, made his debut against Portsmouth at Portman Road. McGarry said of him "He can play in any position apart from goalkeeper." Having lost 4-2 at Fratton Park earlier that season, we wanted to put the record straight and do the same to them. They had other ideas though and we were two down in fifteen minutes to goals from Harry Harris and Ray Pointer, the fine ex-Burnley and England centre-forward who was playing out the end of his career with Pompey. We were terrible. Colin Viljoen pulled one back with his first ever goal for Town with a header just before half-time. McGarry was unusually quiet during the break as if he'd run out of things to say or swear about. I think even Bill, with his high expectations of us knew we'd tried our best that season and sensed the team were completely flat after going out of the FA Cup. Just as we were about to go out for the second half, he took me to one side and said "Ray, I have a very high regard for you as a player and no one has tried harder than you this season but could you do something for me? Try and get things going as I know the lads are a bit down. I want you to really try and rally them, just get them playing again, can you do that for me?" It was rare for McGarry ever to show there was perhaps a softer side to him. I think in a way he'd left it to me to tell the players he actually cared about them. He didn't know quite how to say it himself. It just wasn't his way. Years later, Joe Broadfoot told me that he'd overheard what Bill had said to me that day at half-time and, as Joe had great respect for Bill, said he was quite jealous of me at the time.

In the second half, with the extra responsibility McGarry had given me, when we put even just a few passes together, I shouted my approval and clapped my hands until we suddenly started to play a bit. Colin Viljoen began to stamp his class on the game. Even as a teenager, Colin showed great poise and calm on the ball, never rushed, like a class batsman playing very fast bowling. He had that ten or so yards of real pace you need to be the complete midfield player. I felt really pumped up by then and, when the ball came to me 25 yards out and fifteen minutes into the half, I struck it with a ferocity Ted would have been proud of. It flew past the Pompey keeper John Armstrong into the top of the net. Colin Viljoen scored two more to complete his hat-trick and a dream debut. After the game, McGarry patted me on the back, just saying "Thanks Ray"; again a very rare occurrence coming from Bill. With that and a 4-2 win over Pompey, it was one of the proudest moments of my career.

We did the double over Crystal Palace in two days flat, winning both games 2-0 away on Easter Monday and by the same score at Portman Road the day after. A maximum of six points over Easter put us into 4th place in the table. We were still too far behind the leaders to have any hope of promotion. A couple of days before our next home game against Millwall, Eileen, along with a few other player's wives had free tickets to go and see Roy Orbison who was touring the country at the time, at the Gaumont Cinema in Ipswich. Although Elvis Presley was Eileen's idol, she loved Orbison's music too. She was really chuffed when they were allowed to meet him in his dressing room after the show where a photo of them with the great man was taken and shown in the local newspaper the next day.

Two days later we avenged our controversial defeat at the Den by thrashing Millwall 4-1 at Portman Road. No one was more delighted than Joe Broadfoot who scored one of the goals against his old club. It was a hard but fair game. At times, we played some brilliant football, outplaying them and almost toying with them, just like Sandie Shaw did later that evening when she won the Eurovision contest with 'Puppet on a String'.

Although we finished in 5th place that season, it was disappointing for the supporters who did us proud that year but we'd failed to deliver. My goal tally that season was 25 goals in 48 games.

Curse of the Jungle Boy

Chapter 16

"Back where Town belong"

Before the season started, we were confident of promotion but McGarry made it clear he wanted to win the 2nd Division outright. We started well with a 2-0 win away to Middlesbrough. Once we'd weathered a fifteen minute opening barrage from our newly promoted opponents, our superior fitness, technique and discipline saw us through with Gerry Baker and I scoring our goals that day. Their biggest threat had come from their young striker, 22 year old John O'Rourke who McGarry had admired for a long time and was to be playing for us by the end of the season.

After the game, we stayed in the North and travelled to the west coast to Blackpool where we had a game on the Monday night. After dinner at our hotel, a few of us went out to a local pub and started talking to some Ipswich Town fans who were staying up there for the next game. Pint after pint went down before Billy Baxter left, leaving me with the Town fans. I've always loved talking football, especially directly with supporters to hear their views, I stayed on, but on this occasion it cost me my first ever fine at Ipswich. When I turned up at our hotel at nearly 1:00 o'clock the next morning, two hours late from the usual 11:00 o'clock curfew for players, there was Bill's No2, Sammy Chung, sitting in reception waiting for me. He just said "You're late Ray, get to bed now."

I'd taken a heavy kick on a knee in the game at 'Boro and was only just declared fit to play the next game against Blackpool two days later at Bloomfield Road. I took another couple of knocks and was struggling by half-time. Gerry was clobbered and had to be substituted so I stayed on for the rest of the game. Calf muscles and ankles were the main targets of defenders and, without doubt, the most battered part of a striker's anatomy in those days. It almost seemed that referees would allow defenders a few 'free kicks' (the painful kind) before they were warned, let alone booked. Some of the challenges refs allowed to go unpunished would have been awarded an immediate Red Card in the modern game. Football was a physical contact sport then although it seems to have gone too far the other way now. Tackling hard, clean and fair was one of the great skills in football. Now that seems to have become almost extinct in the game. We scored a point in a 0-0 draw that night so three points from two away games was a start anyone would have settled for. I thought I'd escaped with being late on the Saturday night but McGarry called me into his office the day after our return. He told me he wasn't best pleased with me as I was the senior professional in the team. He fined me £20.00 and the matter was soon forgotten.

Our chance to access Town's potential against a 1st Division club came in the Second Round of the League Cup against Southampton at Portman Road in mid September. On paper they had a very strong attack with Terry Paine, Jimmy Melia, Ron Davies, Mike Channon and John Sydenham, all playing that night. There was no question of fielding weakened sides in the League Cup in those days. It was regarded as a very important competition. We were two up in twelve minutes. They fought back but I completed my hat-trick in 63 minutes and added a fourth one minute from time to make the final score 5-2. We went out in the next round at Stoke City 2-1 although I was glad to have scored our goal as I'd not scored for a few games; especially as it was against Gordon Banks who they'd just signed from Leicester City. A couple of weeks later, Stoke made an offer for me and Town gave me permission to talk to them. I decided to stay put as I was happy at Ipswich as was my family. It was nice though to think that I could still attract a 1st Division club at the age of 31.

In the league, we went from strength to strength including a 4-0 win over Brian Clough's Derby County at Portman Road. After the game, Eileen had a question for Cloughie when he walked into the players lounge, asking him what Derby was famous for. "Obviously not our football on today's performance," he replied. Eileen explained that our daughter Jane had to go to school the following Monday with the answer so Brian added "Crown Derby China and Rolls Royce engines." Eileen was to have another exchange with Brian a few years later when I was coach at Brighton. The same weekend, Millwall lost 2-1 at The Den to Aston Villa. Referee Norman Burtenshaw was carried off unconscious after being surrounded and attacked by rioting Millwall hooligans. This time, things had gone too far. It was bound to happen eventually. It was a sign of the times. There seemed to be demonstrations almost every week in London, not about referees but mostly about the war in Vietnam. Publicans were also protesting at the time, parading through London in their hundreds with banners complaining about what 'the breathalyser' had done to their trade after Barbara Castle had introduced it in October that year. Although it was a good thing and the number of road deaths went down, beer sales went down as well so the breathalyser was about as good for publicans as hippies were for the hairdressing trade.

In the last week of October, Town sold Gerry Baker to 1st Division Coventry City. It came as a shock to me. I thought that, if Town were going to mount a serious promotion challenge, this wasn't a very positive move. You couldn't blame Gerry for taking the chance to move up a league and an increase in his wages. Despite Gerry's more wayward lifestyle off the field, he was a good pro when it came to training and doing the business of scoring goals. The 58 that he scored in 135 league appearances were a great contribution in Town's slow recovery through some desperate years. One of my most amusing memories of Gerry happened shortly before he left the club. By that time, he'd probably written off more cars than I've had in my life. One morning, we were training on the practice pitch at Portman Road when a policeman on a large motorbike appeared, drove across the ground, finally coming to a halt on the centre of the pitch, bringing our five-a-side game to a standstill. After switching off his engine, he climbed off his bike and asked which one of us was Gerry Baker. With his usual charm and smile, Gerry walked towards the policeman and said in his broad Glaswegian "Ay, that's mee's officer!" confessing that he'd left his latest car, a white Ford Anglia, parked halfway up a lamp post in town the night before! Gerry said it was the lamppost's fault as its light wasn't on so he hadn't seen it! As 'the breathalyser' had just come into force, he probably thought it best not to report the accident at the time. Gerry, despite his obvious Scottish roots, had been born in New York to Scottish parents and, because of this link, went on to win a few international caps for the USA. He was not just a very good footballer but also one of the nicest people I ever met in the game, always great company with a wry sense of humour, especially over a beer and a good game of cards. I missed him both as a fellow striker and a friend when he left.

I don't think it was any coincidence his leaving coincided with one of the leanest goal scoring periods of my career, a run of twelve games in which I only found the back of the net twice. The week Gerry was sold, Town bought Bobby Hunt from Millwall to replace him. We had the Saturday off as our game at Crystal Palace was postponed because of a waterlogged pitch at Selhurst Park. On Guy Fawkes night the day after, the worst rail crash in the history of British Railways took place when a train travelling from Hastings to Charing Cross London, was derailed by broken tracks at Hither Green in South London. 49 people were killed and dozens more injured. It was a tragedy in which I was to be involved through football over a year later. For a while, it overshadowed the national crisis of the Foot and Mouth outbreak that year that went on for months with the north being the worst hit area.

Thousands of poor animals were slaughtered. All race meetings were called off as was the RAC Rally and a lot of football matches as well. Hunting and fishing was also banned in many areas so at least some creatures benefited like foxes and fishes. With both games against Millwall still to play, Bobby Hunt was to find out that sometimes the hunters become the hunted.

Bobby played his first game in the 2-1 win against Aston Villa, a tough game in every respect. Billy Baxter suffered such a bad cut in a sickening clash of heads with their centre-half Bill Turnbull that he had to go off to hospital where he had a general anaesthetic before the wound was stitched up. He was kept in over the weekend for observation. Turnbull also gave me the chop, not in the usual leg area but more like a full-blooded karate chop on the back of the neck. I missed the whole of next week's training with severe headaches. To make matters even worse, Bobby Hunt twisted a knee in training. With Billy out, Danny Hegan was made captain for our next game against Rotherham at Millmoor. I played upfront with Charlie Woods, one of a few makeshift strikers that I was to be paired with for the next two months. Rotherham already looked destined for relegation. We won 3-1, leaving us well placed just a few points off the two promotion positions. Like most teams in a successful season, we went through a shaky period losing three out our next four games; 1-0 away to QPR in London then both our next two home games 2-1 to Portsmouth and by the same score the following week to Middlesbrough just before Christmas that year. The game against Portsmouth was played on a treacherous pitch and a snowstorm with ex-Town player Bobby Kellard having another fine game against us. Judging by some of his tackles that day, I don't think any of us were on his Christmas card list! Most annoying about the loss was that Pompey went top.

The Middlesbrough game a week later was my 300th appearance for Ipswich Town; one I remember more for the pain that it left me in. We were two down inside fifteen minutes, both from their fullback Hickton, the second being from a dubious penalty. I managed to pull one back ten minutes later when I scored almost lying on my backside in my 'laid-back style'! I should have had a penalty later on when Bill Gates blatantly hauled me down. The referee, a Mr New from Portsmouth, didn't give it. Having lost at home to Pompey the previous week, anything to do with my home town wasn't helping our cause at the time. Boro' hung on to take both points by a mixture of luck and brutal defence including a massive kick on my shin that probably would have broken my leg but for my shin-pad. This was from their centre-half Bill Gates, the older and much fiercer brother of Eric Gates who later played for Ipswich Town. It goes without saying who was the more skilful of the two. He was booked for the challenge and the day after, my shin was badly swollen almost from knee to ankle. A few weeks later Gates was suspended for seven days and fined £10 by an FA Disciplinary Committee for what they called 'persistent infringements', a slight understatement in my book. When I think of the tackling in those days, it seems a miracle how George Best survived to play at the level he did for as long as he did without ever getting a broken leg or a bad ligament injury. Ted once told me a story that he'd heard about a Chelsea v Man. United game when George walked past Ron 'Chopper' Harris after the game. Ron asked George to stop for a second and George said "What's up Ron?" to which Ron replied "Stand still George, I just want to see your face!" George asked "Why?" Obviously with reference to George always showing him a clean pair of heels, Ron said "Because all I ever see is your fucking arse!" My most outstanding memory of George Best was strangely not on the football field and probably not one many will remember. It must have been before 1967 as it was on black and white TV. George was on a beach in his swimming trunks in some foreign climate, bouncing a six inch diameter plastic ball on and off his right foot, then to left and back without losing control of the ball. I almost had to pinch myself to believe what I was watching, like watching a man from another planet or universe, with such skills you were never likely to see again.

As usual, I went to Felixstowe and stood in the sea to help heal my injured leg. Eileen and I had often talked about emigrating to a warmer climate. It seems nearly half the nation had inquired about going to Australia. The day after the Middlesbrough game, Harold Holt, the Prime Minister of Australia, on of the safest men in the country you would have thought, disappeared without trace, either swept away by strong currents or eaten by sharks whilst swimming off a beach in Victoria. Although the North Sea was freezing at the time, it was at least safe to have a paddle without getting your legs ripped off by some shark. I think the only ones who weren't too unhappy when I was injured were my two young daughters as it meant another day out at the seaside, more candy floss, spending more of Dad's money in the games arcade in the Felixstowe Pier Pavilion, followed by fish and chips! One person who was definitely fed up with the treatment being meted out to me was Eileen.

Although my shin was still sore, I was fit enough to return for the two back to back games against Millwall on Boxing Day at home and at The Den three days later; games not exactly guaranteed to bring out the best of seasonal cheer or goodwill in those either playing or watching. The game at Portman Road was a fiery, bad tempered game ruined by non-stop petty fouls. Eamon Dunphy was a very skilful midfield player but he had an obnoxious side that could get right up your nose. He was talking to the ref all through the game, trying to influence his decisions. The ref he stuck to his guns and awarded Ipswich two definite penalties in the game. Frank Brogan scored from both, the second giving us a 2-1 win in the last minute of the game with Frank celebrating by swinging on the crossbar like a performing chimpanzee. Wisely, this was not at the end where the Millwall supporters were; it could have caused a riot. When the referee blew for time seconds later, he was surrounded and jostled by some of the Millwall players, having to be escorted off the pitch by several policemen. After the game, a few of the Millwall players said they were going to file complaints of assault against the local police but nothing ever came of it. Frank really should have had a hat-trick of penalties as I was literally 'cut' down from the back when in the area but the ref didn't give it. The challenge left me with yet another bruised calf and a gash as well; not a serious one but still needing a few stitches after the game. It was all just part of the 'thrills and blood spills' of being a professional footballer in those days.

The return game four days just before the turn of the year at The Den wasn't a pleasant experience for their ex-player Bobby Hunt. He was barracked whenever he came anywhere near the ball. It didn't worry Bobby who gave us the lead shortly after half-time. Bryan Conlon equalized for Millwall. We held on for a precious point with Billy Baxter fearless and strong in defence. The ref, a Mr E Wallace, a tough no nonsense referee from Swindon, took a tight hold on the game from the start. There were plenty of hard tackles and challenges; one from their centre-half Barry Kitchener that left me with a dead leg ten minutes from time.

I missed a game before returning against Huddersfield Town at Portman Road in mid January but more brutal treatment was in store for me. Like us, they had some talented and skilful players such as Frank Worthington, Trevor Cherry and Roy Ellam who all went on to play for Leeds United. It was a game remembered for its physical battles and was another bruising encounter. I remember Worthington going through a sort of crowd pleasing ritual before the game near the touchline, bouncing a football from right foot to left foot then up to his thighs and back again. He was a very gifted player with superb skills. Had he been a more prolific goal scorer, he would have been a world beater and played many more times for England than he did. Their centre-half that day was Under-23 Welsh International Ray Mielczarek who they'd just signed from Wrexham. He must been given instructions before the game to 'look after me' as he was my near executioner on the day. Almost from the very first whistle, he chased me around the field like a modern day 'RoboCop' gone completely mad. It was as if he'd turned into the rogue alien robot dressed as a policeman who chased Arnold Schwarzenegger in the film Terminator 2. He was almost taking chunks out of me. I found out after the game that it had come to the point when Eileen had seen enough. She thought that the referee wasn't giving me enough protection and left her seat in the wives enclosure in the West Stand. She very nearly managed to get onto the pitch before being physically restrained by club officials! God knows what she would have done to Mielczarek if she'd managed to get out there, probably a fierce knee-bone uppercut to the groin area, bringing him painfully to his knees. When he was finally given his marching orders late in the game, he became the first player ever to be sent off in a League game at Portman Road, thankfully before he had the chance to finish his mission which, in 'Terminator' terms, could have been to pin me by the throat to the nearest goal post! I have always wondered what I would have done if Eileen had come on the pitch that day. I have a slightly comic vision of Eileen chasing Mielcrazek with myself and a couple of policeman in hot pursuit.

Without the physical attentions of my more violent namesake Ray, I managed to seal the match with a goal in the 80th minute adding to Colin Viljoen's 60th minute opener and Town ran out 2-0 winners. It was in the words of Town archivist John Thorne, 'a notorious match that did little credit to either side'. The one player who really rose above it all that day was Danny Hegan who showed some dazzling skills. His performance was that of a master midfield player; a show of skill that George Best (who Danny idolized) would have been proud of. He shone out above all the physical axes that were wielded around for most of the game. What was most surprising was that only two players were booked in the game, Worthington and Mielczarek before he was sent off. My goal in that game was only my second in nine games and some supporters had started to voice their opinions from the terraces that I was over the top. During this lean spell, McGarry gave me his full support. "Don't worry Ray, I know you're trying your hardest, I'll stick by you," and he did.

Going out of the FA Cup a week later 3-1 to 1st Division Chelsea was like our exit from the League Cup, the usual blessing in disguise. More important was the seven goal thriller at Carrow Road in the local derby against Norwich City with Colin Viljoen notching up his second hat-trick for the club in a 4-3 win. The ever goal-hungry Hugh Curran scored twice for City that day. I was to find out, after my Testimonial at Ipswich just over a year later, that Hugh also liked his grub, especially after midnight.

A week later we made the usual 'pointless' trip to Carlisle and were hammered 4-1. The air was blue in the dressing room after the game as McGarry really let us know what he thought of our performance. Carlisle is only about 40 miles from the Scottish border and not a trip many southern clubs looked forward to. It was a good incentive to get promoted to avoid the long journey up there every season and possibly minor consolation for Plymouth Argyle, almost 450 miles away who were relegated that year.

Just before the start of the run-in to the end of the season, McGarry was allowed a rare dip into the transfer market, pulling off a deal vital to our final push for promotion by signing striker John O'Rourke from Middlesbrough. Town also bought Peter Morris, a strapping, hard tackling midfield player from Mansfield Town, very much McGarry's type of player. Since Gerry Baker had left, things hadn't been easy up front for me as neither Ron Wigg nor Bobby Hunt, with all respect, were in the same class as Gerry. I'd also been paired with a few makeshift strikers alongside me including Charlie Woods, Eddie Spearritt and Colin Viljoen before O'Rourke arrived. He'd once been a youth with Arsenal and Chelsea but neither of their managers at the time, Bill Swindin or Tommy Docherty, thought he would make the grade as a 1st Division striker. O'Rourke was very self confident and probably handsome enough to have made it as a male model. Though he was far from being a physical presence in the box, he was signed to score goals, not to mix it or ruffle up big defenders; that was my job. I didn't mind taking the heavy challenges and going in hard to help create the openings for John to score. I was now 31 years old and beginning to be referred to as 'the old warhorse' and it wasn't for nothing.

In his first game against Cardiff City at Portman Road, O'Rourke immediately became a crowd favourite by scoring twice in a 4-2 win and went on to score 12 goals in our last 15 games. This alone almost paid back the £30,000 Ipswich had invested in him, a very modest fee for a very good player but then Ipswich never did pay much for their strikers as they bought me twice for a total of £20,000!

It wasn't till the very last game that we made sure of winning the 2nd Division title. It was at home to Blackburn Rovers who were a good side then and not far behind us in the league. We only needed a draw on the day. I settled a few nerves by opening the scoring after 26 minutes. I couldn't see much on or anyone to pass to when the ball came bouncing towards me, about thirty yards out in front of the old North Stand so I hooked the ball into the air over the defender who'd come to challenge me, wrong-footing him and turned to chase the ball. It bounced on the edge of the box and their keeper, Adam Blacklaw, was a bit slow to come out. When he tried to punch the ball away, he came nowhere near it. I jumped up with one of my highest ever leaps to head the ball over him and into the net for one of the best opportunist goals I ever scored. They equalized just before half-time and, in true Town style, we kept our supporters on edge for the rest of the game. There were thousands of relieved faces all round when the referee blew the final whistle with the score level at 1-1. We'd won the title outright.

The champagne was soon flowing like water in the dressing room. It was great to see Mr John and Bill McGarry so happy. Even though some players didn't care for Bill, even hated him, as far as I was concerned they were men you really wanted to win for. Mr John had guided the club back to the 1st Division after many years in the wilderness. Bill McGarry was now no longer the 'nearly man' having just missed out on promotion with his previous two clubs Bournemouth and Watford. It was also a great moment for Billy Baxter and I. We were the only two surviving players from the Championship winning side of 1962. I think Billy had a sort of love-hate relationship with McGarry. When the press asked him how he felt after the game, he said "Naturally I'm very pleased for myself and the team but my first thought is for the manager. If ever a man earned this it was him." Billy was so right.

Later on that evening, we were taken by coach to a hotel in nearby Felixstowe where Mr John had laid on a large reception for us. The champagne flowed again. 'Hermann's Hermits' were touring the area at the time and appeared in the bar later that evening with their lead singer Peter Noone. We asked him if they'd give us a song but he politely declined our request. Winning promotion was one thing but expecting to be entertained by the Hermits was obviously pushing things too far!

The booze was still flowing in the bar at 2:00am in the morning when Danny Hegan and myself, the two who were reckoned to still be in reasonably good shape, were paired in a drink-off which was to down six single whiskies each as fast as we could. "On the count of three," said Mr John, "One..two..three!" and we were off. I think Danny had most of it down his throat and, when I finished, I had it dribbling down my chin and shirt but Mr John called it a draw, thankfully not calling for a replay. Even as things were, I was as sick as a dog the next day.

It was a very proud moment for me when the team was photographed with the shining, brand new 2nd Division Champions Trophy. It was a replacement for the old one which had been melted in a fire at Coventry City, winners of the division the previous year. Apparently it was worth £400 but the honour of being the one to hold that cup was worth a lot more to me than that. It was a new cup and also the start of a new and exciting era at Ipswich Town in which I was to play some part. When that photograph was taken, I was just over two months short of my 32nd birthday and feeling pretty tired. That was not surprising as I'd run my heart out for the team in all the 42 League and Cup games that I'd played, scoring a total of 22 goals. I think I'd shut up most of the doubters who'd said I was finished sometimes during that season. Now for me, just one thing remained. That was to see if I was a man for all the seasons of the sixties, back in the 1st Division where I'd made my debut for Portsmouth over ten years before in 1958.

Chapter 17

"Exit Bill"

Although we didn't think we were going to win the championship as we'd done in 1962 the year after being promoted, McGarry was confident that we had a strong enough attack to take games to opponents rather than sit back hoping for a few scraps to come our way. Billy Baxter and I were the only two who'd played in the 1st Division before and I think we were able to help one or two of the players who were doubtful of their ability to adapt to the step up in class. It was a very strong league at the time. Unlike the 2nd Division, you had more time on the ball, although keeping possession of it was now crucial. Mistakes were more liable to be punished.

The season started well against my old club Wolves in which I played provider, crossing for John O'Rourke to head home the only goal in a 1-0 win. After losing away 3-0 at Sunderland, I scored my first of the campaign against Leicester City at Filbert Street, putting one past a very talented young keeper by the name of Peter Shilton who was understudy to Gordon Banks before he went to Stoke. I was getting a lot less stick from defenders which was a relief after the previous two years. It showed. In all of the next six games, we were unlucky to lose at home to Leeds 3-2 and Arsenal 2-1.

At the time, Leeds United were fast becoming the best team in England. They were not popular, mainly through jealousy I think. The way they played was setting the standard for all to follow and being noted by every football coach in the country from schoolboy level to the professional game. They played total possession football from defence right through to attack. As most football followers of that era, I can remember listening to their games on the radio, just imagining all the tight triangles of passing movements they were playing in, moving from one end of the pitch to the other: "Bremner Giles Madeley, Giles Bremner Madeley, Bates, Hunter Giles" went the commentary as they kept possession of the ball. Looking back on the years I played in the game and after as a coach for some years, to me the example Leeds set in those days and for years to follow was learned, then somehow unlearned. Now the game seems so much more about pace and physical strength. I may be wrong. I have to say that England will not win another World Cup until they can find players who can hold the ball and put more than just a few passes together, not just square passes but ones that can really penetrate high class international defences. We could do with a new Alan Ball (two more preferably). He was one of the top midfield players I ever saw and played against. No wonder Don Revie tried to buy Alan from Blackpool before he decided to stay in his native Lancashire and signed for Everton.

With three wins and three defeats in our first six games, we were giving as good as we were getting. A 1-1 draw at Manchester City confirmed our potential but the whole of Norfolk must have celebrated the following Tuesday when Norwich City knocked us out of the League Cup 4-2 at Portman Road. It started a mini collapse. We lost our next two games to Sheffield Wednesday and Liverpool before steadying the ship with a 2-2 draw at Southampton.

In late September with the sun still hot on our backs at Portman Road, I was doing battle against Stoke City and Gordon Banks again. I was marked by Dennis Smith that day, a young bruiser of a centre-half. If he couldn't soften you up with his challenges, he didn't have a second plan. I stuck two past Gordon that day and Town run out 3-1. Alf Ramsey was at the game and it was good to remind him that I could still beat the best goalkeepers in the world. A rare thing happened in the game. Danny Hegan pointed out to the referee, Mr Kirkpatrick, that Stoke City had kicked off in both halves; Ipswich had only kicked off once in the game after Stoke's goal. A few days later, Danny raised even more eyebrows by putting in a transfer request. With this came the first signs of unrest in the club that season.

Danny said his wife had never been able to settle in Suffolk and wanted to get back to her native north-east. He was also unhappy with McGarry continuing to play him as a right winger due to the long-term injury to Joe Broadfoot. Even though Danny was playing well in this position, he knew his best position was on the right side of midfield. I also think he was missing his best mate Gerry Baker. When Danny finally left Town for West Bromich Albion, it was not far from where Gerry was living in the Midlands. When they were at Town, if you saw one of them nine times out of ten you saw the other. They were almost inseparable and the greatest of friends. Danny was such a key player that his request was at first rejected and he was held to his contract which still had almost a year to run.

It certainly wasn't anything to do with the way the team was performing. Despite losing five games, we'd won four and drawn two and were in 10th position in the table; a lot better start than most had predicted. I'd scored nine goals in 11 games. Those who'd expressed doubts about me still being able to cut it at the top level were beginning to have to eat their words. 'Jungle Boy' was back at the age of thirty two and still scoring goals in the top flight of the English league.

In the first week of October we made our first trip of the season to London, to play the very fashionable Chelsea of the time. After just 4 minutes, I scored one of my best goals that season with a first-time volley from a Derek Jefferson cross that fizzed past a motionless Peter Bonetti, the reserve England keeper at the time. It wasn't to be our day at Stamford Bridge. They had a talented young striker, Ian Hutchinson, who started our downfall that day. Part of his armoury was a long throw that had to be seen to be believed. It was a secret weapon and potentially lethal to defences who'd never seen it before. It completely mesmerised the usually unflappable Billy Baxter who ended up putting the ball in his own net after 15 minutes. We conceded another soft goal to John Hollins and Alan Birchenall added another to finish us off 3-1. It was no disgrace to lose to a talented Chelsea side but it was the start of a poor run of form losing five out of the next six games. We returned to London just three days later. It was during the Tuesday evening game against QPR at Shepherd's Bush that our third daughter Suzanne Marie was born. Having given birth to our second child Liza Anne during the FA Cup match at Mansfield Town in 1963, perhaps Eileen was having her usual 'kittens' just thinking of me playing which may have bought both births forward a few days!

Talking of creatures, there was nothing imaginary about the one I was to confront shortly before Suzanne Marie's christening later that summer in Portsmouth. The ceremony was to take place at our local church and I had reserved an upstairs room in a nearby pub for the reception afterwards. About an hour before the christening, I went to the pub to take in one or two things that we were providing ourselves, including a large cake Eileen had made for the occasion. As it was a Sunday and past the lunchtime closing hour of 2:00pm, the pub was closed. When I arrived, the publican allowed me access through his backyard. I was just about to get back in my car when a huge Alsatian dog came out of the back door and approached me. He seemed quite friendly and jumped up on his hind legs, placing his front paws on me in what I thought was a friendly embrace. I was patting him on the head and giving him the old 'Good boy, you're a lovely boy aren't you' routine (you often wonder if this makes them even worse) but the dog had obviously decided I was up to no good in his backyard and sunk his large front fangs into my chest. It was a good job I wasn't four inches shorter or it could have been my throat! I had been hacked and almost kicked to pieces many times on the football field and never lost my temper but, on this occasion, I reacted like a man possessed. Though I'd managed to push the animal off, he still had me backed up against a wall. It was either him or me I thought. Just behind me happened to be a rusty old mangle. I turned around quickly, picked it up and launched it at the dog accompanied by loud swearing and shouting. It did the trick. The dog turned with a whimper, retreating to the back door of the pub with its tail between its legs. Through all the commotion and shouting, the landlord never appeared. Not wishing another encounter with the Alsatian, I drove myself straight away to the casualty ward of Portsmouth General Hospital where I revealed the fang marks that looked like Dracula had just siphoned a couple of pints of blood off me. They patched me up and gave me a jab of something, probably tetanus. Later on, at the pub after the christening, I told the landlord what his dog had done to me.

"Oh! He was just being friendly, just showing he liked you!"
"Yeah sure!" I replied and opened my shirt to show him the gauze and plasters over the wounds on my chest, telling him it was a good job I wasn't a few inches shorter as it could have been my throat! This dog's bite was certainly worse than its bark and I thought about reporting it to the local newspapers. Then I thought that they'd probably come up with something like *Jungle Boy Crawford savaged then fights off killer dog with mangle'* or something equally silly so I decided not to.

The downside of the evening that Suzanne was born is that we lost 2-1 to bottom of the table QPR; a game we'd expected to win. A few days later, Peter Morris put in a transfer request as he was unhappy playing in the reserves. There was a growing sense of unrest amongst the players, not helped by being the lowest paid in the 1st Division. The same probably went for McGarry as manager who'd lived with the frustration of managing a club on a shoestring budget for so long. This could well have influenced his decision to leave the club just over a month later.

Four days later on the Saturday, a 4-1 thumping at home to Newcastle United after leading 1-0 at half-time did nothing to improve morale. Peter Morris was recalled in our next game away to Nottingham Forest to strengthen the midfield. We managed to stem the tide a bit, winning 2-1 with goals from John O'Rourke and myself but we couldn't seem to recapture the form that we'd started the season with and went down 1-0 at home to Spurs then away to Burnley by the same score. Our luck seemed to have deserted us as well. In the Spurs game, we had a blatant penalty claim turned down after fifteen minutes when Frank Brogan was hacked down in the box by fullback Joe Kinnear. Then, ten minutes later, I witnessed one of the worst tackles I saw in my whole career when Alan Gilzean, with both feet off the ground and studs showing, took out Frank Brogan with a flying knee high tackle to fell his fellow Scot. It was nothing short of assault that could easily have finished Frank's career there and then. It was a similar challenge to the one that finished Colin Harper's career when Ipswich Town played Lazio in Rome in the UEFA Cup in 1974. What was most amazing was that the ref didn't even book Gilzean although he was booed every time he touched or came near the ball for the rest of the game. All we had from the referee, Derek Nippard who refereed Ipswich Town's cup final win over Arsenal nearly ten years later in 1978, was a free-kick while Frank was being carried off to the dressing room. Luckily his knee was just very badly bruised. Typically as often happens, the one man who shouldn't have still been on the pitch, Alan Gilzean, scored just after half-time. We laid siege to the Spurs goal for the rest of the game and, but for the brilliance of their goalkeeper Pat Jennings who McGarry had discovered at Watford, we would have won comfortably. For much of the second half, their goal was more like a coconut shy. We peppered it with shot after shot. Bill Nicholson conceded after the game that Town were unlucky not to have scored at least a point. In the highlights of 'Match of the Week' on the Sunday afternoon, neither the penalty incident nor Gilzean's tackle on Brogan were shown, much to the annoyance of many Town supporters, and the players as we used to watch it as well. The programme was produced by Anglia TV in Norwich and many believed, with good reason, that they were jealous of Town's 1st Division status. They believed that crucial parts of games were being edited out in order to see Town in as poor light as possible; the Spurs game was a classic example of this. I've always thought that both clubs would want to see each other prospering. It can only be better for the region in encouraging home grown talent to come through if nothing else.

Despite losing narrowly at Burnley which was our fifth defeat out of six games, we managed to stop the rot with a 2-2 draw at home to Everton. Joe Royle gave them the lead after 8 minutes which I cancelled out after twenty minutes with a rare long distance effort from 25 yards out, side-stepping a defender before striking a shot into the roof of the net. Their keeper, Gordon West, never saw it until it flashed past him. Peter Morris, much more renowned for his long distance shooting, celebrated his return to the first team by crashing in our second from even further out to share the points in a 2-2 draw.

Manchester United away at Old Trafford is the one game every footballer wants to play despite the poor results you usually get there. On the Wednesday before the game, I went down to Kent to take part in a charity match against southern league Hastings FC to raise money for the relations and victims of the Hither Green railway disaster the year before. Reg Flewin, the Hastings manager, had asked me if I could play and Bill McGarry agreed. It was for a good cause. There was a good crowd of over 5,000 people to watch the game on a heavy, rain soaked pitch. Near the end of the game, I felt a strong twinge in the back of my right leg and I knew I'd done a hamstring, most likely torn it. I came off the field straight away. I think Reg was even more worried than I was at first and said to me "God, what will Bill McGarry say?" He then asked me if I could possibly hide it. I said I'd try which is what I did. I didn't dare tell Bill what had happened. He'd given me the day off training the next day, Thursday, as he thought that playing a game the day before was enough exercise for two days. I was sore when I turned up on the Friday morning before leaving for Manchester. As was normal the day before games, we didn't do much physical training apart from a bit of head tennis and a few half-hearted sprints. Although I was a lot slower than usual, nothing was said. I managed to conceal my injury. I didn't regret playing in the Charity game. A pulled muscle wasn't much in the scale of things compared to all those who'd lost their lives at Hither Green.

I lasted only ten minutes of the game at Manchester United in front of a crowd of 45,769 before pulling up with my hamstring. It was one of the least sensible decisions I made whilst I was a professional. I should have told McGarry that I was injured the day before. Fullback Tommy Carroll replaced me which at least strengthened the defence but Tommy did a thigh muscle within a few minutes of coming on. He bravely carried on with a heavily strapped leg and with Mick Mills doing a good marking job on George Best and Hanks having a blinder in goal, we came away with a 0-0 draw. My injury hadn't worsened and McGarry was content that we'd at least gained a point. He possibly had other matters on his mind seeing what was shortly to follow.

A few days later, without any build up or warning, the bombshell dropped. Bill McGarry was there one minute, then gone the next to be the new manager of Wolverhampton Wanderers. I was shocked as were all the team and Town supporters as well. Bill was one of the best managers Ipswich ever had; in the top three, up there with Ramsey and Robson. Getting Town back into the 1st Division within three years had been a great achievement. Ipswich owed him a huge debt of gratitude for what he'd done for the club. I think he felt that he'd gone as far as he could with Town and needed a new challenge. We all do sometimes whatever job or profession we're in. He was the second biggest influence on my playing career after Ramsey. Though not all the players liked his manner or his methods, he was undoubtedly a motivator. I was grateful for the new found confidence that he'd given me after signing me from West Bromich Albion. When Bill left, I missed playing for him as I'd done when Alf left Ipswich and after Cullis was sacked by Wolves. I wanted to play my very best for these managers to repay them for having faith in me. It was as if things were not quite the same when they'd gone. As is natural, I was most loyal to those who treated me well. I would run and work for them all day with dog-like obedience to the point when I was ready to drop. The prospect of a new 'owner' at Ipswich was always going to be hard to adjust to. I think it stemmed from my feelings of insecurity and the lack of confidence I felt in my childhood and early youth when my loyalty could be stretched almost to the point of worship for anyone who gave me even the slightest bit of self belief in my ability. In a way, when McGarry left for Wolves, I had lost my master and mentor, leaving a psychological gap for me that wasn't going to be filled by anyone else however qualified or good they were as a manager.

Curse of the Jungle Boy

Chapter 18

"Enter Bobby and Some bloke called Ray Crawford"

After Bill had left for Wolves, Cyril Lea took over as caretaker manager. Although Cyril was still registered as a player to be used as an emergency defender if necessary, his main role was as reserve team coach. The team held up well for a few games. We drew 2-2 away to West Ham, won 2-0 away to Coventry City and brushed aside West Bromich Albion 4-1 at Portman Road. "Who needs McGarry?" many said. Four consecutive defeats followed; three in the league putting us only a few places above the relegation places and another going out of the FA Cup. Moral sank quickly to a low ebb. Life as a player had sometimes been hectic and sometimes explosive under McGarry but he always had an urgency and energy about him that kept us motivated. After Bill left, the whole place felt empty without him. You noticed the silence everywhere from the dressing room to the training ground. All the passion for the game and the intense desire to win that Bill had instilled in us seemed to have gone with him.

The first of those defeats was just before Christmas, away to Newcastle United where we lost 2-1. On the way back on the train from the north-east, I was talking with Mr John over a drink. He brought up the subject of what I planned to do when my playing days were over. I said I'd like to emigrate to South Africa and perhaps finish my playing days there, mentioning how well Roy Bailey had done. He had a good job in television and was also the director of the Football Association of South Africa. Mr John took me completely by surprise when he said if that's what I wanted to do, he wouldn't stand in my way and that I could go wherever I wanted on a free transfer when my contract ended in June. He said I'd earned it for helping Ipswich Town achieve what they had in my nine years with the club. As I was only a few months away from my 33rd birthday, it was time to seriously consider my future and explore all the options that were open to me. This was the best one I'd had up to that time.

With Danny Hegan and Peter Morris already on the transfer list and Town without a manager, the boat didn't need rocking any more than it already was. We agreed not to announce it straight away. Eileen was as excited as I was when I told her the news and I immediately wrote to Roy Bailey in Johannesburg to tell him that I'd be available on a free transfer at the end of the season and that I intended to finish my playing days in South Africa. As things turned out, the old saying of not 'counting your chickens before they have hatched' could not have been nearer the truth.

Just a few days into the new year, we were knocked out of the FA Cup 2-1 at Everton. I found an interesting reference to this game on the Internet from an Everton fan site called www.bluekipper.com. It was a supporter describing his memory of this game as an 8 year old boy. Part of the letter reads:

'I walked up the steps and saw the Goodison pitch for the first time, it is a sensation that can only be compared to the birth of your offspring, the memory is etched in your head for eternity. I stood for a brief moment awestruck. The image is as clear today as it was 32 years ago. It was 1969 and we were playing Ipswich at home and I WAS THERE. The blues made my day by winning 2-1 Royle and Hurst scored for us, and some bloke called Ray Crawford scored with his hand for them (latter day Maradona). etc.. etc.
Keep up the good work fellas, it's a top site. Steve Enty Winsford.'

Well Steve, everything you say is right, apart from one vital error. *'Some bloke called Ray Crawford'* wasn't me as you have declared (loved that one Steve - almost made it the title of the book!) but instead my fellow striker John O'Rourke who scored our goal in the 50th minute with a low drive from a Colin Viljoen cross. I have to plead '**NOT GUILTY**' to this terrible deed that has been etched on your memory for 32 years now! I am grateful for the comparison with Maradona, though not for the reasons he is most remembered for by England fans; for his *'Hand of God'* goal as he himself named it against England in the World Cup in 1986. However, I have to concede that you are not completely wrong in what you remember. I just think you have your games mixed up. My variation of the 'Hand of God' occurred two weeks later in our League game with Everton at Goodison Park which I will come to shortly.

After seven games without a goal, I returned to scoring ways with a goal against Burnley at home in a 2-0 victory. Mick Mills substituted for me in the second half and scored his first goal for the club to secure two vital points. The day after the game, Mr John went to London to interview both Billy Bingham and Bobby Robson for the vacant manager position. Most were expecting Billy to get the nod because of his greater experience but he called off his interview saying that he'd decided to stay at Plymouth and Robson was appointed manager. It wasn't the easiest of times for him to take over. The week before John O'Rourke had joined Danny Hegan and Peter Morris on the transfer list and I was about to announce that, on the strength of what Mr John had promised me, I intended to go to South Africa at the end of the season.

Our first game with Robson in charge was away to Everton in the league. On the Friday night we stayed at the Lymm Hotel in Cheshire which had some football history as the Brazil team of 1966 had stayed there during the tournament. It was only a stone's throw from where Bobby Charlton lived at the time. The following morning, we were sitting in the lounge after breakfast reading the newspapers when I noticed a young lad of no more than about twelve years of age who kept walking past the reception area and looking at us. As he was wearing a blue and white scarf, I thought he was probably an Everton fan. It was a foul day and he looked a bit rain soaked and miserable. I put my paper down and walked towards him.

"Are you alright, are you waiting for someone?" I asked him. He told me he'd taken the first train from Chesterfield at 7:00am that morning and that he was in fact an Ipswich Town fan.
"You're Ray Crawford aren't you?" he said.
"Yes, I am," I said and asked him if he'd like to join us.

Of course his face lit up. After introducing him to a few of the players, I bought him a plate of sandwiches and a pot of tea and he soon warmed up. I asked Bobby Robson if we could take him under our wing for the rest of the day to which Bobby agreed. He travelled up with us on the coach to Goodison Park. He became our mascot for the day. We had a few spare tickets so we made sure he had a good seat in the ground.

Now I can explain to Steve when *some bloke called Ray Crawford scored with his hand*. It was the 18th of January 1969 in front of a crowd of 41,725 at Goodison Park. The pitch, like Everton's nickname 'The Toffees', was an absolute quagmire that day. It was like pulling your boots in and out of sticky black treacle. Jimmy Husband put Everton one up with a header after 27 minutes. About ten minutes later, I equalized with probably my best goal that season. Danny Hegan found me with a pass on the edge of the box and Roger Kenyon, who was marking me, had been a bit too close so as I clipped it round with my left foot, turning him and giving me just the yard or so of space and the split second you need to get in a shot. The ball sat up perfectly for me to hammer a left-footer which screamed into the net. A few months later, it was voted by viewers of Anglia 'Match of the Week' as goal of the season. Half-time score 1-1. As we walked off the pitch, we were covered in mud and the referee, Mr Fussey, told us to change into a clean strip. As we only carried a few extra ones, we had to borrow Everton's away strip for the second half.

After 52 minutes came the moment, Steve, that has been *'etched in your head for eternity'*. Frank Brogan floated a high cross into their box. I went up to challenge for it with their keeper Gordon West. When I realised it was too high for me to head, I raised my arm and the ball hit my hand then cannoned off my shoulder into the net. Mr Fussey allowed the goal to stand despite the protests of the Everton players. I suppose I should have owned up at the time but when I think of all the dozens of perfectly good goals that I had disallowed in my career plus all the penalties I didn't get, this was the only volleyball like one that was allowed to stand. If you think that, in cricket these days, if the umpire doesn't give a batsman out, very few players 'walk' any more even though they know they're out but it makes up for the times they've wrongly been given out. The game became very heated after that. Frank Brogan was booked for kicking the ball away after he'd clearly been fouled and their centre-half Roger Kenyon gave me a heavy kick and yet another bruised calf.

Alex Brown soon equalized for Everton who should have won the game in the third minute of extra time when they were awarded a penalty after Jimmy Husband had collided with Billy Houghton in the box. Billy was furious when Mr Fussey blew and pointed to the spot, claiming Husband had run into him deliberately and was expecting a free-kick to be given Town's way. With only seconds to go, Alan Ball ran up and whacked his shot well to David Best's right. The ball struck the post rebounding to Alan who joyfully tapped the ball into an undefended net thinking that he'd notched up the winner. Unfortunately he'd forgotten the rule on penalties that another player must touch the ball before the penalty taker can strike the ball again. Mr Fussey rightly disallowed the goal. He blew for time a few seconds later giving us a 2-2 draw and another vital point. Well Steve, yes, I do confess but at least we've have the right game now!

Robson was happy with a point and so was the young lad we'd adopted for the day. We took him on the coach as far as Coventry where he caught his connection back to Chesterfield. On the way, we stopped for a meal and he sat beside Bobby

Robson, looking a little shy but it was good to see the thrill that the day had given him. It reminded me of the day my Dad took me to see my first match at Fratton Park. It had been a good day. In view of what was to happen with my plans of going to South Africa, it probably would have been better if I'd not scored quite so many goals as I had by that time of the season. The curse of 'the hand of God' one was soon to be on me!

On the Monday of the next week with a new manager at the helm, I thought it was time to see Mr John to confirm the free transfer he'd offered me the month before. I was so confident it would be approved by the Board, I'd already put my house on the market. When I spoke to Mr John, he said things had changed since our initial conversation. With three first team players on the transfer list and Eddie Spearritt on his way to Brighton that week, the free transfer he'd offered me was now by no means a foregone conclusion. He said he'd put my case forward as strongly as possible to the Board. Billy Houghton had put in a similar request. He wanted to finish his playing days in the north, preferably with his native Barnsley and wanted to be released for a small fee at the end of the season. Billy had a similar problem to me in that he'd proved himself a reliable defender at the top level and wasn't going to be sold off cheaply.

My intention of leaving at the end of the season was inevitably released to the local press. I told them I was finding it an increasing strain keeping my fitness up to demands of 1st Division football and that people perhaps didn't realize the injuries that I'd carried into many games that season. I continued by saying that although I had a place in the 1st team at the time, in this game you are in one minute then out the next. I didn't want to end my time at Ipswich playing for the reserves. I wanted to go out at the top level of English football if I possibly could. When asked if I had any intention of going into management or coaching when I'd finished playing, I said "No" as I thought it was too 'cut throat' for my liking. I also emphasized that whatever was decided at the Board meeting as to my future, I would never walk out on Town and would honour my contract. I said I didn't think it would come to that. I thought the club had my best interests at heart.

Unfortunately it was the start of a messy, complicated and frustrating time for both me and the club. Robson's first comments on my request were an indication of what was to follow when he said "Nothing has been settled yet as there are a lot of loose ends to tie up. I understand he wants to play in South Africa and, if that is the case, we will keep his registration as a player." One thing for sure was that Ipswich were trying to bring in as much revenue as they could. Eddie Spearritt was sold later that week to Brighton for £10,000. Town as usual were probably running at a loss and Robson was only too aware of this.

At this time, I thought Bobby might offer me an improved contract for the next season but he never once approached me to at least talk things over. Perhaps he thought I was 'old wood' that could be chopped out for at least some half decent fee. My gut feeling is that Bobby was more than ready to unload the older players at the club at the slightest chance to avoid any re-occurrence of the nightmare of player power that by all accounts had led to his downfall as manager of Fulham. McGarry had left him the legacy of a good youth policy and some very promising young players. I think Bobby was expecting to rely on it too soon and pick the fruit before it had ripened. He nearly had the chop the next season with many supporters calling for his head when Town were in deep trouble. If it hadn't been for Mr John's support, he almost certainly would have done but Mr John once said that it takes a new manager at least two years to find his feet and quite rightly stood by Bobby.

Meanwhile, Syd Chattowitz, the chairman of the Johannesburg club Rangers, had contacted Ipswich Town asking about my availability at the end of the season on a free transfer and for permission to approach me. He was told he'd have to wait for the outcome of the Board meeting. Along with his inquiry, Roy Bailey was quoted as saying that 'Crawford will find the going in South Africa a lot easier. He still has three to four years of football left in him and should be an asset to South African football'.

Robson's first home game in charge was against a star-studded, Manchester United side with Stiles, Willie Morgan, Brian Kidd, Bobby Charlton, Dennis Law and the master himself, George Best, in their line-up. They'd been playing two matches a week for much of the season so I think we were a lot fresher than they were at the time. Their League form had dipped due to their commitments in Europe. We were just below them in the league. A new record gate turned out for the game and the turnstiles were closed 45 minutes before the kick-off. After six minutes, I went in to challenge Nobby Stiles and ended up on the deck holding my head. I don't know what part of him hit me but Nobby, almost true to his name, was very 'knobbly' all over. Whichever part of him connected with you it usually hurt! Cyril Lea tended to my sore head as the referee Gordon Hill lectured him and the crowd booed. Nobby's challenge may have been to even things up. Earlier in the game, Billy Baxter had gone into George Best with an eye-watering tackle, right on the very edge of fair and foul. We dominated most of the play. Twelve minutes from the end of a game that had been littered with petty fouls, the storm that had been brewing between Billy Baxter and George Best ended up with George throwing a punch at Billy who retaliated and more punches were thrown. Luckily it was away from the play and behind the ref's back. Denis Law, known to be very volatile on occasions himself, was the unlikely peacemaker. Denis was a world class striker, one of the greatest of all time. If he had a weakness, it was reacting too easily to the strong challenges you had to expect as a striker in those days. He could be pretty nasty too. John Elsworthy said he once spat at him for very little reason although Dennis was still a teenager with Huddersfield Town at the time. Apart from breaking someone's leg, spitting in the face of a fellow professional is the probably the worst thing you can do on a football field.

This incident caused United to lose concentration. In the very next minute, Danny Hegan threaded a defence-splitting, thirty yard pass through to me, about ten yards outside their box. I saw Chris Barnard rushing through the centre. I flicked the ball first-time into his path. Just as he was about to shoot, Tony Dunne, their fullback, stretched to intercept but only succeeded in lobbing the ball over the advancing Alex Stepney into the net. Danny Hegan brought two more brilliant saves from Stepney before the final whistle blew. Danny was without question the man of the match. He'd given a performance that day that his idol George Best would have been proud of. The 1-0 win took us above United on goal difference. We had scored 41 goals to their 31 and conceded 44 compared with their 37. On paper, there wasn't that much to choose between the two teams. The game was my 350th appearance for Town. Little did I know that it was to be my last ever league game at Portman Road. It was a pity that I didn't manage to sign off with a goal that day.

On the Monday after the game, Robson was supposed to be meeting the Mayor of Ipswich which had been arranged for that afternoon but instead he was lying fast asleep on the operating table at Ipswich General Hospital. Bobby had left the ground with blood pouring from his nose after sustaining a bad cut and a broken nose in a collision with centre-half Bobby Bell in training earlier that day. There was no malice involved and although Bobby, that is Bobby Bell, was not renowned for going in lightly, it was just one of those unfortunate accidents. Two days later, I was effectively to get my nose 'bloodied' as well. The outcome of the Board meeting was that I was to be given a testimonial at the end of the season but not to be given a free transfer when my contract expired. I was to be put on the transfer list along with Billy Houghton. The reasons were that I was still an asset to the club and they couldn't afford to let me go without any compensation.

I would have to be replaced which would require a substantial fee to bring a new striker to the club who was going to score 20 plus goals a season for them in the 1st Division.

Fair enough, though I did wonder whether the Board had stopped to think they'd already benefited very well financially from my transfers since they first signed me from Portsmouth over ten years before in 1958 for £6,000. Quotes vary on how much I was sold for to Wolves. It wasn't less than £40,000 before buying me back from West Bromich Albion for £15,000 in 1966. Ipswich Town had made a healthy profit from their initial investment. It was perhaps ironic that the week I was transfer-listed, I went with Eileen to the Gaumont Cinema in Ipswich to see the one of the Spaghetti Westerns as they were called, starring Clint Eastwood in the film 'For a few dollars more' which just about summed it all up.

Robson, having come out of hospital with bandaged nose and matching black eyes, did actually have a word with me at this point, telling me I was too good a player to go to South Africa yet. He thought there was enough mileage left in me to command a reasonable fee in the transfer market. He also told me that when he retired as a player at Fulham and went to Canada to manage Vancouver that a fee had been required by Fulham to release him. The moment Johannesburg were told there would be a fee of at least £10,000 to buy me, they dropped their interest. They were in the habit of signing up overseas players only if they were on free transfers. So on the transfer list I went. I wasn't at all happy with the decision of the Board but I just had to accept it. Trying to explain to Eileen that we were no longer going to South Africa was not so easy. She was so furious that she went to the ground and had a big showdown with Robson. She said and did things that are unmentionable in this book. I think what the Board feared most was if things didn't work out in South Africa, I could return to England and sign for another club, meaning that Ipswich were losing an asset without any compensation. They had a point. It almost turned out like that. There were many ways of looking at it but I just kept on playing doing the best I could. I was disappointed that Mr John had gone back on what he'd said about giving me a 'free' at the end of the season. I still respected the great man and bore no ill will against him. I valued his friendship and wasn't going to say anything that might have changed that. I have always thought it was a great pity that Bobby Robson just failed to win the World Cup for England. If he had, Mr John would have gone down in history as being the chairman who produced the only two managers to ever achieve this.

As it was the 5th Round of the FA Cup on the following weekend, we had no match. With frozen pitches and snow blizzards all over the country, games were being brought backwards and forwards. Leeds were getting behind with their fixture list because of their European commitments so our game at Elland Road was brought forward to the next Wednesday evening. On the eve of that game, Ipswich Town announced that Charlton Athletic had contacted them with a view to signing me. Eddie Firmani, their manager, could speak to me regarding personal terms. Robson said it depended on the results of our next few games as to when the transfer would be allowed to go through. We were still too near the relegation zone for comfort. I spoke to Firmani on the phone who told me there was a club house I could move into straight away. He also promised me twice the salary that I was on at Ipswich but you had to take into consideration that the cost of living in London was going to be almost twice as high as living in Suffolk. I told him I was interested but would have to wait until Ipswich were willing to let me go. It was a strange situation of Robson's making, showing his inexperience as a young manager. I was on the transfer list but I wasn't actually for sale at the time! This was to cause both him and the club more than a little embarrassment in the weeks to come. By not being willing to sell me straight away, he was conceding how much Ipswich relied on me to get goals for them. I kept wondering why he made no attempt to persuade me to stay. Bobby was no doubt a coach of great potential but still had a lot to learn about the art of man management.

As the freezing conditions continued, our game at home to Coventry the following weekend was postponed. Our game against Arsenal the following Tuesday evening went ahead because of Highbury's revolutionary, under soil heating. It was a memorable game ending in a 2-0 victory for Town over the mighty 'Gunners' with a brilliant O'Rourke header and my 17th of the season. This turned out to be the last goal I scored for Ipswich Town. After the game, I spoke with Bill Nicholson the Spurs manager who'd watched the game, in the Marble Hall there alongside the bust of Herbert Chapman, one of the great Arsenal managers of the past. He knew I was on the transfer list but asked me how Robson could possibly let me go. If it had been up to him, he would have tried to talk me out of leaving. I took this as a great compliment from one of the greatest managers in the history of English soccer. Sadly Bill has passed away now but I will always remember that conversation with him.

Our next game against West Bromich Albion was also postponed because of the weather which was having a big say in terms of my future - no games, no points, no transfer. Since I'd been transfer-listed, more than a few supporters had written to the 'Football Star' saying this was hardly the treatment I deserved. That weekend, one fan was so annoyed he was about to make a drastic protest.

"Sir - I am distressed that the management of Ipswich Town saw fit to put Ray Crawford on the transfer list instead of allowing him to emigrate. Presumably they were motivated by a desire to show firmness, but letting Crawford go need not have set a precedent. Anyone who claimed similar treatment should have been told 'You do as much for the club as Ray Crawford has done, then you can go anywhere'. One is entitled to assume that Mr Robson influenced the Board in their decision. This being so, he has forfeited the respect of at least one keen Ipswich supporter, who moreover, feels compelled to make a protest which will cause himself considerable sadness. I intend no longer to watch football at Portman Road, with two exceptions. First, I shall attend Crawford's testimonial match at Portman Road. Second, in the event of his new team being drawn to play Ipswich, I shall attend in order to support the opposition."
Mr M.F.H Vulliamy, 'Football Star' February 22nd 1969.

At the beginning of the next week, things became even more complicated when Bert Head the Crystal Palace manager asked if he could approach me and Robson agreed. I travelled up to London and Bert impressed me with the set-up there. Like Firmani, he also said he would double my salary. At least I had a choice now although Robson was furious when it was leaked in the press. He commented "Palace have been interested from the start but I had not heard from them for a while. Bert Head rang me to speak to Crawford and, as a favour to the player, I agreed. I am very annoyed that this confidential matter has come into the open. I am determined that the Crawford transfer will not develop into an auction." Funnily enough, another letter from a Town fan had said that I was being treated and auctioned off like a 'Prize Bull'!

Personally I didn't mind this. A transfer can be a bit like an auction with the highest bidder who can also agree terms with the player getting their man or the 'antique' some may have considered me in football terms at that time. Since Ipswich had listed me, surely they should have been looking for as much as they could get for me? The Belgian club Standard Liege also approached Ipswich in the same week. They were not given permission to talk to me. The Board were, by now, getting more than a little embarrassed by the whole situation. More complications were to follow.

Our next two scheduled Saturday games were away to Wolves and at home to Leicester City. Robson said they would be my last two games for Ipswich. The day of the Wolves game was also the 6th Round of the FA Cup but Leicester, due to the long spell of freezing weather, had still not managed to play their 5th Round tie against Liverpool at Filbert Street. The FA had ordered the winners to play Mansfield Town who'd reached the 6th Round the next weekend when we were due to play Leicester. This meant that, if Leicester beat Liverpool, our game would be postponed. Robson, who was by now under strong pressure from the Board, said that only in the case of Leicester winning would my transfer be allowed to go ahead. In fairness to Charlton, it couldn't be put off any longer and Town had a cushion of ten points above the relegation places. Almost everybody and Robson, fully expected Liverpool would win so that Leicester City would be my last game for Ipswich the following weekend. It looked a safe bet as City were struggling only one point above the drop zone. When I ran out onto the pitch at Molineux that weekend against Wolves, I didn't think it would be my last game for Town. Derek Dougan by then had become an idol there. Since 'The Doog' and I had gone our different ways after leaving Portsmouth over ten years before in 1958, in one way or another we'd survived and succeeded at the top level of the game. There were chances for both sides but we generally controlled the game. I should have scored with only their talented young keeper Phil Parkes to beat, crashing a shot against the bar but it just wasn't to be that day for Ipswich or me. In the dying seconds of the game, Mike Kenning, who always seemed to score against Ipswich, scored again just as he'd done for Charlton Athletic and Norwich City before. This time it was to salvage a 1-1 draw that Wolves hardly deserved.

Liverpool were held to a draw by Leicester City at Filbert Street. We were still odds-on to win the replay two days later on the Monday night, meaning that Leicester would be free to play Ipswich the following weekend in what Robson said would be my last game for Ipswich Town.

Chapter 19

"Sold and sacked"

On the Monday night, the totally unexpected happened when Leicester City beat Liverpool 1-0 at Anfield in their FA Cup 5th Round replay. Their young keeper, Peter Shilton, had a blinder including saving a Tommy Smith penalty. It was a shock result; not the result Robson had banked on at all. Our game against Leicester City was postponed immediately. After training the next day, Bobby went off on a scouting trip to Wales to watch Swansea play Bradford City that evening to see if City had any players who could possibly be included in a player plus cash deal for Billy Houghton as they hadn't been offered the £15,000 Robson was looking for. Unknown to me, before leaving, Bobby had announced to the press that I still couldn't go even though Leicester City had won. I didn't find out about this until Firmani, whose patience had all but run out by then, rang me at home later that day saying he was coming down to Ipswich the following morning to get things sorted out once and for all. He told me he'd expressed his views very strongly on the matter when Mr John had rung him to tell him of yet another change of plan.

Robson arrived back at Portman Road early the next afternoon. In an emergency Board meeting, he was overruled, finally allowing my transfer to go ahead. The Board said they couldn't go back on what Bobby had assured them although he did have a point saying that he had my best interests at heart. A home game had been re-arranged against Manchester City the Tuesday evening after the postponed Leicester game and it would be fitting for me to play my last game for Town in front of the home fans. I would have liked that too but, at about 4:30 that afternoon in the presence of Eddie Firmani who'd been waiting patiently at Portman Road for most of that day, I finally put pen to paper and signed for Charlton Athletic for £12,000. What a cheek when I come to think of it! Now almost exactly ten years and over 270 goals later, my value had only gone up six grand. I never did know much about antiques!

I will never blame Mr John for how my time with Ipswich finished. I know football is as much about running a business as a football team. Failure to recognise this by any chairman, Board or manager, is asking for disaster. With South Africa ruled out, for Eileen the next best thing she could have wished for was moving to London which was much closer to Portsmouth. It was also a slightly safer place to live. The same day that I signed for Charlton, the Kray twins Ronnie and Reggie, were sentenced to 30 years in jail after a 39 day trial. It had taken almost as long before Charlton finally signed me, so in a sense my trial was over as well.

The same day that I became a Charlton Athletic player, another deal went through when Ken Hancock was sold for £7,000 to Spurs as cover for Pat Jennings. Ken hadn't been on good relations with Robson from his very first day in charge of training. He said that Robson had 'treated him like a child'. Bobby was quickly coming to terms with the business side of managing a poor club but losing good, experienced players in doing it. By selling Eddie Spearritt, Hanks and myself, Bobby had shown signs of his future prowess in the transfer market but Mr John had to bail him out of deep trouble the next year when many supporters were calling for his neck. The 'old heads' he'd been all too quick to see the back off, could have helped him avoid the crisis he was to find himself in.

After a quiet debut in a 1-1 draw at home to Carlisle United, I opened my scoring account for the 'Addicks' at Carrow Road against Norwich City. I took a lot of stick on that day having played in so many derby games for Ipswich against them. I had the last word scoring the only goal of the game. One thing that immediately struck me at Charlton was the very generous pre-match meals the players were allowed, of steak and toast followed by rice pudding and as much tea or coffee as you liked; a relative feast compared to my previous clubs. It was a bit over-indulgent. In a way, it went hand in hand with the drinking habits of some of the first team players. It hadn't taken me long to realise that many of them were boozing and clubbing almost every night of the week, including Friday nights before matches. I went as far as mentioning this to Firmani, but he wasn't strong enough to deal with it, so it went on. I'd known of some very good players who were guilty in this respect but were still good enough to produce the goods on the day. Most of the players at Charlton weren't good enough to burn the candle at both ends and still maintain the necessary performance levels. After the win at Norwich, we needed to win almost every game and a couple of draws soon after put paid to any hopes of promotion.

At the end of the season I returned to Ipswich for my testimonial at Portman Road. Ironically it was against Wolverhampton Wanderers managed by Bill McGarry who, ahead of the game, had kindly said "Ray is without doubt the best player I have ever worked with. I regard him as a wonderful example of a professional sportsman both on and off the field, so I am very pleased to bring the Wolves team here to Portman Road tonight. He is the only player I would do this for, and I wish Ray all the best for the future."

I was completely taken aback by a crowd of 16,474 loyal supporters that evening who greeted me when I ran out onto the Portman Road pitch for my last ever appearance in a Town shirt. To be honest, I hadn't expected even half that number to turn out. If I'd had any doubts about supporters not forgiving me for leaving Ipswich twice for other clubs, those doubts were removed that night once and for all. I will remember that night with great pride for the rest of my life. Just for the record, Town won 6-0. The result didn't matter; it was just kind of McGarry and Wolves, one of the great clubs in English soccer to honour me in this way, especially as they were on a tight schedule, leaving for their close season tour the next day.

My Testimonial raised about £3,000 that night, and, after paying the ground staff and laying on the food and drink for the reception at the First Floor Night Club in Ipswich, it left me with about £1,800 pounds. I didn't care about the money so much but I was annoyed when Hugh Curran, who'd played for Wolves that evening, came up to me asking for more food after midnight. I said I was sorry but there was no more food. All the restaurant staff had gone home. He then told me what he thought of me in no uncertain terms but I just ignored him as he was half pissed anyway.

When we arrived home early the next morning, most important to me that night was not only been all the loyal fans who turned up but also what the two most influential managers in my career had said before the game to the crowd and the players. Sir Alf Ramsey was the guest of honour that evening and, after being introduced to all the players, many of whom he knew very well of course, he said ...

"Ray is one of the Ipswich Town all-time greats, and I am grateful to have had the privilege of being able to share part of his career with him."

With the crowd cheering after that tribute, I was chocking back the tears. I defy any man who wouldn't have felt the same way.

Chapter 20

"Sacked"

Three months later after pre-season training at Charlton, we were fit and ready to go. I sensed a better attitude in the team as a whole. There was one problem before the season started in that the player's contracts didn't include any win bonus. Michael Gliksten, the club chairman, felt he'd paid out the season before without getting the results so he didn't see why he should pay out again. I think this was the only time that we fought together as a team in my whole time there, telling him that, if we played well, attendances would improve but, if he took it away, it would have the reverse effect. He finally relented at 4:00pm the day before the 1969-1970 season started with our home game against Preston North. It was just as well he did as all the players, including myself, had agreed to strike if necessary.

We justified our win bonus. We were unbeaten after six games with four victories and two draws, going top of the 2nd Division. I'd scored four goals including a brace against Sheffield United. Unfortunately, the next half dozen games were as bad as the first six were good, drawing three and losing three including a 5-0 thrashing away to Swindon Town and an even worse one at Bristol City 6-0. The last of those six games, a 1-1 draw away to Hull City in late September 1969, was to be my last game for Charlton Athletic.

Firmani and his coaching staff didn't seem to have any answers to the loss of form and failed to restore the confidence of the team. It wasn't helped by a lot of the players lapsing back into the bad habits of the previous season. If you are being professional in your approach, you expect the same from the players around you. If you know some of them are behaving irresponsibly in their private lives, somehow you feel distanced from them which usually shows when it comes to match days. I'm not saying everybody at my previous clubs were saints. It was usually only the odd individual or two. I felt I was in the minority; separate from them both on and off the pitch. I was beginning to find it hard to motivate myself and starting to suffer from the same low morale that was running through the whole club.

After the poor results, Firmani started to have the first team in for extra training on Sunday mornings. On the morning after a 4-0 defeat away to Huddersfield Town, having missed two games through tonsillitis, I joined the first team squad for training on the Monday morning. There was a rumour going around that we were going away for a few days training. No-one knew where or exactly when. I went to see Firmani to ask him if there was any truth in this as Eileen and the girls had all gone down with flu. A doctor had been round to see them and told me they should all stay in bed for the week. Eddie denied the rumour. For some reason, he kept us all in the dark. Several of the players said they wouldn't go if the rumour turned out to be true, complaining that not enough notice had been given in consideration for their families and anything they might have prearranged for those days. I was used to the no-nonsense style of McGarry who expected discipline from his players but would also do his very best to be honest with you and help you if you had any problems off the field.

The Tuesday morning after training, I again asked both Firmani and the first team coach whether we were going away but they still both denied it. After training that afternoon, Firmani called a meeting with the first team. He told us to be ready to leave at 10:00am the next morning for special training at Bisham Abbey and that we would be away until the Saturday game at home to Blackburn Rovers. I reminded Firmani after the meeting that my family were ill and if I could be excused from the trip to look after them. He wasn't prepared to listen and said he expected to see me the next morning ready to leave with the first team squad.

When I returned home, Eileen was very ill, trying to nurse the children when she should have been resting. I told her to get back into bed and rang Firmani to explain the situation again. He told me bluntly that failure to turn up the next morning could lead to severe consequences. I put the phone down thinking what a two-faced bastard he was. Needless to say, I didn't turn up the next morning and the day after I received a letter from Charlton Athletic informing me that my contract with the club had been terminated. I'd been sacked for the first time in my career. It didn't surprise me but my conscience was clearer than theirs. I'd stuck with my family when they needed me. Their health was more important than a couple of training sessions with a club that was out of order. A week later, Eileen and my daughters had recovered but I was out of a job.

I appealed against my dismissal and that great man of the PFA, Cliff Lloyd, represented my case to the FA. On the day of the hearing, he looked at me gravely and said "We haven't a chance of winning you know Ray. I know the committee and the way they think." He was right. They backed the club showing the same lack of sympathy or consideration that Charlton had shown to me and my family. At the tribunal, the club added to their case against me that I'd missed the two games previous to the Bisham Abbey trip, making a big fuss about it even though I was able to give evidence of a doctor's certificate confirming that I had tonsillitis at the time. As Cliff had predicted, I lost the appeal.

Any club that treats honest players like they had dealt with me, hardly deserve another word. As they say, "what goes around, comes around". They had neither the quality in depth nor the discipline to achieve promotion. As the season went on, Charlton went from bad to worse finishing third from bottom of the 2nd Division. I had little pity for Firmani who was sacked before the end of the season with his sidekick, Theo Foley, taking over. Perhaps the 'Curse of Jungle Boy' had struck again? Two seasons later, they were relegated to the 3rd Division with gates down to 3,000 until Andy Nelson, my old mate from Ipswich took over. He'd been manager at Gillingham and learned about management from Alf Ramsey in his time at Ipswich. It only took Andy one season to get Charlton back up into the 2nd Division in 1974-1975.

I was now unemployed for the first time in my life and signed on the dole at the local Labour Exchange. I just sat around the house wondering what to do next and even thought of giving up football. I'd rarely been as down in my whole career and just kept torturing myself as to how everything had gone so wrong since I'd left Ipswich Town. Ironically, Eileen had never been so happy. In those uncertain days, we were perhaps closer than at any other time of our married life. She tried to lift my mood, sometimes dragging me into central London to shop with her and the girls. On one outing, we went to Harrods in Knightsbridge. We were looking around the famous food hall there when I was approached by quite an elderly lady who asked me for my autograph. I was very surprised that she'd recognized me. She told me she was a keen football fan and a lifelong Chelsea supporter. I signed with my best wishes on the back of her shopping list. Whether she knew it or not, I didn't tell her I'd just been sacked by Charlton. Neither did I think of it at the time that I could easily have had a job at Harrods. With a couple of references from Mr John, an ex-Etonian and Sir Alf Ramsey, I possibly could have been earning more by perhaps selling expensive carpets to Arab sheiks and the aristocracy of London rather than continuing with a career in football! The trouble was that, even though I was only 33 years old, in terms of being a professional footballer I was getting on a bit which somehow made me feel old as a person as well, not realizing how young I still was with my whole life still ahead of me.

After a few weeks of head scratching, wondering which way to turn, completely out of the blue came a phone call from the ex-Cardiff player Steve Gammon who was then manager of Kettering FC in the Southern League. Steve was about the same age as me and I'd played against him a few times when I was with Ipswich. He told me the club was near the bottom of their league and, though they were playing quite well, were in need of a goal scorer. He hoped that I might be able to help them out. Under FIFA rules, I could sign for a non league club without a transfer fee but not a League club unless a transfer fee was paid. As the wages weren't enough to survive on, Steve had mentioned the possibility of a job working for the club chairman's dry cleaning business. With no other irons in the fire, I arranged to go up and see them. I probably should have waited for another league club to come along but I panicked. Unemployment had come as a big shock to me. I figured it wouldn't do any harm just to have a look at the set-up there, to meet Steve and find out what the chairman had to offer in the way of a job to top up my wages. I'd been to their stadium the Rockingham Ground years before in 1961 when Alf Ramsey took an Ipswich team to play out a 2-2 draw in a friendly on the official opening night of their floodlights. Since then, it had changed out of all recognition with new dressing rooms and new stands. The whole ground had a more professional feel about it and was certainly well up to 4th Division standards at the time. Some big name players had been there before, including Derek Dougan, Ron Atkinson, and Jack Froggatt the former Portsmouth player. Steve Gammon had represented Wales at Under 23 level and impressed me a lot, as did the chairman in the way he talked about his ambitions for the club. It didn't take me very long to make the decision and, after agreeing on my wages, they took me out to a very expensive restaurant for lunch. When we returned to the club later that afternoon, I signed for Kettering FC.

I made my debut at home to Burton Albion and it was not the greatest start I could have made. We were awarded a penalty in the first half. As the regular penalty taker was injured at the time, I was volunteered to take it. I stepped up and made good contact with the ball but their keeper made a fantastic save, probably knowing full well who I was. With great embarrassment, I told everyone at half-time that Alf Ramsey had once banned me from taking penalties at Ipswich! But football like most other sports is a great leveller. I made amends by scoring my first goal for Kettering in the second half.

After a few weeks of travelling up by car, Charlton told me they wanted me out of their club house in London. I asked the Kettering club chairman if he could find us a house to rent. He obliged very quickly and we moved up there a couple of weeks later. Soon after that, I took up the chairman's offer to work in his dry cleaning business. There were no more leisurely afternoons playing golf, going to the races or watching TV. I was now Ray Crawford, the dry cleaning salesman, driving around in a white van, knocking on people's doors asking if they needed any clothes cleaning. I felt a bit like a jumped up ice cream salesman except the Mr Whippy music wasn't blasting out of the van. I was grateful for the chance to earn some extra cash. It was still winter and more often than not, cold and raining as I drove from estate to estate and trudged from house to house. The worst thing about it wasn't the cold so much but the fact that I found the job mind-numbingly boring. It wasn't long before I started asking myself what on earth I was doing asking people if they needed any clothes cleaning, having been playing and scoring against Arsenal at Highbury in the 1st Division no more than six months before? In opting to play non league football, I'd effectively relegated myself as a player all of five divisions in less than a year! With all respect to Kettering FC, I'd done it all very wrong after Charlton had sacked me.

People used to turn up at their front doors in all states of dress, some women without much on at all. One miserable afternoon as it poured with rain, a man with a cigarette hanging out his mouth and a huge belly bulging inside a string vest stretched to its limits, stood before me in his doorway. It was just like a sketch from 'The Two Ronnies'. After I'd given him my usual sales talk, he gave me a long hard look and took a deep drag on his fag before telling me to 'Piss off!' and slammed the door in my face. I turned back to my white van with the rain running down my face, my hair drenched and matted to my head, saying angrily out loud "I've had enough of this crap!" I stuck it out though as I couldn't afford not to.

It made me long for the weekends to arrive and the games to come. I was banging in the goals with a few hat-tricks already to my name in the short time that I'd turned out for Kettering. A chance meeting with one of the all time greats of football was to be the turning point of my time there. One Saturday, we played Hereford United who were player-managed by the legendary John Charles, once of Leeds United and Juventus fame. In his time there, he'd probably become the most loved Welshman in Italian history scoring no less than 260 goals in 543 games, helping them to win three championships and two Italian cup finals. He'd always been a big chap. He was carrying a bit of extra weight by then but he'd lost none of his heading or passing skills, making up for his loss of pace with good positional play. He scored with a bullet of a header that afternoon giving our keeper no chance as it flew into the net. It was a privilege to see him play for the only time in my life and also to join him for a drink in the club bar after the game. He told me this was to be his last year as a player. We compared notes about our careers. Just before we parted company, he said to me "Ray, you should still be playing in the Football League," confirming what I had already realized. From that moment on, the advice of the great man was constantly in mind until the end of the season by which time Kettering had climbed from near the bottom to finish mid-table in their division. I scored over 20 goals in 34 games for them. I felt I'd done my bit to help them out as they'd helped me. The thought of playing in the Southern League for another season and, much worse, being a dry cleaning salesman for another year made me determined to get back into league football. The only problem was how to go about it. Help was soon at hand from a loyal old friend, Ted.

Having kept in contact with Ted since leaving Ipswich, I told him in a phone call that I thought my career was going nowhere. Ted suggested I approach Colchester United, saying they were a good club to play for and that Dick Graham was an excellent manager. I took Ted's advice. I had to ask Eileen to ring Dick Graham as I couldn't personally market myself. It's a strange law that a player can't approach a club offering his services as a player yet the wife can ring on your behalf! Dick told Eileen he was very interested in signing me and that he would sort things out between Kettering and Charlton; both clubs might expect a fee. True to his word, Dick arranged everything and within a week had bought me from Kettering and paid Charlton £1,000 for my contract. We moved back to Ipswich, only eighteen miles from Colchester where we still had a lot of friends. It was a great feeling to be back in league football again. It was one of the best moves of my career and also a chance to chase the goal-scoring record of my hero Jimmy Greaves.

Chapter 21

"Giant Killers"

When the new season started, Dick Graham soon impressed me with his deep understanding and knowledge of the game. He had previously been coach at West Bromich Albion and Crystal Palace. Our pre-season training nearly killed me. Apart from that, it was always interesting. Dick kept ringing the changes which kept us thinking all the time. He also expected a high level of professionalism from all his players, both on and off the field. One of the first things that struck me was that he never overdid the planning and tactics before games. He thought it made players over cautious and not adventurous enough. He was also very open minded about how games could go and encouraged us to think for ourselves as much as possible. I'd never known such an original approach from a manager before.

Before the start of the season, Mr Graver, the Colchester United chairman, said he'd give me ten pounds for every goal I scored. This didn't apply to the rest of the players which I thought it was a bit unfair so I turned his offer down, telling him that I couldn't score goals without the help of my team mates. What I should have done was keep my mouth shut and ask him to put it in a pot for me and the lads to have a good piss-up at the end of the season. As it was, I'd kissed goodbye to three hundred and forty quid as I scored 31 goals in all competitions that season. The old warhorse had looked 'a gift horse in the mouth'! With hindsight, the only problem was that Mr Graver resigned well before the season ended.

It took me a few games to get going, finally breaking my duck with both goals in a 2-0 win at Barrow. Shortly after that, Dick Graham had to go into hospital to have a kidney stone removed. He caught flu after the operation and was away for over a month. Dennis Mochan, the 1st team trainer took over. We went on a run of poor results including a 4-1 thrashing at Bournemouth with their rising young star Ted MacDougall netting all four. The same night, Jimi Hendrix, one of my favourite musicians whose brilliant guitar play I'd always marvelled at, died from a drug overdose in London.

By the time Dick came back, I'd scored 8 goals in 12 games including my first hat-trick for the club in a 3-0 win over Crewe Alexandra. We were in the lower half of the 4th Division. Results soon improved and we went on an unbeaten run winning five of our next eight games including a 1-0 win over York City at Layer Road when Alf turned up from nowhere to watch me score the only goal of the game.

I scored my second hat-trick of the season in the first round of the FA Cup against the Sussex county side Ringmar at Layer Road. I made a little bit of football history that day. I'd become the only player ever to have scored hat-tricks in the FA Cup, the European Cup and the League Cup. Whether this record still stands I'm not sure but I was the first to this 3xCups hat-trick. Dave Smith, the local football journalist, wrote of my achievement "In my view, Crawford is one of the most underrated players of all time and perhaps this record will help put this right". It was a great compliment although I didn't think I had anything more to prove. Through the FA Cup that year, I was to leave one final reminder of what I done in the past and was still capable of, just a few months before my 35th birthday.

In the next game, a 4-0 home win over Brentford, an unusual thing happened which you might expect to see on TV's 'A Question of Sport' in the 'what happened next' part of the quiz. We were already two up after fifteen minutes when Chic Brodie, the ex-Manchester City keeper, was involved in a freak accident. Suddenly from nowhere, a dog rushed onto the pitch (was it 'Dick's Dirty Dog'?) and started to chase the ball which was rolling towards Chic in his goal area. Just as he reached down to collect the ball, the dog crashed into him leaving Chic in a painful heap on the ground. It took him several minutes to recover in which time the dog had disappeared; probably sent off for violent conduct?

Two weeks before Christmas, we reached the 3rd Round of the FA Cup beating Cambridge United 3-0 at Layer Road. The next week, Dick bought Brian Lewis from Oxford City and Dave Simmons, a big striker from Aston Villa. It soon paid dividends. We beat Lincoln City away on Boxing Day 2-1 with goals from the two new signings. Although we went into the New Year only 9th in the division, we had a lot of games in hand.

Just after the turn of the year, one of my Colchester team mates Brian Hall, suggested a business proposition to me. He said he'd seen vacant premises in a prime shopping area in central Colchester, about two hundred yards from the Town Hall, which he thought would be a good place for a sports shop. I had no business experience at all. After having a look at the place, I thought it was a great idea. I asked Eileen what she thought of it and she told me to leave it well alone. I didn't listen and without getting any advice or consulting a solicitor, we went ahead like two hog-headed idiots. I put up £1,300 to rent the shop and buy the necessary stock. It doesn't sound much now but it was a lot in those days. I naively thought that, when I finally hung up my boots, it would be a nice little nest egg to fall back on. In time, it only proved to be a very rotten egg. We should have gone in as a Limited Company, allowing us the option of voluntary bankruptcy if things didn't work out. I was like a child playing with fire and had lit the long fuse of a financial time bomb that was eventually going to blow up in my face.

We were drawn against Barnet in the next round of the Cup, the first time the 'U's' had reached the 4th Round of the FA Cup for twelve years. The game was postponed twice because of the weather. We finally managed to play on the Tuesday evening, three days after the worst ever crowd disaster in Britain at Ibrox Park when 66 people had died shortly before the end of a local derby game between Rangers and Celtic. We won a hard game at Barnet with the only goal of the game coming from a thirty yard blockbuster from Mick Mahon. In the next round away to 3rd Division Rochdale, I came a real cropper in the game. I opened the score with a classic far post header but, in my follow through, I collided head first with the post as well. I had a very strong nut as big Ron Yeats found out in one of my last games for West Bromich Albion against Liverpool at Anfield when he lost his temper and head-butted me. I just stood there as he staggered backwards holding his head. He'd come off a lot worse than me but heading a post at pace was pushing things too far. I came to lying flat on my back with the blur of Dennis Mochan slowly coming into focus and a large policeman hovering over me, looking as if he wasn't about to inform me of my rights; more like a priest about to read me my last rites! I recovered after lengthy treatment but so did Rochdale who came back strongly to be 3-1 up with only five minutes to go. By that time, many of the travelling Colchester supporters had left the ground. They missed two late goals, again from Brian Lewis and Dave Simmons and we scraped a 3-3 draw. Dick's investment was producing instant dividends.

On the Monday morning, we were down at the seaside preparing for the replay at Layer Road that evening. As Dick Graham said in his memoirs of that day, we were training on a green patch of grass not far from our hotel and the sea when a little boy appeared from nowhere with a radio in his hand. He went up to Dick and said "By the way mister, do you want to know who you're playing in this round of the cup? You're playing Leeds United at Colchester," and we all cheered at the news.

The replay was easy and we won 5-0. The same day things were boiling up at Portman Road. My old mate Billy Baxter, club captain and the only remaining player from the Championship winning team, was suspended by Ipswich Town for comments he'd made in a Sunday newspaper, saying that the "club was going to the dogs". Billy was suspended for 14 days and it was the start of a sad and controversial end to Billy's brilliant career at Ipswich, one of the most loyal players through thick and thin Town has ever had. I can't put that too strongly or without very strong feeling.

The weekend before the Leeds game, I gave warning that I was in pretty good form, scoring both goals in a 2-1 win in the League against Cambridge United at Layer Road, bringing my tally to 22 goals for the season. The day before, Shepard and Mitchell had landed back safely in the Pacific Ocean after a four and a half hour walk on the moon. Although it's not an expression I ever used, a week later we were to be 'over the moon' as well. There were lots of other events outside football in the week leading up to the game. London Bridge had been sold to the 'Yanks' and gone to Arizona in the USA, Mick Jagger had married Bianca in St Tropez, the Minister for Education, Margaret Thatcher at the time, had been called 'Thatcher, the Snatcher' after taking away the free milk that school kids drank everyday at school (the best thing I remember from my schooldays) and Cadbury's had brought out a new selection of chocolate coins to match the new ones. Decimalisation was to kick in for real the next week. After decimalisation, there were only 100 new pence as opposed to 240 in the old pound. It caused a lot of confusion and head scratching to work out the value of the new coins when shopping. The new one pence coin was a lot lighter than the old one and so a lot less painful on the head if you were hit by one! Literally overnight, coin-throwing fans were reduced from 240 throws to a 100 throws for one pound. You could say that footballers had benefited from the 'change'! By coincidence, the bookies had given us odds of 100-1 to beat Leeds.

With six of the team over thirty, we'd been nicknamed 'Grandad's Army'. There was also plenty of winding up from both sides in the days leading up to the game. Billy Bremner said "Where's Colchester?" and I'd returned fire by saying "I can score against Leeds as easily as a farmer knocks off rabbits". There was some truth in my prediction. I'd scored 5 goals in my previous 4 games against Leeds and my final tally was to going to be 7 in 5.

Leeds flew down on the Friday, the day before the game and booked in at the Royal Hotel in Clacton where Revie always insisted on staying when Leeds were playing in that part of the south–east; he was incredibly superstitious. On this occasion, he hadn't even allowed his wife to make the trip as apparently Don had banned her from all away cup-ties. The last one she'd been to Leeds had lost. Dick Graham was a bit superstitious as well. We weren't far away, just a little way up the coast from them at the same hotel at Holland-on-Sea where we'd stayed before all our Cup games that season. We had a few things in our favour apart from the home advantage. Billy Bremner, the Scottish equivalent of Alan Ball, was ruled out the day before the game through injury. We also thought we could get at them in the air as Jack Charlton was recovering from a broken nose, making heading a football an unpleasant prospect. Norman Hunter was a very good defender on the ground but he was not so strong in the air. We knew that, Gary Sprake, their keeper was a great shot stopper but had become increasingly unsure on crosses. All week up to the game, we practised crosses from all angles, time and time again. The crosses were designed to reach Dave Simmons and myself just outside the six-yard box, a sort of no-man's land for keepers when they're not sure whether to stay on their line or come out and catch the ball.

A lot has been said and written about the game. I won't be able to do it any more justice than the reconstruction of the game by BBC Radio of which I have a copy. It was directed by Brian Moore; for me simply the best TV football commentator of all time with John Motson coming a close second. For me, Brian and Ron Atkinson were the 'bacon and eggs' of TV football commentary. Brian has sadly has passed away now so I'd like this recording to be a tribute to him as well as Colchester United. I was always a fan of his and myself one of his. Not long before he died, Brian did a TV series called 'The Brian Moore Interviews' and I will always be grateful to him for the honour of being the subject of one of those programmes in which he introduced me as being 'one of the most devastating goal scorers of all time'. In the recording, there is a Narrator, H.M. is Hal Mason, the club historian, I am R.C., D.G. is Dick Graham, G.S. is Graham Smith our keeper and D.C. is David Coleman, the BBC TV commentator of that day.

D.G. "Leeds were probably the most feared side in Europe at the time, the equivalent of Colchester beating Barcelona, Juventus or Milan."
Narrator: "February the 13th 1971 and another day when the FA Cup turned the form book upside down. On one hand, Colchester United of the 4th Division, an unspectacular collection of players who'd seen better days. On the other side, the mighty Leeds United, simply the best side of their generation. Leeds couldn't

lose, but of course, they did."

G.S. "It was not a fluke. If anybody watches the game they can see that Colchester played delightful, penetrative football and we were prepared excellently by Dick Graham and we went into the game believing that we could win. If you ask any of the players playing, none of them were surprised. We won on merit and, on the day, eleven humans beat eleven humans from Leeds."

R.C. "We played well. We had a manager who planned everything. He was a crafty old devil and he knew Leeds needed the wide open spaces. I mean Elland Road is a big ground and they used to ping the ball around and get teams to chase it, so Dick obviously thought that if he could make the pitch seem smaller, it would help us out. He put some benches along the side and sat the stewards and the first-aiders on them and, on the film, I think you can see a chair on each corner with somebody sitting in it. He really was a crafty old devil!"

Narrator: "That was Ray Crawford, ex-England and Ipswich centre-forward who scored twice that afternoon. Before him, goalkeeper Graham Smith who also had an important part to play in this most unlikely tale. Unlike most upsets, this one took place in the 5th round, the last sixteen. Colchester had already achieved much by reaching this stage although their play hadn't always been impressive."

H.M. "Well, they'd struggled against a Sussex County side Ringmar in the 1st Round and they weren't very impressive against Cambridge in the second or Barnet in the third, then at Rochdale of course we were three one down with five minutes left and half the Colchester supporters had gone home and didn't see the dramatic equalizers by Lewis and Simmons."

D.G. "When I knew we'd got Leeds, I got them all together and I said 'Now look, the week before we play Leeds, you're probably not going to see anything again like this in your lives. There's going to be all the media coming down here. It's going to be the match of the round. I said what we've got to do is decide that we're going to enjoy every moment. We're not going to get upset. We're not going to fall out with anybody. We're going to welcome them and make sure that they remember us. At the time I think Leeds had gone nineteen matches and only lost one. We'd gone 23 or 24 and only lost three and I think they had eight current internationals in the side whereas I only had one former international in my side and that was Ray Crawford. We went to Holland-On-Sea and stayed there the night before and on the morning of the match I just went for a walk and I sat on a bench on the promenade there. It was a lovely morning, the sea was calm and I had no doubt in my mind at that moment that we were going to beat Leeds. I had no doubt at all. I may have, on the way to the ground, got a few butterflies but the atmosphere in the dressing room before the match was absolutely marvellous.

There weren't the usual nervous fidgets which you often see with some of the lads when they're a bit worried. It was a nice feeling. We certainly knew a lot more about Leeds United than they knew about us. I mean they were on the television every weekend and so I personally knew all I wanted to know about their players. In fact I think I was one up on Don because he only saw us play once. We certainly knew more about Leeds United than they knew about us."

G.S. "I think that maybe they had come to Colchester believing that it was a formality and I suppose they weren't allowed to get into their stride. We hustled them, harried them and they may have been surprised by the quality of the soccer we played. Believe it or not, I wasn't very busy during the game. Leeds did not pose a great threat to us as we actually took the game to them. The first goal was worked by Brian Lewis putting a free-kick deep into the six-yard area as we knew that Sprake was weak on cross balls. Anything played into that area he was reluctant to leave his line. He was worse than me in actual fact. Ray Crawford was lethal with his head and Brian Lewis could put the ball on a postage stamp and bang, it happened; that was the first goal."

R.C. "I remember going down the left hand side and Jack Charlton pulled me back to give the free-kick away and Lewy came up and of course we'd been training all week on these free-kicks and Brian Lewis put over this cross on the edge of the six-yard box, Sprakey came half and half and I headed it in and we went one up."

D.C. "Now this free-kick could be awkward because any ball in the air is a real test... the kick being taken by Brian Lewis... oh and Sprakes missed it!... and Gibbs... Crawford's got it!!... Ray Crawford... who's scored so often at all levels of football has done it again... eighteen minutes gone... and 4th Division Colchester lead Leeds one nil!"

G.S. "The second goal was a ball played through the middle, played out wide. I think it was Brian Gibbs. Again another cross whipped in, Crawford went for it with Reaney and the ball went in off the post, and it was a goal."

D.C. "Kurila... Gilchrist... good ball... Gibbs... Crawfords there... and Simmons... two nil for Colchester!!... and Leeds in the most desperate mess."

R.C. "Gibbo just knocked this ball in early and I came running in and actually headed the ball onto Paul Reaney's back and the ball just dropped and I suppose being a striker you're always looking for something and the ball just sat there beautiful for me. Sprakey came out to pick it up because Jack Charlton had called him and as he came out I just swung my left foot at it and it went in off the post. Big Simmo was following it up anyway so if it had come out he would have got it and we went two up and that was the score at half-time and I remember Norman

Hunter put his arm on my shoulder and said 'Do you know what Ray, I could have got that first ball but I thought Sprakey was going to come and get it' and I just laughed and he went in his dressing room and I went into mine."

Narrator: "Half-time, Colchester two Leeds nil, both goals to Ray Crawford. It was hard enough for those who were there to comprehend. As for those who weren't, Hal Mason explains."

H.M. "I was doing the scorelines for the PA on that day and when I went over with the first goal the bloke on the other end said 'Are you sure you've got the score the right way round?' I said 'Yes fine' and when I went through again on twenty-five minutes and said 'Colchester two Leeds nil', he said 'Pull the other one!' He really genuinely thought I was joking and it was a hell of a job to convince him I had given him the correct score! When it got to three, well he was speechless... so was I!"

D.C. "Cooper for Leeds... turning into trouble... Crawford... Lewis for Colchester... and Simmons one against one here... Simmons and Reaney... it's there!!... And the scenes at this ground... really... what can one expect... 4th Division Colchester three, Leeds United nil and no one can complain or quarrel about that not being a true reflection of the game."

R.C. "I remember getting the ball just inside their half and playing it out to Brian Lewis who hit a first time ball, must have been a good forty yard ball down the middle. Sprakey came out, Reaney went in, they got in a bit of trouble and big Simmo went in and headed it into the net and we were three up and of course we were in the crowd celebrating with them. I can see it now, just like yesterday. On their worst day you'd probably think we might get a draw, to be three nil up against them was fantastic."

D.G. "I had two of their players, man to man marked and I gave John Kurila the job of marking Allan Clarke and John Gilchrist marking Johnny Giles and it worked like a charm. Then Don Revie changed his set-up. He moved Giles up front and Allan Clarke into midfield."

D.C. "It's a corner and one has the feeling now Leeds have accepted they've got a match on their hands... they're three nil down and it's taken a long time for them to come to the boil... they've pushed nine men into the eighteen yard box for this corner and Colchester have got ten back... and it's there!.. Hunter!... significant that very few of the players have taken the bother to congratulate Hunter... Leeds are now down to the serious business of staying in the FA Cup."

G.S. "Someone threw a carton of orange juice from the crowd. I even dropped that actually. It hit me and went on the floor. I was busy moaning to the referee and throwing the thing in the back of the goal and the corner was taken. I rushed out for it but, having said that, I had no excuse as a goalkeeper as you have to

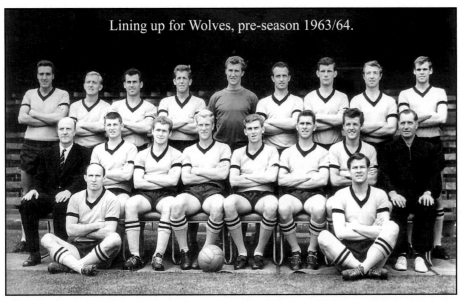

Lining up for Wolves, pre-season 1963/64.

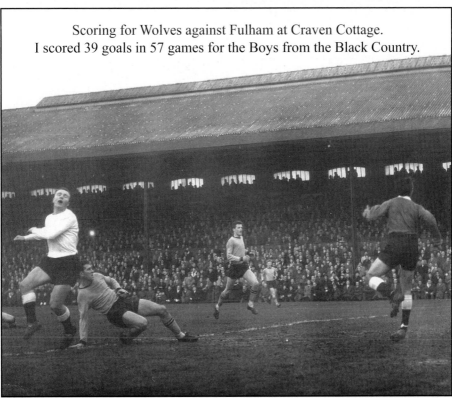

Scoring for Wolves against Fulham at Craven Cottage.
I scored 39 goals in 57 games for the Boys from the Black Country.

Scoring against Blackburn to win the 2nd Division Championship for Ipswich in the 1967/68 season.

The Ipswich Team show off the 2nd Division Championship Trophy.

Relaxing on the Golf course with Joe Broadfoot and Charlie Woods, my Ipswich team mates.

I have always been a sharp shooter. A night out in Southport with Bill Baxter and Ken Hancock.

Having a laugh with Crystal Palace winger Mark Lazarus.
Defender John McCormack is in the background.

Signing on at the dole office in London after being sacked by Charlton Athletic. Wife Eileen and daughter Suzanne were there to support me.

Me playing for Colchester against Rochdale. I have just scored but followed through and headed the post.
It looks like the post won.

The Colchester players celebrate after my second goal against Leeds.

The 'Crawfords' the day after Colchester beat Leeds.
Jane, Liza, Eileen, Me and Suzanne.

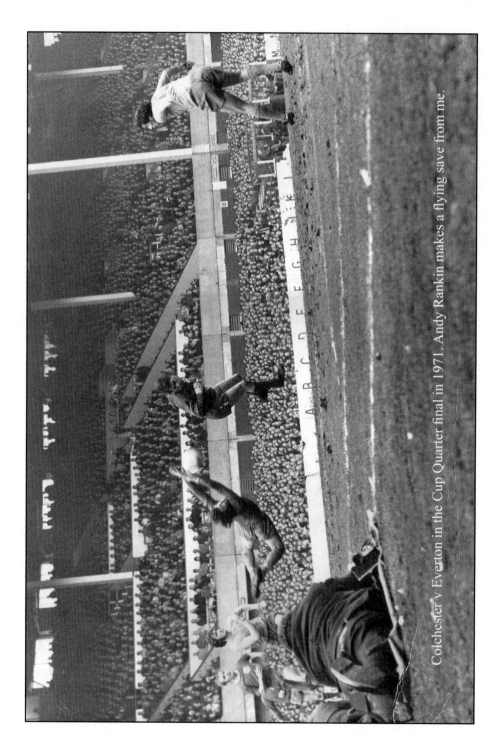

Colchester v Everton in the Cup Quarter final in 1971. Andy Rankin makes a flying save from me.

First team coach at Brighton in 1972/73 season until Cloughie arrived
and then I was on my bike back to Portsmouth.

Me and Bobby Robson at his testimonial match in 1979.

A tearful time for me unveiling the statue to the great man Sir Alf.

I was proud to be asked to unveil the statue of Sir Alf Ramsey.

Lady Ramsey is to my right.

Ipswich Town re-union celebrating 40 years since winning the Championship.

Me and my lovely wife, Carol.

Me with Ted Phillips, Mick Mills (in background) and John Wark on the pitch after induction into the Ipswich Town Hall of Fame, 2007.

Even at 71, I am still proud to wear my England Cap.

concentrate and if you come for the ball you've got to get it which I didn't do.

The second goal was an excellent goal, very well worked. Bates picked the ball up on the edge of the eighteen yard area, played it forward to Johnny Giles who was about fourteen yards out and he hit a very good shot into the top corner and I was still diving when the ball had hit the back of the net and come out."

D.C. "Bates... Jones... Giles... yes!!... and Johnny Giles so cool and so assured with that left foot and Leeds are now really back in with a chance."

D.G. "When they got back in the game at 3-2, they really did turn it on but it was a terrific finish. I mean if it had finished 3-0, I don't think it would have been the same."

Narrator: "Leeds turned it on to such an extent that they nearly equalized four minutes from time. They didn't, because Colchester's goalkeeper Graham Smith made the most famous save of his life."

D.C. "Lorimer... round the back of the defence... Jones YES!!... Oh what a save!!... And that must be one of the saves of the season and if Colchester survive this last four minutes, Graham Smith deserves a special Cup medal."

G.S. "The ball came right across the six-yard line. I was at my near post to cut out anything coming in low. The ball was whipped across. Mick Jones was centre goal and smashed the ball in and I just turned and I suppose it was an instinctive reflex save although I moved my feet very well and managed to hold onto the ball as well. Dick Graham said that when he saw that save he knew we had won the tie."

Narrator: "But it didn't last. These things rarely do. In the quarter finals, Colchester went to Everton and lost five nil. The following season they were drawn at home to Shrewsbury in the 1st Round and they lost 4-1."

G.S. "I look upon it with great fond memories, thinking how lucky I was to have taken part in a something which for me was a little bit of magic that happened to me and I was so proud to have been involved and to have played with a great bunch of lads under a great manager. It was wonderful, absolutely marvellous."

R.C. "I got more publicity and more acclaim for that one game, I mean we won the championship at Ipswich, we won the 2nd Division twice, I played for England twice and the Football League three times, moments I remember vividly in my career and there I was playing for a 4th Division side and every year I get invitations to go places possibly on the one game, so really it rates very highly, and I can go through that game as if it were yesterday."

(End of recording)

In the bath after the game, we were singing 'Grandad', a recent chart topper and drinking Moet & Chandon Champagne supplied by the chairman, some of which Simmo and me drunk out of our boots. My prediction about scoring against

Leeds being as easy as a farmer knocking off 'rabbits' hadn't backfired. In my prime, I would probably have scored four in the end as I had two good chances to finish the game off but my legs had almost given up on me by then. Billy Bremner later said that his main claim to fame was not playing for Scotland nor all the titles and medals he won playing for Leeds United but that he hadn't played in the FA Cup against Colchester United!

It was said that Dick climbed the walls of Colchester Castle that night. I think it was just a couple of steps on a stepladder for the photographers. Desmond Hackett, who'd sworn to eat his hat if Leeds lost, certainly didn't eat it. To his credit, he ate a chocolate replica he had specially made of it a few weeks after the game. After the dressing room celebrations, the players just parted like we did after any weekend game. I watched the highlights on a TV at a nightclub in Ipswich with the Sunday team that I was coaching. Just to give you some idea of the sort of bonuses you had in those days, as a senior player I was paid £70.00 for that game.

Just over a week later, Leeds United were due to play Ipswich Town at Portman Road. It had been nearly two years since my transfer to Charlton and since then I'd had time to think about the circumstances under which I'd left Town. The more I thought about it, the less happy I was. Rather than ask for a couple of tickets, I rang up the club a few days before the game, leaving a message for Jack Charlton to leave tickets for Eileen and myself on the evening of the game. Before games, there were always envelopes waiting for players of both home and away teams which could contain anything from requests for tickets, autographs or messages; all kinds of things. When I arrived with Eileen on the evening of the game, we went to the ticket office. The tickets were waiting for us and Jack had kindly obliged. Leeds were chasing the 1st Division Championship title whilst Ipswich were struggling near the bottom of the table. Leeds overpowered Ipswich that night with some brilliant football that not many teams could have lived with and won 4-2. Billy Baxter wasn't playing for Town that night as he'd just finished his two week suspension from the club and was getting back to full fitness after the lay-off. I wanted to thank Jack for leaving us the tickets. After the game, I waited with Eileen outside the dressing rooms for him to appear.

After about five minutes, the door to the home dressing room opened and out walked Billy Baxter with one hand bandaged, followed by Tommy Carroll. I went to greet Billy but, from the moment I saw him, I could tell something was wrong. He quickly told me he'd just had a big bust-up in the dressing room with Bobby Robson. It wasn't the place to talk about it so we drove off to into town and went for a drink at the Golden Lion pub on the same square as the Town Hall where we'd celebrated nearly ten years ago in front of thousands of Town fans after winning the championship. On the way there, Billy, who was still club captain, said he'd gone up to the Players Lounge with Tommy Carroll, straight after the game. He was totally taken aback when he arrived there to find he'd been banned from going in by Bobby Robson. Billy said he was absolutely furious, 'saw red' and went down to the dressing room to confront Bobby. A punch-up took place that was to end Billy's time at Ipswich Town. In my mind, although Billy's action was wrong, Bobby had gone too far in making an example in this way of one of Town's greatest ever players. Weighing up the situation, I had to side with Billy not only as a friend but for what he'd achieved for the club he'd served so well for eleven years, winning two 2nd Division title medals in 1961 and 1968 and another for winning the 1st Division Championship in 1962, making 473 appearances for Town, second only to Tommy Parker's record at the time. Banning him from the Player's Lounge was just adding fuel to a fire that should have been put out and forgotten long ago. Bobby's man management, as I had also felt in my case, had fallen a long way short of the mark. I was never able to thank Jack for his tickets that night and Billy never played for Ipswich Town again. He was sold to Hull City a few weeks later, never returning to Portman Road until he was finally persuaded to 28 years later. Mr John said "I never imagined that we would part in this manner". Nor did I.

Three day's later on the Friday evening, Colchester notched up a 1-0 win at Aldershot, taking us to 5th place in the 4th Division. We had a few games in hand but were starting to get into a fixture pile up; often the drawback of having a good cup run. This was to take its toll on a small squad that wasn't getting any younger. Harry Catterick, the Everton manager, was at the game and apparently left well before the end, obviously thinking he'd seen enough as we had drawn 'The Toffees' at Goodison Park in the 6th Round of the FA Cup. Odds on the 'U's winning the Cup hadn't changed. We were still 100-1 against. It may have been different if we'd been drawn to play at Layer Road. At the end of that month, Dick Graham was voted the February 'Bells Whisky' Manager of the Month, following Bobby Robson who'd won it the month before. That was before the incident with Billy Baxter. Maybe either the nomination or the Scotch had gone to his head a bit?

After the Leeds game, I'd had many invitations inviting me to open or attend local functions. I couldn't accept all of them but one invitation to go to Canada to play in an exhibition match was one I couldn't refuse. I was invited along with Bobby

Cram, the club captain, and our families on an all expenses paid trip to play an exhibition match in Vancouver. Dick Graham kindly gave us permission to go and we flew out to Washington on a Sunday then onto Vancouver where we were put up in a top class hotel. Jack Charlton had been invited as well although he stayed in a different hotel to us. At least I finally had the chance to thank him for the tickets - better late than never! We were given the use of a huge car and the first automatic I'd ever driven. We visited all the local sites, including the place where Errol Flynn died. We saw killer whales leaping and diving at the outdoor aquarium there which the kids loved. One evening, as we were going down to dinner in the lift (lifts were to become quite interesting places for Eileen and I over the next few months), we spoke briefly to a couple and told them what we were doing in Vancouver. They happened to be in the hotel trade. Later that evening, they approached us and offered us a job running one of their hotels. They actually thought we came from London. They thought the way we talked would go down well with the sort of clientele who used their hotel. It was a generous offer. The salary was good. Even though I was nearly 35 years old, I wasn't ready to hang up my boots yet. It was to be another 16 years before I finally turned my back on football. I can't remember much about the game we played out there. Bobby Cram was so impressed with the place, he emigrated there when he'd finished playing.

The turning point in our push for promotion came, strangely enough, in the warm up at Layer Road for the game against Exeter City when Dave Simmons suddenly collapsed after one of his knees had given way. Dave never played again that season. I missed his power and support up front which had taken a lot of pressure off me since his arrival. Another bombshell dropped on the morning before the game when Dick Graham handed in his resignation. Nobody knew about until halfway through the next week. We drew 1-1 with Exeter but we really needed to win all our home games to have any chance of promotion. We made up for it two days later on the Monday evening when I scored both goals in a 2-0 win against Scunthorpe at Layer Road. Two days later the whole club was in shock when Dick announced his resignation, saying he'd no intention of changing his mind. He was very upset about something. He said that it wasn't just an issue between him and Mr Graver but more of an accumulation of events. Mr Graver resigned the very next day and Dick withdrew his resignation. We never found out what had upset Dick. By Saturday, it was all over as if nothing had happened, smoothed over by a local estate agent Roy Chapman who'd immediately taken over as club chairman. I banged in my 30th goal of the season in a 1-0 win over Southport.

It was the worst week of the season off the field. Dave Simmons had just returned home after a few days in hospital and then had another accident. He was walking down the stairs when his leg gave way again. He crashed through a glass door at the bottom of the stairs, cutting his arm very badly. With Dave out for the season, the wheels really started to come off the push for promotion with just seven games to go. There were more injuries to come. We lost 4-0 to division leaders Notts County, assuring them of promotion. In the game, reserve keeper Brian Sherratt, standing in for the injured Graham Smith, collided with our own Brian Garvey and was carried off unconscious, then taken to hospital with a broken shoulder blade. Brian Lewis also broke his arm in the game. We lost by the same score at Oldham five days later which ended any real hope we had of promotion.

We rallied well for the last three games with two wins and a draw but promotion was lost. I scored my 24th and final Football League goal in a 3-0 home win over Crewe. The next game, a 1-1 draw with Stockport was my last ever league appearance in English football. Brian Gibbs' goal in that game was a very important one. It made us the top goal scoring side in the 4th Division that season, qualifying us for the Watney Cup plus a prize of £4,000. I was very proud to be voted player of the year by the Colchester supporters. Any player at my age, nearly 35 years old, would have found it difficult turn down the offer I was to receive in the next few months.

At the end of the season, the club treated the players and their families to a two week holiday in Spain. We left Colchester at 6:00pm in the evening and arrived at our hotel in Benidorm at 1:00am in the morning. While I was getting the key to our room, Eileen and the girls, Bobby Cram and his family and two of the lads went in the lift. Eileen pressed the button for the third floor. The lift went straight down to the basement where it stayed! An engineer was called in but they were stuck in there for almost an hour before the lift was repaired. This was only the start of the problems. At about 2:30am, when most of the party had settled into their rooms, there was suddenly a lot of shouting and commotion in the corridor outside our room. I rushed out to see what was going on only to see John Kurila comforting his wife who was clearly in a state of shock. Dick Graham's wife had decided to have a bath in the room above them before going to bed but had no way of knowing that when she pulled the plug out, there was no drainage pipe attached to the plug hole. The water had poured through the ceiling, giving John and his family an unexpected shower that they hadn't bargained for!

But that wasn't the end of it. The next morning when everyone assembled in the dining hall for breakfast, there were no waiters or a manager in sight. There were unpacked boxes of crockery stacked up against the walls. Dick, after a quick look in the kitchen, said there was a chef there but he was unpacking cooking utensils and just shrugged his shoulders when asked for an explanation. It soon became clear that the whole hotel from the lift to the plumbing was a long way from being finished. The whole place was quickly becoming like a stage for a 'Carry On' film. We were all hungry so we went out to find somewhere to eat. Just before lunchtime, we were moved to a another hotel nearby. We thought this would be the end of the snags but, when Eileen and I opened the door to our room, we were confronted by an embarrassed looking couple hastily covering up in bed who obviously had their own ideas of how an afternoon siesta should be spent! Retreating quickly with our apologies, I followed a now fuming Eileen downstairs to reception (she didn't risk taking the lift). Anybody who says the English put up with everything without complaining, should have heard Eileen that afternoon. She really gave them the complete ear-full! The day ended with Dick getting his drink spiked. Everyone suspected Brian Lewis had done it as he was the drinks and fags expert. Lewy loved both of these and, without them, probably could have been one of the best players in the country. Jimmy Hill rated him very highly and later took him to Coventry City. After the chaos of the first day, the holiday passed without further alarms.

Before the start of the next season, we took part in 'The Watney Cup', an experimental tournament in which players could only be offside if they were inside the 18 yard box. I played in the first game at Layer Road against Luton Town who were in the 2nd Division at the time and we won 1-0 with a penalty from Brian Lewis. A few days later, Dick Graham called me into his office and told me he'd had a phone call from Durban City's London based agent, enquiring about the possibility of signing me. They'd probably seen my exploits against Leeds United in the FA Cup and thought there must still be some mileage left in the 'old warhorse'.

Although I was happy at Colchester and the family had settled down in Ipswich again, we'd always wanted to go to South Africa. Dick and Colchester United were very fair to me. After an emergency Board meeting, they agreed to let me go. I will always be grateful to Dick for salvaging me from the scrap heap of non league football. But for him and Colchester United, my career in football may well have come to an end a lot sooner than I would have wished.

By then, Jimmy Greaves had decided to call it a day and retired from football, leaving me as the highest scoring striker still playing in British football at the time. I could have carried on and chased Jimmy's record of league goals but I thought it was now time for me to bow out as well. I hope all Colchester United supporters who may have thought I was disloyal at the time will now understand why I had to go.

Chapter 22

"Black and White Boots"

Just a few days after leaving Colchester and a twenty four hour flight later, we arrived at Durban Airport on a very hot, humid Sunday afternoon. It was winter out there when we stepped off the plane but it was like getting out of a cool fridge and stepping into a hot oven. We were tired after the long flight. It was as a boost to our morale when we were picked out by two representatives from Durban City FC who took us away in a smart Mercedes saloon straight to the Durban City ground where my new team were to play against East London United that afternoon. I couldn't help thinking on the way there of when my ship had stopped in Cape Town all those years ago on the way back from my National service in Malaya where I'd played alongside almost every single race of people under the sun, but this was going to be the exact opposite of my experience there. Although we'd heard a lot about apartheid and racial segregation back home, seeing it 'in the flesh' and the madness of it all at close hand was going to be a big culture shock for us.

I'd only been in South Africa for about an hour when I saw my first familiar face. It was a lot chubbier than when I last saw him. It was the same Johnny 'Budgie' Byrne that I'd made my England debut with ten years before in 1961 against Northern Ireland. He was now the Durban City player-manager. Johnny had put on quite a lot of weight. He was still full of life and as chirpy as ever. Most people who ever met me said I never stopped talking but it was still hard to get a word in as Budgie was still a champion chatterbox! He introduced me to the Durban club chairman, Norman Elliot, nicknamed 'The Silver Fox'. We watched the game from the Director's box with Eileen and the girls. Not far from the end of the game, we were all fighting off our nodding heads which were bobbing up and down, in and out of sleep. It was a welcome whistle when the game came to an end. We were invited to their clubhouse for drinks. They told us that Eileen and the girls would have to stay in the family room. Neither Eileen or myself liked this. It was our first experience of a society divided by colour, sex and race. It was at a time when the rule of apartheid was at its strongest there.

It wasn't long before some of my new team who'd played that afternoon turned up, including Johnny Haynes, Les Green (ex-Derby goalkeeper), Greg Farrell (an ex-Cardiff winger) and another player called Charlie Mann. It was good to see Johnny again. He looked bronzed and very well. He was now even less mobile than when I'd played alongside him in my England debut but he was still a very fine passer of a football. Johnny would have been a great player in any era of the game. I never saw the ball passed better, long or short, so accurately with either foot as he did. That evening, we were taxied with all our luggage to a hotel where we were to stay until the club house Durban City had organized for us had been modernized and re-decorated.

I was already very fit having done my pre-season training with Colchester United. I started playing for Durban City straight away. Matches were played in the evenings when it was a lot cooler for the players. Because of the apartheid ruling, there was a league for black teams and another for whites and football grounds were divided into sections for black and white supporters. When whites played against black teams, they were regarded as training matches and played behind closed doors with no crowds allowed to watch. I hadn't been there long before I played in one of these games against a local black side. After the game, we went to a buffet that the club had laid on for the all the players and their wives and children with both teams mixing freely. I thought this was getting a bit more democratic and sensible after what I'd already seen. We were about to leave and I went into the kitchen to sign some autographs for the staff who'd laid on such a good spread for us to share. When I went into the kitchen, I witnessed one of the craziest scenes I've ever seen in my life. A couple of the kitchen staff who were all whites as blacks were not allowed to prepare food for white people, were smashing the dinner plates we'd eaten off by throwing them into a large metal wheelie-bin. I'd had a few drinks so at first I saw the funny side of it, laughing as I said I thought only managers did this with teacups in the dressing room after losing games, like Bill McGarry who'd been a champion teacup thrower at Ipswich. When Bill retired from the game, he emigrated to South Africa and married a black lady. Even he might have been disturbed at the amount of crockery smashed after every black and white game. I was then told they were always told to smash the plates because the black players and their families had eaten from them. I couldn't believe what I saw that day. Whilst on South Africa and McGarry who lived out his days there, another thing I find hard to understand is that the week Bill died, there was no one minute silence before the next game at Portman Road as is customary for players and managers who have served their clubs well. For a man who did so much for Ipswich Town after Milburn left the club, in all likelihood saving them from going into 'free-fall' as they call it these days (like Portsmouth did ending up in the 4th Division in 1978) not to be shown the respect he richly deserved, was a disgrace in my opinion. Ipswich Town are normally very good in this respect. In Bill's case, they were very wrong. One minute's silence wouldn't have been long considering what he achieved in the years he gave his all to the club.

After spending six weeks in a hotel, it was a relief when we finally moved into our club house. It was an all wooden construction with four bedrooms and ideal for the kids because it wasn't far from the sea. We couldn't have been given a warmer welcome than we received from a pretty, young, black lady called Beauty who was to be our housemaid. In our short time out there, Beauty was to become and treated as one of the family and was true in every sense of her name. She'd been an orphan as a child and lived in a large shed at the bottom of the garden. She'd done it up brilliantly. To Beauty, it was the only home she'd ever been able to call her own. It was always spotlessly clean and she was so proud of it she always invited people who were visiting to go and have a look inside. Eileen thought Beauty's talents were wasted as a maid. She thought Beauty could have made a very good interior designer. She was wonderful with the girls too who came to adore her, taking them out shopping with her and to the local parks. Although Beauty had never learned to read or write properly, she had a wonderful imagination. I remember standing by the doorway of their bedroom, listening to the stories she invented right off the top of her head as she sat there on the side of their beds. She would then give them a gentle kiss on the forehead before they drifted off to sleep.

The laws about mixing race were crazy. When I used to drive Beauty back to see her adopted family for the weekend, she had to sit in the back of the car. If Eileen took the gardener home, he was allowed to sit alongside her in the front passenger seat. I never did quite work that one out. We soon realized there wasn't any escape from apartheid in almost every aspect of living out there. It never failed to anger Eileen when she saw large signposts up everywhere of 'Whites Only' beaches, 'Whites Only' toilets, 'Whites Only' buses. The segregation was in every public place and in all sports, not just football. The week we moved into our house, I went by myself to do some shopping for Eileen. Having bought all that we needed, I went to the counter to pay. I'm a polite, patient person by nature. After being brushed past by about four black people who were not before me in the queue, I enquired quietly why I wasn't being served. The woman at the checkout smiled at me, before pointing at a notice by the shop door which said 'Shopping for Blacks Only' which I hadn't seen. All I could do was smile back in embarrassment and leave the shop in disbelief at the stupidity of it all.

During our time there, a 55 year old South African doctor, Philip Blaiberg, became Dr Christian Barnard's second revolutionary heart transplant patient and was given the heart of a black man who'd collapsed dead with a brain haemorrhage on a beach in Cape Town. It seemed like a case of double standards that this man, just because of his colour had been banned from sharing the same beaches as whites but it was alright for Blaiberg who was white to share the heart of a black man. Beauty only saw the funny side of it and giggled when we talked about it. It just summed up what a 'heartless' regime it was.

Not long after the plate smashing incident and as a reaction to the stupidity of all, I decided to make my own protest and perhaps inject a bit of humour into a game. I borrowed a pair of white football boots from Les Green the ex-Derby keeper. It was very rare to see football boots in any colour other than black in those days. It was my chance to have a snipe at the whole system out there. I wore Les's white boots in the first half, then one black boot and one white for the second half which amused the black section of the crowd no end and became my party-piece for a few games. Unfortunately, it didn't last long. One afternoon, before an evening kick-off, the team met up us usual in a hotel in Durban for our pre-match meal and team talk. Les asked a young boy to keep an eye on his car for a couple of hours. When he returned to his car later that afternoon, the back window had been smashed, his kit bag stolen and with it the white boots as well so that was the end of my small protest about apartheid.

The one moment that always stands out in my memory above all my experiences out there, came during a home match played in a rain storm. I hit a shot at goal that missed the target and broke a black man's umbrella in the crowd behind the goal. He started waving his smashed umbrella at me. On impulse, I decided to go into the crowd, something I had never done in my life before. I slowly climbed up the ten or so steps of the stand behind the goal to where the man stood. The crowd made way for me as I came nearer. When I reached him, I put up my hands to give the 'sorry' gesture and his face lit up into a wide smile showing only two shining white teeth behind it. I quickly arranged with him to meet me outside the ground after the game to give him some money to buy a new umbrella. After shaking his hand, I made my way down the terraces and the applause I received when I stepped back on the pitch was one of the most emotional moments in my whole career in football. After the game, I found the man waiting just outside the entrance to the ground as we'd arranged and I gave him enough money to probably buy three new umbrellas. That day, I'd made a new friend. In future games, he was always there behind the goal in the same place, waving his umbrella like mad whether it was raining or not with the same toothy grin I will never forget.

Not all of the South African whites out there were in favour of apartheid. Some of the 'tourist footballers' as you could have called us, though not agreeing with it, accepted it as just another way of life. One day, Eileen had just been to the shops and was taking a bowl of fresh fruit down to Beauty in her little home at the bottom of the garden. Jean Fascione, the ex-Chelsea player's wife was in the garden next to us and asked Eileen what she was doing. When Eileen told her, Jean said she shouldn't let her have fresh fruit. She should only give her old fruit that was either going off or past its best or Beauty would think we were going soft. Eileen gave her a piece of her mind, telling her she didn't treat anyone differently whether they were black or white.

Although playing for Durban City was great at the time and the children loved it as it was a great adventure for them, just like a never ending summer holiday, Eileen soon started to feel homesick. She said she would like to return home to our families and friends. I was missing home too. I think many people who go abroad with the idea of spending the rest of their lives there, find that, after a while, the pull of their roots and your home country is hard to resist.

The last game I played for Durban City was in the final of their version of our FA Cup Final. It was in Johannesburg against Cape Town. I met up with Roy Bailey and his family who'd had lived there since leaving Ipswich and emigrating to South Africa in 1964. Roy had done well and made a good new career for himself in television. We went to see him and his wife Pauline the night before the final. There was a youngster there getting into everything! The next time I saw the little terror, he was playing in goal for Manchester United, true testimony to Roy Bailey as a great goalkeeper that his son Gary Bailey was that man. Much to my sadness, Roy died in 1996 of an incurable illness. It was the loss of a good friend, ever since the day Alf had introduced me to Roy in the old 'Chicken Hutch' dressing rooms at Ipswich in 1958.

We drew 1-1 with Cape Town the next day, then won the toss to stage the replay at Durban City a few days later with the odds stacked in our favour. Everyone thought it was just a formality that Durban would win the Cup. Our chairman Norman Elliot said we'd win the replay easily but all it did was to stir up the pride in Cape Town and their manager Frank Lord who'd been one of the great journeymen in English soccer before retiring at Plymouth Argyle in 1968. His team were not ready to admit defeat and went on to win the replay 3-1.

It was then time to go home. The day we left to go back to England, Beauty cried, asking if she could come back with us. It was a very sad moment the day we left Beauty standing there in front of the house, waving goodbye to us. We all waved back until we could no longer see her from the taxi that drove us to Durban airport.

Chapter 23

"The Seagulls and Never say never again"

Having sold our house in Ipswich before leaving for South Africa, we had nowhere to live when we returned shortly before Christmas that year. Eileen's father had sadly passed away by then and her mother said we could stay in her three-bedroomed house in Portsmouth until we had sorted out things. As well as needing to find somewhere for the family to live, I also needed to find a job. I was reading the sports papers of the local paper one morning and noticed that nearby Brighton & Hove Albion, 'The Seagulls', were having trouble scoring goals. I knew Eddie Spearritt from my Ipswich days was playing there. I gave him a ring asking him if he could approach the Brighton manager at the time Pat Saward, the ex-Aston Villa and Irish International, on my behalf. A few days later, I received a letter inviting me for a week's trial. I was immediately impressed with Pat. He was full of life and enthusiasm with some original and exciting ideas about training. He certainly liked a good lifestyle too. He had a boat in Brighton harbour as he loved the sea. In his time, he had also been a model, telling me that he had no less than fifty suits in his wardrobe at home!

Pat was on a small budget to get promotion to the 2nd Division. One of his best ideas had been to get Brian Bromley on loan from Pompey. 'Brom' as he was known, was single and living in Portsmouth at the time. Pat asked me if I could give him a lift every day to save on the train fares as Brian didn't drive. Most days, when I arrived at his digs, 'Brom' was still asleep when I knocked on his door. After letting me in, I would have to watch him whilst he slowly drank a big mug of strong black tea with the leaves floating in it before he was ready to go. As a player, he was a class above most of the Brighton lads, a good passer of the ball with a good work rate and, just like his tea drinking, was never rushed in anything he did on the pitch.

I did well enough in my trial week for Pat to ask me to stay for another month just to see how things went. The club tried to get my registration forms from Durban City but they wanted a fee and I think their chairman, Norman Elliot, was annoyed about me leaving them. Pat kept faith in me by extending my trial period to three months. By then, we'd been staying at my parents for a few weeks as things hadn't worked out living with Eileen's mother. I think her father had always been the peacemaker between Eileen and her mother in the past. Without him, it wasn't long before they were constantly rowing. There'd been a strong underlying tension between them ever since the death of her brother Tim in the motorbike accident not long before I first met Eileen. Shortly after his death, her mother had said it would have been better if she'd died and not Tim and Eileen had never forgiven her for what she'd said. The tension soon turned to a bitterness, bordering on hatred. I just couldn't live in that atmosphere. I knew it was time for us to move on before things became any worse. My parents came to our aid until we finally moved into a Brighton FC club house.

As it happened, the moment I started at the Goldstone Ground, results picked up and the goals started to flow. There wasn't the same need for my services as a striker. With Durban City still holding my registration forms, I couldn't play anyway. Pat offered me a contract to coach the youth and reserve teams which I accepted. I went to Lilleshall to get my coaching badge and there I was, a few weeks later, working with the players, something I said I'd never do but was enjoying every minute of it - 'never say never again' as they say. Meanwhile Eileen was given a job working from home making dresses for a London firm and the three girls were at school in Brighton. Life was good and we felt more settled than for some time. Unfortunately, my finances were soon to become very unsettled.

Just before I'd gone to South Africa, the first shop I'd opened with Brian Hall had done quite well so we'd opened another in Sudbury in Suffolk. Brian told me not to worry as he would run the shops while I was away. I hadn't been at Brighton long when, one evening Brian rang me to talk about our shops, saying that he was looking forward to seeing me when Brighton Reserves came up to play Colchester Reserves, to discuss the future of the business. He told me things were going well and that all the profit the shops had made had been ploughed back into the business to buy more stock and that he was going to send me account sheets as soon as possible. He also put to me the possibility of opening a third shop. Though I hadn't put much time into the running of the business, I'd not had a penny from my initial investment and told him I wasn't interested in opening a third shop. I already had my hands full with my coaching job at Brighton and wouldn't have the time to help in the running of an expanding business. I said to Brian that if he could give me the back the money I'd put in for the start up costs, in effect buy me out, I'd be happy to let him take over the whole business. He agreed and said he'd get a solicitor to sort out the necessary paper work, then get back in touch with me.

A few weeks later, I was taking a training session on the pitch at the Goldstone Ground when I was called in to answer an urgent phone call. I took the call on the telephone in the tunnel that leads out on to the pitch. It was a solicitor named Mr Scott who told me that the High Sheriff had gone into our two shops and taken all the stock to cover bills that hadn't been paid. It was a hell of a shock. Telling Eileen was one of the most difficult things I ever had to concede. She'd been against the idea of the sports shops from the very start. Mr Scott followed his call by sending me a list of all the companies the business owed money to. Amongst the list of creditors was Vic Keeble, the ex-West Ham and Newcastle striker, who I knew from in the year I played for Colchester United. He'd loaned Brian £1,000 to buy a new van for the business. He was very sympathetic towards me and easy going about being paid back the money he was owed. I met up with Vic again in 1980 when I was manager of Fareham Town and Vic was secretary of Chelmsford City FC. I took on all the debts of the business and through a Court Order paid them off monthly. It took two years to clear the amount owed. Having had my fingers burnt once, this was not surprisingly my last ever venture into business.

On the plus side, not long after I'd joined Brighton, Jimmy Hill made contact with me and invited me to play for his 'Goaldiggers' team who played for charity. It was made up of ex-professionals and we played on Sunday afternoons. Jimmy Hill had played at the highest level in the 1950's and early sixties alongside Johnny Haynes, Jim Langley and Tosh Chamberlain. Though the man with the famous beard was never a prolific goal scorer, he was an outstanding player and always gave 100 percent. When Jimmy had finished playing, he became the chairman of the PFA, the Players Football Association and, in 1961, brought about the end of the maximum wage of £20.00 per week. Johnny Haynes became the first ever player in England to earn £100 a week. At Ipswich, our wages went up to £30.00 a week with an extra £5.00 for playing in the first team plus £4.00 for a win and £2.00 for a draw. He then became a manager, then chairman of Coventry City who became the first club in the country to have an all seating stadium for their supporters. Jimmy was very modern in his thinking. City became the first club to have an all seated stadium at Highfield Road. Although wages would have gone up eventually, players of his generation and those who followed owe him a lot to him for the justice and fairness he brought about. Present day players may well not be aware of the debt they owe Jimmy as well.

'The Goaldiggers' went all over the place to play and abroad as well, once playing in The Bernabau Stadium against Real Madrid who'd beaten Eintracht 7-3 to win the European Cup and included some all time greats including the famous Hungarian Puskas, Di St'fano and Gento. Another good trip was to the Sudan where it was unbelievably hot. We were all surprised by the standard of skill shown by their team. We also visited Khartoum and saw where General Gordon was killed in the massacre there. When Jimmy signed a long term contract with the BBC to present their new 'Match of the Day' programme, along with his commitments as chairman of Coventry City, it was sadly the end of 'Goaldiggers' - he just didn't have the time to run it any more.

My last game for them was at Windsor in aid of the Duke of Edinburgh Award funds. My daughter Suzanne wasn't behaving very well that day. I told her before I went out to play that, if she was good, she might be allowed to have tea with the Queen. She quietened down a bit. I could still hear and see her playing up in the stand where she sat beside Eileen, Jane and Liza. When the game started, Suzanne was sitting right behind the Duke of Edinburgh himself who received a few kicks in the back from Suzanne, much to Eileen's embarrassment. Seats were quickly changed to stop the Duke taking any more punishment! Needless to say, Suzanne didn't go to the palace to have tea with the Queen and cried all the way home to Brighton. In that game, we were awarded a penalty and up stepped the greatest goal scorer I ever saw. It was a very nervous Jimmy Greaves who told the goalkeeper not to move, meaning he was not to try and save it as Jimmy didn't want to miss a penalty in front of a royal dignitary! Jimmy put away the penalty and looked as relieved as if he'd just scored the winning goal in an FA Cup Final! A few weeks later Jimmy told the papers that he was an alcoholic and his life was hell; thankfully he is fine now.

At the end of my first season in 1972, Brighton won promotion to the 2nd Division. I was given a contract for the next year to continue as reserve and youth team coach. There wasn't much money to spend on new players so Brighton wanted to get the youths coming through as quickly as possible and get into the Under-18's South East Counties League. I went to the FA in London to put forward their case. After a few weeks, our application was accepted. With the little money his budget allowed that summer, Pat bought Barry Bridges, the famous ex-Chelsea and Birmingham winger, Steve Piper who later went to Portsmouth and a small lad called Tony Towner who went on to play for Wolves and Charlton. By then, I had some good youth players coming through. Inevitably, there were a few that weren't going to make the grade, one of them being an 18 year old youngster,

Francis Frazer. A few days after Francis had been released, his mother, Mrs Frazer, came to see Pat to ask him why. Pat asked me to be on hand in case he needed me to back him up if she wasn't happy with his reasons. Unknown to me as I waited outside Pat's office, was that she was the wife of none other than the notorious Frankie Frazer, once the hit man for the Kray brothers! Though I never found out what was said in that meeting, it didn't last very long and Mrs Frazer came out with a contented smile on her face, soon followed by Pat who was not looking quite his usual calm self. "Ray, I've changed my mind about the boy, Frazer" he said, "I think he's got more potential than we thought" and young Francis was given a two year contract straight away!

Unfortunately Brighton were relegated to the 3rd Division that year, and, to be honest, I was happy to be Brighton's scout that season. It was better at weekends to be a long way from a club that was in trouble all that year. I travelled all over the country, mainly looking for a good defender. The furthest I went from the south coast was a trip to Morton in Scotland to check out their centre-half. I can't recall his name but I do remember going to watch another Scot, Billy Rafferty, who was playing for Coventry City at the time. Brighton were a long way short of meeting the asking price of both players so neither of them were bought.

After being relegated and a few months into the next season, Pat Saward was sacked by the chairman Mike Bamber. It was surprising after what Pat had done for the club. It was perhaps not just because of the poor results. There was a rumour around that there'd been ill will between them since Mike hadn't been invited to Pat's wedding that year. Though I owed a lot to Pat for giving me the chance to get back into football and into coaching, I also had a lot of respect for Mike. I'd known him for a couple of years since my days at Colchester United and before he'd become chairman of Brighton. In 1971, in an earlier round before the Leeds game, we'd knocked out his team, Ringmar, from the FA Cup and I'd scored a hat-trick in our 3-0 win there. He owned a hotel and a night club. At the end of that season, Mike invited me and my family to stay at his hotel for the weekend during which I was to open the local summer fete. Since that time, I'd regarded Mike as a friend and a man I could trust. He was also popular with the Brighton players and staff. There was always an open invitation to spend Monday evenings 'on the house' at his night club in Ringmar.

Mike was very ambitious and went for a big name to replace Pat. They didn't come much bigger than Brian Clough at the time. From the very first day he arrived at the club with his other half in football terms, his former club mate and ex-Middlesbrough goalkeeper Peter Taylor, I wasn't sure if I'd be able to work with Brian. Although he achieved results, he had a reputation for being abrasive and stubborn; a man who did things his way with little time for anyone else's ideas or opinions.

Before his first match in charge, he took the players to stay overnight at a hotel in nearby Lewes. He invited me and Glenn Wilson who'd taken over as caretaker manager after Pat's dismissal, for a drink in the hotel bar. He bought us both a pint before disappearing with Peter Taylor. Two hours later, Brian hadn't come back so I left. Glen stayed at the bar and with Brighton FC as it was his life. I wasn't prepared to be treated like that and I soon found out that the way he spoke to people was as I'd expected. Alf had shown me that you could get results without any threats, swearing or ill will. Sometimes Cloughie liked to surprise the players with a sudden change of routine. One day, he kept the players sitting in the dressing room for two hours before training. I don't know why. You could say it was a bit like Alf making us train without footballs at Ipswich. The way he managed it was different. It left a sort of threatening pressure on the players that I didn't agree with.

One day he was going to take the players for a late afternoon training session at the Sussex University ground. It was winter at the time, getting dark at about 4:00pm and I knew the ground had no floodlights. I pointed this out to Brian Sheridan, another coach who'd come to Brighton with Peter Taylor. He told me no-one told Brian anything. It was situations like this that made up my mind to leave Brighton. I knew Portsmouth were starting up a new youth policy so I applied for the position of youth team coach there. I was given the job and it was a great feeling to be joining Pompey again. It had taken a round trip of nearly fifteen years to get back to the club that I still held close to my heart.

Shortly before I left Brighton, Eileen had a dig at Cloughie. Just before a game, he went into the room where the player's wives met before a match. Many of them were smoking and he told them in his usual blunt way that he would like them to stop. Most of them just smiled but not Eileen. She said "Brian, I don't smoke but, if I did, it wouldn't be anything to do with you!" Exit Brian. Take it from me, if Eileen had something to say, she would say it. We had some real battles in our life together.

I was looking forward to my new job. I still had to resign from Brighton so I went to the manager's office. Brian wasn't there at the time and Peter Taylor offered to pass on my resignation but I said I wanted to do it myself. When I caught up with Brian later that day, he was alright about it and just commented on how much money Pompey had squandered on new players and how bad they still were (he was dead right about that), before shaking my hand and wishing me good luck. Maybe he was a bit relieved that he wouldn't get any more flak from Eileen too!

Brian wasn't with Brighton for long after I'd left and Mike Bamber was so furious when he left them for the manager's job at Leeds United that he told one of his staff to put all of Brian's belongings, paper work, anything he'd left behind in a box and leave it on the roadside outside the entrance to Brighton FC! Cloughie only lasted five weeks at Leeds. It was hardly a secret in the game that he'd despised the club for years during the Revie era. You wonder if he just took the job to tell the players what he thought of them. I found out the feelings of the Leeds players in his short time there when I teamed up with John Kurila against ex-Leeds United players Peter Lorimer and Mick Bates. This was many years later, on a BBC radio programme called 'Extra Time' about the Colchester versus Leeds FA Cup game in 1971. After one of the questions, Peter mentioned what Cloughie had said in his first meeting with the Leeds players, telling them they'd cheated to get all the medals they'd won and told them to throw them into the nearest rubbish bin. I think Brian may have made a very good England manager but we never found out. I think he blew his chances in that five week fiasco at Leeds before he was sacked. The players no doubt had a large say in his quick downfall there. No doubt the FA took serious note of Brian's short spell in charge of a side full of international players. After that, it was unlikely they would ever have given him the England job. It was a shame. Brian had more tactical know how than almost any manager in the history of English football and, like Alf Ramsey, could get average players to perform well beyond their ability. I think he would certainly have gained results as England manager if he could have curbed some of his more unusual ideas about the man management of senior players and internationals. One of my favourite Cloughie quotes was "If football was meant to be played in the air, there would be grass in the sky." In that respect, Leeds United should have been perfect for him because they were probably nearest to the concept of total football than any other English club at that time but he blew it.

Whether Cloughie would have made it as National soccer coach we will never know. Some of his offbeat ideas might not have gone down well at that level and, like Revie, he loved the everyday contact with his players which you are starved of at international level. That's why Alf was perfect for the job. He was his own man, never feeling the need to be breathing down his players' necks day in, day out, week in, week out. With the talent Bobby Robson had in Italy 1992, in my opinion the best team England have ever had with the likes of Gascoigne, Waddle and Hoddle, natural ball players we've hardly seen the like of since, it was our best chance of winning the World Cup since 1966. To be honest, I think the present England team is a little overrated. They can't seem to hold the ball for more than a few passes. They haven't the all-round ball skills to do it. A lot of people complain about the number of foreign players in the premiership these days. They've been imported because we're not producing enough players who have those sort of skills. Jimmy Hill kept banging on about it for years that we were falling behind on skill compared with our international opponents and I don't think a lot has changed.

Chapter 24

"Return to Pompey"

In December 1973, I started my new job as coach of the Portsmouth youth team. It had been abandoned by George Smith in the 1960's and the club was trying to build it up again. At first, I had a mixture of talent to work with. Some were almost no hopers, others were average and I had just four apprentice professionals, Peter Ellis, Phil Figgins, Andy Stewart and Chris Bartlett. As the majority of them had daytime jobs, training was twice a week on Tuesday and Thursday evenings from 6:30-8:00pm. The club were looking ahead to the next season when they hoped to get into the Under-18's South East Counties League to play against the likes of Arsenal, Chelsea, West Ham and Spurs. I only had a few months to get the team up to scratch. At the time, they were playing in the 4th Division of the Hampshire League, not really suitable for teenagers as it was literally fully grown men against boys. By the end of the season, after numerous trials and coaching sessions, the club put together a full team of apprentice professionals. They would spend the morning training then, in the afternoons, work at Fratton Park doing jobs like cleaning boots and the dressing rooms before working on the pitch under the guidance of Gordon Neave and Pompey legend Duggie Reid who'd had taken over the job of groundsman when his playing days were over.

My afternoons were spent scouting, watching local schoolboy matches looking out for future football stars. If I thought any of the boys looked promising, I would approach their schools and ask for permission to invite them for coaching. This was held twice a week in a small gymnasium, playing 3 a side, a very quick way to assess the skill levels of young players. The enjoyment I had from coaching was immense. Most of the them had natural ability. It was just a matter of telling them certain things and letting them progress with good habits. By sheer hard work, we entered the Under-18's South East Counties League for the 1974-75 season.

Around the time of my arrival, the club chairman, John Deacon, had given the manager John Mortimore a small fortune to splash out on new players including Ron Davies from Southampton for £25,000, Peter Marinello from Arsenal for £100,000, Paul Went from Fulham for £155,000, Malcolm Manley from

Leicester City for £50,000 and Phil Roberts for £50,000 from Bristol Rovers. I thought the club was really going places but Tony Barton, the club scout, told me that Deacon had cocked up almost all of these buys. Although he'd put a lot of his money into the club, Tony and ex-Pompey player Ron Tindall, the club's general manager, were experienced in negotiating deals with other clubs. Deacon had stuck his nose in and was taken to the cleaners, paying far too much for most of these players, especially Marinello. Malcolm Manley was probably the best buy. Sadly, he suffered a serious knee injury forcing him to retire at the end of that season. Only Phil Roberts turned out to be a good long term investment. As so often happens when throwing a lot of new players together and hoping for instant success, it doesn't guarantee they will gel together with the existing squad, however good they are. In this case, it didn't pay off and Pompey finished in 15th place in the 2nd Division that season; well below Deacon's expectations.

It was great to be working for Pompey again but some important promises that the club had made when I signed hadn't been honoured. These included a club house and car. I'd spoken several times to Mr Deacon about it. He just kept saying they were still waiting for an ex-player to leave the club house that they'd reserved for us. When pre-season training started in August 1974, I was working very hard to prepare for the new season, leaving Brighton at 7:30am, not getting home much before 9:30pm, six days a week. I had little spare time to spend with my family and, although the £40.00 I was being paid a week was alright, it was nowhere near enough for the hours I was putting in. I couldn't go on as things were. I had my coaching badge so I contacted the FA and asked them if they could find me a job abroad. They asked me for some references. I asked the most influential man in my career and still the top man in English football at the time, Alf Ramsey, who helped me out with a letter that I still have today.

Only a week later, I was offered a job in New Zealand to manage the North Island club Gisborne; by all accounts a well run club. Eileen was also keen to go. I accepted the offer and organized the necessary medicals for the family. We went to New Zealand House in London where we were given the okay. The day I handed in my resignation, Deacon asked me to talk it over. Eileen came over from Brighton to hear what he had to offer. Deacon told me straight away that he was very grateful for the great job I was doing with the youth team and how much the club's future depended on the youngsters coming through. He then assured me that the club house would be ready for us to move into by the end of the month. I would have the use of a club car within the next few days. I still wasn't sure. When he told me my wages would be doubled to £80.00 a week, I agreed to stay after discussing it with Eileen. The next day, I wrote to both the FA thanking them for their trouble and to Gisborne FC apologizing for changing my mind. Deacon was true to his word. Within a month, we'd moved into a club house and I was given a club car, a white Ford Escort. Another improvement which made life easier for me was the club's investment in a new, blue Mercedes Benz 18 seater minibus. The previous season, I'd not only had to use my own car, not a very powerful Morris 1100 at the time, but also find volunteers to drive the rest of the team to away matches. Getting the petrol money back from the club that I'd forked out to the other drivers plus my own as well had been another problem. Now, everything seemed to have fallen into place and I felt I could devote all my energy to coaching the Pompey youth team.

After a poor start to the season, John Mortimore, who'd hardly been given a chance, was sacked after just five games. With the promise of more funds to spend on new players, Deacon persuaded Ian St John, the ex-Liverpool and Scottish international, to give up his position as manager of Motherwell and take over the helm at Portsmouth. Ian was greatly misled on false promises. The river of money had dried up and it wasn't long before he realized he was taking on a mass of problems and a club in rapid decline. Despite this, Ian was ready to give his all and was a great bloke to work with, trusting my judgement and letting me get on with coaching the youth team.

One of the problems with the Pompey 1st team was that the forward line had names but no firepower, with Ron Davies at centre-forward expected to thrive on a good supply of crosses from Peter Marinello, but both were struggling in this respect. At 31, Ron had been a great centre-forward in his prime. By then, he had lost a lot of his mobility and, unless the ball was put on a sixpence on his head, he was unlikely to score. Peter could dash up and down the touchline all day but had a problem a winger can do without. In one training session, Ian St John was trying to get him to cross the ball at pace. All Peter had to do was run past a marker and cross the ball but he just couldn't do it. The more he tried, the worse he became. It ended up with Ian stomping off cursing loudly. He wasn't a happy manager with a centre-forward who could hardly leap any more and a winger who had trouble crossing the ball. Peter's days at the club were numbered. First out was Ron to Manchester United in exchange for George 'Stroller' Graham, one of Arsenal's famous double winning team of 1971. George, even in his heyday, had never dashed around the pitch. One day on the training ground at Eastney Barracks, Ian and his second, another Scot, Billy Hunter, were trying to get him to run faster, pulling George along by the arm like a reluctant mule! He certainly lived up to his nickname but with his ability to read the game so well, the team slowly improved. But for George, the team may well have been relegated that season. Pompey survived in 17th place and at the end of my first full season as youth team coach, we finished in a respectable mid-table position in our first season in the Under-18's South East Counties League.

Not long into the new season I had a phone call from Reg Tyrell who I'd known at Ipswich when he was chief scout before Bobby Robson took over. I respected Reg as a scout. He'd taken a lot of good players to Ipswich in his time there including Mick Mills and Clive Woods, that brilliant all-round player and winger. Reg pinched Mick from Pompey after George Smith had scrapped the previous youth policy. He went on to make over 700 appearances for Ipswich and was capped 42 times by England. At the time, Reg was assistant manager at Bournemouth. He was unhappy with his contract and was looking for a new job. I said I'd ask Ian about a possible job and, happily for Reg, he was taken on to do some scouting for the club. As well as being a good scout, Reg was brilliant at weighing up the strengths and weaknesses of young players and in which positions they were likely achieve their best potential. None more so than in the case of Steve Foster, an 18 year old young striker that Southampton had released, telling him he wasn't going to make the grade. It was quite unusual the way I managed to bring Steve to the club.

I had a call from Harry Bourne, a local school teacher who was also in charge of Portsmouth and Hampshire school teams. He told me about Steve's situation, what a good player he was and gave me his address in Gladys Avenue, Portsmouth where he lived with his mother. Football clubs and coaches used to get many calls like this. When you followed them up, more often than not, they were nowhere near making the grade. In those days, you couldn't afford to ignore any tips. For all you knew, you could be missing out on the new George Best; you just never knew. Everything is a lot more structured and clinical these days. With all the academies around that so many clubs have rightly adopted, any young talent is quickly sifted out of all the thousands of possibles. I followed up Harry's tip straight away and called at Steve's house the same evening. His Gran answered the door and said she didn't know where Steve was. His mum was at a works disco at the local Alders store. So off I went and, after a brief explanation at the door, I was allowed in, entering a hall of deafening music with flashing kaleidoscope lights everywhere. I probably looked like a worried father looking for his teenage daughter. I found Steve's mother and told her, nearly having to shout as the music was so loud, "POMPEY ARE INTERESTED IN SIGNING YOUR SON

STEVE!" asking her to get Steve to contact the club as soon as possible. Steve contacted us early the next day and signed for Pompey in October 1975 to get his career back on track again.

When Reg came to watch the youth team in training games, he always amused me by the way he talked in numbers when referring to players. Fullbacks were 'that number 2 or 3', centre-backs as 'that number 5 or 6', wingers as 'that number 7 or 11' and so on. The first time that he saw Steve play in a training game, it wasn't long before he said "That number 9, he's no centre-forward but he'd be a good number 5." A few weeks later Steve was picked to play at number 5, centre-half in his debut for Pompey, making eleven appearances that season and went on to win three England caps in 1982.

Shortly before the end of the season, on April 2nd 1976, Eileen gave birth to our fourth daughter, Claire Louise. Eileen was 40 years old by then and had a difficult pregnancy due to high blood pressure. To monitor her condition for possible toxaemia, she was admitted to hospital three weeks before the birth and happily all went well. My joy was soon to be mixed with disappointment and sadness. The season ended in disaster. Pompey were relegated to the 3rd Division and Reg Tyrell, who'd clearly not been well for some time, was taken seriously ill shortly before he was due to take the youth team to a tournament. I was on holiday at the time so Ian stepped in and took over. Sadly, Reg died not long afterwards. It was the loss of a good man and both life and football were poorer without him.

Although the state of a club is only judged by the results of the 1st team, there was some consolation in that the youth team I was slowly building up again did well in the Under-18's South East Counties League. Many of them were about to be plunged in at the deep end of 3rd Division football well before they were ready. Andy Stewart had already been a classic example of what can happen to a young player if you do this. Andy had made his debut for Pompey at the age of seventeen at the end of the 1974 season and scored two goals in four games. Deacon hailed him as a new Jimmy Greaves. Andy only made a handful of appearances the next season before his confidence was shattered, finally ending with him dropping out of the big time to play the rest of his career in the Southern League.

Like myself, a few of the youth team came from Landport, a rough estate in Portsmouth and had little experience of travel or holidays. To broaden their horizons, I arranged a pre-season tour to take part in an Under-18's tournament in Holland. One of the boys, Kevin Clements, was a very poor traveller and likely to be sick before you even made it to the end of the road! He said it helped if he could see the road coming up so he sat in the passenger seat beside me. We'd just driven onto the A3 when suddenly, without warning, Kevin stuck his head out of the window and threw up or out as was the case. Unfortunately for me, the wind was blowing the wrong way and a lot of it came flying back coating me with half his breakfast! We made it to Harwich without any further alarms and took the ferry over to the Hook of Holland. As I expected, most of the lads went to the bar during the crossing. I already knew some of them liked a drink as the previous season I'd had more than a few phone calls reporting them drinking in various pubs and clubs. They weren't doing anything I didn't do at their age, it was just all part of growing up and they never caused any trouble.

When we docked in Amsterdam, they made their way back to the bus only to find that two of them were missing. I waited for a few minutes but had to drive off as I was holding up the traffic behind me on the ferry. I parked up with a sense of panic wondering whether they'd gone to sleep somewhere or, even worse, had become so drunk that they'd fallen overboard! To my relief, I soon noticed two youths with their arms around each other, come staggering down the ramp as pissed as farts. One of them was Leigh Barnard, a fitness fanatic not used to alcohol at all who could almost get drunk at the sniff of a beer towel. Supporting him was one of the usual culprits, fifteen year old Alan Knight, a very talented young keeper and a great kid; well, most of the time! I was very relieved to see them. The lads were paired off to stay with families in Amsterdam who'd kindly agreed to put us up. I had the luxury of an apartment all to myself. The boys were well looked after. Although I couldn't keep my eyes on them the whole time and they partied hard, they did the job on the pitch. We were up against many good European teams. Most of the Dutch players seemed incredibly tall. They all seem to be in Holland. I was proud of my lads as we finished up runners-up in the tournament and brought home some silverware. Short as it was, I think some of the lads grew up quite a bit on that tour which was just as well considering many of them were about to be thrown in at the deep end of professional football and were shortly to be known as the 'Pompey Babes'.

In September, only weeks into the new season, Pompey were near the bottom of the 3rd Division and the club's financial crisis had finally come to a head. Home gates were down. These were desperate days for the club. One week, the bank even bounced our pay cheques. From somewhere, the club had to find £25,000 in two months to clear its most pressing debts. It was then that the fans started a fund raising scheme called 'SOS Pompey'. Even Bruce Forsyth was involved, raising a large sum of money for the club by giving a one man show to a full house at Portsmouth Guildhall. For my part, to help pay for the youth team expenses, I started up keep-fit classes with the assistance of Henry Stenhouse, Chief Petty Officer on HMS Vernon and two local sports instructors, Sid Holly and Mike Brady, all keen Pompey fans who charged nothing for their services to the club. Men were invited to attend for one hour, two nights a week and asked to make a donation of no less than £1.00 a session. Each session consisted of 20 minutes running, 20 minutes on the exercise machines and 20 minutes of football in the gym. Help came from many sources. If it hadn't been for the generosity of Derrick Meakins, the owner of a local sports shop, the lads wouldn't have had a strip to play in. Pompey were absolutely skint. Eileen, even with a new baby, three young children and a house to run, contributed as well, saving money by making sandwiches for the boys when they came in for special coaching and for the youth team on away matches.

My lot were hungry and thirsty little rascals as they proved one evening on an away trip to Aston Villa who had the likes of Gordan Cowans and John Deehan playing for them in the FA Floodlit Cup. We travelled up by coach and stopped off just outside Oxford at a Travel Lodge where I told the lads they could order a light meal like toast with poached or scrambled eggs. When I went to settle up, I received one hell of a shock as the greedy bastards had ordered almost fifty quid's worth! It was a lot of money in the mid-seventies and an amount Pompey's budget didn't run to. I had to dip into my own wallet to make up the balance of the bill. This wasn't unusual for anyone employed by Pompey at the time.

SOS Pompey helped towards the cause but it wasn't enough to raise the money needed in such a short time. Ian St John knew he had to get in some money fast and get the wage bill down as well. All excess baggage had to be thrown off Pompey's sinking ship so Alan Stephenson, Bobby Kellard, Ken Foggo and Paul Went were sold and George Graham went to Crystal Palace in exchange for a young striker named David Kemp. Although Pompey managed to pay off the required £25,000, they'd lost a lot of experienced players forcing Ian to blood many of the youth team into the tough physical demands of the 3rd Division. This soon resulted in half the 1st team being under 19 or 20 years old. In at the deep end along with Steve Foster, went Peter Denyer, Keith Viney, Clive Green, Phil Figgins, Dave Pullar and Chris Kamara. They came to be known as the 'Pompey Babes' and I was so proud as I watched them slowly help pull Pompey round. They brought a lot of spirit to the team which had been lacking with the older players. Chris Kamara, who Henry Stenhouse had recommended to me when he was a young lad in the Navy, was probably the most skilful of them although he was a stubborn, mule-headed character and not easy to manage. I had a big fall-out with him after substituting him in a away game in London. He was treating the game just as a stage to show off his skills. I told him at half-time, it's a team game. He wouldn't listen so I took him off and put his nose well out of joint. He went on to play for Leeds United, Swindon and Luton amongst others and had a great career in the game. He eventually managed Bradford City and Stoke City and I bet he told his players there it was a team game!

Graham Roberts was another teenager who played for the youth team. After Bournemouth had scrapped their youth team, I had a phone call from Tony Nelson who was on the coaching staff there recommending Graham to me. He told me that he'd been released by the club and was working on the family's market stall in Bournemouth. He didn't have a phone number so I wrote to him asking him if he'd like to come for a trial which he agreed to. He was a very strong, well built young lad, playing as a striker at the time. He was so brave, it was almost frightening to see him go in to head the ball as defenders were about to kick it. He was totally fearless. Ian thought he'd make the grade and put him on non-contract terms. After Ian and myself had left, Jimmy Dickinson released him as he thought he wasn't good enough. Graham never made an appearance for the Pompey 1st team. Then in stepped my old mate Dave Best, the former Portsmouth keeper I'd once played alongside at Ipswich Town who'd also realized Graham's potential. David took him to Weymouth where he continued to improve. It wasn't long before the bigger clubs started to sniff around. He was about to sign for West Bromich Albion when, at the last minute to the annoyance of their manager 'Big Ron' Atkinson, Spurs stole in to buy him. He played for Glasgow Rangers and was capped six times by England before his career was sadly finished by injury. Another local boy 'done well' as they say.

I still loved to play and was turning out for 'The Showbiz Entertainers' who played for charity on Sunday afternoons mainly on the South Coast. They all loved football. Amongst their numbers at the time were Dave King, our captain Robin Nedwell from 'Doctor in the House', Richard Beckinsale from 'Porridge', Di Bradley, star of 'Kes', big Mike Redfern, the 'Oxo' man whose TV wife was Lynda Bellingham, Geoff Hughes from 'Heartbeat', Jack Sheppard who was Wycliffe, Jack Smethhurst from 'Love thy Neighbour', singer Paul Young and Adam Woodyatt who later starred in 'Eastenders'. Our manager was Hugh Elton, a television and film extra who dressed up at half-time as a drag queen which always went down well with the crowd.

One weekend, Hugh rang me to say they were short of players so I took a few of the lads with me, Neil Hider who now coaches the kids at Pompey, Chris Kamara and Kevin Clements. They loved the chance to mix with the stars and also the crates of booze supplied by our sponsors, Newcastle Brown Ale. After the games, we'd usually go to a night club for the evening and Hugh would pull in a few girls for the entertainment of the entertainers. One weekend, I persuaded Ian St John to play in one of our games. That day he was in the entertainers team alongside Richard Beckinsale, Dave King and TV presenter Fred Dineage. Fred was no footballer. He always played on the wing where he could joke with the crowd. Ian was so passionate about football. Even though it was only a charity match, he really wanted to win the game. After Fred had completely bungled a few passes to him, Ian had seen enough and shouted out "Don't give it to him, he's fucking hopeless!" and so it went on whenever it looked like Fred might get the ball. In a way, I think Ian made it even more amusing for the crowd, though perhaps not for poor Fred who was once director of Portsmouth FC!

Despite the success of SOS, Pompey and the young lads giving their all, Ian's time at the club ended after a 2-0 defeat at Mansfield Town and a bust-up with Deacon, leaving Portsmouth still in danger of relegation with just three games to go. Ian hadn't been given a fair chance, having been promised thousands of pounds to rebuild the team which he never received. Jimmy Dickinson took over as manager after Deacon had talked him into it. Jimmy had been offered a coaching job by George Smith when his playing days were over but had turned it down. In 1968, he had taken the post of club secretary and Public Relations Officer for the club, a position he was ideally suited for. He loved his work, enjoying the peaceful routine of his job and going to the 'Pompey Pub' for his lunchtime sandwich and half of bitter. It was a cruel option that the chairman gave Jimmy, playing on his great loyalty to the club he'd served so well. Jimmy had never managed a team before, let alone one that was so close to his heart and on the brink of relegation.

At the time I was with the youth team in a 6-a-side tournament at a holiday camp in Brean Sands near Weston-Super-Mare. Most of the teams we were up against were in the South East Counties League. There were also teams from the West Country, including Bristol Rovers, who had a young lad called Gary Mabbutt playing for them. I expected some of the lads to go out for a drink in the evenings. I told them not to overdo it and I didn't mind as long as they gave 100% on the pitch.

Both West Ham and Millwall were at the tournament. For obvious reasons, there was a bit of tension between them. One incident nearly had our lads into trouble. Some of the Millwall youths decided it would be funny to write 'PFC' in boot blacking on all the doors of their West Ham rivals, trying to stir up trouble between them and our lads. I knew they had nothing to do with it and stood my ground when fingers were pointed the next morning. To their credit, although my boys were last in bed each night, they were the first up for breakfast and were producing the goods on the pitch. The one thing that did let them down on the trip was showing a lack of respect to Bertie Mee, one of the elder statesman in the game who'd managed Arsenal to the league and cup double in 1971. They'd nicknamed him 'Bertie Bassett' and started to call him this within earshot. This came to a head one evening when two of my lot became so pissed that they lost their bearings and ended up falling through a fence opposite to where we were staying, making a hell of a racket. Bertie Mee looked out of his upstairs window to see what all the commotion was about and asked them what they were doing, only to get a stream of abuse back from the youngsters. Bertie reported this to me. I decided it was time to show the whole team who was boss and that this was pushing things too far. The next morning, I assembled the whole squad and tore them off a strip before taking them down to the beach and making them run up and down the sand dunes. It's a painful exercise if you do it for long enough. They knew they'd been out of order and took their punishment without any moaning. We'd done well in the tournament getting to the semi-final before getting knocked out. We were about to take part in the play-off for 3rd and 4th places when I had an urgent call from Jimmy Dickinson asking me to help him out. Ian had been sacked. I obviously couldn't refuse. We went straight back to Portsmouth without even taking part in the play-off.

I was reluctant to take on the job of first team coach. I was totally committed to the youth team. Jimmy was very persuasive so I accepted his offer with Billy Hunter taking over as youth team coach. Jimmy didn't have much time for Scotsmen. What a mug I was to take the job. I was still learning as a coach. Both Jimmy and I were pitched together into a situation we weren't ready for. I remember taking training on my first day in the job when the plan was to finish with a thirty minute game. Jimmy said he'd come and watch but never turned up. Afterwards I went to see him in his office and asked him why. "I was going to but it's a bit cold out there today," he replied.

Jimmy started well enough getting a vital point in a 0-0 draw at Preston. We needed two points from our last two games and the 3-1 win over York City was enough to see Pompey safe with two goals from 19 year old Clive Green and one from David Kemp, definitely Ian's best ever signing for Pompey. His 15 goals in 33 games surely saved Pompey from relegation to the 4th Division for the first time in the club's history. There was nothing on the last game which we lost 4-3 away to Swindon. In the first half, we were terrible. At half-time, all Jimmy could say was "Just think of our supporters out there who've come all this way to watch you play" and that was it. When the players had left the dressing room, he said to me "Ray, I very nearly swore at them." I knew from that moment, Jimmy wasn't going to make it as a manager. Having had so much natural ability as a player, I don't think he could put into words what had come so naturally to him. As far as Jimmy was concerned, either you could play or you couldn't. He was a kind person and a gentleman but I think those stressful years as manager at Portsmouth no doubt contributed to his early death after a heart attack in 1982 during a game at Rotherham United, after which he shortly died. Jimmy should have been left as club secretary but his great loyalty made him take a job that finally killed him.

One event on my return to Pompey gave me more satisfaction than any other. Ron Greenwood, who had moved upstairs to general manager at West Ham, contacted Portsmouth regarding our young goalkeeper Alan Knight. I was on my summer holiday at the time and received a phone call from Jimmy Dickinson asking if I could come into the club to see him. He told me Ron Greenwood was travelling down from London to discuss the signing of Alan Knight, our youth team goalie who was just 16 at the time. Ron arrived at Fratton Park to do business but I had already talked Jimmy out of selling Alan. I said that we have to keep this boy as he will be great for the club. The £6,000 they offered was not enough anyway. Ron was a bit upset as he knew Pompey were in financial trouble and thought we would bite his hand off for that sort of money. He also knew that Jimmy was a gent and and would find it hard to say no. I stood my ground and said a firm 'no deal' which turned out to be a great decision for the club as Knightsie went on to play 801 games for Pompey in a career that spanned 22 years.

Chapter 25

"Farewell Pompey Again"

The next season, I was forced out of Portsmouth Football Club for the second time in my career. I was alleged to have hit a man in the Pompey Supporters Club room. He was a local hairdresser who owned two salons in the area and had given one of my teenage daughters a job as a trainee. All seemed to be going well until she'd been working for him for a couple months when Eileen, who always sensed very quickly if something was worrying any of the girls, found out he'd taken advantage of her. When she told me, I was so furious that I went round to see him at his home straight away. His wife was devastated when I told her what he'd done, then he told me to hit him but he was such a pathetic figure, I left it at that. I told him that if he even so much as came near my daughter again, I would do more than just hit him.

My warning wore off quickly as he continued to be a pest. He was involved with the Supporters Club and it was difficult to avoid him as he was always at after match functions which Eileen and I went to as well. The snide comments he was making were pushing things too far and I found just his very presence sickened me. When our eyes met, there was usually a smirk on his face. I decided it was time to report it at a higher level rather than take action myself. I went to see Deacon asking him to deal with it. He said he couldn't help me as it wasn't a club matter but later changed his mind on this.

Things came to a head after an evening game at Fratton Park. By the time I had arrived in the Supporters Club room, Eileen had slipped into an argument with the man who was getting very lippy. He then said something which overstepped the limit and I went for him. He turned and ran for the door but I caught up with him and grabbed him just as he opened it. The force of our collision cracked his head against the edge of the door leaving him bleeding above the eye. Seeing he was cut, I just shook him and swore at him telling him never to speak to my wife like that again. I may as well have whacked him as things turned out. He was talked into reporting it to the police by some of his mates who'd witnessed the incident.

A few days later at about half past midnight, I'd just returned home from an evening reserve game in London and was making a cup of tea when there was a knock at the door. It was a young police officer who asked me as they say 'to accompany him' to the police station. I made a statement and then they asked me to remove my belt, shoelaces, my watch and rings before being taken to the cells. For the first and last time in my life, the cell door, 'the slammer' as it's called, crashed behind me leaving me in an eerie silence. There was just a wrought iron bed and a chair to sit on. The few hours I spent in that cell seemed like an eternity. I wondered how I could have ended up like this. It was one of the most welcome sounds when I finally heard the key turning to unlock my cell door. From there, I was taken to another room, given a cup of tea and charged with ABH, 'aggravated bodily harm', then released. They took me home by which time it was nearly five o'clock in the morning.

With a court case hanging over me I continued to help Jimmy as first team coach. It wasn't easy as word had circulated about what had happened and a lot of people knew why. A month later, my case was heard at Portsmouth Crown Court where I was fined £120 and warned as to my conduct over the next twelve months. As if the fine wasn't enough, a few days after the hearing, I received a letter from Deacon informing me that I'd been suspended for an indefinite period on no pay. Effectively, it meant I'd been sacked. I'm sure he saw this as an opportunity to get rid of me. The way I saw it, he knew Jimmy couldn't do the job but couldn't sack a club legend because of the uproar it would have caused amongst supporters and his head would have been on the block. With me out of the way, he could bring in someone with more experience which he did; Frank Burrows, the ex-Swindon player. I remember meeting Frank the day I left Pompey, advising him not to trust Deacon. I said to him "You'll think you're doing okay and see the light at the end of the tunnel then he'll sack you" and that's exactly what happened. Frank was sacked after he'd made the best of an almost impossible job.

A few weeks later with no money coming in, I went with Eileen to sign on the dole at the DSS Office in Cosham. We arrived there early but it wasn't until 11:30am that we managed to see one of their advisors. She was a young lady who, after listening to us, politely said we were not entitled to any benefit as I'd been suspended and not sacked and that I would have to take the club to court to get any compensation. Eileen was furious. She told her loudly that a lot of people were fiddling the system, getting money they weren't entitled to and that we'd both paid income tax and national insurance for over twenty five years and it was the only time we'd ever asked for help. The young lady said she was sorry but there was nothing she could do. Eileen said if that was the case she would go to Tescos, fill up a trolley with food for the children and walk out without paying, then, when arrested, she would tell the police and the newspapers she'd done it for the children.

After this, our young advisor asked us to wait while she had a word with the manager there. She returned about five minutes later and told us to come back that afternoon to collect a one-off payment we could cash at a Post Office. She also advised me to apply to the 'Unfair Dismissal Tribunal' in Southampton which I did straight away.

I was looking forward to it. I was not only confident of winning my case but also leaving Deacon with egg on his face. On the day of the hearing, just over a month later, I arrived ten minutes before it was due to start. Deacon was already there with a big time solicitor from London that he'd hired and Bill Davis who'd taken over Jimmy's job as club secretary. I'd only just sat down when Bill came over to me and told me the club were no longer going to contest the case and had decided to pay me the 15 months left to run on my contract. I felt sorry for Bill. He was the one sent in to tell the court officials and he looked as sick as a parrot when he came out after being given a rollicking from the chairman of the tribunal for wasting their time. I came out of the building to the waiting press and TV cameramen. I was only too pleased to talk to them with a winning smile for the cameras. I went to a local pub with them to celebrate. The down side of the whole affair was that the club couldn't afford to pay me off in one lump sum. It was agreed that I would be paid on a weekly basis.

I had an unexpected bonus not long after this when a man called Reg Locke came around to my house to see me. He rolled up in a smart Rover V8 followed by another car. Reg was not a registered scout but loved football and Pompey. He was also a real character that you couldn't help but like. You could name it, he'd 'been there, done it!' including some time in prison. He wasn't the least bit embarrassed about his colourful past. Reg had come around to say how sorry he was to see me go. He said he wanted to get some of his mates down from London to beat up the person responsible for getting me the sack. I told him that it wasn't my style and just to let things be. There were many sides to Reg but above all he was a very generous man. As he turned to leave, he threw some keys at me.

"What's this?" I said.
"They're for the Rover out there, it's yours for keeps Ray. Everything's up to

date and the log books there as well." The car was only a few years old and in very good nick. Reg had recently been banned from driving and insisted I have it before being driven off in the other car. It was good to think I still had some loyal friends.

Although things were never easy in my second spell with Pompey, mainly due to the never ending financial chaos of the club and leaving as I did hurt a lot, it was an experience I wouldn't have changed for anything. I felt I'd done a good job helping to get the youth scheme going again and leaving a nucleus of players that the club could build on for the future. After I'd left, they also had the benefit of my bringing Steve Foster to the club, selling him for £150,000 to Brighton, easing the financial problems of the club that I'd always loved even in my 15 year exile. Though nothing could never had made up for all the years I would liked to have been a Pompey player, I felt I'd put the record straight when I remembered what Freddie Cox had said to me all those years ago "Ray, I am sorry to say this but you have no future left at this club." In the end, I'd proved him wrong even though I was out of a job again. I left the club with my head held high. When George Smith scrapped the youth scheme at Pompey in 1961, he'd said there were "no talented young footballers in the area, only fish" but I think I'd also proved him wrong. By the time I left, you could say that Cox and Sparshatt were lousy fishermen as I was one of those ones 'that got away'. When Pompey first sold me off to Ipswich Town in 1958, they were relegated to the 2nd Division and, after they'd shown me the door for the second time, perhaps the 'Curse of Jungle Boy' struck again for the final time. At the end of the season, Pompey were relegated to the 4th Division for the first time in the club's history.

Chapter 26

"Fareham Town FC and the real world"

Though all the publicity I'd had was not the type you could wish for, at least I didn't have to market myself and was soon approached by Fareham Town FC. They were playing in the Hampshire league at the time and had won many trophies in the previous few years. A step up to pro-status was on the cards. Their Chairman Roy Grant, signed me for the position of first team manager. I was given the immediate priority of putting a new team together strong enough to gain promotion and join their closest rivals Gosport Borough in the Southern League. Roy also owned a taxi and coach firm called 'Hellyers'. As the club obviously couldn't afford the money that I'd been on, the chairman employed me as a driver in his business to top up my wages, much like my time at Kettering FC.

It was nearing the end of the season when I started there. They were doing well in second place but the chairman told me he was annoyed that some of the players were turning out for a Sunday league team as well. With this in mind, I used the remaining games of the season to sort out the players that I wouldn't retain for the next year. We finished second behind Newport, a very good side from the Isle of Wight managed by ex-Pompey player Derek Edwards. Then I had tell the players who I had decided to release and why; something I'd never had to do before. I know it didn't make me popular but I strengthened the squad by bringing in some of the youngsters who hadn't made the grade at Portsmouth.

The plan was to get the club into the Southern League at the end of the season. After just six weeks, we were bottom of our league. I realized the changes I'd made had resulted in some resentment from the remainder of the old team towards the new recruits I'd brought in.

As neither the chairman or myself were happy with the situation, it resulted in us having words and I told him to stick his job 'where the sun doesn't shine'. We didn't speak to each other for weeks but slowly the old and new players forgot their differences and started to play more as a team. We finished second in the league and were promoted to the Southern League. I now understood how many things you have to take on as a manager. I was able to put into perspective all the problems Jackie Milburn had when stepping up from non league football to the highest league in England with Ipswich Town - management is a very complex and stressful job at any level. Just try it and you will know what I mean.

In the close season, I managed to persuade Ray Hiron to come back to the club where he'd started as a youth before going to Portsmouth in 1964 where he scored 110 goals in 324 games. Ray was over six feet tall and very thin and one of the few players Billy Baxter of Ipswich Town never liked playing against. Billy once said to me "I wish he had more meat on him. He's all bones, knees and elbows. When they stick into you, it's just like being jabbed in the Army again!"

Another player I signed was Dave Reid from Leatherhead, son of Pompey's Duggie Reid, a player remembered for his thunderous shot. I also brought in the ex-Pompey striker Andy Stewart, making the squad a lot stronger than the previous year. We had a good first year in the Southern League, reaching the first round of the FA Cup for the first time in Fareham Town's history, eventually going out 3-2 at Merthyr Tydfil. The next season, after a run of poor results, Roy Grant sacked me, replacing me with the very man who'd used his players in his Sunday league team. I'd always known that being a football manager was a job in which you could produce wonders one week then get kicked out the next. This show of double standards finally made me call it a day after twenty two years in the professional game.

It didn't take me long to find a job. I went to the local Employment Office where I saw a job advertising for a 'Merchandiser' in the area we lived. I wrote off for it and, after an interview, I started to work for a company called 'Lloyd Coopers'. The wages weren't that great but it was a start. My job involved visiting 'Cash and Carry' stores and warehouses in the area to merchandise food lines such as 'Oxo', 'Tetleys Tea', 'Terry's' sweets and chocolates, 'Nestles Coffee', 'McDougalls', 'Fray Bentos' and 'Kraft'. One of the places I visited regularly was Nurdin and Peacock who had a large warehouse in Portsmouth. I had a hand in starting up a team there made up of employees which started in the 4th Division of the Meon Valley Sunday League, playing mainly in small villages around the Portsmouth and Southampton area. It took us six years to get into the 1st Division and although we never won it, we came second in our best season and won both cup competitions over the years in that league. I still loved to play and the thrill of scoring goals kept me playing till I was 56. It was not long after a game in which I had had some touchline abuse from an unexpected source that I finally gave up the game. It was from two plump ladies, a bit like the couple in the old cookery programme 'Two Fat Ladies' who told me from the touchline that I should be ashamed of myself. It wasn't fair that I was playing against young lads because I'd once played for England. There I was, 56 years old and still upsetting the crowd! We won 6-1 that day but a few weeks later I decided to hang up my boots once and for all, binning them to resist any further temptation to play the game that I'd loved since I was just a child.

I was working at Nurdin and Peacock one morning when a young lad who worked there, brought my attention to an article in the day's issue of 'The Sun' newspaper. It was by Kevin Beattie, the great former Ipswich and England player who was writing a series of articles about his life in football at the time. He alleged in the article that he'd seen me having a punch-up with Bobby Robson in the showers when I was at Ipswich Town. I phoned my old friend Pat Godbold who was Bobby's personal secretary in his time there, to find out if Kevin was at the club in my final few months there. Pat said he would have been only 14 years old then. He may have been involved with the club but she'd no idea where Kevin had picked up this story. If there'd been any sort of punch-up while I was still at the club, it would more likely have been with Eileen who was furious with Bobby after he'd denied me a free transfer, putting a block on us going to South Africa.

At first I looked on it as being just a bit of fun as I went on my daily visits to other 'Cash and Carry' centres, being called names like Tyson and other famous boxers. I thought it would all blow over and be forgotten in a few days. But it carried on and after a couple of weeks it began to annoy me. I no longer saw the funny side of it as it just wasn't true. I decided to seek legal advice and arranged a meeting with a local solicitor called Mr Solvetti who agreed to take on my case.

I didn't hear anything for a few weeks by which time, according to some, I was right up there with the greatest boxers of all time. My Dad, having been a professional boxer, would have been proud of me had it been true. When Mr Solvetti eventually rang me, he said 'The Sun' newspaper had agreed to an out of court settlement and, shortly afterwards, I received a cheque for £1,000. 'The Sun' also paid Mr Solvetti's fee so I owed him nothing but a big thank you.

It wasn't quite the end of the affair though. Not long after the libel case, when my contract with Nestle came to an end, I received an invitation from them to watch a game between Crystal Palace and Ipswich Town at Selhurst Park. The company had a private corporate box. I thought it was just their way of saying thank you for all the work I'd done for them. There was more to it than I'd imagined.

When Eileen and myself walked in to their box, we were greeted by two smartly dressed men, one of them Nestle's top man. After exchanging handshakes, he reached into a pocket and produced a black and white photograph. "Take a look at this," he said, handing me the photo. I immediately recognized myself though it was a lot younger version and I was signing an autograph for a young boy who looked to be in his early teens. He asked me "Do you know who that young boy is?" Of course, I hadn't a clue as I'd signed hundreds during my career but, just as I thought it might be him, he said with a smile "Well actually it's me, at fourteen years of age!" He went on to tell me that the picture was taken at the Vetch Field ground, home of Swansea Town, after making my debut against them for Ipswich Town in 1958. He also showed me the programme for the game which he'd kept for all those years and there was another surprise to come.

He turned to the man standing next to him, introducing him to me as his brother. He said that he worked for 'The Sun' newspaper. Before I could speak, he said "I know what you're going to say Ray, but I knew it wasn't you!" He went on to say that Kevin Beattie didn't get it wrong about the player who'd had the bust-up with Robson but the editor had told him to change it to 'Ray Crawford' as I was more well known and it would sell more papers! Town drew 1-1 with Palace that afternoon and, though it wasn't a great game, it was another experience and another link with the past, one of many I owe to my career as a footballer.

Chapter 27

"Nothing is forever"

I was working in the Makro superstore in Fareham, Hampshire when one of the lads who worked there came to tell me that he'd heard on the radio that Alf Ramsey had died. It caught me totally unprepared and I was soon almost in tears. They're a decent lot there and were very kind to me as they knew how sad I felt. Even though I knew Alf had been very ill for some time with Alzheimer's disease, you have a feeling you get about people who have touched your life in a powerful way that they are almost indestructible and will go on forever.

About two weeks later, I received a letter from Ipswich Town Football Club, inviting me to attend Alf Ramsey's memorial service at St Mary-le-Tower Church on Saturday 15th of May 1999. I wouldn't have missed it for anything. It was a celebration of Sir Alf's life and the club he'd served so well did him proud that day. Though it was also a sad day, it was good to meet up with most of my old Ipswich team mates there and some of the 1966 World Cup winning team, apart from Bobby Moore who sadly died in 1993. Both Bobby Charlton and his brother Jack were there and one of my old mates told me Jack had picked me out and said I'd given him more trouble than most in his career as a defender; a great compliment from a great player who was respected by all his fellow professionals.

It was less than a month later, when my life started to take its biggest turn since the day I'd met Eileen at the South Parade Pier dance hall in Southsea over forty years before. I was usually first up in the household but, on that morning Eileen was up long before me. It was 7:00am when I came down stairs to find her watching the TV breakfast news. She said she wasn't feeling too well, felt a bit faint and was having trouble with her breathing. I told her to rest, made her a cup of tea and cooked my breakfast. I usually started work at 8:00am. By that time, Eileen was looking very pale and her breathing had become worse. She told me not to worry. She already had an appointment that morning at our local surgery to see Doctor Harrison, a very good doctor who'd once been Pompey's club doctor. I rang him as soon as the surgery opened at 8:30am, describing Eileen's condition as best I could. With no hesitation, he told me to call an ambulance straight away.

When I told Eileen, she was having none of it, telling me not to worry and that she'd be alright. I knew how stubborn she was so I rang all our daughters asking them to come round as quickly as possible, keeping my voice low so that Eileen couldn't hear, telling them to persuade her to go into hospital.

I stayed with Eileen until the first of the girls arrived, then went off to work hoping that the combined wills of my daughters would be too much for even Eileen to resist. I was relieved when I had a call an hour later from my eldest daughter Jane. She told me that they'd taken their mum to the Queen Alexandria Hospital in Portsmouth where she was undergoing tests. When I came to see her later that day, the doctors told me Eileen was being treated for a blood clot and she was on a strong dose of 'Warfarin' which helps to thin the blood. By visiting time, the next day on Friday evening, she seemed to be back to her old self as the girls and I laughed and joked with her at her bedside. The doctor said it would take a bit longer for the drugs he'd prescribed for her to have their full effect. She could go home after two more days in hospital on the Monday. We left her that evening thinking all was going well and that Eileen was going to make a complete recovery.

The next morning my daughter Claire rang to say she was going to pick up her sisters and meet me at the hospital later on at visiting time. She was going to bring some fresh clothes for her mum to wear on the Monday that she was due to leave hospital. When I arrived in the ward at 11:30am, I sensed straight away that all was not well. She didn't seem to want to talk much. I just sat there by her side her holding her hand. After a while, she said she wasn't feeling well. I quickly found a nurse and asked her to come and see her. After a quick examination, she told me she would deal with it and suggested I go for a walk. I went outside to my car thinking it was just a minor setback in her recovery. In no way was I prepared for what had happened when I returned to the ward about fifteen minutes later.

The nurse was waiting for me as I walked in and she showed me to a nearby office telling me the doctor would be there soon to speak to me. Even then as I waited in almost complete silence, there was no way I could imagine what I was about to hear. The doctor came in after a few minutes and it was when he pulled up a chair and sat beside me, gently placing a hand on mine that I feared the worst.

"I'm afraid I have bad news for you. Your wife has just died." A cold shiver went through me. I just couldn't take it in at first. "I'm afraid she had a massive heart attack. There was nothing we could do to save her."

He told me he suspected Eileen's death had been caused by a blood clot reaching her heart. I told him Eileen had slipped and fallen down the stairs of our house a few months before. Although she had just a few scratches and bruises, Eileen had been suffering from dizzy spells ever since. The doctor said the fall could well have started a blood clot but it wasn't easy to diagnose them as they can be just like a time bomb waiting to go off.

I had to try and keep myself together as the most difficult part of the morning was to come. All my four daughters were on their way to see their mother, fully expecting her to be full of life as she'd been the evening before. About half an hour later, they started to arrive, one with pillows, one with some snacks from Marks and Spencers, one with sweets and flowers and Claire with a new nightie. When I told them the news, we wept together in a round huddle, hardly knowing what to do or to think.

A few days later, the local vicar came round to see me to arrange the day of the funeral. I told him Eileen had always said she would prefer to be cremated rather than buried. There was a large turnout on the day of the funeral and the Portchester Crematorium was full of family and friends to see Eileen on her way. The service was accompanied by songs of her favourite singer Elvis Presley. We'd also arranged for 'Come on Eileen' to be played as her send off when we left the hall. Although Eileen had gone well before her time, in her sixty four years she'd lived a full life. We'd raised four lovely daughters together who she was totally devoted to and given them the very best of everything she could. It still makes me laugh when I think the only time she ever was annoyed with them was if they rang up when she was watching her favourite soaps 'Eastenders' or 'Coronation Street'!

At the turn of the century, it seemed I didn't have much to look forward to. I'd known for sometime after Alf's memorial, a project had been put in place to make a statue in his memory. On August the 7th 2000, I received not only an invitation from the Ipswich Town Supporters Club to the opening ceremony but also a request from Lady Ramsey that I should be the one to unveil his statue on the day. I was absolutely thrilled to bits that this great honour had been given to me. I immediately accepted the invitation, proudly telling all my family and friends. I then arranged my work to fit in around the day of the ceremony and everyone at work wished me well. I think it was perhaps another turning point in my life. I was going to return to Ipswich again, just as I'd first done when Alf had taken me there as a young man over forty years before.

"So that takes us up to today and that's about where I came in Sir Alf, I mean Alf!"

It's dark now but for the yellow streetlights. I wonder if Alf was listening and of course I will never... Christ look at the time! I'm going to miss the last train if I'm not careful and started to walk quickly towards the station. Ten yards on I'm sure I heard a voice behind me which stops me in my tracks.

"Ray, thank you for telling me your story, I enjoyed it very much and thank you for entertaining me!"
"Thanks Alf, I'll be back before long. I'll never stop coming back here till the day I die, you know that, must rush now!"
"Oh, but just one last thing Ray, thank you for not mentioning I liked the occasional secret fag!"
"No worries Alf! Bye, see you soon!" I say as I turn once again and make for the old bridge over the river that leads down to the docks, as I make for the station once again.

EPILOGUE

It has been over five years since I unveiled the statue of Sir Alf and, as promised, I've been back to Ipswich many times to say hello to the great man again although I might never have seen him again as a few months after the event I had my first ever road accident. I was travelling from Fareham's Makro 'Cash and Carry' to Chichester on the M27 and had just pulled into the middle lane doing about 65 mph when my Vauxhall Cavalier was suddenly given a huge shunt in the back from another car, sending me spinning into the crash barrier. Both the police and an ambulance were at the scene very quickly. I had a bump and a cut above my right eye, a sore ankle and the usual whiplash injuries. The other driver who hit me wasn't injured. It turned out he was in the Royal Navy on his way back to Portsmouth at the time. He told the police his car had been blown by a freak gust of wind into the back of me. When a police officer had inspected his car, he found a mobile phone lying on the floor leading him to think his story was most likely not true. The police and ambulance people were brilliant and could not have been kinder. My car was a write-off and I was back on the treatment table again. It took a few months of physiotherapy at St Mary's Hospital in Portsmouth to get me right. The other driver involved was given a caution.

During the months after the accident, home was so quiet and lonely without Eileen and I started to drink more than I'd ever done before. I know alcohol is no escape from reality and only a short-term fix but, most evenings especially at weekends, I'd taken to boozing quite heavily. Then along came Carol who I met through work and helped me pick up my life again. We saw each other for over 4 years before getting married. I've finally retired from managing my Sunday League side as I wanted to spend more time with Carol. She's not a football fan and works all week for the NHS. It's nice to have the weekends free to go out together. She also loves a good book, getting through a couple a week. I now have the bug as well, mainly preferring books about sport, especially autobiographies. As for my old team mates at Ipswich, we had a get together in April and I met up with John Elsworthy who is still the same gentle giant that he was as a player and also Larry Carberry and John Compton. Andy Nelson moved to Spain to live out his years in the Mediterranean sun but, tragically, Billy Baxter, one of the finest athletes I ever saw, had to have half his leg amputated and was then diagnosed with diabetes. He is as brave as ever and still likes his round of golf. On the sad side, Rocky Stephenson, Kenny Malcolm, Jimmy Leadbetter (Jimmy died a month after the World Cup 2006) and Tom Garneys, all great players for Ipswich Town in their time, have all passed away.

After the World Cup in August 2006, Carol and I were invited to spend two days at the Savoy Hotel in London with no expenses spared to launch E-ON as the new sponsors of the FA Cup. The last time that I'd been there was in 1962 when Ipswich Town were presented with the 1st Division Trophy and the players were given their medals. I was very proud to be there again to take part in the celebration of the greatest domestic football cup competition in the world. John Motson, the famous BBC commentator, was running the show and introducing the players to the guests at the function. I hadn't seen 'Motty' for some time so, before he came to me, I thought I'd have a bit of fun. I stood in front of him and asked if he knew who I was. We've all aged a lot so I was quite relieved that I was still recognizable. It only took John only a few seconds to come up with my name! He was just as quick to identify Jim Montgomery, the ex-Sunderland keeper who was standing beside me. Other ex-players there were Ray Clemence, Peter Barnes, Joe Royle, Tommy Booth, Mike Sumerbee, Peter Reid, Lou Macari, Steve Perryman, Dave Mackay, Frank Clark, Sir Trevor Brooking, Ian Rush and Ricky George. All of them had some connection with memorable games in the FA Cup with my particular feat playing for Colchester United and scoring two goals in the 3-2 win against Leeds United 1971. Some consider this to be the biggest giant-killing in FA Cup history. Also attending the launch was Graham Taylor the ex-Watford and England manager, Gordon Taylor the ex-Bolton player and now chief of the PFA and Brian Barwick, chief executive of the FA.

It's now the second week of July 2007 and in the last month my old mate Derek Dougan, 'The Doog', most famous for his years at Wolves and Dave Simmons my old strike partner from my Colchester days have both sadly passed away. My old Ipswich buddy, Brian Siddall, has also died at the age of 77. I will always remember Brian as having terrible pre-match nerves. One of the first games I played alongside him was in 1958 away to Sheffield United at Bramall Lane, just a couple of months after I'd joined Town. As we were leaving the dressing room with our studs starting to clatter on the hard concrete outside, a desperate cry came from the toilets shouting "Hey, wait a minute! Hey, wait for me!" It was Brian, again suffering from his pre-match nerves. Another of my old team mates Reg Pickett, who played alongside Brian many times for Ipswich Town, is still going strong. When I go and see him, I take him out to a nearby pub as Reg still loves a pint and so do I. I also never fail to remind him that I still have more hair than him! Reg still follows the fortunes of Pompey very closely and we were both so pleased that Harry Redknapp and the boys did so well last season.

My Mum and Dad have both passed away now. My father died some years ago and my mother just last year at the age of 89. I have 3 grand children; one a girl called Chloe and two are boys - Oakley who is 4 years old and Jack who is 11.

Well, that's me up till the present date and I've just turned seventy-one. My memory is still good which is one of the reasons why I did this book. None of our championship winning team of 1961-62 or McGarry's side that won promotion in 1968 ever wrote their memoirs so, as well as being my story, I hope it pays tribute to some of the great players who graced the famous turf of Portman Road and should never be forgotten. The last thing I heard about one of those players, Danny Hegan, was that he was working at Butlins Holiday Camp in Minehead doing a bit of football coaching for kids on holiday. Danny would no doubt of been a millionaire these days with the talent he had.

I can count myself lucky as I've had a wonderful life and travelled all over the world, staying in the best hotels and eating at the best restaurants. I know what money can buy, but more important than anything, I still have my health and that's the one thing money can't buy. Many have not been so lucky as me in this respect. I hope you will bear with me for just a minute longer, as I'd like to bring your attention to '**Motor Neurone Disease**' which perhaps has not had as much publicity yet as other life threatening diseases.

I first saw the devastating effects of MND when it took the life of a good friend of mine, Richard Page. When I was youth team manager at Pompey, his 16 year-old son Chris was playing in the team. Richard and his wife Lillian were lovely people and we soon became close friends. Chris looked to be a possible new Alan Ball with his red hair but didn't quite make the grade. Despite this, Richard and Lillian still remained our friends. Not long after this, Richard was diagnosed with Motor Neurone Disease which attacks the muscles in the body. His health rapidly declined. Lillian told me that he always locked up at night as part of his routine even though he was very ill. The night he died, he asked Lillian to lock-up and told her he was going to bed. She followed him up a while later to find him lying on the bed, finally at peace with the world. It was if he knew he was going to die that night and, when Lillian told me, I had tears rolling down my face. The great Don Revie, once player then manager of Leeds United and England, died of the disease at the age of 62 in 1989 and the legendary Jimmy Johnstone of Celtic and Scotland, one of the greatest wingers the game has ever seen, died from the disease in 2006. The effects of MND have to seen to be believed. In the end, you have arms and hands you cannot move as they have shrivelled away to nothing but bone and flesh and you age well beyond your years. As the condition worsens, there comes a time when you need help every day as you can't do much for yourself. You can't dress yourself, you can't even feed yourself, and there's the humiliation of not being able to go to the toilet by yourself. When I see the horrific things this disease does to a fellow human being, I think it's time everybody sat up and became more aware of it.

Another very good cause that I would like to bring your attention to is the 'Oakley Waterman Foundation' that provides holiday respite caravans for terminally ill children and their families. Former Pompey player Dave Waterman and his wife Lorraine whose son Oakley tragically died of cancer at a very young age founded it. On this account, I will be dividing **all proceeds** that I receive from any sales of 'Curse of the Jungle Boy' towards research into '**Motor Neurone Disease**' and the '**Oakley Waterman Foundation**'. It possibly won't be much but, if it serves to bring more attention to these very good causes, my call will have been answered.

Finally, I must say that if anyone has been offended or hurt by anything I have said in this book, I apologize with all my heart. I have tried to avoid this as much as possible but, when you go back so far into your past as I have, sometimes mistakes are made. I hope it is all as close to the truth as possible.

Thank you so much for buying this book.

Ray Crawford.

Ray Crawford's Career Statistics

Season	Club	Total Apps	Total Goals	League Apps	League Goals	FA Cup Apps	FA Cup Goals	League Cup Apps	League Cup Goals	European Cup Apps	European Cup Goals	Charity Shield Apps	Charity Shield Goals
1957-58	Portsmouth	17	9	16	8	1	1						
1958-59	Portsmouth	2	1	2	1								
1959-60	Ipswich Town	33	26	30	25	3	1						
1960-61	Ipswich Town	37	18	36	18	1							
1961-62	Ipswich Town	44	40	42	40	1		1					
1962-63	Ipswich Town	50	37	41	33	5	1	4	3	4	8	1	
1963-64	Ipswich Town	49	33	42	25	2							
	Wolves	6	2	6	2	1							
1964-65	Wolves	35	26	34	26	1							
	Wolves	26	15	23	13	3	2						
1965-66	WBA	5	2	5	2			2	1				
	WBA	11	5	9	4			2	1				
1966-67	Ipswich Town	12	8	12	8	4	3						
1967-68	Ipswich Town	48	25	42	21	1		2	1				
1968-69	Ipswich Town	42	21	39	16	1		2	5				
	Ipswich Town	32	17	30	16	1		1	1				

Club games

	Club	Total Apps	Total Goals	League Apps	League Goals	FA Cup Apps	FA Cup Goals	League Cup Apps	League Cup Goals	European Cup Apps	European Cup Goals	Charity Shield Apps	Charity Shield Goals
	Portsmouth	19	10	18	9	1	1						
	Ipswich Town	353	227	320	204	18	5	10	10	4	8	1	0
	Wolves	61	41	57	39	4	2						
	WBA	16	7	14	6	0	0	2	1				
	Charlton Athletic	22	7	21	7	0	0	1	0				
	Colchester United	55	31	45	24	7	7	3	0				
	Club totals:	**526**	**323**	**475**	**289**	**30**	**15**	**16**	**11**	**4**	**8**	**1**	**0**

Representative games

		Apps	Goals
	England	2	1
	Football League	3	5
	FA XI	1	
	Representative totals:	**6**	**6**

		Total Apps	Total Goals	League Apps	League Goals	FA Cup Apps	FA Cup Goals	League Cup Apps	League Cup Goals	European Cup Apps	European Cup Goals	Charity Shield Apps	Charity Shield Goals
	Grand Totals	**532**	**329**	**475**	**289**	**30**	**15**	**16**	**11**	**4**	**8**	**1**	**0**

HILSEA MODERN BOYS' SCHOOL

EACH FOR ALL

SPORTS AND ATHLETICS

This **CERTIFICATE** is presented to

Raymond Crawford

FOR AN OUTSTANDING PERFORMANCE IN

Athletics, Cricket & Football

July _____ 1951

L. F. Street
Head Master

You can be in
STANLEY MATTHEWS
boots !

The boots he plays in do make a difference to a player. 'Course they do. Even a star in the game couldn't shine in ill-fitting footwear. Stanley Matthews knows that. He wanted the best—and he helped to make them. They're C.W.S. He always plays in them. So do many other famous professionals. That's how good these football boots are. They have refinements, advised by Stanley Matthews, which put them way ahead of others. Try on a pair. Play in the kind of boots that Stanley Matthews wears. They'll improve your game.

Boys'
7 to 10   11 to 1   2 to 5
20/3   22/6   26/9
Men's 34/-

C.W.S
STANLEY MATTHEWS
FOOTBALL BOOTS
Obtainable at all Co-operative Footwear Branches

Cooperative

Co-operative House, Fratton Rd
129, Kingston Road
107, High Street, Cosham
100-106, West Street, Fareham
15 Stoke Road, Gosport
Lavant Street, Petersfield

Portsea Island Mutual Co-operative Society Ltd.

My first Football boots

ENGLISH SCHOOLS' SHIELD 3rd ROUND

AT FRATTON PARK
(By kind permission of the Directors)

SATURDAY, DECEMBER 2nd, 1950
at 11 a.m

PORTSMOUTH

TOOMEY
(Technical)

ROGERS
(St. Lukes)

EDWARDS (Capt.)
(S. Grammar)

CRAWFORD
(Hilsea)

LEWIS
(North End)

WATTS
(Hilsea)

TOUT
(S. Grammar)

...KELD
(...Grammar)

CLUCAS
(Hilsea)

CUMMINGS
(Hartley)

USMAR
(S. Grammar)

MOODY
(Ashley)

W. E. RANN (Isle of Wight)

MILLS
(Hartley)

SEYMOUR
(Ringwood)

FLOOD
(Brockenhurst)

MANUEL
(Hartley)

STACEY
(Christchurch)

HOYLE
(Christchurch)

SCOTT
(Ashley)

PITMAN
(Christchurch)

NEW FOREST

ATKINS PRINTERS, PORTSMOUTH

Portsmouth Juniors' outside-right, Crawford, beats Ariesey defender.   P.M. 824

City Representative XI 1950-51. Ray Crawford is bottom right

Hampshires score double

TROUNCE 55 COY RASC 9-2 IN KL GARRISON CUP SOCCER FINAL; CRAWFORD THE STAR

THE 1st Bn. Royal Hampshire Regiment "Tigers," as expected completed a double yesterday when they routed 55 Coy Royal Army Service Corps by 9-2 in the Kuala Lumpur Garrison Cup final on the HQ Malaya ground. Earlier they had won the league.

But what was not expected was the ease which they disposed of their opponents yesterday.

Getting in top form the winners' speed precision passing were too much for RASC.

Left-winger Crawford, showing plenty of dash and speed scored four goals. He also paved the way for another two.

Wicks, the skipper, gave a sterling performance in the wing-half berth. He had the opposing forward well policed and opened up the game with clever, cunning moves.

The Service Corps forwards were unable to combine effectively and their defence was none too steady against the fierce raids of the Tigers.

After 10 minutes of even exchanges the Service Corps were the first to take the lead. Mitchell, Tigers right full-back, was pulled up for obstruction in the penalty area. Centre-half Dobinson scored from the spot.

Equaliser

Stunned by this setback the Tigers hurled their might against the R.A.S.C. and within two minutes left-winger Crawford equalised with a blazing shot off a pass from right-half Wicks. This goal spurred the Tigers to greater efforts and in 34th minute right-winger Rule gave them the lead. Later Crawford took the half time score to 3-1.

Hampshires dictated play for the major part of the second half but the Service Corps fought on with courage and determination.

In the 15th minute Wicks sent across a lovely centre for inside-left Newton to head the ball into the net. Two minutes later a combined move by the Hampshire forwards resulted in centre-forward Salt increasing the lead to 5-1.

The Service Corps made sporadic raids but this had no effect on the agile Hampshire defenders.

Tigers took a 6-1 lead when right-winger Rule put centre-forward Salt with a through pass. Salt beat Knight with a fierce drive from 15 yards out.

The Service Corps did not give up fighting. They "pulled their socks" and stormed the Tigers goal-mouth and their courage was rewarded when inside-right Hughes reduced the lead.

Hampshires scored their last three goals through Crawford (2) and Salt (1).

Capt. Hugh Slocker refereed. Teams were:

1st Bn Royal Hampshire Regiment, Thomas; Pickard, Mitchell; Wicks, Hellard, Softly; Rule, Hunt, Salt, Newton and Crawford.

55 Coy. Royal Army Service Corps; Knight; Loone, Draper; Way, Dobinson, William; Steward, Hughes, Aindra, Heagman, and

Hamps Enter Caldbeck Cup Semi-final

KUALA LUMPUR, Sat.—The Royal Hampshire Regiment beat Royal Army Service Corps, South Malaya, 4-2 in their Far East Land Forces Caldbeck Cup soccer competition (South Zone) at the Headquarters Malaya Command stadium here today.

The Royal Hampshire Regiment have now qualified for the semi-final of the Malaya Zone.

RASC gave a fighting display, and had a fair share of the exchanges, but poor finishing by their forwards robbed them several good chances.

Left-winger Ray Crawford proved to be the matchwinner for the Hampshires. He netted two goals, and was the key man in the attack.

After ten minutes, Newton opened the score for Hampshires with a mighty shot that gave the RASC goalkeeper, Drummond, no chance to save.

The Service Corps came near to equalizing in the 18th minute, but centreforward Stewart's shot went inches wide.

Ten minutes before the interval, Newton, gaining a pass from Crawford, put the Hamps two-up with a rising shot.

After the resumption, Crawford took the tally to 3-0 with a fine fierce left-foot drive. RASC, staging a storming rally, reduced the lead through Westom off a pass from left half Richards.

Against the run of play, Crawford netted the fourth goal for Hampshires, but centre-forward Steward managed to reduce the lead for the RASC five minutes before the end.

Royal Hampshire Regiment: Thomas; Pickard, Mitchell; Terry, Hellard, Softly; Rule, Hunt, Salt, Newton and Crawford.

RASC, South Malaya: Drummond; Taylor, Draper; Davies, Astley, Richards; Way, Smillie, Steward Brennan and Westom.

(right) My 'oppo' Brian "Smudger" Smith just before leaving on a mission into the jungle. Soon after this picture was taken, he was accidentally shot and killed.

(above) Lining up with the Malayan Team, waiting to be introduced to the Vietnamese Prime Minister.

Portsmouth pre-season 1957/58.

Ray Crawford (left) in the match at Fratton Park today. F.N. 671

Lining up with Pompey

Back row: Bill Albury, Jimmy Dickinson, Norman Uprichard, Phil Gunter, Cyril Rutter, Alex Wilson.
Front Row: Peter Harris, Derek Dougan, Me, Jack Mansell, Jackie Henderson.

Crawford Weds—Then off to Match

RAY CRAWFORD WEDS.—Youthful admirers were present in for[...]
Pompey footballer, Ray Crawford, was married to Miss Eileen [...]

The Bride Went To Fratton Park

After playing for Pompey on Saturday, Ray Crawford was met outside the ground by his bride, formerly Miss Eileen Inkpen, to whom he had been married before the match. He was also met by young admirers who reckoned that Ray's pen-work for the day had not ended with the signing of the register.—E.N. 6737

TIME MARCHES ON.—Pompey footballer Ray Crawford glances at his watch on his day of two appointments — one for his wedding to Miss Eileen Inkpen and the other to play at Fratton Park.—E.N. 6707

'Jungle Boy' comes to town

...and friends

PORTSMOUTH
Colours: Royal Blue Shirts, White Knickers

Gunter 2   Beattie

Phillips

Harris, P. 4   Chapman 8   Hayward 5   Dickinson 3 (Capt.)

7   Saunders 9   Howells 6

Referee: Newman 10   Campbell 11

Mr. E. T. Jennings (Stourbridge)

Linesmen:

Red Flag: Mr. T. Clapperton

Yellow Flag: Mr. W. H. J. Cole

Leadbetter 11   Phillips 10

Belcher 6,   Crawford 9

Malcolm 3   Nelson 5

Bailey

IPSWICH TOWN
Colours: Red & White Shirts, White

Spectators are EXPRESSLY FORBIDDEN TO CROSS PL...

At first glance, this is not Ipswich Town returning on an economy class ferry from a close season tour of Europe! We are returning from Bawdsley to Felixstowe during the big freeze of 1963.

HOW TO DO IT

TED PHILLIPS

TEDS THUNDERBOLT SHOOTING—TIMED AT 90 M.P.H. MEANS HE NEEDS VERY CLOSE MARKING

Bazooka THE CHEW OF CHAMPIONS

Was this a crib sheet for opposing defenders who had to face Ted Phillips of Ipswich?

'Bazooka' chewing gum wrapper with Ted on the ball.

Key men in the Ipswich title-winning team. ROY STEPHENSON, RAY CRAWFORD, DOUG MORAN and JIMMY LEADBETTER with ALF RAMSEY

Local derby v Norwich, I'm on the prowl.

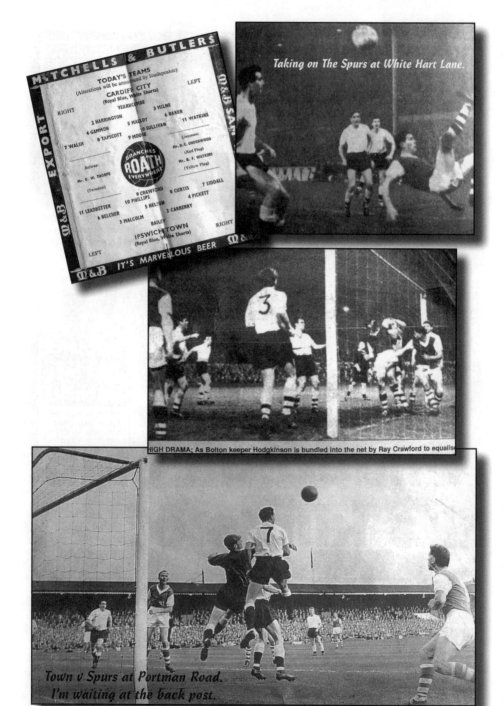

TODAY'S TEAMS
(Alterations will be announced by loudspeaker)

CARDIFF CITY
(Royal Blue, White Shorts)

RIGHT   LEFT

YEARNCOMBE

2 HARRINGTON   3 MILNE

4 GAMMON   5 MALOT   6 BAKER   11 WATKINS

7 WALSH   8 TAPSCOTT   9 MOORE   10 SULLIVAN

Referee:
Mr. G. W. THORPE
(Swindon)

Linesmen:
Mr. D. C. UNDERWOOD
(Red Flag)

Mr. B. F. WATKINS
(Yellow Flag)

9 CRAWFORD   8 CURTIS   7 SIDDALL

10 PHILLIPS   5 NELSON   4 PICKETT

11 LEADBETTER   6 BELCHER   3 MALCOLM   2 CARBERRY

BAILEY

IPSWICH TOWN
(Royal Blue, White Shorts)

LEFT   RIGHT

Taking on The Spurs at White Hart Lane.

HIGH DRAMA; As Bolton keeper Hodgkinson is bundled into the net by Ray Crawford to equalise

Town v Spurs at Portman Road.
I'm waiting at the back post.

Flashback to 1962 when Ray Crawford's header landed the opening goal in the 2-0 Ipswich win against Aston Villa

The lads in training.
Roy Stephenson, Doug Moran, Me , Ted Phillips, Jimmy Leadbetter.

Ted's torch trick bags the birdies

I PLAYED with and against some great characters. One of the funniest was Ted "Thunderboots" Phillips, my strike partner at Ipswich.

He was a natural sportsman, a good fast bowler and a terrific runner.

Ted lived in the country and was a pretty good poacher — he was always bringing in pheasants.

Word got round that he was lethal with a catapult, but Ted let me into the secret. He said he used to take a torch out into the woods at night, shine it into the pheasants' eyes, and they'd just fall out of the trees into his arms.

I remember one training run. Ted and a pal nicked a bottle of milk from a milk float as they ran past.

When we got back to the ground, the milkman was banging on Alf's door to demand the money for his milk!

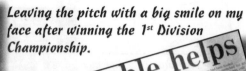

Leaving the pitch with a big smile on my face after winning the 1st Division Championship.

Crawford's double helps Town to title

THEY were called the miracle team of all-time — and no wonder!

CHAMPIONS: Ramsey's Division One winners — (back row) Bill Baxter, Larry Carberry, Roy Bailey, John Compton, John Elsworthy. (Front Row) Roy Stephenson, Doug Moran, Ray Crawford, Andy Nelson (captain), Ted Phillips, Jimmy Leadbetter

Parading the Trophy outside Ipswich Town Hall.

		P	W	D	L	F	A	Pts
ONE	**Ipswich**	**42**	**24**	**8**	**10**	**93**	**67**	**56**
	Burnley	42	21	11	10	101	67	53
	Tottenham	42	21	10	11	88	69	52
	Everton	42	20	11	11	88	54	51
	Sheff Utd	42	19	9	14	61	69	47
	Sheff Wed	42	20	6	16	72	58	46
	...n Villa	42	18	8	16	65	56	44
	...t Ham	42	17	10	15	76	82	44
	...nal	42	16	11	15	71	72	43
	...n Wdr	42	16	10	16	62	66	42
	...City	42	17	7	18	78	81	41
	...pool	42	15	11	16	70	75	41
	...ester City	42	17	6	19	72	71	40
	...Utd	42	15	9	18	72	75	39
	...kburn Rvrs	42	14	11	17	50	58	39
	...ngham City	42	14	10	18	65	81	38
	...verhampton	42	13	10	19	73	86	36
	...s Forest	42	13	10	19	63	79	36
	...am	42	13	7	22	68	74	33
	...iff City	42	9	14	19	50	81	32
	...sea	42	9	10	23	63	94	28

FIRST DIVISION GOAL SCORERS 1961/62

Ray Crawford	(Ipswich)	33
Derek Kevan	(West Brom)	33
Ray Charnley	(Blackpool)	30
Ted Phillips	**(Ipswich)**	**28**
Roy Vernon	(Everton)	26
Ray Pointer	(Burnley)	25
John Dick	(West Ham)	23
Peter Dobing	(Man City)	22
Bobby Tambling	(Chelsea)	20
Jimmy Greaves	(Tottenham)	20
Derek Pace	(Sheffield)	20
Barry Bridges	(Chelsea)	19
John Fantham	(Sheffield Wed)	19
Alan Skirton	(Arsenal)	19

11 players
have scored five goals in a single match in the European Champion Clubs' Cup

Owe Ohlsson	IFK Göteborg	Linfield FC	6-1	23.09.1959
Bent Løfqvist	B 1913 Odense	CA Spora Luxembourg	9-2	13.09.1961
José Altafini	AC Milan	US Luxembourg	8-0	12.09.1962
Ray Crawford	Ipswich Town FC	Floriana FC Valletta	10-0	25.09.1962
Nikola Kotkov	PFC Lokomotiv Sofia	Malmö FF	8-3	10.09.1964
Flórián Albert	Ferencvárosi TC	Keflavik	9-1	08.09.1965
Paul Van Himst	RSC Anderlecht	FC Haka Valkeakoski	10-1	14.09.1966
Gerd Müller	FC Bayern München	AC Omonia Nicosia	9-0	24.10.1972
Claudio Sulser	Grasshopper-Club	Valletta FC	8-0	13.09.1978
Søren Lerby	AFC Ajax	AC Omonia Nicosia	10-0	24.10.1979
Mikhail Mikholap	Skonto FC Riga	AS Jeunesse Esch	8-0	21.07.1999

Ray Crawford of Ipswich Town FC.

Sir Alf Ramsey says . . .

One of the most difficult things in life is to satisfy yourself that you are doing a job of work as well as you ought to. Whilst I have considerable doubt as to my ability to pay a high enough tribute to Ray Crawford, there is no doubt in my mind, and indeed minds of others, that Ray has qualified in all aspects of his profession.

Others will provide in this programme details and facts of his career whilst others who have been associated with him will remember his humour, his loyalty, his determination, his ability and perhaps most of all, the great amount of work he put into his game and the uncanny way he had of being in the right spot at the right time to score his goals.

Ray is one of the Ipswich Town's all time greats, and I am grateful to have had the privilege of being able to share part of his career with him.

Football will always be indebted to players such as Ray, may the future bring even more success to him.

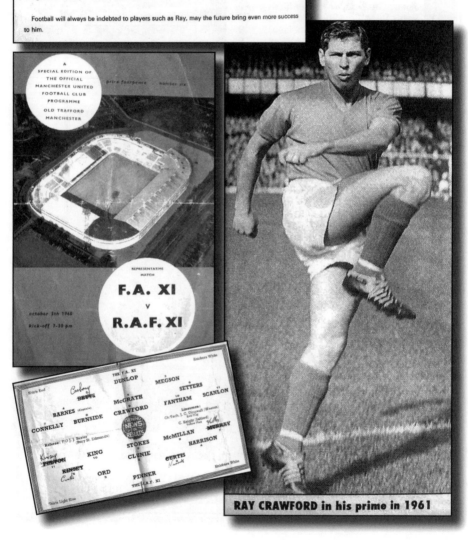

RAY CRAWFORD in his prime in 1961

HOW THEY WILL TAKE THE FIELD

Any alteration in the teams will be announced on the public address system

Irish League
(Green Shirts)

11 HAMILTON Distillery

6 J. E. SMITH Ballymena

10 MORRISON Coleraine

4 JOHNSTON Glenavon

3 STALLARD Derry City

5 TWENTYMAN Ballymena (capt.)

9 COYLE Coleraine

2 GILLILAND Linfield

8 BRUCE Glentoran

4 CUSH Portadown

7 HUMPHRIES Ards

Football League
(White Shirts)

7 CONNELLY Burnley

4 RAY Sheffield W.

8 HILL Bolton

2 HOWE (GWM) West Brom. A.

10 CRAWFORD Ipswich

5 LABONE Everton

6 BANKS Leicester

3 SHAW Sheffield Utd.

10 FANTHAM Sheffield W.

6 MILLER Burnley

11 HARRIS Burnley

Referee: J. Adair, Belfast

Linesmen: S. Cornwall and H.

REJECT CRAWFORD CAPPED

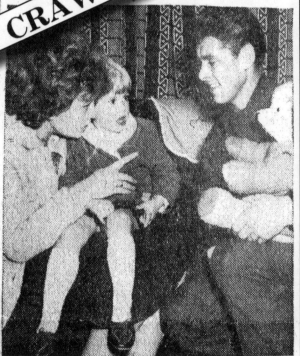

ENGLAND NEW BOY . . . Ipswich centre forward Ray Crawford at home last night with his wife Eileen and baby daughter Jane.

INTER-LEAGUE MATCH

IRISH LEAGUE
versus
FOOTBALL LEAGUE

OFFICIAL PROGRAMME

WED. 1ST NOV. 1961
KICK-OFF 7.30 P.M

WINDSOR PARK
BELFAST

6D

Ray Had A Moderate Match Says His Father

(By LINESMAN)

Mr. George Crawford, father of Eng...

EX-PROFESSIONAL boxer, George Crawford, was back trimming hedges at the Canoe Lake, Southsea, today after the excitement of going to Wembley yesterday to see his son, Ray, play centre-forward for England for the first time.

Ireland forced a 1—1 draw as England played disappointingly.

"I thought Ray had a moderate match, but he did not get the assistance he needed," said Mr. Crawford. "I'm not just saying that because I am his father. It was the view of those around me in the crowd as well.

"The other forwards kept trying shots, instead of passing. If no-one puts the ball through to the centre-forward, he cannot get the goals.

"Ray repeatedly asked for the ball, but it did not come to him. In the second half he kept being out to the wings to get it for himself."

Mr. Crawford wished he had been able to have a chat with his son. But it was not possible before the match, and afterwards he had to hurry to catch the coach home.

"BIG RESPONSIBILITY"

"I expect Ray was on edge. It was a big responsibility for him.

"I wish his Ipswich teammate, Ted Phillips, had been playing for England, too. Phillips has that great firing power and would have combined well with Ray."

Still, Mr. Crawford had the satisfaction of seeing Ray provide the pass for Bobby Charlton to score England's goal. Now he is hoping that after the tension of his England debut, his son will get further chances — and make the trip to Chile for the World Cup.

Mr. Crawford, whose home is at 13, Blackfriars Road, Southsea, is foreman of the Canoe Lake grounds.

He has worked there since the day after he left school 32 years ago, and from his very young days he was never interested in soccer until Ray made his way through the Portsmouth Schools team and then to the Pompey Juniors side and first team.

His sport had been boxing, in which he had professional experience.

The Division Three boy and the 'Jungle Boy' play for England

VIC HUNTER, the Irish goalie, deals effectively with a high ball despite the close attention of England's centre forward, RAY CRAWFORD

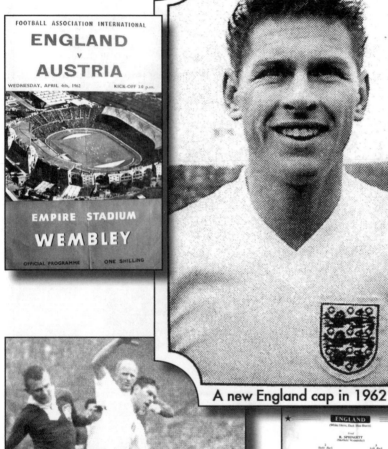

A new England cap in 1962

RAY in action for England against Austria

ENGLAND
(White Shirts, Dark Blue Shorts)

Goal
R. SPRINGETT
(Sheffield Wednesday)

Right Back   Left Back
J. ARMFIELD   R. WILSON
(Blackpool)   (Huddersfield Town)

Right Half   Centre Half   Left Half
S. ANDERSON   P. SWAN   R. FLOWERS
(Sunderland)   (Sheffield Wednesday) (Wolverhampton Wanderers)

                Inside Right   Inside Left
                R. HUNT   J. HAYNES (Capt.)
                (Liverpool)   (Fulham)

Outside Right   Centre Forward   Outside Left
J. CONNELLY   R. CRAWFORD   R. CHARLTON
(Burnley)   (Ipswich Town)   (Manchester United)

Referee:
P. SCHWINTE
(France)

                                              Linesmen
                                              A. VUILLEMIN
                                              (France)
                                              Touch Flag
                                              J. HERBERT
                                              (France)
                                              Goal Flag

J. RAFREIDER   J. BUSEK   A. KNOLL
(Dornbirn)   (Vienna)   (Vienna Sportklub)
Outside Left   Centre Forward   Outside Right
11   9   7

        E. FIALA   E. HOF
        (F.K. Austria)   (Vienna Sportklub)
        Inside Left   Inside Right
        10   8

K. KOLLER   K. STOTZ   R. OSLANSKY
(Vienna)   (F.K. Austria)   (Vienna Sportklub)
Left Half   Centre Half   Right Half
6   5   4

        K. HASENKOPF   A. TRUBRIG
        (Vienna Sportklub)   (Linz A.S.K.)
        Left Back   Right Back
        3   2

                G. FRAYDL
                (F.K. Austria)
                Goal
                1

AUSTRIA
(Red Shirts, White Shorts)

'999' The three West Brom centre forwards in 1966. John Kaye, Jeff Astle and me.

Goal machine

Ray Crawford 'The Baggie'.

Wearing the old gold of The Wolves.

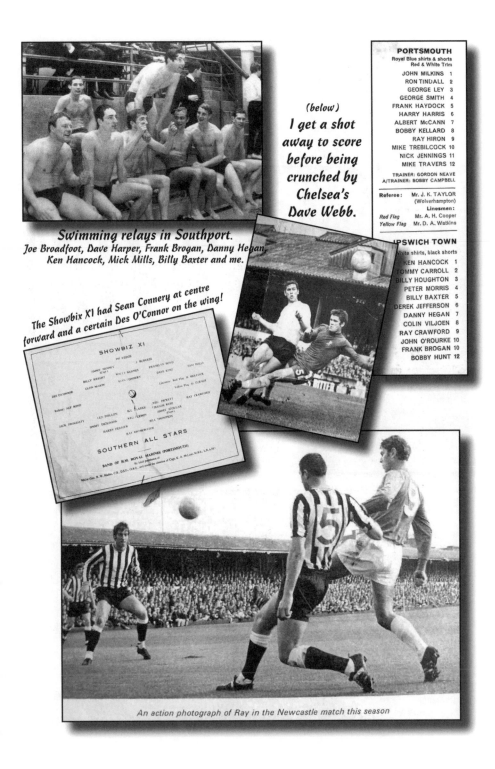

Swimming relays in Southport.
Joe Broadfoot, Dave Harper, Frank Brogan, Danny Hegan,
Ken Hancock, Mick Mills, Billy Baxter and me.

(below)
I get a shot away to score before being crunched by Chelsea's Dave Webb.

PORTSMOUTH
Royal Blue shirts & shorts
Red & White Trim

JOHN MILKINS	1
RON TINDALL	2
GEORGE LEY	3
GEORGE SMITH	4
FRANK HAYDOCK	5
HARRY HARRIS	6
ALBERT McCANN	7
BOBBY KELLARD	8
RAY HIRON	9
MIKE TREBILCOCK	10
NICK JENNINGS	11
MIKE TRAVERS	12

TRAINER: GORDON NEAVE
A/TRAINER: BOBBY CAMPBELL

Referee: Mr. J. K. TAYLOR
(Wolverhampton)
Linesmen:
Red Flag Mr. A. H. Cooper
Yellow Flag Mr. D. A. Watkins

IPSWICH TOWN
White shirts, black shorts

KEN HANCOCK	1
TOMMY CARROLL	2
BILLY HOUGHTON	3
PETER MORRIS	4
BILLY BAXTER	5
DEREK JEFFERSON	6
DANNY HEGAN	7
COLIN VILJOEN	8
RAY CRAWFORD	9
JOHN O'ROURKE	10
FRANK BROGAN	10
BOBBY HUNT	12

The Showbiz XI had Sean Connery at centre forward and a certain Des O'Connor on the wing!

SHOWBIZ XI

SOUTHERN ALL STARS

BAND OF H.M. ROYAL MARINES (PORTSMOUTH)

An action photograph of Ray in the Newcastle match this season

Bill McGarry says . . .

Ray Crawford is without doubt the best player I have signed in my managerial career. He is the best player I have had working for me. I regard him as a wonderful example of a professional sportsman both on and off the field. I am very pleased to bring the Wolves team here tonight to give him a good send off from Portman Road — He is the only player I would do this for — All the very best Ray, for the future.

Ray gets tangled with Phil Parkes of Wolves in his last First Division game for the Town.

Town's strike rate

Town players	Games	Goals	Strike Rate
Ray Crawford	354	228	.6440
Ted Phillips	294	181	.6156
Tom Garneys	274	143	.5218
David Johnson	112	50	.4464
Gerry Baker	151	66	.4370
Sam McCrory	103	42	.4077
Paul Mariner	339	135	.3982
Bill Jennings	111	44	.3963
Alan Brazil	210	80	.3809
Alex Mathie	138	48	.3478
Trevor Whymark	335	104	.3104
Frank Brogan	223	69	.3094
Bryan Hamilton	199	56	.2814
David Johnson (1972-75)	178	46	.2584
Eric Gates	384	96	.2500
Chris Kiwomya	260	64	.2461

RAY'S ROLL CALL

FULL NAME: Raymond Crawford
BORN: Portsmouth

DATE OF BIRTH: July 13, 1936

DATE SIGNED: September 9, 1958

DEBUT: October 10, 1958, won 4-2 at Swansea Town

TRANSFERRED: From Ipswich to Wolves, September 1963; from West Bromwich Albion to Ipswich, March 1966; to Charlton Athletic, March 1969

LAST GAME: March 1, 1969, drew 1-1 at Wolves

CLUB RECORD: Total appearances 354 and 228 goals

✪BEST GAME FOR IPSWICH?

"We had so many good times during my time there that it's hard to pick one game out. During my second spell at the Club we won the Second Division title again and we drew at home with QPR 1-1 to clinch it and I scored the goal. Also when we beat Inter Milan 2-1 at home and I flicked the ball through the keeper's legs to score. They were both pretty special moments for me."

the RAY CRAWFORD story 1959-69

RAY CRAWFORD'S BENEFIT NIGHT
29th APRIL, 1969

PROGRAMME
IPSWICH TOWN F.C.
PAST v FUTURE
KICK OFF 6.30 p.m.

IPSWICH TOWN v WOLVES
KICK OFF 7.30 p.m.

PRICE ONE SHILLING

ray says . . .

I should like to thank all my old team-mates and friends who have turned out tonight, especially the "old- timers" who have come out of retirement to join in the fun.

A special word of thanks to Bill McGarry and the Wolves for coming along too and good luck in the States in the coming weeks.

Many thanks to all the people who have helped put these games on for me tonight. They may not have been on the pitch but they were part of the team.

Finally "Thank you" to everybody who bought this programme and who were at the match.

All the Best,

RAY

Ray in control in the last Division 2 match of last season versus Blackburn Rovers

ten glorious years of ray . . .

Ray Crawford is one of the most prolific goalscorers of his time. Jimmy Greaves and Roger Hunt are the only two players in the game today who have scored more than Crawford, and only Greaves' striking rate is better.

Crawford has netted 262 goals in 416 League games, scored over 30 in cup-ties, one for england, and seven in European Cup ties. He is the only Englishman to have scored five goals in a European game which he did when Ipswich won their home leg against Floriana 10-0.

In 13 years since he returned to Britain from soldiering in Burma has played over 500 games — first with his native Portsmouth, then with Ipswich, Wolves, West Bromwich, Ipswich again and now Charlton — and has won two England caps, played in four European Cup ties, and won First and two Second Division championship medals with Ipswich. This is the full league record:

Season	Club	Div.	Apps.	Goals
1957-58	Portsmouth	1	16	8
1958-59	Portsmouth	1	2	1
	Ipswich	2	30	25
1959-60	Ipswich	2	36	18
1960-61	Ipswich	2	42	40
1961-62	Ipswich	1	41	33
1962-63	Ipswich	1	42	25
1963-64	Ipswich	1	6	2
	Wolves	1	34	26

Season	Club	Div.	Apps.	Goals
1964-65	Wolves	1	23	13
	West Brom.	1	5	2
1965-66	West Brom.	1	9	4
	Ipswich	2	12	8
1966-67	Ipswich	2	42	21
1967-68	Ipswich	2	39	16
1968-69	Ipswich	1	30	17
	Charlton	2	7	3

By NORMAN GILLER

RAY CRAWFORD is ready to fight Charlton Athletic in court following their decision yesterday to sack him.

The former England centre forward has been given two weeks' notice for refusing to join the first team in a week-long training session at Bisham Abbey.

He joined Charlton from Ipswich for £12,000 in March, and still has nine months to run on his contract.

Trouble?

Crawford will seek the advice of Players' Union secretary Cliff Lloyd today before deciding whether to go ahead with a legal war against Charlton.

The 32-year-old one-time Ipswich, Wolves, West Bromwich and Portsmouth striker made allegations last night of dressing-room troubles at Charlton. He said:—

❝ The atmosphere has been terrible. Supporters have been writing in vicious letters accusing the players of excessive drinking.

This is all rubbish, of course. There has been no heavy drinking, but the rumour got around the club that we were being ordered away for special training because of a lack of professionalism.

I was not told until the last minute that we were to go to Bisham Abbey for a week's training. I just couldn't do it at such short notice.

My wife, Eileen, does not like being left at home on her own with our three young daughters. I like to make arrangements for her to stay with relatives.

Surely I have the right to give my family priority. I have always been a conscientious professional footballer, but on this occasion I could not do what the club wanted of me.

Notice

Manager Eddie Firmani informed me that he would be taking disciplinary action.

The next I knew I was handed a letter giving me 14 days' notice for supposed persistent breaking of my contract.

It looks like I will have to go on the dole when my 14 days are up. The club retain my registration and I am not able to play for anybody else unless they pay a transfer fee.

I shall go to the players' union, the League, the F.A. or maybe even the courtroom to try to get what I consider is justice. ❞

The Crawford case is likely to end up in front of the League Management Committee of which Charlton chairman Mike Gliksten is a member.

Eddie Firmani, Charlton manager, said last night: "I have taken disciplinary action against Crawford because he broke his contract.

"I have informed both the League and the F.A. of the situation, and as far as I am concerned it is final."

EDDIE FIRMANI

CLIFF LLOYD

RAY CRAWFORD . . . TWO WEEKS' NOTICE

Playing for Charlton, albeit briefly.

Ray Crawford, centre, and his wife Eileen talk to Professional Footballers' Association secretary Cliff Lloyd at the Great Western Hotel before today's hearing.

Now Crawford faces vital FA meeting

Ray with his wife Eileen and their latest arrival, Suzanne, born on the evening the "Town" played Q.P.R. this season. Ray has two other daughters, Jane and Liza.

Ray Crawford

Dick Graham's faith in the former Ipswich striker has paid handsome dividends. Signed in the close season from Kettering, he was twice with Ipswich.

Sitting it out for Colchester.

STAR CHOICE
FOR
STAR PEOPLE

Ford

CANDOR
MOTORS

Sliding in to score for The U's

Almighty upset: Ray Crawford climbs to head his first goal as Colchester inflict FA Cup humiliation on the First Division leaders Leeds United in 1971

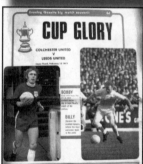

CUP GLORY

COLCHESTER UNITED
V
LEEDS UNITED

BOBBY

BILLY

COLCHESTER LEEDS THE CUP GIANT-KILLERS

PAXMAN LEADS IN DIESEL POWE
MAKE PAXMAN YOUR GOAL AND BECOME A WINNER

COLCHESTER UNITED

Colours: Blue and White

1 Graham SMITH
In top form in the revival run.

2 Micky COOK
Continues to impress everyone with his progress.

3 Brian HALL
His spectacular goal swung the Aldershot match.

4 Bobby CRAM
An over present.

5 Brian GARVEY
Also 100 per cent. and outstanding at Exeter.

6 John KURILA
Out to prove that undoubted ability against his former club.

7 Ken JONES
The skipper is bang back on the goals trail.

8 Brian GIBBS
Owns a tremendously high work rate.

9 Roy MASSEY
His second goal of the season at Exeter.

10 Ray CRAWFORD
Earning rave notices in away matches.

11 Mick MAHON
Running into peak form.

12

Linesman: J. E. BENT (Hemel Hempstead) Red Flag

DANGER! RAY AT WORK

ONLY 15 months ago former England striker Ray Crawford signed on the dole at Catford labour exchange in London.

His Soccer career looked in ruins after struggling Second Division Charlton had cancelled his contract when he refused to attend a special training session at Bisham Abbey.

Within two weeks he seemed doomed to end his playing days in one of football's backwaters when he signed for Southern League Kettering.

But today he strides out to face mighty Leeds United, one of the best club sides in Europe. Once again Crawford basks in the nationwide spotlight.

This one-time Portsmouth, Ipswich, Wolves, and West Bromwich Albion forward faces up with Fourth Division Colchester United on their small Layer Road ground, hoping to

play a leading role in one of the season's biggest Cup shocks.

Now approaching his thirty-fifth birthday, Crawford has made a startling comeback in his adopted home of East Anglia — scene of his greatest triumphs.

During his two years with Ipswich — the first under the now England team manager Sir Alf Ramsey — he scored more than 200 goals.

This season with Colchester he has again found the goal trail being on target 25 times so far.

"I must admit I never thought I would play in the Football League again after I joined Kettering," recalls Crawford, whose wife lives in Ipswich.

"Dick Graham, Colchester manager, had been interested in me when I was on the transfer list at Charlton, but the fee was too high.

"He tried again when I moved to Kettering and I'm happy to say he succeeded.

The most fantastic result you'll ever see

COLCHESTER 3 LEEDS 2

They DO come back.. Crawford proves it

RAY CRAWFORD, 35 next July, streaked in sweat and glistening with liniment, strolled like a giant off the smallest pitch in the League.

But once for a few yards. Then they swarmed over the touchline walls and carried him towards Colchester's dressing-room.

A triumphant thing — leaderless and the chant whooping and ecstatic — swirling the form of a wonder runt.

The conqueror is not a lot, flowing, dance-floor player, limping, sporting, charging over the course in one go — to climb into the dressing-room, and drag Daniel and the crowd.

Leeds, always a better white ball, slammed the ball. His tousled across goal-close. His his... the DG's a ball, the Don needs.

MIKE LANGLEY REPORTS

A Colchester corner stood like fail in thirty-two spirits — to a Cooper mare like a corner.

Leeds, with a better goal. Then the DG's at drive, and Giles scored.

A Colchester corner libeled to put. Crawford needed bend into the net, above. Jones deflected Lorimer's one event, and Giles put over for him.

Leeds, stirring down to two and pushing together concentrating across in points, restricted Don East Ambition appeared that they were taking the ... finalline.

Only Charlton, of course, harrying furiously and sending the Herder into a befuddled glaze. He scored the first. And when N.O. comes to Colchester's first-round reared and player in the town.

Shot Bengy passed his head under the first time slowly in very ... Mee says ... too ...

The dole

The ... alone Crawford through his career and that, to mark of sheer feverish effort, was his fifteen back. I remember him when he scored Portsmouth fourth-division position, after his difference from Jungle Buy.

I followed him through the dole street, for £5,000 fee shell friends and all the mental Division by the pitches.

BOY DAVID KO?
DERBY

By Stan Liversedge

EVERTON 1 DERBY 1
DAVID JOHNSON is the...

They DO come back..
Crawford proves it

RAY CRAWFORD, 35 next July, streaked in sweat and glistening with liniment, strolled like a giant off the smallest pitch in the League.

But only for a few yards. Then they swarmed over the touchline walls and carried him towards Colchester's dressing-room.

A triumphant throng—bandsmen and the mayor, schoolboys and pensioners—saluting the hero of a volcanic cup-tie.

MIKE LANGLEY
REPORTS

In the dressing-room it was a riot. Cameras, microphones, directors, reporters, supporters, the popping of corks, and almost buried in the hubbub, a bond of Fourth Division players who had just whipped one of Europe's finest teams.

Said Crawford: "The last 20 minutes were hell. We'd gone and Leeds knew it. They were all over us. I was scared we'd never hang on."

Never mind the last 20 minutes. It's the first 70 they'll cherish in East Anglia for years to come.

The dole

I've followed Crawford through his career and this, in terms of sheer personal effort, was his finest hour. I remember him when he joined Portsmouth from fighting Malayan guerillas and we christened him Jungle Boy.

I followed him through the days when, for £3,500, he shot Ipswich out of the Second Division to the League championship and launched Alf Ramsey towards his knighthood.

I saw his two games for England in 1961 and, when he was signing on the dole just over a year ago, I thought I'd seen the finish of the Crawford story.

Lorimer's corner, shook his fist at slacking team-mates, and slung Cooper and Giles forward.

Jones, always a brave white ball, answered the call. He headed across goal. Giles hit the bar. Did it again, and Giles scored.

A Charlton header flashed wide. A Cooper header was saved. Jones side-footed Lorimer's low cross, and Smith saved. Then shot over the top.

Leeds, making space at last and putting together sophisticated strings of passes, reminded these East Anglian upstarts that they were facing the Cup favourites.

Only Crawford, of course, bursting through and sending Sprake into a left-sided dive, relieved this pressure.

The crowd prayed for the whistle. Then it came. With wild scenes in Colchester's dressing-room and silence in the losers.

Don Revie popped his head round the door long enough to say: "No excuses." And there weren't.

COLCHESTER: Smith 8; Cram 8, Garvey 7, Kurila 6, Hall 6; Lewis 8, Gilchrist 6, Gibbs 8, Mahon 7; Simmons 8, ★CRAWFORD 9.

LEEDS: Sprake 5; Reaney 5, Charlton 5, ★HUNTER 8, Cooper 6; Bates 5, Giles 6, Madeley 5; Lorimer 6, Clarke 5, Jones 7.

Ref: D. Lyden (Birmingham) 7.

● *MANAGER Dick Graham is mobbed by his happy band of Cup heroes.*

RAY CRAWFORD (left) and fellow scorer DAVE SIMMONS celebrate Colchester United's FA Cup victory over Leeds

I WAS READY TO PACK IT IN SAYS CUP HERO CRAWFORD

Colchester United 1971.

Bobby Robson says . . .

Ray's departure from Ipswich came all too soon after I became Manager. I was rather disappointed at this because I have always regarded Ray as a true professional and would have liked to have had him on our staff. As a player he always gives that little extra that is so valuable to a team and I know how the Ipswich supporters appreciated his hard work on the field. I have played with him — in the England team — and realised then he was a 110% player.

Very best wishes Ray for your future success.

All time top goalscorers in 1968.

I am in special company.

Jimmy Greaves

Roger Hunt

Ray Crawford

Ray Charnley

football is my life

I started my football career with Portsmouth's youth team soon after my 15th birthday. We played in the South East Counties League and for the next two years I was the regular left winger.

Before I left to do my National Service, manager, Eddie Lever, signed me as a professional at a weekly retainer of £1 a week.

For the next 18 months I was hunting down terrorists in Malaya with the Royal Hampshire Regiment, and it was because of this experience that I became known as "Jungle Boy" when I returned to football in the 1957-8 season.

I soon made the Portsmouth first team and made my league debut against Burnley at Fratton Park. It was not a very good game for me, but I was given another chance the following week. For five weeks I held my place then I broke my ankle. Four months later I got back into the first team and finished the season as an accepted first teamer.

Early the next season Eddie Lever left Portsmouth and Freddie Cox, now manager of Bournemouth, took over. At that time we were at the bottom of Division 1 and changes had to come. Very soon after this I went on the transfer list — Freddie Cox thought that I was too inexperienced — and Ipswich Town made an offer for me. I went along to see them play and wasn't very impressed with what I saw. However I was talked into the move and came to Portman Road.

At the time the Town were somewhere near the bottom of Division 2 but newly-appointed manager Alf Ramsey had other ideas. Every Ipswich supporter knows the story of the exciting years ahead. I was the Baby of the team in those days and I was really on top of the world when I scored the winning goal to beat Aston Villa, for us to take the Division 1 championship.

Continued

football is my life *continued*

It was during this time, of course, that I played for England. The first game was a great thrill, but I didn't think I deserved a second chance. However, it came my way out of the blue one Sunday afternoon.

I had taken a hard knock on the Saturday afternoon and was limping badly. I was at home doing a spot of decorating when Mr. Ramsey called to see me. It appeared that Walter Winterbottom, then England team manager, had been on the 'phone enquiring if I was fit to play for England against Austria on the Wednesday. What would you have done ? Mr. Ramsey quizzed my ankle so I gritted my teeth and walked across the room normally. I must have put on a good show because I was soon on my way to London to join the England party.

I struggled through training without giving any signs of the pain I was in. I was lucky enough to score the first goal early in the game and felt much better. When I returned to Ipswich the manager sent me for an X-ray and a chipped bone in my ankle was diagnosed. I was out for a couple of games but it was well worth it.

Soon after this I felt that the time had come to move and I was transferred to the "Wolves". After 18 months with the famous Midlands club I was on the move again, this time just down the road to West Bromwich Albion. I didn't really settle down and when Bill McGarry contacted West Brom to see if a deal could be arranged I jumped at the chance to return to Ipswich. Ipswich Town fans have always been very good to me and my family and I hope I have repaid their support.

It was a great thrill to help win another Second Division championship last season. It was an even greater thrill to score goals in the First Division this year, but I have realised that the pace is too hot there for me now. I hope to be remembered at Portman Road for the good times and will always look back on my time here with pleasure.

Being a professional footballer today is a good life. I have had the chance to travel and meet people in all walks of life that I would never have had in any other job.

● RAY CRAWFORD, the Durban City forward, got up well to beat Mario Ungarotti, the Maritzburg defender, for this high ball.

Pleasure maker

CAPE TOWN CITY
(Gold jerseys and white shorts)

1. V. Lovell or P. Wicks
2. E. Yard
3. B. Kinsey
4. K. Scott
5. J. Klers
6. J. Morrison
7. T. Brimacombe
8. G. France
9. J. Regan
10. I. Towers
11. T. Coleman
12. B. Anderson
14. T. Claxton
15. P. Kerr
16. D. Gie.

REFEREE: Mr. S. Stonestreet

The beer with the taste that can't be copied.

Plesier -bier

DURBAN CITY
(Blue and white hoops, black shorts)

1. L. Green
2. A. Bermingham
3. A. Munro
4. R. Keetch
5. D. Forsythe
6. J. Faccione
7. G. Farrell
8. J. Haynes
9. R. Crawford
10. R. Mann
11. R. Cooke
12. A. Milne
13. B. de Leuer
14. M. Chislett
15. J. Byrne.

LINESMEN: Messrs Bill Gultic and B. McNaughton

Die bier met die smaak wat niemand kan namaak nie.

City, down to 10 men after centre-half Dave Forsyth had been sent off the field for an alleged offence against Dave Underwood, the Maritzburg striker, brought Ray Crawford, their centre-forward, back in defence and appeared to be content to end with a share of the points.

NATURALLY, IT WAS THE NEW SOCCER IMPORTS WHO WERE THE CENTRE OF ATTRACTION AT NEW KINGSMEAD YESTERDAY.

THERE WAS CITY'S ALAN BERMINGHAM SPORTING A NIFTY LINE IN HOT PANTS —

MARITZBURG'S JOHN KEITH IN SOME NOT-SO-HOT PANTS

AND CITY'S RAY CRAWFORD, WHO CHANGED HIS WHITE BOOTS AT THE INTERVAL, FOR A BLACK PAIR.

(HE MUST HAVE COTTONED ON THE POLICY OF SEPARATE DEVELOPMENT MIGHTY FAST!)

AGAINST THAT SORT OF COMPETITION KEITH KNEW HE'D HAVE TO PULL OUT A BIT MORE - SO HE HAULED HIS JERSEY OUTSIDE HIS SHORTS

HALF WAY THROUGH THE SECOND HALF ALL EYES WERE FOCUSSED ON KEITH'S SHIRT REACHING TO MORE FASHIONABLE MIDI LENGTH

AND ONLY THE FINAL WHISTLE SAVED HIM FROM BEING THE FIRST PLAYER IN THE N.F.L. TO APPEAR IN A MAXI!

DESPITE THAT SORT OF OPPOSITION FROM THE YOUNGER SET, WE THOUGHT THE MOST STYLISH PLAYER ON THE FIELD WAS "THE OLD MASTER" JOHNNY HAYNES!

LEYDEN

BRIGHTON & HOVE ALBION 1972

Youth team coach at Pompey.
Actor Jack Smethurst gives a
young Chris Kamara a lift.

Meeting Lawrie McMenemy at a bash.

Coach Ray Crawford.

Lining up with Portsmouth FC, 1976/77.

WELL DONE ● Former Pompey, Ipswich and Colchester centre-forward Ray Crawford presents trophies to Port Solent United players. Left to right, back row, are Karl Warner, Gareth Watkins and Shawn Purslow. Front row are Ian Pinner and Kevin Clements

CLEANING UP: Ray Crawford on one of his supermarket visits

If only we still had...

GREENE

PAYING THEIR RESPECTS: Blues legend Ray Crawford, right, at the funeral of Roy Stephenson today with Town chairman David Sheepshanks

FAREHAM TOWN FOOTBALL CLUB

Season 1979-80

Southern League Premier Division

OFFICIAL PROGRAMME 10p

Ipswich Town F.C.C. Supporters Club
invites you plus guest to
the unveiling of the
Sir Alfred Ramsey Statue
On Tuesday August 22nd at 12 noon
Reception: Centre Spot 11:30
Buffet Lunch: 12:30

R.S.V.P. to Philip Horsley, 169 Hamilton Road, Felixstowe IP11 7DR
Tel: 01394 278244

Meeting up with my old Ipswich team mate Jimmy Leadbetter.

49 years on, back in the home dressing room at Fratton Park.

A Pompey get together with old teamates Johnny Phillips (left) and Keith Blackburn (centre).

Have a laugh with another old Pompey and Town stalwart Reg Pickett.

Milan Mand Suite

Crawford's league career record

club	season	appearances	goals
	1957-58	19	9
Portsmouth	1958-63	197	143
Ipswich Town	1963-64	57	39
Wolves	1964-65	14	6
West Brom	1965-68	123	61
Ipswich Town	1968-69	21	7
Charlton	1970	45	25
Colchester	total	496	290